When Solidarity Works

Why do some labor movements successfully defend the welfare state even under the pressures of neo-liberal market reform? Why do some unions (and their allied parties and civic associations) succeed in building more universal and comprehensive social policy regimes, while others fail to do so? In this innovative work, Cheol-Sung Lee explores these conundrums through a comparative historical analysis of four countries: Argentina, Brazil, South Korea, and Taiwan. He introduces the notion of 'embedded cohesiveness' in order to develop an explanatory model in which labor–civic solidarity and union–political party alliance jointly account for outcomes of welfare state retrenchment as well as welfare state expansion. Lee's exploration of the critical roles of civil society and social movement processes in shaping democratic governance and public policies make this ideal for academic researchers and graduate students in comparative politics, political sociology, and network analysis.

Cheol-Sung Lee is Associate Professor of Sociology at the University of Chicago. His research interests lie in comparative welfare states and politics of inequality and specifically in the evolution and transformation of modern welfare states. His work has been published in *American Sociological Review*, *Social Forces*, *Sociological Theory*, *World Politics*, and *Comparative Political Studies*.

Structural Analysis in the Social Sciences

Mark Granovetter, editor

The series Structural Analysis in the Social Sciences presents studies that analyze social behavior and institutions by reference to relations among such concrete social entities as persons, organizations, and nations. Relational analysis contrasts on the one hand with reductionist methodological individualism and on the other with macro-level determinism, whether based on technology, material conditions, economic conflict, adaptive evolution, or functional imperatives. In this more intellectually flexible structural middle ground, analysts situate actors and their relations in a variety of contexts. Since the series began in 1987, its authors have variously focused on small groups, history, culture, politics, kinship, aesthetics, economics, and complex organizations, creatively theorizing how these shape and in turn are shaped by social relations. Their style and methods have ranged widely, from intense, long-term ethnographic observation to highly abstract mathematical models. Their disciplinary affiliations have included history, anthropology, sociology, political science, business, economics, mathematics, and computer science. Some have made explicit use of social network analysis, including many of the cutting-edge and standard works of that approach, whereas others have kept formal analysis in the background and used 'networks' as a fruitful orienting metaphor. All have in common a sophisticated and revealing approach that forcefully illuminates our complex social world.

Recent Books in the Series

When Solidarity Works

Labor–Civic Networks and Welfare States in the Market Reform Era

CHEOL-SUNG LEE

The University of Chicago

CAMBRIDGE
UNIVERSITY PRESS

CAMBRIDGE
UNIVERSITY PRESS

One Liberty Plaza, New York NY 10006, USA

Cambridge University Press is part of the University of Cambridge.

It furthers the University's mission by disseminating knowledge in the pursuit of education, learning and research at the highest international levels of excellence.

www.cambridge.org
Information on this title: www.cambridge.org/9781107174047

© Cheol-Sung Lee 2016

First published 2016

Printed in the United States of America by Sheridan Books, Inc.

A catalog record for this publication is available from the British Library

Library of Congress Cataloging-in-Publication data
Names: Lee, Cheol-Sung, author.
Title: When solidarity works : labor-civic networks and welfare states in the market reform era / Cheol-Sung Lee.
Description: New York, NY : Cambridge University Press, 2016. | Includes bibliographical references and index.
Identifiers: LCCN 2016026207 | ISBN 9781107174047 (hard back: alk. paper)
Subjects: LCSH: Labor movement–Developing countries. | Labor unions–Political activity–Developing countries. | Social movements–Developing countries. | Solidarity–Developing countries. | Welfare state–Developing countries. | Developing countries–Social policy.
Classification: LCC HD8943 .L44 2016 | DDC 330.12/6–dc23
LC record available at https://lccn.loc.gov/2016026207

ISBN 978-1-107-17404-7 Hardback

To my parents

Contents

Figures

Tables

Preface

This book explores how labor–civic solidarity evolves in civil society and how it builds welfare states. I wrote this book for several different audiences: those who hope to explain the development and retrenchment of the welfare states in developing countries, but have become dissatisfied with the existing welfare state literature focusing on rich democracies; those who wish to explore the critical roles of civil society and social movement processes in shaping democratic governance and public policies; and finally those who are interested in the evolving processes of different forms of organizational solidarity for collective actions.

The book is a combined version of two earlier projects: one started with my 'going-underground' project, in which I wanted to investigate how different forms of labor–civic solidarity emerged during authoritarian repression eras in developing countries, and how they eventually evolved into different forms of labor organizations during democratic consolidation eras. The other project, published in *World Politics* in 2012, explored how different configurations of civic networks played a role in steering party and union elites' political decision-making regarding the retrenchment or expansion of the welfare states. In the project, I first developed the notions of embeddedness and cohesiveness to capture how unions develop linkages with formal governmental and non-governmental civic organizations. In the combined project, my new task was to illuminate a historical process in which labor–civic solidarity evolves around specific social policies.

To achieve this goal, I had to raise the bar beyond a structuralist argument, which is typical in conventional network analysis. I had to analyze different layers of labor organizations and civic associations to investigate the historical evolutionary processes of labor–civic networks and their changing structures over time. In order to accomplish this task, I interviewed the top leadership of the major unions and labor organizations in four developing countries through referrals and soliciting contacts and information for years. In South Korea, I approached and met with top experts in social and labor market policies, which opened my eyes to the ideas of 'policy networks' and 'policy capacity', as well as leading me to develop the notions of 'policy embeddedness' and 'mobilization'-based organizational capacity. During the interview processes, I had to discard many of my earlier hypotheses and devise new theoretical tools to explain novel and deep realities which I could not detect from secondary documents. Thanks to the interview data, I was able to interweave detailed historical contexts and field-level voices with associational network data. It was a process of letting each node in a network produce a voice and tell its story. Through this process, I was able to explain how and why different social policies evolved in policy and mobilization fields and became institutionalized in different ways. It was an eye-opening experience to walk into the structure of an existing network, and to see smaller or newly evolving structures within larger underlying structures. Through such experiences, I came up with the argument that the evolving or devolving configuration of labor–civic solidarity and its mobilization and policy capacity effectively accounts for variations in the retrenchment and expansion of social policies.

This book also has another origin, which traces back to my experience as a college student and as a graduate student during the tumultuous democratization periods in the 1990s in South Korea, more than 20 years ago. At that time, I bumped into several older students who had prior experiences as disguised workers for union movements at local factories. Retrospectively, it was the time when the revolutionary fervors of the 1980s evaporated and democratization opened a new political space for those radical entrepreneurs. Some of them stayed around their old college campuses briefly and then ventured out to build new labor and civic organizations. Others quit their movement careers or lived as professionals in relevant fields.

For the last 20 years, I have been hoping to launch a study on those who 'went underground.' I wanted to investigate more seriously why they went into factories and poor neighborhoods, why they came out of there, why and how they built contemporary forms of labor and civic organizations, and what they achieved or failed to achieve. I wanted to walk into their histories and reorganize them with the analytical measures and languages I have acquired since then. I thought it would be critical to understand their career trajectories, including goals, strategies, actions, and resources, in order to reveal how contemporary labor politics institutionalized around certain routines and practices. I also thought it would be essential to put the evolving process of labor politics in the larger context of civil society development or multi-organizational fields, so that we could investigate not only labor organizations' internal capacity, but also their embedded institutional features in the larger associational field. I assumed that such efforts would help advance our knowledge especially in the study of the welfare state in recently democratized/democratizing developing societies, filling an important gap between social movement/organizational analysis literature and welfare state literature.

Writing this book, I am indebted to many people. First of all, I would like to thank labor and civic leaders who willingly shared their time and experience with me. They provided not only historical data on labor–civic solidarity through their vivid memory, but also diagnoses and analyses of labor and civic politics in different societies. They served as the most essential grounds for this book. The data collection was financially supported by an NSF Award (No. 1260191, "Identity, Networks, and The Origins of Participatory Democracy"). I thank Francois Nielsen and John D. Stephens, who were my dissertation advisors and have continued to support my research since then. Mentors at UNC-Chapel Hill such as Evelyne Huber, Ken Bollen, and Charles Kurzman also kept offering me valuable advice whenever I needed it. Peter Evans was an important supporter of this project from its early inception to its late development. He encouraged me to keep pursuing this project by inviting me to his research group. David Brady, Art Alderson, Andrew Schrank, and Kraig Beyerlein helped me to sustain my journey in several workplaces in the US by providing emotional as well as intellectual support. I am grateful to my colleagues in the Sociology Department at the University of Chicago: Andrew Abbott, Edward Laumann, Dingxin Zhao, Elisabeth Clemens, James Evans, Andreas Glaeser, and Terry Clark, who continually encouraged me to develop a serious – in a Chicago sense – project, and gave me invaluable feedback at various stages of this book project. Marco Garrido, Kimberly Hoang, and John Levi Martin read several chapters of this book and delivered incredibly insightful comments. Kyung-Hee Choi and Bruce Cumings in the East Asian Studies program also encouraged me to pursue this agenda at its very early stage. Several portions of this book were read by my other colleagues: I thank Jason Beckfield, Seok-ju Cho, Kentaro Hirose, Chang-whan Kim, Yong-kyun Kim, James Montgomery,

Jong-Hee Park, Monica Prasad, Ross Stolzenberg, and Andrew Schrank for their thoughtful feedback. Especially, Seok-ju Cho, Kentaro Hirose, James Montogomery, and Ross Stolzenberg's critical comments helped me to build more rigorous game theoretical models. Students of my "Welfare States, Poverty, and Inequality" and "Sociology of Civil Society" class read several chapters and offered critical and challenging comments on them. Participants in several workshops and colloquiums gave me diverse and in-depth feedback: I presented a part of this book project at the Social Movement Workshop, sponsored by the Kellogg School of Management, Northwestern University; the Department of Sociology Colloquium, Indiana University at Bloomington; the Watson Institute, Brown University; the East Asia Workshop and Comparative Politics Workshop, University of Chicago; the Institute for Developing Nations, Emory University; the Center for East Asian and Pacific Studies, University of Illinois at Urbana-Champaign; the Department of Sociology Colloquium, Choong-Ang University; the Korea Labor Institute; the Department of Sociology, Seoul National University; and the Beijing University-Seoul National University Sociology Department Joint Conference. During my stay as a visiting professor at Seoul National University, members of the Sociology Department gave me thoughtful feedback and provided an ideal research environment for this project. In particular, Kyung-Sup Chang and Keun-Sik Jung gave me thoughtful scholarly advice regarding writing a book and its value. Also, for the last two years, several colleagues in the "SSK-Multiple-Inequality Project", Byung-yu Cheon, Ji-yeon Chang, Jin-wook Shin, and others, provided ample support to my research and stay in Seoul.

The research in this book has been partially supported by a Research Grant of the National Research Foundation of Korea (Social Science Korea NFR-2014S1A3A2044833) received by the research team, largely for the network data collection in South Korea. Also, Su-Mi Eŭn, Duk-jin Chang, and Kuk-jin Kang allowed me to use and update their network data for this research. Without their generous support, a significant portion of this book project would not have been possible at all. Many other graduate students here at the University of Chicago or at other universities in four countries helped me to collect interview data from labor leaders. Aparajita Das, Nicolas Damin, Deni Rubbo, Wilson Santo, Hsiao-Yu Chen, Mariana Toledo, Monise Picanço, Marina Barbosa, Lucas Amaral, Myŏng-sŏn Mun, and Chris Dunlap helped me conduct interviews or transcribe and compile interview data. Nathan Gonzalez, Stephen Klein, Wan-zi Lu, Andrew Proctor, Benjamin Rohr, and Nuannuan Xiang spent significant time providing substantive comments as well as copyediting the several versions of the manuscript.

Some parts of this book were drawn from my articles, either unpublished or published elsewhere. Segments of Chapter 1 were drawn from a paper I published in *American Sociological Review* (August 2007) with the title "Labor Unions and Good Governance." Chapters 3 and 9 were developed from my article published in *World Politics* (July 2012) under the title "Associational Networks and Welfare States in Argentina, Brazil, South Korea, and Taiwan." One section in Chapter 4 (The origins of cohesiveness and embeddedness) was built on my forthcoming article in *Sociological Theory* (September 2016), "Going Underground: The Origins of Divergent Forms of Labor Parties and their Successes in Recently Democratized Countries." One section in Chapter 7 (on Argentina) and another section in Chapter 8 (on Taiwan) were built on and expanded from an unpublished paper I wrote with Maria Akchurin and Jean Yenchun Lin.

Two anonymous reviewers provided an almost article-length set of comments, which I digested for months to improve the book. Mark Granovetter advised me on incorporating findings from network analyses into the text seamlessly. Robert Dreesen, an editor at Cambridge University Press, asked me whether I had a book draft three years ago, and then waited three years while I came up with something from nothing. I thank him for the suggestion and subsequent patience. I also thank Cassi Roberts, Helen Flitton, and Luke Finley for their careful managing and copyediting work.

My wife, Kyung-Jin, and my kids, J. J. and Ana, have always been with me, reminding me that I should enjoy life as well as work. Without their presence, I would not have been able to sustain my desire to accomplish good work. I also sincerely thank my parents-in law for their continuous encouragement. Finally, I would like to express my deepest gratitude to my parents for their unconditional love and support.

Abbreviations

ANDES-SN	National Union of Teachers of Higher Education Institutions (Sindicato Nacional dos Docentes das Instituições de Ensino Superior, Brazil)
CAUP	Catholic Association for the Urban Poor (S. Korea)
CCC	Classist and Combative Current (Corriente Clasista y Combativa, Argentina)
CCEJ	Citizens' Coalition for Economic Justice (S. Korea)
CFL	Chinese Federation of Labor (Taiwan)
CGT	General Confederation of Labor (Confederación General del Trabajo de la República Argentina)
CGT (Brazil)	General Confederation of Workers (Central Geral dos Trabalhadroes, Brazil)
CMAP	Christian Medical Association for the Poor (S. Korea)
CNTA	National Confederation of Food Workers (Brazil)
CONDSEF	National Federation of Federal Public Servants (Brazil)
CPA	Catholic Peasant Association (S. Korea)
CSP-Conlutas	National Coordination of Struggles (Brazil)
CTA	Argentine Workers' Central Union (Central de Trabajadores de la Argentina)
CUT	Unified Workers' Central (Central Única dos Trabalhadores, Brazil)
DIEESE	Inter-Union Department of Statistics and Socioeconomic Studies (Departamento Intersindical de Estatística e Estudos Socioeconômicos, Brazil)

DLP	Democratic Labor Party (S. Korea)
DP	Democratic Party (S. Korea)
DPP	Democratic Progressive Party (Taiwan)
FDA	Free Democratic Alliance (Party) (S. Korea)
FERAESP	Federation of Rural Workers of the State of São Paulo (Brazil)
FKI	Federation of Korean Industries
FKTU	Federation of Korean Trade Unions
FLACSO-Argentina	Latin American Faculty of Social Science in Argentina
FPV	The Front for Victory (Frente Para la Victoria, Argentina)
FS	Força Sindical (Brazil)
GNP	Grand National Party (S. Korea)
HRMA	Human Rights Movement Association (S. Korea)
HRN	Health Rights Network (S. Korea)
HCSE	Health Care Service for Employees (S. Korea)
KCTU	Korean Confederation of Trade Unions
KDHS	Korean Dentists for Healthy Society
KDMU	Korean Democratic Metal Union
KEF	Korean Employers' Federation
KFEM	Korean Federation of Environmental Movements
KFMA	Korean Federation of Medical Activist Group for Health Rights
KGEU	Korean Government Employees' Union
KHMU	Korean Health and Medicine Union
KIHASA	Korean Institute for Health and Social Welfare
KLSI	Korean Labor and Society Institute
KMT	Kuomintang, Chinese Nationalist Party
KHU	Korean Hospitals Union
KPA	Korean Peasants' Association
KPDS	Korean Pharmacists for Democratic Society
KPTSU	Korean Public Transportation and Service Union
KPTU	Korean Public Service and Transport Worker's Union
KSIU	Korean Social Insurance Union
KTU	Korean Teachers' Union
KWAU	Korean Women's Associations United
MFE	Ministry of Finance and Economy (S. Korea)
MST	Landless Workers' Movement (Brazil)
MTA	Movement of Argentine Workers (Movimiento de los Trabajadores Argentinos)
NAFITU	National Federation of Independent Trade Unions (Taiwan)

NAHC	National Association for the Health Care (S. Korea)
NCHIU	National Conference for Health Insurance Unification (S. Korea)
NCTU	National Council of Trade Unions (S. Korea)
NHIS	National Health Insurance Service
NPA	National Peasants' Association
NPS	National Pensions Service
NPSU	National Pensions Service Union
NKP	New Korea Party (S. Korea)
PAAHR	Physicians' Association for Action for Human Rights (S. Korea)
PJ	The Judicialist Party (Partido Justicialista, Argentina)
PMDB	Party of the Brazilian Democratic Movement (Partido do Movimento Democrático Brasileiro)
PMPHC	People's Movement against Privatization of Health Care (S. Korea)
PSDB	Brazilian Social Democracy Party (Partido da Social Democracia Brasileira)
PSPD	People's Solidarity for Participatory Democracy (S. Korea)
PT	The Workers' Party (Brazil)
RHCS	Regional Health Care Service (S. Korea)
RHCU	Regional Health Care Service Union (S. Korea)
RING	National Assembly of Students – Free (Brazil)
SHR	Solidarity for Health Rights (S. Korea)
SNHMA	Solidarity Network of Health and Medical Associations (S. Korea)
SUH	Solidarity Union for Hope (Union for Non-Standard Workers, S. Korea)
SUS	Unified Health System (Sistema Único de Saúde, Brazil)
TAMI	Taiwan Association of Machinery Industry
TCTU	Taiwanese Confederation of Trade Unions
TLF	Taiwanese Labor Front
TLSA	Taiwan Labor and Social Policy Research Association
UNE	National Union of Students
WAU	Women's Associations United (S. Korea)
WP	Workers' Party (S. Korea)

PART I

I

Introduction

PUZZLES AND RESEARCH QUESTIONS

The past few decades were the era of neo-liberalism. Since the 1980s, two central prongs of state institutions – their regulatory power over markets and their protective functions as a collective safety net for citizens – have been under serious attack, initiated, on one hand, from the forces of global capitalism, and on the other hand, from the domestic agents benefiting from globalization.

After the Golden Era of economic growth and welfare state expansion in rich democracies, these two main components of state institutions have faced retrenchment. Social democracy and leftist politics, which had long thrived on strong and comprehensive unions and their allied parties, face serious challenges from centrist and right-wing political forces carrying out market reform agendas encompassing privatization, deregulation of labor markets, and the retrenchment of welfare services.

In contrast to rich democracies, in developing societies the era of neo-liberalism coincidentally overlapped with the era of democratization and democratic consolidation. The advent of democratic political institutions dramatically facilitated democratic contestation among different social forces in middle to upper-middle income developing societies in Asia, Latin America, and other non-Western parts of the world. As a result, the need to respond to citizens' demands for redistribution via social welfare became one of the most important items on the political agenda; this was so for leaders of political parties and other formal organizations, such as labor unions, in many 'democratized' developing countries. In other words, the institutionalization of democracy "provides subordinate classes and reformist elites with better opportunities to channel and

3

realize their (re)distributive demands" via progressive taxes and social policy programs (Lee 2005, p.163). Democracy makes it possible for middle and lower classes to perceive the existence of alternative political parties and policies. Eventually, democratic political contestation enables "actors committed to redistribution" to rise and consciously pursue their policy goals (Huber and Stephens 2012, p. 11).

However, accelerated economic globalization in the late twentieth century drove leaders and citizens of new democracies into increasingly vulnerable positions vis-à-vis economic crises, shocks, and fluctuations in world markets. This implies that the social forces that drove civil society's resistance and challenge to authoritarianism in the 1980s, simultaneously or very soon after democratization, had to face pressures for neo-liberal market reforms. In some countries, therefore, the main pillars of state institutions were under construction with democratization, when neo-liberal agendas started permeating both the market and civil society, greatly constraining the opportunities for the politics of redistribution.

Under these opportunities and constraints, the newly emerging leaders of democratization and labor movements were forced to solve several puzzles regarding the expansion and the retrenchment of existing labor market and social policy institutions – sometimes as challengers, and other times as allies to government incumbents. They had to make choices regarding (1) which policies to defend or relinquish; (2) which social and political forces to ally with; and (3) which strategies to utilize in challenging or lobbying the incumbent state. Under such circumstances, political elites in new democracies, just as in developed countries, have shown markedly different responses to these pressures from below and outside. Some countries have enjoyed dramatic expansion of the welfare state, while others have suffered radical retrenchment in the public sector. While some labor-based party leaders, as incumbents, chose to introduce radical neo-liberal market reforms to existing pro-labor regulations, others chose to protect or expand regulations. What factors account for these strikingly different trajectories of the development and retrenchment in social policies and labor market institutions in emerging economies with newly institutionalized democracy? Why do some labor movements successfully defend their core labor market institutions and social policies even under the pressures of neo-liberal market reforms, while others do not? Why do some unions (and their allying parties and civic associations) succeed in building more universal and comprehensive social policy regimes, while others (that are equally large, strong unions) fail to do so?

To answer these questions, this study initially conducts a deep case study of South Korean labor movements and their roles in developing or defending social and labor market policies. While the book devotes significant attention to the comparative studies of four cases in its latter parts, I initially put a heavy weight on the South Korean case. The case provides an ideal historical laboratory to test my theories: South Korea not only witnessed one of the most rapid economic developments in modern history but it also saw the institutionalization, in only a couple of decades, of one of the strongest labor movements and civil society sectors among developing countries. The strength of the Korean labor movement was astonishing in its heyday, as its general strike in 1996–97 played a decisive role in toppling four decades of authoritarian rule. In the late 1990s, South Korean labor–civil society solidarity achieved the creation of a universal social insurance scheme unprecedented among developing countries for its comprehensive scope. The South Korean story of social and labor market policy development also provides one of the most intriguing 'negative' cases, as its neo-liberal turn in the 2000s under the (first and) second reformist regime(s) was stunningly deep and abrupt. However, here too, the case offers interesting variations to explore: its pension program and labor market regulations were vulnerable and subject to the retrenchment drive by the state and capital, but its national health care program has been well-defended by a durable labor–civic solidarity. The growth and decline of South Korean labor movements, their heroic solidaristic endeavors as well as tragic internal struggles and subsequent declines, are at the center of these institutional changes in social and labor market policies[1]. Under this framework, what factors account for the dramatic expansion and equally dramatic retrenchment of social and labor market policies in South Korea over the nearly three decades following the transition to democracy? Do the same factors explain both the expansion and the retrenchment outcomes, or are different factors at play in each case? What roles have labor and civic organizations played in those policy changes and what were the contents of the labor–civic solidarity? What can the South Korean case teach scholars of social movements and welfare states in general?

Next, the study extends its focus to a comparative historical analysis of four countries: Argentina, Brazil, South Korea, and Taiwan. I justify my case selection as follows: they have achieved medium (Argentina and Brazil) to upper (South Korea and Taiwan) levels of development, and thus social demands for public provisions of welfare have emerged in functional, demographic, and political contexts; in turn, the expansion or retrenchment of social policies has become a critical battleground in formal politics. In addition, all four countries experienced democratization in the 1980s and subsequently consolidated democratic political institutions in the 1990s and the 2000s. Significantly, all four countries suffered economic crises in the late twentieth century: the two Latin American cases have had endemic and chronic debt crises and extremely high inflation, situations that were exacerbated in the 1980s and 1990s, while the two East Asian cases suffered from the Asian Financial Crisis in 1997 and subsequent recessions, though the degree was less severe in Taiwan. These similarities allow us to control for some alternative economic, political, and structural factors that might otherwise account for variations in the dynamics of welfare states among these countries. Second, I intentionally chose two East Asian and two Latin American countries with relatively similar cultural and geopolitical histories. In this way, I can readily control for several known or unknown region-specific factors. Taiwan and South Korea share very similar modern histories such as colonization by Japan; American political and military influence during the Cold War and ensuing ideological confrontation; rapid state-led, export-oriented economic development under authoritarian regimes; and strong Confucian culture. Argentina and Brazil also share geographical and cultural similarities such as Catholic-dominant religious identities, as well as highly unequal and volatile economic structures; traditions of populist politics; and the pronounced influence of large landlords and international capital.

Finally, despite their similarities, these four developing countries have considerable and potentially quite illuminating diversity in the histories of their social welfare regimes. First, the development and retrenchment of welfare states in Argentina and Brazil provide intriguing cases for comparison. These two countries have followed sharply different trajectories of social, political, and economic transformations in the 1990s and 2000s. While Argentina has embraced neo-liberal market reforms on public sector and social policies after experiencing a serious debt crisis, Brazil has not adopted them wholeheartedly. Argentina has launched a relatively radical privatization of pensions, cut the public share in total health spending, and decreased benefits in family allowances. Brazil, by contrast, has not only durably resisted market-oriented reforms of key social policy areas such as pensions but it has also dramatically increased government spending for total health care expenditure.

The recent development stories of the welfare states in South Korea and Taiwan are no less intriguing. During the course of democratic consolidation both countries introduced not only universal health care and national pension programs but also basic old-age pension and long-term care insurance, mainly targeting the disabled and the elderly population living under the poverty line (basic income and pension) or those of middle-class origin (long-term care insurance). In addition, both countries introduced government-guaranteed basic income as a social assistance program. However, even if these two countries share many pre-existing conditions and commonly operating causal forces, such as the growth of influential pro-welfare civil society groups, there is also a growing and significant difference in how they deliver on their social policies. On the spending side, Taiwan has maintained its overall social expenditure at a higher level than South Korea, thanks to its generous income-maintenance policies, mainly in the form of direct cash transfer programs. On the institutional side, however, South Korea has succeeded in launching more universal types of programs with greater potential to increase spending in the future.

These differences between Argentina and Brazil and between Taiwan and South Korea become even more puzzling given that the major retrenchment in Argentina was propelled by a labor-based party, the PJ (the Justicialist Party), whereas the implementation and expansion of key social policies in Taiwan were driven by the right-wing (semiauthoritarian) party, the KMT (the Kuomintang, the Chinese Nationalist Party). Why did a formerly labor-based party suddenly betray the poor and working class in Argentina but not in Brazil? Why did the right-wing (formerly) authoritarian party initiate the expansion of key social policies in Taiwan? Why are universal social policies gaining increasing popular support in South Korea, deepening traditional right-wing versus left-wing partisan confrontations along the line of targeted versus universal policies, while politicians in Taiwan have been jockeying to provide more generous cash transfer programs, regardless of partisan affiliation?

Answering these puzzles requires the introduction of further complexities into the cases. In Brazil, both the centrist government (Cardoso) and center-left government (Lula and Dilma) introduced moderate reforms with varied levels of support from unions. In Argentina, however, different segments within the same PJ introduced completely

TABLE 1.1. *Expansion and Retrenchment of Income Maintenance Policies in Four Developing Economies: 1990s and 2000s*

	Argentina	Brazil	South Korea	Taiwan
Major Expansion				
Health Care	None	Administrative rationalization (progressive allocation to municipalities) (2002)	National Health Insurance (2000) Long-term care insurance	National Health Insurance (1995) Long-term care insurance (2007)
Old-Age Pension	Privatized pensions reappropriated by the state by 2008	None	National Pension (1999) (*Single pillar*) Basic old-age allowance (2007) Basic (non-contributory) Pension (2014)	National Pension (2008) (*fragmented*) Basic old-age Allowance (2008)
Family Allowance and Social Assistance	Assistance to unemployed Expansion of Conditional Cash Transfers in the 2000s	Conditional Cash Transfers (Bolsa Familia)[a]Non-contributory Pension for elderly, disabled, and rural poor gradually Expanded	Government-guaranteed basic income (2000)[b]Child Care Subsidy expanded (since 2010)	Minimum living expenses (2008) Free institutional care to elderly (1993) Medical subsidy to children (2002) Child Care Subsidy (2008)

Major Retrenchment

Health Care	Public benefits decreased	None	None (privatization attempts failed)	None (attempt failed)
Old-Age Pension	Partial privatization (1993) Reduction in minimum pension guarantee (1995)	Eligibility and benefits adjusted (1998) Pension reform (eligibility) attempt failed (2012)	Pension replacement rate lowered (60 to 40%)	Pension reform (individualized account) postponed (2014)
Family Allowance and Social Assistance	Benefits decreased	None	None	None

Source: USA Social Security Adminstration 2014/15.
Note ᵃ: Conditional upon children's school attendance and vaccination.
Note ᵇ: The official title of the law is the National Basic Livelihood Security Scheme (NBLSS).

different levels and forms of reforms: the Menem regime launched one of the most radical market reforms in modern developing economies, as just discussed, while the Kirchners reversed course as drastically as Menem, restoring existing labor market institutions and social policies (see Table 1.1). While labor market reforms in Latin America followed similar trajectories to their social policy reforms, in the East Asian cases they diverged: although Taiwan introduced more moderate reforms gradually, South Korean democratic reformist regimes enacted an abrupt lifting of existing labor market regulations, allowing lay-offs, and introduced radical flexibilization measures such as laws on dispatched workers and indirect employment. Particularly, the second reformist regime (Rho regime) introduced a significant number of market-oriented elements into pensions and health care systems: a strong impetus behind building a universal welfare state in South Korea suddenly halted after the turbulent 2000s. One of the most impressive stories of the expansion of universal social policy provisions suddenly moved to become a story about the serious retrenchment of several key social policy areas during the 2000s and after.

How could these marked differences and ideological incongruences between parties and policies (i.e., radical reforms under labor-based or labor-friendly regimes) be explained? What theoretical resources do modern social sciences (especially political sociology, political science, comparative political economy) provide to account for these variations?

To answer these questions, this book introduces the notion of 'embedded cohesiveness' (EC) to the comparative study of the welfare state. Based on the social movements literature and organizational studies of network analyses, the book builds two theoretical concepts of solidaristic linkages, cohesiveness (unions' ties to incumbent political parties or labor parties), and embeddedness (unions' ties to civic associations), which will be discussed in detail in Chapter 3, and then explains how the state and unions interact with respect to the retrenchment and expansion of social policies. By these 'ties', I imply "interorganizational solidaristic linkages," by which leaders and members in "multi-organizational fields"(Curtis and Zurcher 1973; Minkoff and McCarthy 2005) exchange their resources and negotiate their ideas with the goals of contentious mobilizations, policy deliberation and channeling, and electoral interventions. With this network-driven, actor-centered framework, this book explores how leaders of labor and civic organizations mobilize and institutionalize divergent repertoires of social solidarity regarding social policy agendas, and how they channel those policy agendas into state institutions through the politics of threat and persuasion. In short, the book develops a society-based explanatory model of the welfare state, in which labor–civic solidarity and union–party alliance jointly account for outcomes of welfare state retrenchment as well as welfare state expansion. The theory and findings of this study are expected to offer a novel approach to analyzing welfare state outcomes not only in democratized developing countries, but also in a larger set of rich democracies and new democracies.

JUSTIFICATION FOR THIS STUDY: IMPORTANCE OF UNIONS AND THEIR LINKAGES TO CIVIL SOCIETY

Now I turn to the importance of unions and their linkages to civil society, respectively, before I develop the primary causal mechanism of this study. It is a well-established fact that labor unions and their influence have declined in many societies (Western 1995, 1997), and the four countries being studied in this book are no exception. Nevertheless, I find that it is still important to emphasize in each country the role of the union as a component of (civic) associations or of the larger civil society for the following reasons.

Why Unions Matter

I contend that unions are unique civic associations that play a decisive role in balancing and configuring the relationships between the state, the economy, and civil society.

First, *labor unions, in contrast to other voluntary organizations, can directly affect production activities through institutional or non-institutional means.* Unions' cooperation with employers and the state can boost overall economic activities, both via nationwide neo-corporatist institutions (Garrett 1998) and via firm-level cooperation (Hicks and Kenworthy 1998). National- or industry-level union confederations play a critical role in wage bargaining and restraint (Western 1997), which is indispensable for constant economic growth at a national level. In sum, although the connectedness of unions to other civic organizations is relatively weak, unions' political and economic significance cannot be underrated because unions are the only civic organization that can cooperate with the state and employers to improve the production and distribution of economic resources and interests.

Second, *labor unions are one of the strongest mass movement organizers that can establish a position against state coercions, and they are the framing centers for alternative viewpoints of the world.* Labor unions have the option to withdraw workers from production lines for their own interests or for more general interests. When their economic and political power is exerted beyond factories, unions can have a tremendous impact on the existing power structure and social order in a country (Fantasia and Stepan-Norris 2004) through strikes, wage bargaining, and support for political parties via funding, voting, and resource sharing. In addition, unions build collective identities, coupled with "alternative belief structures," in the process of conflicts and bargaining with employers (Dixon *et al.* 2004; Roscigno and Danaher 2001).

Third, *unions' organizational structure, based on democratic ballots, strengthens workers' involvement with democratic rules and participation, which may lead to organized political participation encouraged by large industrial unions* (Marks 1989). Furthermore, the committed staff of unions, who depend on democratic ballots and material support from workers, also convey strong institutional leadership and resources to the broader community and other social movement organizations (SMOs). As a Brazilian union leader (João Cayres) whom I interviewed testifies, "everybody (social movement organizations) looks for us ... and, if we are available, we try to help within our parameters."

Finally, *unions are one type of civic association that consciously pursue the economic interests of the subordinate or lower classes, which provides a basis for economic justice for democracy and governance.* This distributional justice inherently embraced by unions' goals – better working conditions, higher wages, better fringe benefits, higher security for employment, and better provisions for firm- or industry-level welfare schemes – often easily develops into a societal-level general agenda. Unions' connectedness with other SMOs transfers egalitarian ideas and movement resources through organizational and institutional channels within civil society, thereby enhancing the social legitimacy of union-led reform agendas. When unions are densely connected with other civic associations, the interests of the lower classes are more easily introduced to other political arenas. This ignites and changes the operation of procedural democracy and the way democratic political mechanisms serve the interests of the disadvantaged, as Lipset (1960) pointed out in his concept of "democratic class struggles." Unions are a key node for workers' counter-hegemonic organizational bases that can make up for the lack of power resources of workers relative to those of employers and their allies in the rule of political democracy.

To combine the four points above, unions' unique organizational position and resources, both within civil society and between the state and civil society, afford them greater potential than any other civic association to empower all organizational communities in civil society. Unions' abundant human and material resources can provide other SMOs with organizational resources such as leadership, membership, and egalitarian policy agendas. The long-term solidarity for political and structural reform, or short-term solidarity for policy implementation, between unions and other SMOs greatly reduces the costs of mobilization for marches and demonstrations (Gerhards and Rucht 1992; Rosenthal *et al.* 1985), in turn strengthening electoral support for reformist parties through ballots and lobbying. In sum, *unions can boost the power of entire social movement networks when they are connected to other social movements and community organizations.*

Why Unions' Linkages Matter

A Key Node for Cross-Class Alliance
This study urges labor scholars, scholarship of the state and civil society, and more generally the field of civic associations and organizations to pay deeper attention to unions' linkages to political parties and civil society in analyzing policy or governance-related outcomes.

Power resource theorists in the area of democracy and welfare state development repeatedly argue that class alliance between the middle class and the working class is critical for the transition to democracy, consolidation of democracy (Collier 1999; Rueschemeyer *et al.* 1992), and development of modern welfare states (Esping-Andersen 1990). Recent turns to "relational approaches to collective action" (Diani 2003; Emirbayer 1997) and "social solidarity" (Gould 1995) provide micro-level explanations for class alliances via interorganizational networks. Interorganizational interactions based on shared leaderships and memberships provide an important aspect of social movement mobilization processes (Rosenthal *et al.* 1985). Unions' connectedness with middle-class and community-based civic associations via shared organizational memberships is critical for determining the direction and characteristics of civil society and the state–society relationship.

First, middle-class civic associations help unions acquire knowledge to cope with changing national, regional, and global economic fluctuations; they provide information on global standards of labor and environments that are labor-friendly; and they explore potential but 'realistic' policy options that unions can pursue in their collective bargaining or confrontational tactics against employers and the state. Second, alliances with middle-class and class-neutral civic associations provide unions with 'reformist agendas' that take into account 'general interests' beyond narrow working-class economic interests. For instance, when union leaders discuss environmental issues with new social movement organizations, both groups are likely to draw more support from their communities (Clawson 2003; Rose 2000; Southworth and Stepan-Norris 2003). Third, union members' and leaders' connectedness to prominent middle-class associations, such as professional associations, churches, and other class-neutral associations, allows unions to be more deeply embedded in general community environments, which helps unions build "social legitimacy" (Cornwell and Harrison 2004; Suchman 1995) for their strike activities, collective bargaining, and political campaigns. Historical case studies, such as the Commune of 1871 in Paris (Gould 1995), demonstrate that insurgents' embeddedness in local communities is critical in the formation of collective identities and mass mobilization. Recent demands to move from traditional "business unionism" to "social movement unionism" in US (Eimer 1999; Fantasia and Voss 2004), South African (Wood 2002), and South Korean (Ŭn 2005b) labor movements also suggest that *forging alliances with community and other social movement groups is critical for the success of unions and the development of broader communities.*

A Key Node for Autonomy and Counterhegemony
Both state elites and capitalists attempt to indirectly bridge civic organizations through quasi-civic (state-sponsored) organizations, or to directly co-opt civic organizations through direct economic incentives or populist ideological framing. In this sense, higher social capital does not lead to a deeper institutionalization of democracy or better governance if either authoritarian or populist state elites succeed in penetrating and co-opting (civic or quasi-civic) organizations. Human history in the twentieth century demonstrates that both democracy and autocracy can be based on strong civic associations. Gramsci drew attention to this dual aspect of civil society, contending that a pre-existing strong associational sphere could serve as a microbasis for fascism rather than as an autonomous space for fostering voluntarism and democratic citizenship (Gramsci 1971). Numerous historical examples – the past

and current Peronist regimes in Argentina (Waisman 1999), the fascist regime in 1930s Italy (Riley 2005), and the Nazi infiltration into voluntary associations, including unions, with the voluntary support of German civic associations (Berman 1997; Rueschemeyer *et al.* 1992, Ch.4) – demonstrate that the relationship between the state and civil society is not as simple as the Tocquevillian one-dimensional scale of civic associationism and its positive relationship with democratic governance.

Several elements are important in maintaining the autonomy of the associational sphere from the co-optation strategies of state elites and capital: the strength of unions, the strength of intellectual-based (mostly middle-class) associations and reformist parties, and most importantly the solidarity between the two. In particular, solidarity between intellectuals with working-class origins (organic intellectuals in the Gramscian sense) and intellectuals with middle-class origins (traditional intelligentsia) is critical to prevent working-class unions from being relegated to narrow economic interests. In other words, *solidarity with civic organizations from non-working-class origins provides unions with reformist or community-oriented views of struggles and agendas*. While the working class could resort to pure economism, this would only lead to short-term rewards based on capitalists' and states' co-optation. Solidarity with reformist middle-class and community-based intellectuals opens a longer horizon of struggles, including the institutionalization of democracy and better governance systems at both local and national levels. Visualization of a package of institutional democracy includes democratic class struggles via parliamentary democracy (Lipset 1960). When the working class and unions are convinced that they have a greater chance to pursue their distributional agendas within procedural democracy, they will either build or join reformist movements, which create a deeper institutionalization of democracy, as illustrated in Nordic social-democratic countries (Korpi and Shalev 1980). In accounting for the success of the institutionalization of democracy, it is the working class's connections to broader civic associational networks and reformist parties that matters. Durable solidarity between unions and other civic associations prevents the possible co-optation of some segments of the working class by the state elites and capitalists, simultaneously deterring both the isolation of unions and the subsequent resort of unions to militant unionism. The preceding discussion of the role of unions leads to the key conception of this study, 'embedded cohesiveness.'

OUTLINE OF THE ARGUMENT: 'EMBEDDED
COHESIVENESS (EC) APPROACH'

Through the notion of 'embeddedness of unions in civil society' and 'co-hesiveness of unions with political parties,' this study incorporates the scholarship of social movements, organizational studies, and welfare states into a unified theoretical framework. It extends the scopes of all three fields by developing a 'causal mechanism' that links social move-ments to solidarity as institutions, and then solidarity as institutions to the development/retrenchment of social and labor market policies. I have labeled this project as the 'embedded cohesiveness approach (the EC approach),' which aims to accomplish four novel goals in the fields of social movements, political sociology, organizational studies, and com-parative politics: (1) it builds a theory of the role of labor as a member of the entire civil society by taking into account an "organizational com-munity" (Suchman 1995) perspective; (2) it theorizes the 'contents' of solidaristic linkages by conceptualizing the differences and relationships between policy and mobilization capacities; (3) it theorizes the strategic interaction between the state and social movement sectors by utilizing the notions of network and game theoretical approaches. Based on these approaches, it theorizes the 'mechanisms' underpinning embedded-ness, and its interaction with cohesiveness in engendering social policy outcomes; (4) these efforts will culminate in a theory of the 'politics of expansion' and a theory of the 'politics of retrenchment.' Through the former, the approach will delineate an explanatory model of how such strategic interactions lead to either universal reforms (UR) or selective reforms (SR). With the latter, the approach will propose a model of how state–union interactions engender either radical reforms (RR) or mod-erate reforms (MR).

The embedded cohesiveness (EC) approach could be traced back to the broader literature on the social and political foundations of state cap-acity/effectiveness, a tradition which exploded with Skocpol, Evans and Rueschemeyer's "Bringing the State Back In" (1985) and Peter Evans' *Embedded Autonomy* (1995). The EC approach distinguishes its con-tribution from these previous works by highlighting the importance of 'social (civic and institutional) coordination,' which is anchored in deep social "fabrics" and "milieus" (Habermas 1991[1962]) and becomes materialized by the formerly radical and now 'embedded' leaders of in-tellectual and community origins. The EC approach, therefore, is also in line with Mann's (1986) "social power as organized networks" or "interstitial development" approach[2], in that both frameworks provide a 'society-centered' model. As Evans *et al.* (forthcoming) point out based on Sen's (1999) work, human beings are capable of reflecting on the origins and mechanisms of their suffering and "leading the kind of lives we value"(p. 18). The EC approach ultimately shares this view of human capability, explores the instances exemplifying such capabilities, and intends to theorize the mechanisms of positive and negative cases of 'capability' and 'well-being.' It focuses upon the effectiveness of "social infrastructures" within the state, which did not receive sufficient attention in the state-centric approaches (Skocpol *et al.* 1985) or political-institutional approaches (Ostrom 1990). In the EC approach, the agents building the social infrastructures are doubly embedded – not only in political networks at the center but also in communities of marginalized populations at the periphery. The EC approach is distinct from other similar approaches because of its emphasis on the social and intellectual origins of these agents. They are the ones who were voluntarily engaged in clandestine 'going-underground' activities during harsh authoritarian eras to connect the most disadvantaged social groups, workers, peasants, and the urban poor. The EC approach brings the focus to how such linkages become institutionalized under democratization phases and how they eventually lead to the 'institutions' of 'political power embedded in social power.' This EC approach will serve as an effective theoretical tool to build a 'civil society-based account' of welfare state development in the era of neo-liberal market reforms. In Chapter 3, I develop a concrete causal model that further specifies the logic of the EC approach and accounts for variations in welfare state outcomes with two primary explanatory variables, embeddedness and cohesiveness.

RESEARCH QUESTIONS OF THE EC APPROACH

The EC approach poses the following three research questions. In particular, it resituates the state–labor relationship in the context of a state–civil society relationship by exploring three theoretical questions. First, it reconsiders party–union relationships in an era of globalization, occupational transformation, and economic crises. *Is a close labor party–union relationship still conducive to defending the welfare state and workers' rights?* According to the literature on power resource theory (Esping-Andersen 1985; Huber and Stephens 2001; Korpi 1983), which has been developed on the basis of the close alliance between unions and social democratic parties in Western Europe, the incumbent labor-based party, supported by unions, is expected to implement and defend public policies closer to working-class interests. According to the theory of "political opportunity structure" (Eisinger 1973; McAdam 1996; Meyer 2004), the incumbency of a labor-based party may allow unions to recognize their ally in power and actively take advantage of such an opportunity to promote their interests. Both theories, therefore, predict that solidarity between unions and labor-based parties should lead to more effective resistance against market-based reforms. However, recent literature suggests that there are many factors that weaken such leftist party–union solidarity. First of all, in many societies in which the industrial working class has never comprised the majority in the class structure, labor-based parties had to find other allies such as middle-class white collars, petty entrepreneurs, or peasants (Baldwin 1990; Esping-Andersen 1990; Przeworski 1985) to achieve the leftist incumbency, and such tendencies were even more prevalent in diverse forms of populist mobilizations in Latin America where the size of industrial working class has rarely reached the level of that of Western Europe (Roberts 2002, 2006). Furthermore, the decline in union membership due to deindustrialization and transformation in the occupational structure has resulted in increasing heterogeneity within the working classes and in the weakening of traditional class solidarity (Clark and Lipset 2001; Franklin *et al.* 1992; Kitschelt 1994; Western 1995). Therefore, industrial working-class unions have become increasingly less capable of providing strong electoral support to labor-based parties. In this context, such parties experience pressure to cultivate alternative social bases such as the self-employed or white-collar workers to compensate for the decline in support from the industrial working class (Howell *et al.* 1992: Levitsky 2003b ; Przeworski 1985). This need may urge a labor-based party to turn away from its traditional allies and implement market-based reforms – such as the privatization of public firms, liberalization of labor market institutions, and reductions in social spending – to draw support from the middle classes.[3] This pressure may be increased even further for developing nations under globalization and economic crisis. Therefore, in the latter literature, a close labor party–union relationship may not necessarily guarantee successful resistance against radical market reform.

The first question leads to the second question: *why and how, then, do some unions successfully develop universal social reforms or defend employee rights and benefits against the state's market reforms?* This question may be partially answered by the literature on social movement unionism (Almeida 2008; Clawson 2003; Fantasia and Voss 2004; Lopez 2004; Rose 2000;

Seidman 1994) or inter-movement linkage (Isaac and Christiansen 2002). Unions in post-industrial societies experience pressure to build coalitions with diverse social and political organizations of different class origins in 'multi-organizational fields'[4] to make up for the decline in their traditional bases. With old unions around the globe becoming increasingly domesticated and enervated by rewards and punishment provided by the existing political and economic power, emerging new labor activists have also desired to identify new working-class roles. They refuse to stick with both the economic reductionism and political vanguardism of old Marxists, and instead embrace larger communities and other social groups in their struggles and strategies (Scipes 1992; Waterman 1993). Indeed, recent union movements in the US and other societies have been increasingly involved in housing projects, education, and training, as well as non-economic local and neighborhood-level matters such as environmental issues, to draw more support from wider constituencies. In this social movement unionism, unions' ties with other civil society organizations may provide unions with stronger communal support and movement resources. In such situations, labor rights will be extended to embrace citizenship rights, thereby recognizing the interests of various categories of workers, including the middle class, peasants, the urban poor, small entrepreneurs, and even the non-employed such as retired people and home-makers. In recently democratized developing countries, some societies with strong unions well linked to civil society organizations have consolidated their democratic institutions more effectively than others (Collier 1999; Rueschemeyer *et al.* 1992). Unions that conserve their history of solidarity with civil society groups during democratization movements are more likely to later gain effective support from their allies, thereby successfully building more broad-based solidarity against market reforms. The second question is also relevant to the recent surge of "insider–outsider politics" in rich democracies and some advanced developing societies (Rueda 2005, 2007). According to Rueda, the social democratic party only caters to organized, privileged core union members, excluding marginalized labor market outsiders such as the unemployed or those with non-standard, precarious jobs. He argues that, as a result of the social democratic party's commitment to insiders, labor market inequality could widen between "those with secure employment and those without." (2005, p. 61) This argument is not well supported empirically, as the differences he observed in preferences between insiders and outsiders on active labor market policies are not great (Thelen 2014). Nevertheless, the argument itself is important, because it reminds us that working-class interests are not homogeneous and a labor-based party may not necessarily serve the interests of the entire working class or less-privileged, unorganized workers. The literature leads me to raise a question: *under what conditions do unions (and labor-based parties) promote universal social policies that could reduce the insider–outsider gap?*

The third question explores how the state and labor reach consensus on a reasonable level of (expansion or retrenchment) reform. The literature on corporatism exclusively addresses this question in the context of an interest representation system in which unions are merely functional subsidiaries controlled by the state (Schmitter 1974). For instance, in such a perspective, histories of corporatist regulation of labor organizations in Latin America account for labor's level of restraint (Collier 1995; McGuire 1997). In the (neo)corporatist tradition, unions' cooperative relationships with their partisan allies lead to the development of encompassing, centralized union organizations that can control the behaviors of local unions (Alvarez *et al.* 1991; Calmfors and Driffill 1988; Przeworski 1991), and therefore result in unions' voluntary restraint in wage bargaining. A more nuanced recent study (Murillo 2001) shows how the lack of partisan competition for leadership (in other words, one-party monopoly in union leadership) leads to unions' cooperative behaviors. However, none of these studies explore how unions and the state predict the costs of reforms, militancy, and concession during the course of their sequential interactions, and therefore they do not shed light on the following critical questions: *How does each party achieve the most desirable outcome? Under what conditions are such desirable outcomes more likely to occur?*

In order to answer these questions, I develop detailed mezzo-level theoretical mechanisms for each player's information and action sets in Chapter 3. With concepts such as 'cohesiveness' and 'embeddedness' employed from network and organizational analyses, I highlight the role of the structural positions and capacity of actors in a given associational field in accounting for other players' behaviors as well as their own. I also aim to analyze the state and unions' decision-making processes as strategic choices based on the other players' capacities to resist and on expected behavior with such capacities. Each labor confederation may attempt to select its best action given its past experiences and possibility of future success, but a specific organizational-level strategy as a dominant practice is contingent upon other competitors', allies', stakeholders', and regulators' capacity and strategies. Therefore, a strategic action cannot be adequately analyzed without considering other interacting actors' capacity and strategies within a relevant organizational field (Fligstein and McAdam 2011).

Using these tools, I study the divergent organizational alliance structures and relevant strategic decision-making processes of labor organizations (and their allies). I show that unions' structural positions in larger associational fields inform the state and union leaders of contending players' expected behaviors based on their organizing capacities and commitment to each other, as well as to other relevant actors in the associational fields. From this perspective, I can gain insight into why and how various associational structures in which labor organizations are embedded inform and shape the state and unions' strategies in recently democratized societies.

The EC approach is situated in juxtaposition to traditional approaches in institutional sociology and economics. In contrast to the standard economics approach, it does not posit predetermined preference orders as the starting point, but proposes that "socio-political structure" precedes the order of preference (DiMaggio 1990; Nee and Ingram 1998). In other words, it identifies a causal mechanism in which unions' relationships with the state and larger civil society influence the order of preferences for each actor, which eventually accounts for the actions of unions and the incumbent party. Then, it treats socio-political structure as a signaling mechanism that informs actors of other contending actors' capacities for punishment as well as of their levels of commitment in the pre-existing history of cooperation. Here, the history of cooperation refers not only to bargaining partners but also to the history between one of the bargaining partners and third parties, including other organizational actors in civil society. In this way, I aim to explore a middle-ground of action theory between "over-socialized" actors of sociological neo-institutionalism and "under-socialized"(Granovetter 1985) actors of pure rational-choice theory (e.g. Becker 1976).

The EC approach initially examines how unions are positioned in different configurations of state–civil society relationships. It interprets the structural position of an actor in an associational field as a quasi-institutional mechanism "providing information relevant to the behavior of others"(Hall and Taylor 1996). Then, it assumes that the different orders of actors' preferences informed by network-based socio-political structures will lead to different actions by unions and the state under market reforms. These sequential decision-making processes are summarized in Figure 1.1.

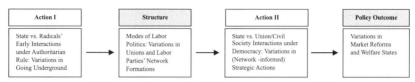

FIGURE 1.1. Causal Sequences

RESEARCH FRAMEWORK

In order to understand the political dynamics of neo-liberal reforms in these 'democratized developing' countries, this study takes an analytical approach, which I label 'actor-centered historical structuralism.' In this approach, I will build a causal framework composed of "long and thick independent variables" and "short and thin dependent variables" (Pierson 2004). As for the former, I will focus upon the relatively long historical formation processes of associational fields consisting of unions, political parties, and other civil society organizations. By 'thick', I mean exploring multiple layers and dimensions of associational fields, in my terms, through the notions of cohesiveness and embeddedness. Regarding the latter, I am interested less in the long-term formation processes of neo-liberal reforms than in the neo-liberal policy reforms as events or actions. Therefore, this study puts more weight on the side of 'independent variable' in terms of length and efforts.

The long and thick design requires incorporating two different frameworks into one. With a long historical approach, this study explores an unlikely time and space by working back to the politics under earlier authoritarian regimes, which may have shaped social and political cleavages for the last several decades (especially in the South Korean case study). With a thick field-based approach, this study investigates the structures of multiple layers of associational fields. By combining these two approaches, it explores how distinctive national associational fields have been structured during the course of democratization. I situate two critical actions in this long and thick design: at the very beginning and at the end of the causal sequences, as illustrated in Figure 1.1.

First, in order to understand the variations in neo-liberal reforms, this study initially explores radical intellectuals' clandestine underground activities in local communities and factories, their subsequent institutionalization processes, and consequential labor politics against or in collaboration with the incumbent state. In other words, it establishes a model of 'going-underground' activities under harsh state repression, and the effects of such activities on subsequent institutionalization of labor-based politics ("Action I → Structure" in Figure 1.1). Second, it further develops a model of the (network-informed) strategic interaction between the incumbent party and unions embedded in civil society ("Action II → policy outcome"). I will call the first causal sequence an 'actor-centered historical structuralism,' while labeling the second causal sequence a 'network-informed game in associational fields.'

Why do I focus upon these two specific modes of actions? I find that the first action by radical intellectuals, going underground, during the authoritarian regime, had decisively shaped the structural features of associational fields in these societies, and the second action by matured political entrepreneurs situated in the associational fields ultimately determined the range and degree of neo-liberal reforms. These actions at the beginning and at the end of the evolution of the associational fields shape the institutionalization of labor politics in each society.

Then, how can this study capture the structural features of the associational field in each society? As I already began to delineate, I propose two concepts to analyze the characteristics of the associational field: cohesiveness and embeddedness. The former signifies the relationship between unions and an incumbent political party or a labor party. The latter captures the relationship between unions and civil society organizations. This study highlights these two dimensions as the most critical factors in understanding the structure of labor politics and their consequences. In short, one part of this book will be devoted to divulging how cohesiveness and embeddedness have been historically shaped in each society, while the other part will analyze how these two explanatory factors account for variations in neo-liberal reforms and social policy expansions across places and times.

A final point regarding the sequential process presented in Figure 1.1 is that this "process-based" (Abbott 2016) argument should not be understood as a set of 'universally constant propositions without concrete variations.' Embeddedness and cohesiveness should be understood as mid-range heuristic devices that capture the structure and configuration of multi-organizational fields. They not only shape diverse actions and policies but also are reshaped into divergent provisional institutional contexts by prior interactions between key actors and larger contexts of global political economy. For instance, embeddedness and cohesiveness may be initially shaped by Action I in Figure 1.1, radical intellectuals' underground activities. Such activities create different modes of labor institutions across societies due to the different cultural and organizational resources they encounter in informal civil society. In addition, labor activists' strategic actions are configured by their own structural resources and other actors' actions (such as those of the state, employers, and other civic associations). These are not universally coherent processes, and instead they retain considerable internal variations due to different actors' different resources and ideas. For instance, Brazilian labor activists originate from strong community-based popular sectors, thereby committing themselves to social movement unionism and larger civic solidarity projects. Alternatively, South Korean activists commit themselves to ideological factions' projects, as historically these activists were engaged in underground activities along factional lines during authoritarian eras. Such initial formation of embeddedness and cohesiveness, and its outcomes (Action II), are exposed to divergent external economic and internal political pressures. For example, Argentine state bureaucrats and labor elites in the 1990s and South Korean employers and bureaucrats in the 2000s embraced neo-liberal economists' ideas wholeheartedly, and attempted to implement them through radical market-based labor and social policy reforms. Because of these reforms, labor unions and civil society had to confront these radical projects initiated by their former allies, labor party or reformist party leaders who were deeply penetrated by neo-liberal ideas and advocates. In contrast to Brazil and Taiwan, labor and civic leaders of Argentina and South Korea could not help but engage in different levels of contentious politics in response to challenges originating in the global economy. Social policy outcomes may vary across societies, again depending upon unions' and civil society's capacities to respond to such reform projects. In short, embeddedness and cohesiveness are continuously reshaped both internally and externally in multi-organizational fields and through their interactions with other key actors, which results in corresponding divergent changes in social policy regimes.

DATA AND ANALYTICAL STRATEGIES FOR CASE STUDIES

These four intriguing cases, all in the shadow of globalization and democratization, prove distinctly valuable for analyzing the politics behind neo-liberal market reforms. The radical transformations these four countries have undergone in their political and economic institutions during the last couple of decades allow me to observe and analyze the institutionalization processes of social movement capacities and their roles in shaping key policy outcomes. In other words, labor and civic organizations in these countries have also been in transition modes from movement mobilizers to policy builders/negotiators. Some unions successfully achieved this fundamental change in their roles, while others failed. Therefore, these four cases provide some of the most exciting stories of labor–civic solidarity in terms of policy and mobilization in the late twentieth century.

Through comparative-historical case studies based on local literature, archival searches of unions' and other civic organizations' documents, and field interviews with key leaders of such organizations, the study will reveal and explain variations in cohesiveness and embeddedness as well as in expansion and retrenchment in social and labor market policies. Its analytical strategy is largely in line with those elaborated by Mahoney and Rueschemeyer (2003) in their influential work on comparative historical analysis, in that I seek "analytic interest in causal analysis" and "contextualized comparisons" of a few important cases with a deep understanding of them that enables "a higher level of conceptual and measurement validity"(pp. 13–14).

My case studies will be conducted in three stages: the first is a deep case study on a single case – South Korea. Consisting of three chapters, it aims to reveal how Korean labor movements emerged, flourished, and declined over the three most recent decades, as well as how Korean labor leaders and their allies have succeeded or failed in building the welfare state. While all focused on South Korea, the unit of analysis of the chapters implicitly varies. It is often the 'union confederations,' as I mostly compare the KCTU's embeddedness and cohesiveness with those of the FKTU, the other large, moderate union confederation. In other instances, however, it is 'policy,' as I will focus on comparing the enactment processes of health care, pensions, and other labor market policies. Within this South Korean case, as discussed above, there exist wide variations in success and failure stories of labor movements and social policies over time. Therefore, I am able to multiply the number of cases across organizations, policies, and times by considering multiple units of analysis and time points. I draw on multiple sources for the South Korean case: the primary source is semi-structured interviews with 56 union leaders of central confederations, industrial unions, and grassroots unions, as well as with several other leaders of civic associations and political parties, and intellectuals deeply involved in labor politics (see Appendix A for the concrete positions and roles of these leaders). I also refer to archival data such as internal union documents, major newspapers, the periodicals of several labor organizations, and, of course, scholarly products on labor politics. Finally, I utilize two-mode network datasets in which civic and labor organizations are co-affiliated with multiple events on joint mobilization and policy formulation efforts in the 1990s and the 2000s in South Korea. With these datasets, I illustrate the structures of associational fields during critical conjunctures to reveal key organizational actors' solidaristic efforts in building or defending universal social policies.[5] This detailed, deep case study on South Korea allows me to reveal the two key underlying mechanisms of embeddedness and cohesiveness, policy and mobilization dimensions that could not be easily explored with shorter case studies or a large N study.

In Chapters 7, 8 and 9, I turn to the second stage of case studies, which are cross-national, comparative historical analyses of four countries. Chapter 7 initially compares two major union confederations' divergent responses to the state's market reforms within two countries in Latin America, the CGT and CTA in Argentina and then the Força Sindical and CUT in Brazil. Chapter 8 extends this within-country comparison to major union confederations in two East Asian countries. I compare the FKTU and KCTU in South Korea, and then the CFL and TCTU in Taiwan. These comparative analyses are based on nearly 90 in-depth field interviews with labor leaders in three other countries.[6] In these case studies, the unit of analysis comes down to the confederation level over several decades. By analyzing two representative confederations within each country over two decades (the 1990s and the 2000s), I expand the number of cases to 16. In this way, my research design mitigates concerns about "degree of freedom" issues (Lieberson 1991; Rueschemeyer *et al.* 1992) in comparative case studies and takes into account multiple potential third variables. In Chapter 9, I expand the focus of the study to comparison of four countries. Using the two theoretical concepts, embeddedness and cohesiveness, and analyses of country-level associational networks built upon *World Values Surveys,* I explain variations in the development and retrenchment of welfare institution. In this final empirical chapter, I conduct cross-national comparisons of the countries' network structures and policy outcomes. The unit of analysis is the country level, as analyses of both network structures and social policy legislations are at the aggregate country level.

OUTLINE OF THE GENERAL ARGUMENTS: BRINGING IN EMBEDDEDNESS

I claim that embeddedness of formal-sector associations, especially labor unions, in informal civil society is expected to contribute to expanding or defending the welfare state for the following three reasons: first, the civil society mechanism leads to a larger welfare state because of enhanced labor leader–voter linkages through effective information exchange and correct evaluations of leaders' trustworthiness, reliability, and performativity. Citizens as voters shape their preferences for policies and political positions based on 'indirect referrals' circulated through relevant personal and organizational networks.[7] Interorganizational ties between labor unions and informal civic associations (especially non-political groups such as churches, sports and cultural clubs, and lifeworld/community-based civic associations) facilitate such indirect referral processes regarding the reputations of formal-sector leaders with pro-labor platforms (insofar as disenchanted voters would drop out of such ties during the course of information exchange). As a consequence, in societies where formal interest bargaining processes with regard to labor issues are strongly linked to informal civic associations, citizens are more likely to build stronger "trust" (Coleman 1990; Granovetter 1985) with formal-sector leaders, especially in labor-relevant sectors. In response to citizens who are well-informed about leaders and have built historical trust with them, party and union leaders will be more loyal to voices from their base and less likely to "free-ride" (Olson 1965) others' efforts, due not only to fear of electoral or non-electoral punishment but also to their "repeated interactions" (Montgomery 1998) with citizens over time and consequential deep understanding of their constituents' welfare needs.

The second element of labor–civic solidarity that potentially contributes to defending the welfare state is the role of social legitimacy in constraining formal politics. Leaders of labor-based parties and unions with high embeddedness are more likely to be those who once undertook going-underground activities (which will be discussed in Chapters 4, 7, and 8) and, therefore, to be fundamentally distinct from machine politicians in terms of their goals and levels of commitment to their base. I expect that these embedded labor leaders, as they emerge from local neighborhoods or at least through repeated communications with them, are more likely to be concerned about policies serving wider groups of citizens at community levels, thereby enhancing their "cognitive and moral legitimacy" (Aldrich and Ruef 2006; Suchman 1995).[8] Such a deep, intrinsic commitment to non-organized segments of civil society, communities, and marginalized populations also leads embedded unions and their leaders to vehemently resist retrenchment drives or to refuse to cooperate with such attempts, thereby contributing to the sustenance of existing social policy institutions (which will be delineated as 'the third proposition' in Chapter 3).[9] Such 'embedded unions' are assumed to be the modern carriers of Polanyi's "the moral entity 'man'," against the egoistical, demoralizing market mechanism, which embed themselves in "villages of cooperation" (Polanyi 1944, pp. 163–69) in local or civic associational communities.

The third civil society mechanism generating welfare state expansion is increased lobbying and negotiation power of labor–civic solidarity based on mobilization and policy capacities (which will be discussed in Chapter 3). In more advanced democracies, union-based policy experts build policy-specific solidarity with experts and citizens in other political and civic associations, which can be illustrated best by the example of 'health solidarity' in South Korea (Chapters 4 to 6). Policy specialists and leaders of upper-level or large unions negotiate, coordinate, and craft social and labor market policies beyond wage negotiations, not only with other civic and professional organizations but also with the incumbent and opposition parties. In these processes, unions with high embeddedness are often capable of waging a policy-based solidarity campaign composed of "constituents" and "sympathizers" (McCarthy and Zald 1977) from a wide range of social classes beyond their narrow working-class base. Such cross-class solidarity based on a specific social policy (when ideally aligned with appropriate 'cohesive channels' with the incumbent party; the fourth proposition in Chapter 3) leads to the provision of more comprehensive social policies, which often translates into a bigger welfare state. In this third route, 'embedded unions' could be deemed not only as "spheres of justice" (Walzer 1984) that preserve "immanent moral structures in their own right"(Alexander 2006, p. 33), but also professionalized, rational organizations that translate community needs into concrete social policy agendas. Overall, then, I predict that highly embedded labor organizations in (informal) civil society, in combination with unions' cohesive channels with the state, will bring in the expansion of more generous and universal welfare programs.

OUTLINE OF THE CASE STUDIES

In Chapters 4 through 6, I conduct a deep case study of South Korean labor politics and welfare politics, applying the EC approach to account for dramatic variations in the expansion and retrenchment of the welfare state over time and across policy domains. Chapter 4 discusses how South Korean radical leftist intellectuals' clandestine going-underground activities (during the harsh authoritarian rule in the 1970s and 1980s) in urban factories evolved into the embeddedness and cohesiveness of labor unions in civil and political societies in the next decade. The chapter reveals the early gestation processes by which those intellectuals eventually institutionalized labor–civic solidarity, as well as labor's channels to the state institutions and political parties. Through this analysis, I present the detailed processes by which a labor-linked associational field emerges around policy domains through divergent activists' endeavors to build 'solidarity structures.' With an implicit comparison of two ideal types and empirical examples (KCTU-PSPD ad hoc solidarity vs. KCTU member unions' systematic participation in NCHIU), I explore how unions' ties to other important civic associations and political parties become institutionalized as variegated modes of cohesiveness and embeddedness. With these historical analyses of the emergence and structuration of labor-linked associational fields, I establish the context in which EC approach accounts for the success and failure stories of welfare state development in South Korea in the subsequent two chapters.

Chapter 5 analyzes how South Korean radical labor leaders built the KCTU (and industrial unions) and subsequently succeeded in promoting a universal social policy reform, the passage of the bill on the integration of national health insurance societies, by participating in a wide range of popular labor-agrarian-intellectual solidarity activity (the National Conference for Health Insurance Unification, NCHIU). It also juxtaposes the KCTU's universal reform strategy with the FKTU's selective reform strategy, which collided in policy arenas during the late 1990s and early 2000s under the D. J. Kim regime, the first reformist regime after the transition to democracy. I then compare the policy and mobilization capacities of the NCHIU's embedded cohesiveness with those of the KCTU-PSPD alliance, and conclude that upper-level organizational alliances seeking policy capacity but lacking mobilization capacity engender a weak version of reform that may not be sustained over time.

Chapter 6 investigates the neo-liberal reforms of social and labor market policies in South Korea during the 2000s and after, under one reformist regime and then two conservative regimes. It initially traces the changes in the two solidarity linkages, embeddedness and cohesiveness, and explore how labor–civic solidarity either managed to sustain or else failed to defend the key components of the universal social policies built in the late 1990s. I focus on the different structures of labor–party and labor–civic solidarity across two policy domains – health care and pensions – and identify durable embeddedness of unions in the health care field around the Korean Federation of Medical Activist Group for Health

Rights (KFMA) and the Health Rights Network (HRN), while observing a sharp decline or lack of embeddedness in pensions. I then show that the solidarity network of the health care field successfully defended the health care system against continual attempts at neo-liberal privatization throughout the 2000s, while the weak(ened) embeddedness of unions in the domain of pensions contributed to severe retrenchments. The chapter demonstrates that the four types of combinational spaces built in Chapter 3 convincingly account for the variations in the changing structure of associational fields and welfare state retrenchment outcomes.

Chapters 7 and 8 move focus to organizational-level major union confederations, examining their strategic decision-making processes in confronting the state's market reform agendas. Still utilizing two notions of solidaristic linkages at the confederation level, I apply the EC approach to analyzing the actions of eight union confederations of four countries. In particular, CGT in Argentina, Força Sindical in Brazil, FKTU in South Korea, and CFL in Taiwan chose restraint rather than militancy when the state implemented labor-repressive or market-oriented reforms. However, I also show that unions' embeddedness, even without cohesive ties to the state, is sufficient to defend their core rights and assets against the state's radical retrenchment drives. CTA in Argentina, KCTU in South Korea, and TCTU and its predecessors (before 1997) in Taiwan did not tolerate the state's repression or market-oriented reforms, especially during the 1990s when their embeddedness reached peak intensity. Finally, if unions are to achieve the best outcome, moderate reform and restraint, they may need both social and institutional coordination processes through embeddedness and cohesiveness. Among the case studies I examine, this ideal mode of civic and institutional coordination has been achieved only in Brazil, but CTA and TCTU's alliances with professionalized civic associations in Argentina and Taiwan have also realized quasi-embedded cohesiveness in the 2000s, under the Kirchners' and DPP regimes respectively, which led to significant expansionary social policy reforms.

The country case studies in Chapter 9 reveal how diverse civic and political associations have formulated divergent structures of associational networks and how variations in these have generated divergent types of welfare states. In the 1990s, in Argentina and Taiwan, party and union leaders' cohesive relationships, disarticulated from the informal civic sphere, allowed them to conduct elite-driven social policy reforms from above, by launching radical neo-liberal reforms (Argentina) or by developing a generous transfer-centered welfare state (Taiwan). In Brazil and South Korea in the 1990s, however, party and union leaders' durable solidarity embedded in wider civic communities enabled them to resist the retrenchment of the welfare state (Brazil) and to implement universal social policies (South Korea) based on bottom-up mobilization and articulation of welfare demands.

In the 2000s and after, however, changing embeddedness and cohesiveness, interacting with structural economic changes and domestic political competitions, produced widely divergent outcomes in social policy regimes. In Argentina and Taiwan, new union movements in collaboration with civil society (CTA in Argentina and TCTU in Taiwan) emerged and helped their political allies take over the state, which resulted in expansionary welfare state reforms. In Brazil, embedded cohesiveness became further strengthened with the PT in power, which led to the most progressive and (too) ambitious version of social policy reform in developing societies. In South Korea, the labor–civic solidarity that achieved the universal social policies in the 1990s and the early 2000s had to witness not only its own stunning demise but also retrenchments in key social insurance schemes.

Overall, through multi-level case studies, I demonstrate that the cohesiveness of unions lacking embeddedness may allow the state to exploit unions' commitment, thereby introducing radical market-oriented reforms of social policies and labor market institutions. I also show that embeddedness of unions plays a decisive role in not only defending the welfare state against market reforms but also promoting universal reforms over selective reforms in these four countries.

In the Conclusion, I summarize the main arguments and their implications, and then discuss the implications of the South Korean case study and comparative case studies. I also revisit theories of the welfare state with the EC approach, and further expand the discussion to broader literature on civil society, development, and democracy. I conclude by explaining how the EC approach provides a new way of understanding theories of social solidarity and welfare state formation.

2

Revisiting Theories of the Welfare State in Developing Countries

INTRODUCTION

This chapter revisits representative theories of the welfare state and considers their virtues and limitations in discussing recently democratized developing countries, before I delineate the EC approach in the next chapter. Theories of the welfare state focused upon rich democracies have largely developed into three schools: (1) a state-centric policy legacies view; (2) power resource theory; and (3) varieties of capitalism (in conjunction with a more recent electoral-system-based explanation). These three perspectives primarily differ in what they deem the 'driving force' behind social policy expansion: the state/policy structure itself, labor unions and allied leftist parties, or employers. Arguments emphasizing 'economic openness' and 'politics of blame avoidance,' which point to the growing need for social policies under global economic fluctuations or the persistent need for welfare states and their continuity in spite of retrenchment pressures, have also claimed their share of attention.

These existing theories of the welfare state, however, have encountered serious challenges in explaining newly emerging welfare states in developing societies. First of all, in such countries democratization and globalization (oriented by neo-liberal market fundamentalism) occurred simultaneously – mostly in the 1980s and the 1990s. Therefore, factors that typically lead to either social policy expansion or social policy retrenchment became confounded under these dually tumultuous circumstances. As power resource theory contends, democratization generated considerable expectations of redistributive politics among newly enfranchised citizens in developing societies. And as the economic openness thesis predicts, the vulnerability of lower-status, marginalized populations to economic fluctuations increased their demand for a social safety net. However, the era of globalization since the 1980s was also marked by market fundamentalism promoted by international financial capital and the IMF. Many emerging market economies suffered financial crises due to their intrinsic balance-of-payment issues or an incapacity to respond to the abrupt movements of international capital. The IMF and the Washington consensus imposed 'market-based solutions' on these countries, which required severe austerity and cuts to or wholesale privatization of public institutions. In short, due to their unbalanced industrial structures, inefficient governance systems, and unequal terms of exchange in international trade, developing societies, and especially emerging economies, suffered through periodic economic crises much more severe than those experienced in rich democracies. Under these circumstances, the risk and income profiles of the competing social forces could change rapidly depending upon international market forces and state policies, with domestic political forces responding promptly to such changes.

However, the dominant theoretical frameworks in the comparative study of the welfare state are built upon the assumption of the long-term structural stability of economic growth and international trade, of state bureaucracy, constitutional structures and veto points, and of the working classes' steadily growing political power. All the conventional theoretical tools for studying welfare states are based on the post-war economic growth of the Golden Age (1945–73), gradually aging populations, and long-term empowering processes for the working classes. To analyze relatively advanced, democratized developing societies – societies in which none of these conditions are fully met – we need new theoretical perspectives which give more weight to short-term coalitions, rapid realignments of political and social forces, and abrupt institutional changes. How could it be that, in just a decade, the same elites could engage in promoting welfare states at one moment and retrenching them at another? Why did the same unions sponsor certain universal social policies at one point and then collude with employers for their own interests at other times – also within just a decade? Can the existing theories of welfare states adequately account for the abrupt expansion and retrenchment outcomes in newly democratized emerging economies in the late twentieth century – especially the four countries being studied in this book? This chapter first revisits each representative theory of the welfare state developed in the late twentieth century and then assesses their applicability in analyzing the variations in welfare states in developing countries. In the latter part of the chapter, I will provisionally explore the utility of new analytical paths – social movement processes and 'configuration of civil society' perspectives – for investigating the distinctive dynamics of the retrenchment and expansion of welfare states in developing countries.

Each of the existing theories has, at different moments, found its heyday in late twentieth-century academic debates. State-centric theory emerged as one of the primary explanations of the rapid expansion of the welfare state in rich democracies in the twentieth century, supplanting the then-prevailing industrialization theory of the welfare state. While the industrialization thesis (Cutright 1965; Wilensky 1975) derived the demand for new social policies from changing family structure (nuclear family) and demographic structure (increasing population of older people) during the course of industrialization,[1] state-centric theory highlighted not only the pioneering role of autonomous state bureaucrats in conceiving, identifying, and implementing (alternative) social policies, but also the enduring role of the legacies of existing social policies (Heclo 1974; Skocpol 1992. A social policy "acquires meaning" (Heclo 1974, p. 4) and therefore creates 'action' or 'new politics.' Later iterations of state-centric theory further argued that the state structure or policy structure itself also plays a decisive role in fostering or deterring social policy development.[2] For instance, the multiple veto points present in federal states were often cited as major deterrent mechanisms against the development or retrenchment of welfare states (Pierson 1994; Skocpol 1992).

Along with the state-centric approach, Pierson's "politics of blame avoidance" earned considerable attention during the late 1990s, as it offered an explanatory tool for the "persistence and continuity of the welfare states" even under the pressure of retrenchment. He contends that "the emergence of powerful groups surrounding social programs may make the welfare state less dependent on the political parties, social movements, and labor organizations that expanded social programs in the first place" (Pierson 1994, p. 147). For Pierson, social policies create their own constituencies. For instance, the elderly may emerge as the very advocate groups who may make the welfare state stand around its own beneficiaries without relying on the founders (Pierson 1996).

He argues that previous approaches also overlook the cost of "assembling and sustaining pro-retrenchment coalitions"(Pierson 1994, p. 155). As a result, "theories designed to explain (expansion) outcomes in a particular context" (p. 156) may not be applicable to retrenchment outcomes under different economic and political environments. Normally, the incumbent political forces will rarely implement retrenchment reforms because it is very difficult to find political strategies to minimize the potential blame they will incur. Because of these disincentives, politicians may not easily launch retrenchment, as demonstrated by a series of unsuccessful reform efforts under conservative regimes in rich democracies.[3]

Following these traditions, many students of the welfare state focusing on developing societies emphasized the role of autonomous bureaucrats in introducing the early forms of social policies. For instance, in both South Korea and Taiwan bureaucrats played central roles in introducing and implementing health care and pensions for employees of the government and large firms (Kwon 2003, 2005). As many social policies were introduced under authoritarian regimes (Mares and Carnes 2009), it was almost inevitable that researchers focused their attention on the importance of bureaucrats, who were the ones to formulate detailed plans for each social policy within the boundaries permitted by the authoritarian dictators. Especially without meaningfully strong interest groups or pressure groups, policy specialists within the state bureaucracy may be the sole promoters of social policies, and they also have the long-term planning capacities necessary to address social policy implementation and budgeting. Thus, in post-colonial state-building processes, state bureaucracy "overdevelops" (Alavi 1972) compared to society, and so has high capacity to coordinate with or enforce the state's agenda on different social forces. In such a situation, the state is easily able to introduce social policies using either its centralized bureaucracy or its corporatistic subsidiary organizations.

Power resource theory also emerged in the 1980s as social democratic welfare states demonstrated that it is possible to promote working-class interests and rights via parliamentary representative democracy without necessarily overthrowing capitalism (Esping-Andersen 1985; Korpi 1983; Stephens 1979). With the support of dense and centralized labor unions that encompass the majority of wage earners, social democratic parties in the Nordic countries were able to retain political power over the long term and therefore progressively expand universal social policies. Even where they were not in power, the strong presence of social democratic parties in competitive elections pushed such expansion by keeping centrist parties, such as the Christian democratic parties, close to pro-welfare forces in other Western European countries (Huber *et al.* 1993).

As scholars of the welfare state began to turn their attention to developing societies, they gave ample credence to power resource theory. In particular, scholars of democratization immediately applied their theory to the development of welfare states in developing societies. As power resource theory assumed that the fundamental power base of social democratic politics originates from the organization of the 'have-nots' in capitalist society, enfranchisement of these have-nots and the mobilization of their demands through unions and leftist parties during the course of democratization will, scholars asserted, eventually contribute to the formation of welfare states in developing societies (Haggard and Kaufmann 2008; Huber and Stephens 2012). It is especially noteworthy that scholars in the fields of both the welfare state and democratization highlight the importance of the 'class coalition' between working classes and middle classes for achieving the best outcomes. Rueschemeyer *et al.* (1992) found that when the working classes form coalitions with the middle classes, which often coalesce with authoritarian elites, the transition to democracy is most successful and durable. In a similar vein, Esping-Andersen (1990) argued that working classes' alliances with peasants or white-collar workers were decisive in promoting universal welfare states in Nordic countries. Therefore, it may be plausible to argue that, in societies where the working classes maintain durable solidarity with the middle classes or some segments of them, democratic consolidation may lead to a larger welfare state.[4]

The emergence of the varieties of capitalism (VoC) school (Estevez-Abe *et al.* 2001; Hall and Soskice 2001; Iversen and Soskice 2009) in the late twentieth century radically transformed the terrain of intellectual hegemony in the welfare state debates. Advocates of this approach adopted, instead of Esping-Andersen (1990)'s celebrated three worlds, a simpler typology composed of 'LME (liberal market economy)' and 'CME (coordinated market economy)'. They then argued that primary institutional differences between two worlds stem from different employers' needs and interests regarding employees' skill investment. While LMEs – paradigmatically, the United States – developed deregulated labor markets and market-based financial and technology transfer systems, CMEs – paradigmatically, Germany – fostered institutional environments in which firms and workers can share information and reputation regarding market and technology shifts. The former encourages labor market actors to invest in easily switchable assets (general skills), while the latter allows employers and workers to develop co-specific skills within firms (firm-specific skills). Especially in CMEs, employers and workers have shared common interests in developing specific skills, which required co-evolving PR (proportional representation) systems. Such consensus-oriented electoral systems historically enabled center-left coalitions to evolve and promote generous redistributive social policies (Iversen and Soskice 2009).[5] In these environments, employers and workers are presumed to build cross-class alliances to lobby the state to enact social policies (Estevez Abe *et al.* 2001; Mares 2003).

Thanks to its influence since the 2000s, many scholars in comparative politics, international development and industrial relations have attempted to apply the VoC framework to developing countries. Schneider and Soskice (2009) treated Latin American economies as a negative variant of VoC – 'Hierarchical Market Economies' (HMEs), in which hierarchically diversified business groups realize their interests through 'institutional complementarities,' reflected in the marginalization of the lower classes, atomistic labor relations, low investment in skill development, and presidentialism. Rudra (2007) also initially employs the VoC categories, but instead ends up with a new regime typology – "productive" vs. "protective" welfare regimes – depending upon each country's developmental strategy. Many others (Haggard 2004; Hall and Gingerich 2009) classify South Korea as a typical CME, with its industrial relations and training systems developed during the developmental era (under the Park Jung-Hee regime).

Finally, the economic openness argument has developed into several distinct versions. In the earliest iteration, Cameron (1978) and Katzenstein (1985) reasoned that economic fluctuations due to trade openness would lead to an increased need to protect vulnerable populations. Garrett (1998) supported this argument by showing that globalization strengthens leftist parties and their redistributive politics. This positive association between economic openness and social provision of welfare, however, has been refuted in the subsequent wave of research. Huber and Stephens (2001) find that globalization has significantly caused the retrenchment of welfare states, at least for the last several decades. Kwon and Pontusson (2010) further provide sophisticated arguments that leftist partisan effects on social spending were noticeable with globalization in the 1970s and early 1980s and in countries in which unions retained their hegemony, but disappeared in the 1990s and after and in countries in which unions suffered decline. In a larger context (beyond the welfare state literature), many theorists of the state and capitalism agreed that market fundamentalism has toppled traditional Keynesian economics, capital has outweighed the state's regulatory or protective roles, and employers have enjoyed greater freedom in terms of capital mobility, flexibility, and efficiency (Jessop 2002; Steinmo 2002; Strange 1997). Recent dramatic increase in financial openness and the amplified voices of international financial capital and their agencies (such as credit rating agencies) are presumed to have enervated the state's policy maneuverability by means of fiscal, monetary, and social policies. Indeed, Swank and Steinmo (2002) found that capital mobility reduces corporate tax rates. In this offshoot of the openness literature, globalization encroaches upon the welfare state and labor market institutions that previously protected workers from ruthless market principles.[6]

In developing countries, economic openness is also known to have diverse effects on welfare state expansion. Globalization retrenches not only labor standards (Mosley and Uno 2007), but also welfare spending (Avelino *et al.* 2005; Wibbels 2006), having especially adverse impacts on the middle classes (Rudra 2008). Globalization tends to strengthen not only the voices of international capital and its domestic partners but also independent bureaucrats who are advocates for market-oriented principles (Babb 2001). Economic crises may be one decisive conjuncture through which globalization forces attempt to eliminate domestic regulations such as labor standards, corporate taxes, and workers' social wages. Scholars using this framework pointed to developmental strategies, often in conjunction with the VoC school's production regime argument, to explain the role of openness in shaping welfare institutions in developing countries. (Haggard and Kaufman 2008; Mares and Carnes 2009; Wibbels and Ahlquist 2011). Wibbels and Ahlquist, for instance, reasoned that countries with scarce labor (in Latin America) adopted ISI (Import Substitution Industrialization) with insurance-based social policies targeting core urban sectors, while countries with abundant labor (in East Asia) adopted ELI (Export-led Industrialization) seeking 'human capital investment' for a larger, general population (over social insurance for targeted groups).

A more decisive element of this competing explanation based on economic openness is that economic crises under globalization may have disastrous impacts on ties among organized citizens in civil society, as well. Economic crises may weaken unions and their cooperatives by indirectly or directly enervating their resource bases and locally entrenched spatial linkages. For instance, retrenchments on labor standards and collective labor rights may adversely affect union activities. New corporate management strategies seeking higher flexibility and individualization of pay scales may create divisions among workers (Pontusson and Swenson

1996), which will weaken the collective bargaining capacity of unions. In addition, geographically dispersed work arrangements by multinational firms and increased capital mobility across borders may also encroach upon unions' organizational power based on geographical concentration in traditional industrial zones. Increasing wage and benefit differentials may further prevent union leaders and members (especially those in high-skilled, high-paid jobs) from building solidarity with other marginalized social forces. Increasingly narrowed and divided working-class organizations, therefore, will stop attracting other social forces into labor-led civic solidarity. Based on this prediction, the final outcome of this process, then, will be decline in both labor–civic solidarity and welfare states.

LIMITATIONS OF PREVIOUS STUDIES

In reviewing the theories that have been developed to account for advanced industrial democracies, I have found that even though the dominant theories of welfare state development retain some explanatory power for variations among these four countries (and other developing countries), they are fairly limited in answering the questions I raise here. The most commonly cited explanations for welfare state expansion – demographic pressure (i.e., increasing old-age population) coupled with the logics of industrialism (Pampel and Williamson 1989; Wilensky 1975) and the theory of economic openness (Cameron 1978; Katzenstein 1985) – may reasonably explain the introduction of universal health care and pensions in Taiwan and South Korea. But these theories cannot explain why the two countries have increasingly followed different institutional paths since the late 1990s, especially regarding the structure of their programs – their universality and generosity.[7] Both theories also have their limits in explaining the different trajectories of welfare policies in Argentina and Brazil, as they have similar levels of openness and demographic structures. For instance, these theories cannot explain why radical retrenchments of pension programs occurred in Argentina and South Korea in the 1990s and the 2000s, respectively, while they did not in Brazil.[8]

Another influential theory of welfare state development, the "state-centric" approach (Heclo 1974; Skocpol 1992), may effectively explain earlier phases of partial, selective social policy developments (targeting state officials and public sector employees) initiated by authoritarian regimes, but the autonomous role of state bureaucrats is less evident in the eras of democratic consolidation. The authoritarian elites were typically content to embrace the core practitioners in the state bureaucracy (civil servants, soldiers, and teachers) and workers in core industries through basic social insurance, but the extension of these rights to regular citizens occurred much later, under growing pressure from the non-insured majority and their newfound organizational power.

In addition, both the role of bureaucrats and the legacies of past policies, which were largely identical in the two East Asian and the two Latin American countries, are unable to provide satisfactory answers to the questions above regarding 'radical departures' of social policies from previous trajectories. In these countries, the state bureaucrats' retrenchment or expansionary reform efforts after the transition to democracy were largely made through close negotiations and coordination with their allies in civil society. The radical departures were possible only in cases where the incumbent partisan leaders had unitary, top-down control over their allies, and where those allies did not have a strong commitment to other civil society forces. Therefore, the state-centric approach works only under specific conditions.[9]

The policy-legacy approach is also questionable with respect to its applicability in developing societies. With developing countries facing repeated and deeper economic crises than advanced industrial countries, policy legacies were indeed easily reversed in either direction: progressive social policies faced sudden retrenchment efforts, while radically universal or progressive transfers were introduced, abruptly nullifying the previous policy trajectories. Even major economic policies were vulnerable to such radical reversals. For instance, facing severe financial crises, both Argentina and South Korea introduced radical market-oriented reforms in public firms and labor market institutions in the 1990s, with each discarding a significant portion of its traditional developmental strategy (e.g. close Bank–Chaebol[10] relationships directed by the government in South Korea). Some policy legacies survived (such as generous Latin American pension programs for public employees), but at the same time domestic economic and political institutions radically and rapidly transformed in order to adapt to uncontrollable outside shocks. Under these circumstances, however, social policy can expand dramatically despite fiscally conservative bureaucrats' and politicians' concerns about the financial cost (Barr 1992). Even under budgetary constraint, policy-makers still have ample choices regarding social policy reforms – such as reallocating within the budget, adjusting entitlement criteria, and raising new or higher social security taxes from beneficiaries and employers. Eventually what matters is whether pro-expansionary reform forces are durable and capable enough to convince voters, the state, and the congress about their reform agendas. The introduction of universal social policy reforms in the late 1990s in South Korea under the financial crisis well illustrates this point. Thus, in these contexts political actors are ready and able to overcome these policy legacies and quickly transform themselves depending upon rapidly changing social bases and allies. In all, in these developing societies, we do not find the same level of policy continuity and path dependency as in industrial countries.

Next, the celebrated VoC approach to welfare state development also faces serious limitations in analyzing the vast majority of societies not belonging to the 'core' of coordinated market economies. First, there is one major difference between Western Europe and developing countries. In the former, the welfare state may have indeed evolved as a part of a larger coordinated production regime. However, in developing countries, such institutional coordination between the state and market rarely emerged: social policies were introduced as a co-optation mechanism by authoritarian regimes, and then became extended to larger populations during or after the transition to democracy. In such processes, firms had neither sufficient time nor capacity to develop coordination systems that would cut across the state and society during their country's developmental eras. Furthermore, far from social policy entrepreneurs, employers were the most consistent and brutal opponents of welfare state expansion in developing societies, as well as the strongest proponents of neo-liberal market reforms. In general, none of the studies within the VoC tradition convincingly demonstrate that welfare states in developing countries are indeed an instance of institutional complementarities organized around different types of skill needs (by employers). In other words, most developing countries do not have strong incentives to coordinate their skill training institutions with social policy regimes: the firms in Brazil and Argentina did not have to compete at a highly competitive level in world markets, while firms in South Korea and Taiwan primarily relied on firm-level welfare provisions during their growth periods.[11] In short, the need for skill specificity has not been an important factor for welfare state formation in these developing countries.

One related theoretical innovation in the welfare state literature is institutionalists' focus on the role of electoral systems in accounting for the emergence of center-leftist governments promoting redistributive measures. Scholars in this tradition explain the variations in the distributional outcomes of welfare states by looking at the presence or the absence of the proportional representation system (PR), which has been known to produce stronger leftist politics (Persson and Tabellini 2003; Iversen and Soskice 2009). It is true that the two Latin American countries have (list) PR systems, while the two East Asian countries have parallel systems, in which only a smaller portion of seats are filled based on PR system (18 percent in South Korea and 30 percent in Taiwan). Although the electoral system variable (and its redistributive impacts) effectively accounts for variations between the two continents,[12] it is not such a useful factor in explaining differences within each continent. Differences between Argentine and Brazilian labor parties, as well as those between South Korean and Taiwanese labor politics, are enormous: well-disciplined participatory governance (Brazil) vs. clientelistic patronage politics (Argentina) and undisciplined ideological factionalism (S. Korea) vs. an internally coordinated but co-opted corporatism (Taiwan) (Lee 2016).

Pierson's "politics of blame avoidance" (1996), when it is applied to developing countries, also has limitations. In developing countries, retrenchments, in the form of privatization, have occurred often. Such institutional changes may not lead to radical retrenchment in terms of overall spending measures, but it will result in a significant reduction of redistributive effects, simply because privatized health care and pension schemes do not redistribute upper-income beneficiaries' shares to lower-income, less capable beneficiaries. Furthermore, in this strategy of institutional neo-liberal reform (as opposed to budgetary neo-liberal reform), benefits are concentrated on the incumbent party and its backers (typically insurance companies, upper-bracket pension and health care beneficiaries, physicians, and drug companies). With the repeated economic crises many developing countries have faced, incumbent parties are under much greater pressure to undertake market-oriented reforms. Pierson's conjecture simply does not hold in these cases. Retrenchments in the form of privatization have been realistic threats and have been actually undertaken to different degrees in many Latin American countries, and many other countries (including South Korea).

Empirical evidence from the cases of this study contradicts Pierson's assertion that, over time, social programs become less dependent on their original builders, such as political parties, social movements, and unions. On the contrary: at least in these developing countries, social programs become more dependent upon those actors, because they rarely create other influential actors with sufficient lobbying and mobilization capacities (such as old-age pensioners in rich democracies). This is the case not only because demographic structures in developing countries have not matured to the same level as in rich democracies, but also, and more importantly, because the other actors who should perceive the harm of retrenchments have not sufficiently shaped their organizational capacities. Again, what matters is how such 'old' forces – workers and parties – rejuvenate their social bases, launch new forms of struggle, and generate new dynamics of solidarity, the core axis of this study. Furthermore, what matters is not only the cost of assembling pro-retrenchment coalitions – Pierson's focus – but also the cost of assembling anti-retrenchment coalitions and their capacity to defend existing social policies.

While the theory of economic openness or crises under globalization and neo-liberalism more broadly may be the most serious contender for the EC approach I propose in the next chapter, it does not account for variations in the cases of this study in convincing ways. First, South Korea achieved its greatest universal expansion reforms during the financial crisis in 1997 and 1998 (which will be discussed in Chapter 5), while Taiwan's expansionary moves were made regardless of economic openness or crises. Argentina may be the only case in accordance with its theoretical expectation. But the economic openness argument cannot explain why the same country (and the same Peronist party) introduced a radical retrenchment after one economic crisis in the early 1990s, while reversing its previous retrenchment decisions after another economic crisis in the early 2000s. Additionally, this theory cannot explain why Brazil managed to preserve core labor rights while its neighbor (Argentina) suffered radical setbacks in social policies in the 1990s after similar economic crises.

The negative impacts of economic crises and globalization on labor movements and civil society actors are not unitary, either: they may have negative effects on both labor and welfare states in Argentina, but not in Brazil. Brazilian labor movements and the PT emerged as the ruling forces in municipal and central governments when economic crises and neo-liberalism prevailed in most of Latin America. South Korean labor movements also reached their peak when economic crises plagued the economy. A recent upsurge of labor movements in the context of globalization (Silver 2003) and the resurgence of leftist parties (Levitsky and Roberts 2011) in the global North and South also contradict this expectation.[13]

Finally, the power-resource school (Esping-Andersen 1985; Korpi 1983; Stephens 1979) also has limited ability to account for the variations in retrenchment and expansion outcomes for the welfare state in developing countries. For instance, the organizational power resources of labor-based reformist parties and unions were largely similar in the 1990s in Argentina and Brazil, and yet it was only Argentina that experienced a severe retrenchment of the welfare state (even under the labor-based party, PJ). Even if the South Korean labor movement is known to have stronger mobilization capacity than its Taiwanese counterpart, it is hard to conclude that labor by itself has played a significant role in the expansion of universal social policies in South Korea. In both countries, networks among intellectuals, and networks linking political parties, labor unions, and other civic associations (all in different ways), exercised a decisive influence on the development of the welfare state.[14] In addition, in all the cases, unions were not necessarily on the side of universal expansion of social policy. Unions' strong alliance with an incumbent political party often led them to accept or acquiesce to severe retrenchment of the welfare state, as illustrated by the Argentine Judicialist Party (PJ)-CGT (General Confederation of Labor) alliance or the South Korean GNP (Grand National Party)-FKTU(Federation of Korean Trade Unions) alliance. The limited explanatory power of power resource theory for the developing world is, therefore a result of, first, its neglect of the role of civic associations in larger associational communities, and second, its unilateral focus on the traditional (leftist) party–union nexus, which is devoid of labor unions' collaborations and coalition mechanisms in a larger associational community. Collier and Handlin (2009)'s U-hub (union–party nexus) and A-net (associational network) approach or a conventional old vs. new social movement (Melucci 1980; Offe 1985) juxtaposition – both of which position labor and associational networks as either replacing or weakening the other – epitomize the narrow focus of previous approaches regarding labor politics. What we need to know regarding the role of unions (and leftist parties) in building social policies is under what conditions they embrace larger civil society and other unorganized social forces and under what conditions they exclusively focus on their own narrow interests.

In short, all of the previous approaches to the study of the welfare state lack one decisive element for analyzing the political dynamics of developing societies over the last few of decades – social movement processes, and their role in linking the state and civil society, on the one hand, and formal and informal civic organizations, on the other hand. These social movement processes are critical for analyzing the development and retrenchment of welfare states in these contexts, because such processes ultimately determine the pattern and structure of 'interest-channeling' as well as 'interest-mobilization' within civil society and between civil society and the state. The generosity and universality of the modern welfare state is fundamentally shaped by bottom-up 'institutionalization' processes that generate pressure for the collective provision of social safety nets and risk-sharing. Most existing theories of the welfare state do not delve into these processes, although two partial exceptions can be found in power resource theory and industrialization theory. The former puts focus on the strengths of leftist parties and labor unions in order to explain the variations in diverse welfare regimes (Esping-Andersen 1990; Huber and Stephens 2001; Korpi 1983); the latter highlights the modernization process itself but, in its causal mechanism, underlines the role of 'interest-group politics' by older people (Pampel and Williamson 1989). However, both theories rarely provide an account of how diverse forms of civic or non-civic associations, with different social constituencies, align themselves in the course of social (democratization) movements, thereby potentially coordinating different interests to forge solidarity movements.

Furthermore, none of the previous theories of the welfare state offer an appropriate framework to reveal how the needs and interests of subordinate classes (working classes and the poor), middle classes (urban white-collar and public sector workers), and the socially marginalized (urban and rural informal labor, non-labor force groups including homemakers and students, the unemployed, and non-standard labor – so called 'precariats') mobilize their common interests through formal institutions "during the course of democratization", rather than in the "already established" form of "democratic political mechanisms" (Lipset 1960). The cases of this study demand that we should explore these neglected civil society networks that emerge and operate through social movements.

As noted earlier, a major difference between developing societies and rich democracies is that the processes of social policy formation have occurred simultaneously with democratization and globalization over a much shorter time span. In advanced industrial democracies, such processes began in the late nineteenth and early twentieth centuries. They had 'maturing' and 'consolidating' periods for social policies, and had sufficient time to coordinate them with labor market regulations, skill-deepening processes, and electoral systems, as VoC scholars demonstrate (Iversen and Soskice 2009; Thelen 2004). As a result, when globalization shattered and reframed the entire global economy in the early 1980s, political, labor market, and social policy institutions in rich democracies had the capacity to sustain or adjust themselves without fundamental changes to these radical transformative pressures. However, developing societies did not enjoy the 'golden era' of the post-war reconciliation between democracy and capitalism. Rather, they were exposed to the ruthless diffusion of neo-liberal market reforms before their political, labor market, and social policy institutions could solidify. In my cases, the efforts of political elites and movements to formulate social and labor market institutions were simultaneously influenced by abrupt economic transitions and events such as trade openness and financial crises, as well as internal political upheavals and regime changes. Previous theories of the welfare state are not formulated to account for these rapidly changing conditions in which democratization movements, new social movement associations, labor unions, and newly organized political parties form varied alliances and coalition mechanisms with diverse forms of collective action in response to abrupt structural changes. More generally, existing welfare state theories are not adequately able to analyze such sequential 'mobilization processes' arising from civil society.

ALTERNATIVES: SOCIAL MOVEMENT AND ORGANIZATIONAL PERSPECTIVES

Theories of social movements have not been given appropriate attention by scholars of the welfare state and labor market institutions. Thus, this project also draws on recent research about social movements and organizational coalition networks (Gerhards and Rucht 1992; Isaac and Christiansen 2002; Stearns and Almeida 2004; Voss and Sherman 2000). On one hand, most students of welfare state development have focused their attention on variations in established political institutions (state-centric and power resource theories), or they have built in larger coordinated institutions across both the political and the economic systems (Varieties of Capitalism school). As their sample has been mostly limited to wealthier democracies, the rich histories of the social movements that occurred long ago and behind the scenes (informing current institutions) have been forgotten or remain unexplored.[15] On the other hand, students of social movements have rarely extended the scope of their dependent variable from mobilization or movement successes/failures to policy outcomes. Only recently has the social movement industry begun to pay attention to policy outcomes as part of their valuable research agendas (Amenta 2006; Andrews 2004; Ganz 2000; McCammon *et al.* 2008; Soule and King 2006; also see Hicks 1999 for an employment of social movement perspective under the power resource tradition).

So, how can we incorporate a social movement perspective into our explanations of the development and retrenchment of the welfare state in these developing societies? A social movement perspective adds three important facets to the framework for this study: first, the formation of a new collective identity/leadership in civil society; second, the impacts of movements on each (divided) stage of a policy-making process occurring between the state and civil society; and third, the (structural, political/institutional, and economic) conditions under which a movement becomes successful or unsuccessful in generating policy outcomes.

The first dimension reminds us of the importance of an initial formation process of 'pioneering leadership', its 'constituents,' and the 'bystanders' around the movement leadership (McCarthy and Zald 1977). Given that the early organizational imprint may affect the later trajectory of an organizational maturation process and its success/failure/limitations (Aldrich and Ruef 2006), it is critical – in order to understand the organizational sustenance, expansion, and atrophy – to reveal the internal and external mechanisms of the early formation of collective identity.[16] Furthermore, early actions by movement leaders under a given structural condition will shape a movement's trajectory by institutionalizing (routinizing) the direction and allocation of available resources, which further shapes and constrains movement leaders' and followers' goals, repertoires of actions, frames, and even organizational forms.

The second dimension leads us to the "mechanisms" (Elster 1998; Hedström and Swedberg 1998) of movement influence on each stage of the policy-making process. The politics of political pressure, lobbying, and negotiation between social movement forces and political institutions is an important focal point of research in its own right. Opening up the 'black box' between social movements and outcomes by examining the pathways of policy initiation, subsequent negotiations in legislative processes (regarding deliberation and passage), and finally implementation (Amenta and Young 1999; Martin 2010), reveals how effective or capable movement forces have been. Opening up the content and trajectories of these processes is critical, because it ultimately discloses to us the actual internal and institutional capacity of social movement forces. Such capacity includes the ability of movement forces to mobilize financial resources, appropriate personnel with relevant skills and expertise, and other means (devices, data, and even knowledge of policies) to achieve their agendas. The quantity and quality of such resources and expertise will ultimately hinge on the degree to which movement leaders and members can mobilize diverse connections through institutionalized channels between their own and other organizations. Depending upon their skill (Fligstein 1997) and expertise in mobilizing and coordinating different movement forces, some movement agendas may successfully draw a wide range of social and bureaucratic support, both by deepening their internal logics and by developing convincing "frames" (Snow 2004; Snow and Benford 1988) that may be consonant with other social groups' interests. Alternatively, movement agendas may fail, due to the limited capacity of their promoters, to develop such a broad social solidarity. In this sense, the 'black box' between social movements and policy outcomes can be opened up only by revealing and analyzing two mechanisms: one, how movement leaders and their supporters institutionalize patterns of solidarity with other social forces regarding a policy agenda (thereby deepening their own capacity), and the other, how they convey and mobilize coordinated policy agendas through established political institutions.

The third dimension reminds us of the importance of the external conditions enabling or disabling movement forces' agendas and actions. The literature on political opportunity structure (Eisinger 1973; McAdam *et al.* 1996; Meyer 2004) has repeatedly taught us that the very political contexts that led movement forces to emerge also helped them achieve their goals. The interpretation of such contexts is so wide that they have ranged from elite division, political allies in power, and electoral success, to the emergence of favorable institutional conditions (availability of procedural or participatory democracy). Opportunity structures could be further interpreted as the larger, macrostructural and macroeconomic changes that may enable mobilization. In such a sense, population growth (Goldstone 1991), state breakdown (Skocpol 1979), and economic crises may be regarded as (political or economic) opportunity structures that may generate the grievances and social discontent that enables the mobilization of social movements with low organizational costs.[17]

This study takes seriously the role of a (political) opportunity structure, and therefore explicitly takes it into account as an external condition or environment. But it does not endorse a unilateral, one-directional role for opportunity structure. The same external condition may be interpreted and utilized in quite opposite ways by different social and political forces depending upon their social position and interests. For instance, an economic crisis could be an opportunity for a pro-welfare force, or it could be a decisive chance for anti-welfare forces to retrench existing welfare institutions. The direction of impact of such structures will be highly contingent upon the quality of movement forces' resource alignments, strategic decisions, institutionalized capacity for coordination with other movement forces, and, eventually, influence on the incumbent regime's responses to a crisis.[18] This study utilizes the role of an opportunity structure as a 'signifying mechanism' by which a movement force decides to reconfigure or utilize its existing solidarity structure in a wider movement community.[19] In this process, movement leaders may misinterpret the changing contexts, and make inappropriate, ad hoc choices based on immediate and un-interpretable situations, all without significant resources and information of their own. Furthermore, as a result of different positions and interests regarding altered circumstances or increased solidarity costs, changing structural conditions may create divisions and new conflict within movement forces.[20] Thus, in addition to considering the positive effects of opportunity structures, this study explicitly takes into account the potentially negative ramifications of changing external conditions on an already established solidarity movement.

CONCLUDING REMARKS: PROPOSING A
CONFIGURATION FOR A CIVIL SOCIETY
PERSPECTIVE

This study, incorporating three key elements of contemporary social movement literature – the formation of new collective identity/leadership, the impact of social movements on each stage of a policy-making process, and the structural conditions enabling or disabling policy adoption – proposes a new analytical model that both builds on and supersedes the 'configuration of civil society' argument earlier introduced by Rueschemeyer *et al.* (1992) and by Collier and Collier (1991). This view was originally developed to explain democratization, but it has turned out to have significant implications for welfare state development in the global periphery (Sandbrook *et al.* 2007). Strong civil society not only tames the state in the shadow of former authoritarianism by installing democratic norms, rules, conventions, and personnel, but it also provides a more favorable environment for the self-organization and mobilization of subordinate social groups. As a universal welfare state requires "community-based solidarity (the moral economy)" to "scale up" to "societal solidarity," (Sandbrook *et al.* 2007, p. 185) it is necessary, in order to build a cohesive programmatic welfare state in the ideal sense, to have strong democratic institutions with densely developed civil society. The explanatory model of this study begins with this exact point and then asks: what if the channeling efforts to scale up community-based solidarity to the political arena are disconnected somewhere or disjointed for some structural reasons? What if influential political, civic, and economic elites maintain their own nexus but are disarticulated from community-based solidarity? Would their strategic choices still be guided by the principle of the moral economy, or would they be guided instead by some other factor or interest?

In order to incorporate these issues into the 'configuration of civil society' argument, I bring into view, in the next chapter, two unexplored factors in accounting for the development or retrenchment of the welfare state in developing countries: (1) the *cohesiveness* of formal-sector organizations (i.e., between state actors and organized formal association groups); and (2) the *embeddedness* of formal-sector organizations in the informal civic sphere (i.e. unions' ties to informal civic asssociations). I will propose that differently configured coalitions and interorganizational structures among political parties, labor unions, and wider civil society organizations produce divergent welfare state outcomes – specifically, variations in the universality and generosity of social policies – in the four developing countries of this study.

I will begin by building a theoretical framework (Chapter 3) that formalizes the notions of embedded cohesiveness and disarticulated cohesiveness and reveals their utility in accounting for variations in the politics of expansion and retrenchment of the welfare state and labor market institutions. In the next three chapters (Chapters 4 to 6), I will delve into one case, South Korea, to evaluate the EC approach. Then, utilizing network analysis of co-membership data, I explore the associational structures of these four countries and build a causal framework to explain the effects of the organizational configurations of formal and informal civic spheres on the politics of welfare states. Detailed comparative/historical case studies in combination with the results from quantitative network analysis, which I call 'network-informed case studies,' will jointly show how my theoretical framework accounts for the politics of social protection in recently democratized developing countries.

3

Theoretical Discussion

The Structures of Associational Networks and the Politics of the Welfare State

INTRODUCTION

How does understanding the origins and structures of associational networks help explain the expansion and retrenchment of social and labor market policies? This chapter proposes a theoretical framework that captures the institutionalization of labor politics through the notion of "associational fields" (Akchurin and Lee 2013). I first construct two social network-based variables, embeddedness and cohesiveness, that capture linkages between formal and informal civic associations as well as linkages among formal civic associations. In turn, I build a combinational space consisting of embeddedness and cohesiveness in which variations in either variable interact with variations in the other, comprising four ideal spaces for generating the conditions and mechanisms of the effects of labor–civic solidarity on the development or retrenchment of social policies.

Next, I develop sub-dimensions for embeddedness and cohesiveness for unions. For embeddedness, I consider dimensions of (contentious) mobilization capacity and policy capacity of unions in their relations with civil society. For cohesiveness, I consider dimensions of (electoral) mobilization capacity and policy capacity of unions in their relations with (incumbent) political parties. The next step is to theorize how reciprocal compensation processes – exchange of mobilization capacity and policy capacity – between labor and civic organizations occur, and then to discuss how such processes matter in explaining social policy outcomes. In delineating these processes, I highlight two aspects of labor–civic solidarity: (1) the politics of mobilization and threat/pressures, and (2) the politics of lobbying and persuasion. Especially regarding the latter, I focus on the growing significance of policy/knowledge capacity for policy-crafting and policy deliberation in national public spheres and in the political battlefield.

As the final step in building my causal framework, I construct network-informed games in which embeddedness and cohesiveness inform unions and the state of the other actors' capacity for punishment and compensation during contentious/institutional politics. I introduce two types of game: one for retrenchment scenarios and the other for expansion scenarios. In the former, I describe four different game structures initiated by the state, which, depending on the levels of cohesiveness and embeddedness, predict different retrenchment outcomes (radical vs. moderate reforms) in social policies. In the latter, I also construct another four game structures initiated by unions, in which cohesiveness and embeddedness play decisive roles in configuring the payoff structures of different expansion outcomes (universal vs. selective reforms). This final step will demonstrate the central importance of the structures of associational networks for understanding divergent responses by the state, unions, and civil society organizations to neo-liberal market reforms as well as to pressures for the expansion of the welfare state.

The last section of the chapter discusses theoretical implications of this labor–civic solidarity (which I label 'unions' embeddedness') model for the comparative study of welfare states. The model has broader implications for the study of the state, civil society, social movements, organizational studies, institutional analyses, and the larger literature on comparative political economy, but I defer my discussion of those implications to the Conclusion chapter.

THE EMERGENCE AND CONSOLIDATION OF ASSOCIATIONAL NETWORKS

In this section, I develop my two variables to theoretically and empirically delineate labor-relevant associational fields:[1] one variable is labor activists' collective political 'goals and agendas,' which then evolve into cohesiveness (labor organizations' political ties with parties – the policy/government sphere), and the other is labor activists' social 'resources and bases,' which develop into embeddedness (labor organizations' ties with civic organizations). Cohesiveness and embeddedness are not clearly differentiated during the protean stages of the authoritarian or pre-democracy eras. Instead they are present in underground communities as political zeal or fervor (for cohesiveness) and informal subaltern ties among leaders and members of different social groups (for embeddedness). Both will eventually evolve into the nuts and bolts of a labor-linked associational field that provide resources and channels for contentious and non-contentious institutional politics during and after the transition to democracy.[2]

Under this framework, these two variables – cohesiveness and embeddedness – are constituted and institutionalized with variations in strength and the form of repertoires employed by labor activists and their allies, who possess varying amounts of "skill" (Fligstein and McAdam 2011) across societies and times. The two variables, therefore, are institutionalized as stable networks of resources, personnel, and ideas among diverse stakeholders. However, these networks may then change over time as organizational actors and, to varying degrees, succeed or fail in their further institutionalization efforts.

The two variables supply content, opportunities, and constraints for labor organizations and their leaders when pursuing strategic actions either against welfare state retrenchment or for expansion. Importantly, labor activists themselves construct the two institutionalized dimensions of a labor-linked associational field. The two dimensions emerge from varying modes of clandestine organizational activities during the authoritarian era, where they are normalized and stabilized as new 'rules' and 'conventions' for building and maintaining solidarity among labor activists. Once these networks are institutionalized, they determine the range of resources, personnel, ideas, and technical expertise which labor activists can mobilize for specific policy-crafting, negotiation, and lobbying campaigns.

THE STRUCTURE OF ASSOCIATIONAL NETWORKS, WELFARE STATES, AND MARKET-ORIENTED REFORMS

In order to better explain variations in welfare state retrenchment and expansion, I bring in two unexplored factors in accounting for variations in neo-liberal reforms and social policy expansions in developing countries: (1) the cohesiveness of formal-sector organizations, including inter-class solidarity between the working class and other classes such as the urban middle classes (coalition among labor-related organizational units), and (2) the embeddedness of formal-sector organizations in the informal civic sphere. I propose that the differently configured coalitions and interorganizational structures among political parties, labor unions, and wider civil society formulate divergent welfare states.

I begin by building a theoretical framework that considers the notions of embedded cohesiveness and disarticulated cohesiveness, as well as their roles in accounting for variations in the politics of expansion and retrenchment of the welfare state in the four developing societies under consideration here. Utilizing network analysis of co-membership data (Borgatti *et al.* 2002; Breiger 1974), I explore the associational structures of these four countries and build a causal framework to explain the effects of organizational configurations of formal and informal civic spheres on the politics of the welfare state. Detailed comparative/historical case studies in combination with the results from formal network analysis, which I call 'network-informed case studies,' will jointly account for the politics of social protection in four recently democratized developing countries in later chapters.

Cohesiveness and the Formation of the Welfare State

This study focuses on the role of formal organizations, especially their interorganizational ties and linkages to larger informal civic networks. It distinguishes between the 'formal institutional sphere' and the 'informal civic sphere.' The formal institutional sphere includes political parties, labor unions, and professional associations, each of which plays its distinctive roles in channeling group interests in the form of formulating and negotiating policy agendas as well as electoral bargaining. These associations are formal organizations, in the sense that they have established bureaucratic structures in which organizational goals, tasks, and agendas are formally codified in core members' routines, activities, and interactions with outside worlds. The institutionalization of organizational routines is internally stipulated as each organization's rules, while externally governed by laws (Aldrich and Ruef 2006; Scott 2008). In this study, I pay attention to two types of formal organization, labor-based parties and labor unions.

Informal civic organizations include churches and cultural activity groups such as singing groups, book clubs, charity associations, and sports clubs. They are the most informal, not (or not yet) politicized, relatively ideology-free or interest-free spaces between the state and family (or individuals). They are the civic space most distant from modern bureaucratized state institutions and interest-based organizations, and they are the closest to informal, private, local community, and family lives. Putnam hoped to preserve this space against modernization and urbanization as the last resort for fostering citizens' reciprocity and civic efficacy (Putnam

1993, 2000). Habermas also claimed that the "lifeworld" embracing this informal civic sphere as a reservoir of "communicative reason" should be defended against the colonizing power of modern bureaucratic systems (Habermas 1984, 1987). It could be Tocquevillian local communities in nineteenth century America or "the Owenite Societies," in which "associations and clubs" are "designed to support plans of Villages of Cooperation," which Polanyi (2001[1944], pp. 177–9) highlighted as "the social" fabric against the penetration of industrial capitalism.

Figure 3.1 displays the specific organizational linkages (solid lines) involved in the cohesiveness of the formal sector. I initially define the cohesiveness of the formal civic sphere as the organizational linkages among the three key formal organizations.[3] First, the linkage between leftist or reformist political parties and labor unions represents traditional social democratic, labor-based power resources (Esping-Andersen 1985; Korpi 1983; Stephens 1979). The linkage "articulates class interests and mobilizes members into (collective) political action" (Huber and Stephens 2001, p. 18). As this linkage becomes stronger, power resource theory predicts that the demand of the working classes for protection of their income and jobs will be more effectively channeled through party structures. In other words, unions' approval or disapproval is essential for the legislative passage of specific reform programs for either the expansion or the retrenchment of social policies. Second, the linkage between unions and the incumbent party (or the state) represents unions' formal or informal lobbying and negotiation channels with the state. When this linkage is strong, corporatism theory predicts that unions' interests may be closely negotiated and represented by the state (Calmfors and Driffill 1988; Crouch 1993; Schmitter 1974), and the state's project (such as wage bargaining or electoral co-optation of the working classes) will be executed through unions in implicit ways. I label the first 'cohesiveness with leftist parties' and the second 'cohesiveness with the state' or simply, 'state–union alliance.' The first and second dimensions will completely overlap under a social democratic party's incumbency, while under a right-wing party's incumbency, the former dimension remains unchanged, but the latter dimension of cohesiveness may not exist or may erode for most democratic, leftist unions. Under a reformist centrist or center-left government, these two dimensions of cohesiveness may incur divisions within unions because different ideological factions may resort to their own allies in different political parties.

The first cohesiveness linkage is relatively stable in a society, as it is literally the cohesive and durable network between unions and labor-based parties that persists in the long term regardless of the parties' incumbency. However, the second cohesiveness linkage could be ephemeral and transitional, because a party's incumbency is determined by electoral competitions, which is often exogenous to unions' capacity. The theoretical framework of Chapter 3 and most qualitative analyses (in Chapters 4 to 8) are primarily based on the second definition (state–union alliance). However, analyses on quantitative associational data in Chapter 9 utilize multiple definitions of cohesiveness in order to show how unions' structural influence on social policy outcomes varies according to unions' ties with different ranges of political actors and institutions. Chapter 9 investigates (1) ties between unions and parties in three ways: ties between unions and (all kinds of) parties (and professional associations) within a formal associational sector; (2) ties between unions and a specific labor-based (or non-labor based) party; and (3) ties between unions and an incumbent party (the state).[4]

In sum, the labor-based organizational ties among these three formal organizations summarize a society's general capacity to represent the institutionalized channeling processes of class-based interests into political arenas. I initially concur with the former power-resource and coalition-building approaches to the welfare state in my conceptualization of the cohesiveness of the formal sector, but this study also develops a different argument from conventional power resource theory. It instead takes into account the "social embeddedness"(Granovetter 1985) of formal politics. In developing countries in which a larger segment of the rural and urban poor is in the informal sector and in which the size of the organized working class is much smaller than in advanced industrial economies, the politics of cohesiveness along the lines of trade unions and political parties does not always function for the development or sustenance of a universal welfare state. Rather, these countries often end up with populist corporatism through co-optation of the working class in core sectors by populist elites (Lee 2005, 2007; Malloy 1979). Absent those formal organizations being embedded in the wider civil society, unbridled formal organizations and their leaders may operate on their own, for their own survival and interests.[5]

Embeddedness and the Formation of the Welfare State

In this section, I contend that the capacity for social and labor market policy formulation of a labor-based formal sector is based not only on its cohesiveness but also on its degree of embeddedness in the informal

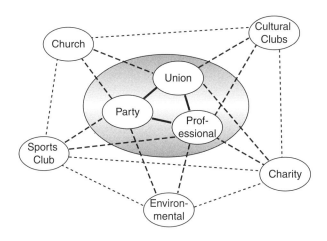

FIGURE 3.1. Illustration of Cohesiveness and Embeddedness in Formal and Informal Civic Sectors

civic sphere (see the dashed lines between three formal and five informal civic organizations in Figure 3.1).[6] I propose that the embeddedness of a specific formal organizational structure in the informal civic sphere addresses two fundamental issues in democratic class mobilization: first, in societies in which formal interest bargaining structure is closely connected to informal civic lives, citizens will build stronger "trust" (Coleman 1990; Granovetter 1985) with formal-sector organizations in charge of interest-channeling and bargaining. Second, in those countries with stronger organizational linkages between formal and informal civic associations, party and union leaders will be more reliably responsive to their constituents' demands for defending or expanding universal social protection, as they not only become more worried about potential punishment by voters in future electoral cycles but also become increasingly engaged in the informal deliberation of a specific policy in the sea of public opinion. Conversely, in societies with weak organizational and institutionalized connections between formal and informal spheres, neither parties nor unions are committed to sponsoring their deeper electoral or organizational bases, and thus they may, if necessary, seek to cultivate new constituencies for electoral survival.

The first argument is based on the long tradition of sociological literature concerning the importance of social relations in the creation of economic trust (Granovetter 1985, 2002; Montgomery 1998); it then focuses instead on the role of social relations in formulating political trust between voters and formal organizations (or their leaders) and building/ retrenching welfare states under neo-liberal market reforms. When citizens are better connected with leaders of formal-sector organizations, they will be exposed to a higher volume of information exchange and will therefore construct a more accurate assessment of the trustworthiness, reliability, effectiveness, and relevance of organizational leaders and their policy platforms. I generally assume that prolonged interorganizational ties over time will facilitate not only this information exchange and assessment but also eventual trust of leaders (insofar as those who have sacrificed trust based on information exchanges would sever ties).[7]

Then, the argument is extended to the trust relationship between leaders of formal organizations and citizens (and their leaders) in both the formal and the informal civic spheres. It emphasizes the role of social relations in constraining and limiting formal politics: it not only allows a partisan formal sector based on labor to advance more progressive egalitarian agendas in welfare politics but also sets a limit on retrenchment in periods of economic crisis. On the one hand, the labor-based formal sector deeply embedded in informal sectors is representative of participatory institutional politics. Those labor-based party or union leaders anchored in informal civic associations are more likely to have initially evolved from the (Tocquevillian) local community as community organizers, who are distinct from the labor aristocracy and machine politicians, or who originated from social movements including going-underground activities. Their collective identities are more likely to originate in residential neighborhoods, as exemplified by the community-based mobilization of the 1871 Paris Commune (Gould 1995), or historically embedded in wide civic mobilization networks. They are more likely to care about the general interests of people of diverse class origins with whom they have interacted in local churches, cultural and sport clubs, and town hall meetings. Therefore, embedded formal-sector leaders are more likely to employ policies that will enhance their "legitimacy"(Suchman 1995)[8] and build social solidarity by serving a wide range of social forces.[9]

On the other hand, the embeddedness of the formal sector in the informal sector may also represent the degree or strength of cognitive "social learning" processes by which political actors reach the "resolution of competing claims" through the exchange of ideas and perceptions (Chalmers *et al.* 1998, p. 565). The aforementioned information exchange and assessment of trustworthiness of leaders' platforms are more likely to abound in the intersections of formal and informal civic sectors. Formal-sector leaders embedded in informal civic spheres will therefore have a greater chance to formulate public opinions, discussions, and debates as well as, further, to craft negotiations and pre-bargaining at these intersections of the formal and informal civic spheres.[10] Formal-sector leaders with high embeddednesss are thus likely to be representative of already negotiated interests and opinions as a form of civic consensus and therefore to be able to channel universal and "programmatic" (Kitschelt and Wilkinson 2007) voices to political arenas. Alternatively, embedded formal-sector leaders are likely to learn how to articulate interests and opinions of different social origins and then to mobilize and convey them into political arenas, utilizing their unique structural positions as "brokers"(Gould 1989; Gould and Fernandez 1989) between the formal and informal civic sectors. Accordingly, embedded formal-sector leaders, as more democratic and programmatic brokers, are more likely to have greater political skills for organizing a wide array of social forces to formulate cross-class alliances.

In addition, embedded formal-sector leaders will resist and challenge the strategic decisions of charismatic or technocratic formal-sector leaders. Thus, even when confronting national debt or financial crises, embedded leaders are less likely to pursue radical market-oriented reform of the existing social welfare system, out of concern for the detrimental effects that such neo-liberal reforms might exert not only on their core constituencies but also on surrounding communities. Instead, they may seek a moderate reform for minimum-level survival in international markets combined with another generous package of social protection for those most vulnerable during the course of the reform project. Because of their origins in local communities and their ongoing ties and relationship of trust with them, they may be able to persuade grassroots civil societies to tolerate the reforms necessary for the survival of the entire nation in the global market (not merely for their own survival), while simultaneously taking care of those most vulnerable to structural reforms.

By contrast, formal-sector leaders who are not constrained by preexisting attachments to the informal civic sphere may be freer to risk implementing more radical market-oriented reforms. Although they may

		Cohesiveness of Formal sector	
		Weak	Strong
Embeddedness of Formal sector	Weak	Weak Loyalty to both the State and Civil Society	Weak Loyalty to Civil Society and Strong Loyalty to the State
		Strong Loyalty to Civil Society but Weak Loyalty to the State	Strong Loyalty to both the State and Civil Society
	Strong		

FIGURE 3.2. Combinational Spaces of Cohesiveness and Embeddedness of the Formal Sector

lose their existing constituency, they may expect to benefit by gaining new constituencies. The formal-sector leaders without connections to the informal sectors may be lacking in institutional and ideological commitments to their old constituency: the poor, the working class, and some liberal segments of the middle class. They will then be more concerned about their own survival in an election than about the welfare of the people they have represented. Formal-sector leaders may abandon their traditional electoral base regardless of political ideology if they can attract new supporters. Thus, in the name of political survival, formal-sector leaders with traditional right-wing tendencies but without solid embeddedness in the informal civic sphere could even resort to left-wing populist mobilization strategies, just as those with past left-wing tendencies might suddenly pursue radical market-oriented reform of the public sector.

Figure 3.2 summarizes the arguments I have made, including two explanatory factors, the cohesiveness and the embeddedness of the formal organizational sector.[11] When formal-sector organizations are disarticulated from the informal civic sphere, incumbent party leaders may boldly attempt to adopt market reform projects developed by other parties, or opposite platforms, as shown in the combination of strong cohesiveness and weak embeddedness. This opportunistic strategy is deemed realistic when party leaders assume that constituents of other political camps are not loyal to their opponents (or other political camps are not cohesive and strong enough to retain their constituents), perceive that new policy platforms could attract more votes than the old platform, and, finally, find that their ideological commitments to their traditional electoral base are out of date, due to industrial and occupational transformation (Burgess and Levitsky 2003), and they therefore need to cultivate new electoral bases for their survival.

However, when the leaders of the (labor-based) formal sector are closely linked to each other and simultaneously deeply embedded in the civic activities of the local community, they will consciously channel a wide range of working-class and middle-class demands into the political bargaining tables among formal-sector organizations, and promote more universal and programmatic social policies to support broader communities as well as their constituents. In the same vein, leaders of the (labor-based) formal sector with strong cohesiveness and embeddedness will vehemently resist the pressures of neo-liberal reform agendas from right-wing parties, government technocrats, and foreign agencies such as the IMF and the World Bank.

DIMENSIONS OF COHESIVENESS AND EMBEDDEDNESS: MOBILIZATION AND POLICY CAPACITIES

In the discussion above when I refer to unions' embedded ties or unions' cohesive linkages, what do those ties or linkages consist of? So far, they may conjure images of "pipes" (Podolny 2001) that carry "information, expertise, trust and other resources"(Kenis and Schneider 1991), as typically implied in social network literature (Knoke 1990; Knoke *et al.* 1996). I suggested in the previous section that the pipes linking two organizations are 'embedded formal leaders' who are jointly affiliated with multiple formal and informal civic associations. However, we should explore further what roles these embedded leaders play in building and maintaining interorganizational linkages, what functions they perform, and what kinds of (policy) outcomes they produce through their networks. This section clarifies and specifies the contents of interorganizational ties and linkages by introducing two conceptual sub-dimensions of embeddedness and cohesiveness: mobilization capacity and policy capacity.[12]

The need of unions to build solidarity linkages with other social and political forces in associational fields arises in two dimensions: one from labor activists' need to engage in professional electoral politics as party builders, sponsors, and lobbyists, insofar as they require their allies to protect and pursue the interests of the working classes in formal democratic institutions. The other dimension emerges from unions' need to construct social legitimacy as a universal policy mobilizer, an interest coordinator, and a representative of all of civil society. To achieve this, unions need to communicate and cooperate closely with other social forces not only to realize their own interests but also to find and pursue general societal interests through contentious and non-contentious politics. In the previous section, the first dimension was conceptualized as cohesiveness and the second as embeddedness.

Now, I further build two sub-dimensions for cohesiveness and embeddedness, which are illustrated in Figure 3.3: one is 'linkages for mobilization capacity' and the other is 'linkages for policy capacity.' Cohesiveness between unions and parties can be assessed in two domains: first, whether unions and political parties have built structures that enable them to share organizational resources for *electoral or non-electoral mobilization*, and second, whether they have established cooperative structures to share organizational resources for the generation of *ideas and policies*. The first aspect of cohesiveness captures a solidarity structure between two (or more) organizations that supports demonstrations against employers and government policies, electoral campaigns, and advertisement of common interests to the public through various traditional and non-traditional venues. More specifically, mobilization capacity can be broken into three components: (1) *intra*-organizational mobilization capacity, (2) *inter*-organizational mobilization capacity, and (3) electoral threat/support capacity. The first denotes the capacity of an organization to incorporate its members into a common category of collective consciousness and mobilize them towards a common goal.[13] The second denotes the capacity to do the same but along with other civic associations. The third denotes an organization's capacity to align and mobilize its policy interests to support its partners or threaten its political adversaries. The first and second components are the ingredients for mobilization embeddedness, while the first and third components comprise mobilization cohesiveness.

The second sub-dimension – policy capacity – involves solidarity structures between two organizations that focus primarily upon the negotiation and deliberation processes behind the production of policy-relevant knowledge (presented in the upper part of Figure 3.3). In this framework, the notion of the policy capacity of an organization has three components: the first component is the capacity to produce or adopt its own policy agendas that satisfy its members; the second component is the capacity to convince potential allies with a policy agenda and further coordinate a 'realistic' alternative that maximizes the shared interests of a policy-based solidarity group through interorganizational deliberation and negotiation; and the last component is the capacity to bring the (coordinated) policy agenda to formal political institutions like the legislature and the state administration, and to negotiate with actors of these diverse bureaucratic and legislative institutions (involving "assistance in lobbying to secure passage of legislation, facilitation of communication within legislative institutions, and provision of substantive information on policy issues and outcomes"(Dark 1999, p. 38). The policy embeddedness of a union refers to the first and the second dimensions, while the policy cohesiveness of a union to the first and the third dimensions.

Both mobilization and policy capacities are ultimately embodied in the networks among unions and other political and civic associations, but the internal contents of the capacities may differ qualitatively across time. For example, during democratization movements or transitional phases, cohesiveness is established through the first sub-dimension – mobilization capacity. In this phase, party and union leaders spend most of their time and resources organizing solidaristic demonstrations and public gatherings, thereby developing personnel and organizational routines and linkages that effectively mobilize more workers and citizens for the demonstrations, petitions, and strikes. During this period, the strength of organizational linkages is primarily gauged by the magnitude and duration of unions' collective struggles and by the degree of threat to the state (and capital).

However, after a certain point, as contentious politics wane and organizations make the transition to electoral and institutional politics, the focus of cohesiveness will shift from mobilization capacity to policy capacity in order to institutionalize the exchange of votes for policies. At this point, cohesiveness is more likely to reflect the capacity of unions to persuade and bind parties and their own members through policy institutions.[14] Especially from the union side, policy cohesiveness implies the existence and operation of channels and venues through which unions or union leaders can convince party leaders and members of the importance of unions' central interests, or of policies proposed by unions. We label the first, mobilization-based solidarity of transitional periods as 'mobilization cohesiveness,' denoted as (4) in Figure 3.3, while we call the latter, policy-based solidarity of settled times 'policy cohesiveness,' which is denoted as (2) in Figure 3.3.[15]

For embeddedness, mobilization capacity and policy capacity comprise two sub-dimensions in analogous ways. The first, illustrated as (3) in Figure 3.3, concerns whether unions and other civic associations have developed solidarity structures that further the developing and sharing of their organizational resources for contentious demonstrations, petitions, and signature-collection drives. This aspect of embeddedness is more likely to emerge from unions' linkages to grassroots, community-level cultural associations. The second aspect, denoted as (1) in Figure 3.3, involves whether they have built legal and professional knowledge networks that cooperatively produce the data, strategies, legal advice, and policy alternatives needed for waging firm-level, regional-level, or confederation-level struggles against and negotiations with the state and employers surrounding labor law, labor market institutions, and social policies. This dimension of embeddedness is more likely to spring from unions' solidarity with expert or intellectual-based, issue-oriented social movement associations.[16]

Such a need for knowledge networks becomes increasingly pressing under globalization and neo-liberal reform pressures, especially for unions in more economically developed social and political systems. First of all, unions must also know what employers and the state know, and intend to do, regarding the national economic situation, and so unions need to be able to diagnose the situation of firms and economies, the implicit and explicit goals and prospects of restructuring plans, and short-term and long-term consequences of specific or general economic policies. Second, unions should be capable of engaging in policy-making processes at firm-level and industrial-level bargaining, and at confederation-level bargaining with the state. Especially as national economies mature, non-contentious negotiations rather than contentious confrontations become the norm of labor–capital relationships. In that context, the availability and flexibility of bargaining-relevant knowledge production will be crucial to unions' capacity and popularity.

Policy embeddedness can be further expanded to include alliance/coalition capability, by which union-based policy experts build policy-based or policy-specific solidarity with other political and civic associations. One Brazilian policy expert, Leandro Horie, whom I interviewed for this project (at DIEESE: Inter-Union Department of Statistics and Socioeconomic Studies), succinctly summarizes this aspect by stating that "it is not enough to just propose a policy. You have to structure it, making it minimally papable for institutional actors that are involved." As policy-wise embeddedness develops, the potential task of knowledge experts gets extended to other social reform agendas, including social policies. As union members and leaders' concerns about their wage structure reaches the question of a "social wage" (Iversen 1999), thereby

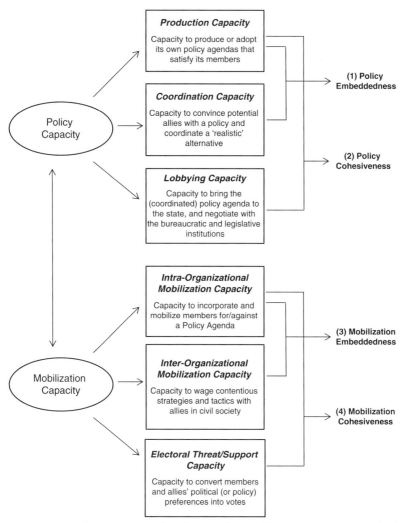

FIGURE 3.3. Components of Policy and Mobilization Capacity and their Relevance to Embeddedness and Cohesiveness

incorporating 'social policy reforms' into their core policy agenda, the level and scope of the expertise required of policy experts within unions changes. Knowledge experts should now be able to understand regime-level institutional structures of social and labor market policies, analyze workers' interests in the current institutional settings, and propose realistic alternative policy formulas. Most importantly, policy experts and leaders at the national center or large industrial unions must be able to craft, negotiate, and coordinate their policy alternatives with other civic and professional organizations in associational fields. In this process, they, as "critical communities" (Rochon 1998), may be able to mobilize new "constituents" and "sympathizers" (McCarthy and Zald 1977), thereby creating policy-wise solidarity across social classes and organizations and augmenting the capacity to channel their policy agenda to political institutions via cohesive ties, or to pressure them via contentious politics.[17]

ASSOCIATIONAL FIELDS AND NETWORK-INFORMED STRATEGIC ACTIONS: THE POLITICS OF EXPANSION AND RETRENCHMENT OF THE WELFARE STATE

In this section, I develop a theoretical model that analyzes the third sequence of the causal flow illustrated in Figure 1.1: strategic actions by the incumbent partisan state and unions under the given structure of an associational field. Cohesiveness is here more narrowly defined as associational linkages between the incumbent party and unions ('cohesiveness with the state' or state–union alliance), while embeddedness is defined as associational linkages between unions and other informal civic associations, as in previous sections. The concepts of policy and mobilization capacity discussed in the previous sections will be reflected in the formulation of 'network-informed games' between the state and unions regarding the expansion or retrenchment of the welfare state. I initially theorize how unions' structural positions in each national associational field, built upon their ties to the state and civil society, relate to the state's and unions' 'preference structures.' In doing so, I expand the concept of associational linkages from trust networks built upon "resource and information channeling pipes" (Podolny 2001) to the 'cost-generating' or 'cost-cutting' mechanisms intervening in the state and unions' policy-relevant actions motivated by their preference structures. In this analysis, the solidarity structures of an associational field will also reflect the organizational capacities of mobilization and policy-crafting efforts, efforts which inform the state and unions of their own or the other players' potential actions and responses. Before the discussion moves to the construction of games (see Appendix C), I propose a revised version of combinational spaces of cohesiveness and embeddedness (see Figure 3.4), reflecting the new consideration of structural positions and preference structures of the state and unions.

Unions' Structural Positions between the State and Civil Society, and Reform Outcomes

I start with the same analytical model proposed earlier, which situates unions of different societies in unique structural positions in each national associational field. In the model, we conceive of unions as actors committed to both formal and informal relationships with other actors in the associational field. The two kinds of organizational relationships, cohesiveness and embeddedness, are deemed as key criteria that may steer negotiators' expectations and interpretations of each other's behaviors. We again pay special attention to the embeddedness of unions in informal civil society, for the following reasons.

First, unions' strong embeddedness in the larger associational field suggests that they have a different preference structure from those of conventional unions, which mainly serve their members' narrow economic interests. Embedded unions may consider non-union members' or the larger community's interests as a part of their own interests (Seidman 1994). As Scharpf (1994) points out, they may "consider the impact of potential agreements on the interest positions of actors who are not parties to the immediate negotiation"(p. 48). For instance, if their negotiations with the state lead to too much sacrifice or disadvantage for the larger community in the long term, they may not seek short-term gains even though the bargaining outcome might benefit their members in the short term. Conversely, if their bargaining outcome is conducive to solidifying their informal social base in the long term at the cost of their short-term interests, they may eagerly support it.

Second, unions' strong linkages to civil society groups imply that they have strong potential to mobilize or demobilize political bases for the incumbent party. In such a case, the state may not consider unions mere economic agents against which they should accomplish wage restraint or labor market reforms, but may instead treat them as political partners in discussing key reform agendas. According to this second point, unions' (policy-wise) embeddedness in the larger associational field may be interpreted as their potential for persuading and drawing larger electorates and civil society forces, for or against the incumbent party (or its policies), beyond unions' own members. Therefore, unions' embeddedness may send a signal to the state that breaking the existing trust (cohesive ties) with unions by introducing unexpected reforms against them or not responding to unions' reform requests may decisively encroach upon the incumbent party's electoral bases.

Third, unions' strong (mobilization-wise) embeddedness also implies that their capacity for disruption in the event of confrontation with the state will be much greater. Unions' contentious politics, supported by the larger civil society, could have deleterious impacts on the national economy through losses in workdays due to strikes and demonstrations, as well as through consequential shortage of products and services (Fantasia and Stepan-Norris 2004). In short, unions' strong disruptive potential in contentious politics (aside from electoral politics) may lead the state to be concerned about the high cost of confrontation with embedded unions, and eventually to make greater concessions or accept unions' proposals for universal provision of social welfare in order to prevent prolonged strikes and mass demonstrations that may diminish state legitimacy.

Finally, unions' strong embeddedness enables unions to take part in collective action at a lower cost to their solidarity, as support from the larger civil society helps them to overcome the "collective action problem" (Olson 1965) resulting from insufficient participation during early

| | | *Cohesiveness* (Unions' Linkages to Incumbent Party) | |
		Weak	Medium to Strong
	Weak	Unions: No (long term) commitment to both the state and civil society;	Unions: Strong commitment to the state, but not to civil society;
		The State: no fear of severe confrontation and electoral loss	The state: no fear of severe confrontation and electoral loss
		→ **Zero-sum Pure Conflict Game**:	→ **Unilateral State Dominance Game**:
Embeddedness (Unions' Linkages to Larger Associational Field)		**(1) Outcome for Retrenchment Game: State's Radical Reform & Unions' Militancy**	**(1) Outcome for Retrenchment Game: State's Radical Reform & Unions' Restraint**
		(2) Outcome for Expansion Game: No Union-driven Reform	**(2) Outcome for Expansion Game: Unions' Selective Reform and State's acceptance**
	Medium to Strong	Unions: Strong commitment to civil society, but not to the state;	Unions: Strong commitment to both the state and civil society;
		The state: Fear of severe confrontation and electoral loss	The state: Fear of severe confrontation and electoral loss
		→ **Unilateral Union Dominance Game**:	→ **Standard Assurance Game**:
		(1) Outcome for Retrenchment Game: State's Radical Reform, Unions' Militancy, and State's Concession/Or Moderate Reform & Unions' Restraint	**(1) Outcome for Retrenchment Game: State's Moderate Reform & Unions' Restraint**
		(2) Outcome for Expansion Game: Unions' Universal Reform and State's acceptance	**(2) Outcome for Expansion Game: Unions' Universal Reform and State's acceptance**

FIGURE 3.4. Network-Informed Strategic Actions of the State and Unions in the Combinational Spaces of Cohesiveness and Embeddedness: Retrenchment and Expansion Games

mobilization. Embedded unions, therefore, may challenge the state's pursuit of radical reforms, or its decision to rebuff unions' reform proposals, more readily and in more effective ways.

These four aspects of unions' embeddedness, interacting with the cohesive linkages between the incumbent party and unions, generate widely divergent structures of commitments and trust relationships for the two actors, as illustrated in Figure 3.4.[18] First, when unions are weakly connected to both the incumbent party and civil society, unions have commitments neither to the incumbent party nor to civil society. Therefore, when the state attempts to implement radical reform drives, unions do not expect any long-term concessions in return for short-term restraint in case of labor-repressive policies or radical market reforms that may encroach upon labor rights and existing social benefits. The state, in the absence of linkages and trust, would not be intimidated by threats of large-scale disruptive politics accompanied by electoral punishment, and therefore would hardly promise long-term concessions. Under this weak cohesiveness and weak embeddedness, unions have neither the policy capacity nor the mobilization capacity to force the state to accept their demands for social policy expansion, thereby failing to change the status quo.

In the second case, when unions have developed strong organizational linkages to the incumbent party but lack ties to civil society, the state and unions' interpretations of each other's behaviors will be starkly different from the weak-cohesiveness/weak-embeddedness case. Unions have strong commitment and loyalty to the incumbent party, but do not have deep commitment to the third party, civil society. Under the circumstance of the state-driven market reforms, they expect long-term concessions from their allies in power, who may implement labor-repressive policies or radical market reforms in an economic crisis, but do not care much about the negative impacts of such reforms on civil society. Under the circumstance of social reform drives for the progressive expansion of social and labor market policies, they may seek to further their own interests with the assistance of the state, thereby introducing selective provisions of social safety nets for unions and their members. However, the fact that they have little commitment to civil society implies that unions cannot resort to other civic organizations and potential allies when they most need them. The state may initially promise long-term concessions with the introduction of radical market-oriented reforms, but may break its promise ex post as there is no strong credible threat from unions, such as society-wide disruption beyond union-led strikes, or electoral punishment driven by a comprehensive civic coalition across social classes.[19]

The third case is the opposite of the second case: when unions have strong linkages to civil society, but not to the state, as the incumbent party is not their traditional ally or they have not developed robust communication channels due to different partisan/ideological origins. On one hand, unions are deeply embedded in civil society, as both members and leaders are co-affiliated with diverse civic and community associations. Unions' interests, therefore, overlap with those found in the larger civic associational field. Unions are expected to behave as representatives of the larger civil society, considering the interests of civil society as part of their own, which has been labeled as the "encapsulation of others' interest" (Hardin 2002). On the other hand, unions' weak linkages to the incumbent party may lead to unions' low expectations of long-term concessions from the state when labor-repressive policies or market reforms are introduced. The biggest difference between this embeddedness without cohesiveness and that of the second case is that the state cannot treat embedded unions as isolated ones, and should not expect them to acquiesce when labor-repressive policies or market reforms are implemented. Embedded unions are less concerned about the cost of strikes and disruptive politics, because allied civil society's mass participation in disruptive or non-disruptive politics through election, media, and street politics greatly lowers the cost of mobilization. In the event that the state implements labor-repressive policies or market-based reforms, therefore, unions are ready to engage in mass demonstrations combined with general strikes supported by civil society. The state will be concerned about the cost of confrontational politics, as this may significantly damage its legitimacy and eventually result in electoral loss in subsequent elections. This implies that in case of union militancy, the state has to pay for the greater cost of disruption, and therefore needs to minimize it to avoid further contentious confrontation. In this case, the state's concession at a reasonable level following union militancy may incur less cost than non-concessionary struggles against embedded unions.[20] Under the expansionary social reform drive initiated by unions, unions' universal reform moves with such large punishment capacity are often not strong and convincing enough to lead the state to accept the universal reforms, but at a very high level of embeddedness, the state may accept unions' universal reform initiative.

The last case is when unions hold strong linkages both to the incumbent party and the larger civic associational field. In this case, unions occupy "brokerage positions" (Gould 1989) between the incumbent party and civil society, in the sense that they not only translate the interests of the larger civil society and convey them to the state (as a representative) but also mobilize and deliver electoral support to the state. As unions are deeply committed to both the incumbent party and civil society, they are responsible for protecting the interests of the larger civil society, including both the middle and working classes, or both organized and non-organized workers. They are also accountable for the incumbent party's good performance in power and electoral success in future elections. In the event of market reforms, they would not allow the state to introduce radical reforms, while convincing other civil society actors about the necessity of moderate retrenchment using their brokerage position. The state may be ready to make concessions to unions, and dare not introduce radical reforms for short-term gains, which may sacrifice its long-term allies' trust and may lead to poor electoral performance and the loss of legitimacy after severe confrontations. In case of expansionary social reforms, unions would be ready to propose universal social policy agendas thanks to their strong policy-wise embeddedness and cohesiveness. Pre-existing policy-relevant channels enable unions to coordinate universal policies among diverse social forces and lobby for the coordinated policies at minimum cost. The state may not be able to resist such pressure to introduce universal social policies.[21]

SUMMARY AND PROPOSITIONS

So far, I have proposed a theoretical model that explains how the divergent structures of associational fields lead to different outcomes in social policy regimes. Highlighting the importance of linkages between labor and formal/informal civic associations, I analyzed two prongs of the politics of reform: (1) the politics of mobilization and pressure through threat and punishment mechanisms, and (2) the politics of lobbying and persuasion (of key policy-makers or legislators, implementers, their beneficiaries and contributors). Utilizing network theory and game theory, I developed two ideal types of games, one for retrenchment and one for expansion, each of which was sub-divided into four different games along the two variables, cohesiveness and embeddedness. I produced four dominant outcomes under each type of game, which reveal divergent processes of utility maximization for the state and unions.

In retrenchment games (see Table 3.1), mobilization capacity matters most for unions' negotiation power, especially mobilization embeddedness. When unions are well-connected to civil society forces in terms of their mobilization capacity, they are capable, even after the state's radical reform drive, of seeking at least 'concessions' via their strong solidaristic militancy. When unions have both cohesiveness and embeddedness, the state will likely not promote radical reforms, given its commitment

TABLE 3.1. *A Comparison: Retrenchment Game vs. Expansion Game*

	Retrenchment Game	Expansion Game
Initiator	The state	Unions (or the state)
Main mode of capacity	Mobilization capacity	Policy + mobilization capacity
Main mode of politics	Contentious politics	Politics of lobbying and threat
Primary locus of solidaristic linkage	Embeddedness	Embeddedness + cohesiveness
Best outcome for the state	Radical reform-restraint	No reform
Best outcome for unions	Moderate reform-restraint	Selective reform-accept
Best outcome for civil society	–	Universal reform-accept

to unions on one hand and its fear of threats by unions on the other. Therefore, in retrenchment games where unions' capacity for 'defense' of their interests is critical, mobilization embeddedness is the main type of capacity required by unions. Mobilization embeddedness most empowers unions to threaten or punish the state through contentious politics (see Appendix C.1 for the payoff structure of the retrenchment game).[22]

In expansion games, the story is more complex. First of all, unions, as an initiator, must be able to propose realistic and convincing agendas, lobby the state, and punish it when it refuses accept their proposals. Unlike the retrenchment game, unions need to overcome the threshold of the cost of reforms in order to make anything happen. The cost of reforms include the costs of militancy, solidarity, and lobbying. In the structure of expansion games, the cost of lobbying can be reduced through stronger cohesiveness, while the costs of militancy and solidarity are implicitly reduced with deeper embeddedness. Second, unions do not have to resort to universal reform (UR), as they have a better payoff structure under selective reform (SR).[23] Given that the state also has a better payoff schedule under SR, the SR-accept equilibrium would be the easiest path for both the state and unions. Therefore, in order to prevent this state–union collusion from occurring to the detriment of civil society and unorganized social forces, civil society needs to maintain durable trust networks with unions, and to persuade unions to stand with civil society and pursue universal reform.

In expansion games, the best-case scenario for society in general is that unions propose and seek universal reform and the state accepts it, because the amount of total benefits from the universal reform (2γ) is greater than that of SR (β) for the entire society (wage earners) including organized working classes (see Appendix C.2 for the payoff structure of the expansion game). Such an outcome is plausible when unions have very strong embeddedness (thereby encapsulating the interests of civil society as their own), or when they have moderate cohesiveness along with strong embeddedness such that they can greatly reduce their costs of lobbying, solidarity, and punishment, while increasing the costs of punishment and rebuff for the state. In this process, unions' policy and mobilization capacity matter, as they need to build a 'policy-based solidarity' with civil society and persuade the incumbent party to accept the proposal. Moreover, policy-wise embeddedness and cohesiveness initially also guarantee stronger mobilization capacity in case of state rebuff. This is so because in expansion games, unions' and their allies' early proposals pre-configure the scope and depth of solidarity that could later be mobilized to punish the state. These differences in retrenchment and expansion games are summarized in Table 3.1.

Based on the previous discussion, I derive the following propositions to be tested in the rest of this book. These propositions have been built on theoretical assumptions and logics (developed in Appendix C), and therefore do not necessarily account for all the details of the empirical cases dealt with in the following chapters. Nevertheless, the four ideal types of games constructed with two network variables, cohesiveness and embeddedness, provide analytical maps to help explain divergent trajectories of social and labor market reforms in different policy domains as well as in different societies and times.

Proposition 1: When unions are isolated both from the state and from civil society (low cohesiveness and low embeddedness), they will likely engage in inconsistent, sporadic conflicts with the state. Under a radical retrenchment drive by the state, unions will be unable to defend their core interests, allowing the state to encroach upon their core rights (labor market institutions) and assets (wage and social benefits). Under a social reform drive by unions and/or civil society, unions will be incapable of advancing either universal or selective policy reforms, lobbying the state, or penalizing the state when the state rejects union proposals. Therefore, reforms will not occur.

Proposition 2: When unions are disconnected from civil society but maintain a close relationship with the incumbent party, unions may either be exploited by the state or seek maximum benefits for themselves, depending upon the economic and political environment. When the state initiates market reform that threatens to appropriate union assets, unions, without their embedded ties, are more likely to acquiesce, which encourages the state to introduce radical market reforms. However, when unions are in a position to launch social reform projects, unions may prioritize their own particular interests, as they do not have serious commitments to unorganized social forces in civil society. Without having to incur significant lobbying costs (thanks to pre-existing channels to the state), unions will likely embark on selective reforms that serve their own interests, and the state will join such a move.

Proposition 3: When unions have durable solidarity with civic associations but do not have direct lobbying channels to the state, they may survive the state's market reform drive, but whether they are able to launch any significant social reform projects depends upon their policy and mobilization embeddedness. Under retrenchment drives, unions are capable of punishing the state, with their ample capacity to mobilize broad segments of civil society around their cause. The state may make concessions or not even attempt retrenchment efforts, depending upon the magnitude of unions' mobilization capacity. When there are social reform opportunities, highly embedded unions may promote universal social policy reforms as representatives of civil society. Such efforts will succeed when unions are able to mobilize a wide range of labor–civic solidarity to punish the state's non-response through contentious or electoral politics.

Proposition 4: When unions have both high embeddedness and (medium to) high cohesiveness, they will be able to coordinate their actions with the state (and civil society). In an era of retrenchment, the state and unions will be able to agree on a 'moderate reform and restraint' solution. Unions' strong mobilization embeddedness and their durable communication channels with the state prevent both the state and unions from engaging in opportunistic behaviors. In an era of expansion, embedded unions may take into account the interests of civil society as their own, and introduce universal reforms in social policy fields, restraining their desire to launch selective reforms – especially under a medium level of cohesiveness.

CONCLUSION

This chapter has developed a theoretical framework that emphasizes the importance of the linkages between formal civic sector associations and informal civic sector associations and their roles in bringing about divergent modes of the retrenchment or expansion politics in welfare state institutions. I explored the patterns and modes of solidarity and their roles in generating different types of social or labor market policy reforms. In particular, I focused on two key network variables, unions' ties with leftist/reformist parties (or the incumbent political party), and their solidaristic linkages with civic associations. These variables capture, at first, trust and commitment linkages, and then, as I further developed their implications, policy and mobilization solidarity. Ultimately, this study considers the structure of unions' political and civic solidarity as the strongest exogenous determinant of the retrenchment or development of welfare states.

My approach introduces two new theoretical perspectives, a 'social movement' perspective and a 'civil society' perspective, into the literature on welfare states. As I discussed in Chapters 1 and 2, I bring "the configuration of civil society" (Collier and Collier 1991; Rueschemeyer *et al.* 1992) and "the outcome of social movements" (Amenta and Young 1999; Amenta *et al.* 2011) into the study of welfare state trajectories. While the former focuses on the 'scaling-up' process of social solidarity and its agendas into political institutions, the latter explores the politics of pressures, lobbying, and negotiation between SMOs and political institutions and their policy outcomes. Incorporating these two perspectives into a unified theoretical and empirical framework, I conceptualize and operationalize two key variables: embeddedness and cohesiveness. Building on notions from network analysis and organizational studies (Gould 1989; Granovetter 1985), I explore two processes: (1) how the working classes (and their allies) grow from "special interest groups" (Becker 1985; Grossman and Helpman 2002) into 'universal interest groups' which exert "weight" or "political power" (Acemoglu and Robinson 2005) on the democratic political process and policy outcomes, counteracting the political power of the wealthy; and (2) how the state responds to the political power of labor-linked civic solidarity networks in pursuing the politics of social policy retrenchment or expansion. The contents of embeddedness and cohesiveness – policy and mobilization capacities – capture the former process, while the basic game theoretical frameworks outline the latter process. Overall, my approach reveals both how such 'political weight' of a social group (unions) is shaped by labor and civic activists in associational 'fields' (Akchurin and Lee 2013; Curtis and Zucher 1973), and how that political weight is perceived by the state and translated into policy outcomes. Examining the logic of these efforts, I have developed four pathways of welfare state retrenchment and expansion, depending upon the levels of cohesiveness and embeddedness.

The proposed theoretical framework of this study accounts for wide variations in both retrenchment and expansion instances of welfare states, variations which current theories of the welfare state fail to explain. In the subsequent chapters, I present detailed comparative historical case studies of South Korea and three other countries to identify variations in cohesiveness and embeddedness, and show how those variables account for the state and unions' interactions regarding regressive market reforms and progressive social reforms. Drawing on those comparisons, I then evaluate my four hypotheses with diverse levels and modes of empirical analyses.

PART II

4

The Origin of Top-Down Solidarity in
South Korea

The South Korean case provides one of the most intriguing stories of labor politics and welfare state development/retrenchment among developing nations. Its labor movement emerged in the 1990s as one of the most militant, alongside its Brazilian and South African counterparts, and attracted worldwide attention. Its political struggle and organizational expansion from 1987 to 1997 not only led to the establishment of an alternative union confederation, but also contributed to the collapse of the conservative regime that had lasted for nearly four decades. The labor movement's dramatic expansion, however, turned into a disastrous decline in the following decade, as it faced neo-liberal economic transformations in South Korea's economy and politics. During these two decades, the growth and then retrenchment of the South Korean welfare state are similarly impressive. With the advent of the 1997 financial crisis, the new reformist regime (the Kim Dae-jung regime) introduced strikingly universal social policy reforms, while its successor reformist regime (the Roh Mu-hyun regime) opened paths toward an equally stunning retrenchment and privatization within the pensions and health care systems. How can we account for these two dramatic changes, one on the labor politics side, and the other on the welfare state side? How are these two changes linked?

In order to answer these questions, this chapter begins analyzing such processes by discussing how radical leftist intellectuals forged alliances with workers' communities during the harsh authoritarian era of the 1970s and 1980s. It explores the early formation processes of the worker–intellectual alliances through which labor leaders eventually institutionalized labor–civic solidarity (embeddedness), as well as labor's linkages to established political institutions (cohesiveness). How and where did this distinctive group of well-organized and militant labor activists emerge in the 1980s, and what roles did they play in cultivating labor politics in subsequent decades?

South Korean labor movements began to erupt in the early 1970s. Around that time, Park Jung-hee, who had led the military coup overthrowing a civilian government in 1961 and was then elected president in three consecutive elections (1963, 1967, and 1971), intensified suppression of workers in support of export-oriented firms, the competitiveness of which was primarily based on low wages. Workers sporadically attempted to organize unions to defend their rights and improve working conditions from the early 1970s, but the authoritarian regime relentlessly oppressed workers' efforts using coercive apparatuses and intelligence agencies – especially after the Park regime announced martial law in 1972 to enforce Park's becoming a lifelong dictator.

Intellectuals and students began to join workers' isolated struggles, after a 22-year-old textile worker named Chŏn T'ae-il immolated himself in 1970, agitating for better labor conditions.[2] They initially approached workers' communities through urban church groups and nighttime community schools (for workers), and increasingly helped workers to organize unions through legal and organizational support. These early moments of 'going-underground' activities were galvanized by Christian missionary workers who ventured into workplaces in the 1970s. Many youth and student members of Protestant missionary groups began underground activities in this period, laying an initial framework for student–worker alliances through the work of Christian faith groups.[3]

In 1979, the dictator Park was assassinated by his close subordinate, Kim Chae-gyu, a chief of KCIA, ending his 19-year rule through his own coercive apparatus. During the turmoil another figure, Chun Doo-hwan, emerged as a leader of the new military junta, which took over the nation in spring, 1980 (see Figure 4.1 for the chronological order of these political events). Against the new ruling military regime, citizens and students of Kwangju waged a huge demonstration against troops deployed in the city on May 18, which led to a brutal massacre of citizens that lasted for nine days. From that point, student movement leaders began to radicalize themselves into revolutionary forces. Thousands of students decided to leave college and become workers in local factories during the early 1980s under the Chun regime. Witnessing the brutal massacre of citizens and the continuing elimination of formal political space under martial law, many leaders and members of opposition movements went underground not only to hide from the intelligence agencies but also to cultivate new revolutionary resources in grassroots communities and workplaces.

During the period, several hundred students per year became workers after dropping out of college or graduating (Koo 2001), as hundreds of riot police squads resided on major college campuses to prevent student demonstrations. These activists "felt obliged to be engaged in labor movements like many others" of that generation, and "thought that there was no other choice than becoming a worker."[4] These students received training on how to get a job, how to get acquainted with blue-collar workers through everyday cultural activities, how to behave as a trusted co-worker, what kind of language to use (or not to use), what kind of clothes to wear, etc. (Lee, N. 2007). As disguised workers, activists were willing to bear the cost of organizing strikes, losing jobs or even being handed over to the police (which meant torture or imprisonment). The size of this movement was unprecedented in the modern era of democratization movements in developing countries. There were so many students-turned-workers in the Seoul-Incheon industrial areas in the mid-1980s that several activists from different universities or different movement organizations say that they "were able to recognize each other in a factory" as they became engaged in the organizing activities of labor unions.[5]

As Hagen Koo (2001) and Namhee Lee (2007) convincingly describe, these students-turned-activists organized numerous study groups in which workers were taught not only their legal labor rights but also revolutionary theory from the Marxist and Leninist traditions. The activists felt obliged to provide workers with the necessary legal information to form unions and bargain with employers, as well as with the intellectual tools to interpret the principles of wider capitalist society. They were eager to equip workers with a belief that they could constitute a strong political force that might be able to correct the deep contradictions of the capitalist economy. Activists attempted to agitate workers into going on strike, utilizing diverse tactics such as sit-ins, demonstrations, and occupations of factories, which greatly contributed to the wave of thousands of strikes during the democratization period in the late 1980s. They also formed thick activists' networks across factories, so that they could wage larger, more threatening strikes beyond a single factory-level struggle. Labor activists in the Incheon and Seoul areas were also united by regional leadership organizations such as the SWC (Seoul Workers' Council) or the IDWC (Incheon Democratic Workers' Council). Without a doubt, such clandestine activities in the 1980s formed the cornerstone of the subsequent organizational and institutional structures of labor politics.

While the most radical and potent group of student movements went to factories, many others remained around college campuses and maintained their status as students. On campus, these students continued expanding leftist 'ideological study clubs.' They were mostly informal, but the leaders overlapped organizationally with formal student associations primarily focusing on students' administrative issues and amenities at the department and college level. Those leaders were chosen by annual elections, and their associations were run by fees collected from students. In the mid- to late 1980s, these associations were established in every university, and those formal and informal student organizations were in charge of freshmen orientations at the academic department level in every single university in South Korea. The majority of students in the 1980s therefore were exposed to leftist ideological study clubs at least during their initial freshmen socialization periods. Student movement leaders, constantly in jeopardy of being captured by state intelligence agencies, maintained these formal and informal organizations throughout the 1980s. By the late 1980s, leaders of South Korean student movements had established a strong, Leninist top-down hierarchical confederation system, of which sub-units reached the grassroots study groups and the upper bureaucracy encompassed nearly all major universities in South Korea.

Based on this durable organizational structure, student movements waged well-coordinated, large-scale demonstrations on and off numerous campuses against the military regime, starting in the mid-1980s. Other civic associations, opposition party leaders, and white-collar workers joined student-led demonstrations in June 1987 after a college student was killed by police during a demonstration. After millions of demonstrators filled the main streets of Seoul and other major cities in late June, the Chun regime eventually succumbed to students' and citizens' request for a democratic election. With this sudden transition to procedural democracy, workers also poured into streets requesting better working conditions and higher wages during the summer of 1987. Nearly 1.2 million workers joined strikes during the year and labor disputes skyrocketed. Workers of large manufacturing firms such as Hyundai, Daewoo, and LG led the surge of strikes and union organizing efforts. Under these new political opportunities, a product of democratization, labor movement leaders, many of whom were disguised students or their allies, were prompted to organize grassroots unions and regional units for solidarity, which were supposed to eventually evolve into a national confederation in the 1990s.

Despite an erupting civil society and citizens' desires for deeper political changes, two prominent opposition party leaders, Kim Dae-jung and Kim Young-sam, failed to form a coalition in the election, with each running as a separate candidate, which helped one of the former military officers, Rho Tae-woo, to become elected president with only 33 percent of the vote in December 1987. Worse, one of the two opposition leaders, Kim Young-sam, decided to join the conservative party in 1989, and was then elected the next president in 1992. Democratization forces had to wait until 1997, when Kim Dae-jung eventually succeeded in ousting the former authoritarian forces from power for the first time nearly in four decades (since Park's military coup in 1961).

In order to understand the emergence of a distinctive, Korea-specific structure of labor politics, it is important to look at a deeper layer of social movement processes during this watershed period. While most literature on the Korean labor movement highlights the 1987 Great Workers' Struggle as a "critical juncture" (Collier and Collier 1991) that shaped the terrain of labor politics, this study underscores a slightly later period – the early 1990s – as the most critical moment for the ensuing development of labor politics.

With the dissolution of the Soviet Union in 1991 and the launch of the Kim (Y.-S.) regime in 1993, many labor activists seriously reconsidered their revolutionary strategies. First, the broken statue of Lenin fundamentally shattered radical activists' belief that socialism would eventually spread to the rest of the world and a revolutionary moment would arrive in South Korea in the near future. Second, the reform drives launched by the Kim (Y.-S.) regime also increased the skepticism of many radicals about the validity of the radical social transformation path. Third, after having reached their peak in 1989, labor movements were witnessing a decline in the early 1990s. Indeed, there were serious debates about whether the labor movement was in crisis or not. During this short period, many early participants in the democratization and labor movements collectively realized that the revolutionary path of a labor or 'Minjung' (民衆, people's) movement was quickly closing in South Korea (Kim, D.-C. 1995). Simultaneously, many perceived the emergence of a new political opportunity structure in which Minjung movements could find their niches within formal electoral politics.

THE ORIGINS OF COHESIVENESS AND EMBEDDEDNESS II: REPERTOIRES IN CAREER CHOICES

Students-turned-labor activists pursued one of three career trajectories. One group of intellectuals – those who remained in or stayed around workplaces – helped local union leaders to build higher union confederations in the 1990s and eventually a labor-based party in the 2000s. The second group of intellectuals, those who left workplaces in the 1980s and the early 1990s, found new careers as the founders of diverse and politicized civic organizations. Finally, the third group went back to school or to normal civilian lives.[6] These intellectuals made critical career decisions at the intersection of individual and historical junctures, which shaped the institutionalization of labor politics for the next couple of decades. The two main explanatory factors I examine in the politics of the welfare state, embeddedness and cohesiveness, have in South Korea been fundamentally shaped by these activists' collective and individual life trajectories.

Figure 4.1 illustrates how these radical intellectuals' conversion choices during the critical transition period later shaped labor-related

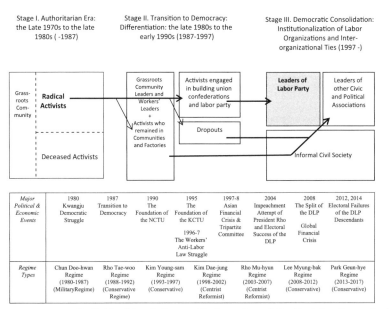

FIGURE 4.1. Individual-level Career Trajectories of Radical Intellectuals from Autocracy to Democracy

political and civil societies. The first group of intellectuals, whom I call 'builders of cohesiveness,' stayed in unions or other labor-linked associations after the 1987 Great Labor Strikes. They kept along a similar career path as founders of a new union confederation and a new labor-based party. First, they found that they needed higher levels of union organization through which workers could bargain with employers and the state at an industry or national level. Labor leaders initially founded regional confederations in 1988 and 1989, and then eventually, in 1990, 1,500 labor leaders founded the NCTU (National Workers' Association) despite the state's severe suppression and surveillance. In the same year, labor leaders in non-manufacturing industries also created a national white-collar workers' confederation. Eventually, union leaders who had been eager to found an independent, democratic union confederation succeeded in establishing the KCTU (Korean Confederation of Trade Unions). The KCTU obtained its legal status from the state in 1997 and remains a major union federation encompassing nearly 580,000 workers as of 2010 (35.3% of the entire organized labor force; MOEL 2012).

It is important to recognize that many students-turned-labor activists relinquished their revolutionary strategies and decided to pursue a moderate, reform-oriented path under procedural representative democracy in the early 1990s. Former revolutionaries poured into the formal arena of electoral politics. Some renounced their ideological faith and became members of existing conservative or reformist centrist parties, while others went on to create a labor party (the Democratic Labor Party, DLP) in 2000, seeking a social democratic reformist path.

The KCTU activists, many of whom were students-turned-workers, participated in building the DLP. As many union leaders' 'class consciousness' was fostered by students-turned-labor activists in the 1980s, it was very natural for union leaders to lend support to the DLP from the beginning. They provided not only resources for electoral competitions but also votes and political guidance regarding major policies in the party platform. This type of activity was often common in the building process of social democratic parties in advanced industrial democracies. Some union leaders directly joined the efforts as key officials of the DLP through co-affiliations, while other unions (and their members) sponsored DLP candidates' political campaigns either by donating or by volunteering. The DLP's 50,000 members were "directly or indirectly linked to labor movements, peasant movements, urban poor's movements, and other progressive civil society groups embracing intellectuals and youth activists … All the main post executives and electoral candidates are nominated and selected directly by its own members"(Im 2005, p. 67). Thus, "the class and regional compositions of DLP are squarely in accordance with those of KCTU"(Im 2005, p. 71).[7]

Overall, South Korean leftist intellectuals and organizations followed a trajectory remarkably similar to that of social democratic parties in Western industrial democracies, despite the shorter time-frame. They wished to create a pure, mass-bureaucratic labor-based party in which blue-collar workers' interests were placed at the center of party agendas, while still attracting other lower or reformist middle classes, such as peasants and urban white-collar workers, who were viewed as allies in a broader working-class solidarity. The cohesive ties between the KCTU and the DLP, therefore, were initially seen as similar to those between unions and labor-based parties in wealthier Western democracies.

Indeed, the birth of the DLP in 2000 was a dramatic realization of theoretical projections that had sprung up among the theorists and strategists of the labor movement in the 1990s. After suffering mass strikes and conflicts between labor and capital in the late 1980s, right- and left-wing theorists and strategists proposed divergent models of labor politics, such as 'social corporatism' (Im and Kim 1991), 'democratic corporatism'(Ch'oe 1996), 'firm-level corporatism,' and 'democratic class politics' (Im 1997).[8] Overall, the founding of the DLP was partially an outcome of labor activists' collective reflections about the need for an organized political body to embody and advance the "democratic class struggle" (Lipset 1960).

While this short story of the growth of cohesiveness between the KCTU and DLP shows that it followed from two decades of labor activists' conscious collective efforts, the embeddedness of unions follows a different story. On one hand, it was an unintended consequence of an 'attrition' process in labor movements. On the other hand, it reflected a conscious effort mainly by a majority faction in the larger Minjung movements, but also by the labor movement, to mobilize civil society around unions. Just as the going-underground movements of the 1980s were unprecedented, so too was their dissolution dramatic. Indeed, even though the going-underground activities occurred on a massive scale, many could not bear the hard work. They increasingly became frustrated with indifferent workers and, as a result, were unable to overcome their own skepticism about workers' role in revolution. Many activists/radicals eventually left the factories, while a few of them "instead became labor counselors, organizers of study groups outside factories, night school teachers, and staff members of labor organizations" (Lee, N. 2007, p. 262).

Overall, then, the top-down solidarity initiated by vanguardist intellectuals in South Korea was short-lived. Although their participation in local workplaces and their communities exercised a deep and fundamental influence on the union movement in the 1980s, going-underground movements began dissipating at the grassroots level in the early 1990s. Simultaneously, many labor-friendly progressive civic associations were built by former students-turned-radical intellectuals. This was the result of the process of their conversion into moderate reformist activists. Eventually this led to an abrupt increase in the embeddedness of labor unions in civil society.[9]

In this sense, the early 1990s was a "gestation period" (Aldrich and Ruef 2006), if not a "critical juncture" (Collier and Collier 1991), not only for labor movements, but also for newly built progressive civic associations. While many labor-linked organizations were conceived and built in the late 1980s, labor–civil society linkages became increasingly dense and differentiated from the early 1990s. Now, I seek to explore the individual-level career choices of radical intellectuals at this juncture, in order to see how their choices shaped the next generation of labor-linked associational fields.

THE EMERGENCE OF COHESIVENESS AND EMBEDDEDNESS: ORGANIZATIONAL HISTORIES

During the authoritarian era, radical intellectuals' political zeal was largely confined to their revolutionary underground organizations. Students-turned-labor activists built inter-factory activist networks at the regional level in the Ulsan, Pusan, and Ch'angwŏn areas (the southeastern industrial belt), as well as in the Seoul and Kyŏnggi-Incheon (surrounding Seoul) areas.

An inconvenient truth in the development of labor politics in South Korea is that factional strife shaped the political terrain of Mingjung movements, including labor movements. Two main factions emerged among radical intellectuals in the 1980s, which were called the NL (National Liberation) and PD (People's Democracy) factions.[10] These two groups viewed the relationship between world capitalism and South Korea, the geo-political situation of the Korean peninsula, and the stages of class relationships in South Korea through two completely different theoretical and ideological prisms. Therefore, their assessments of the ongoing democratization processes differed sharply, which led them to build different strategies and goals during the transition to and consolidation of democracy. Such differences eventually contributed to a peculiar 'factional structure' of cohesiveness and embeddedness in the associational field in South Korea.

According to Im (1997), labor activists in the 1980s identified their roles with regard to three layers: popular movements (through open unions), political movements (through underground revolutionary organizations), and activists' movements. Here, activists are expected to mediate vertically between political movements and popular movements, while simultaneously horizontally linking labor movements and other social movements (Im 1998, p. 92). The divergence between the NL and PD was exposed through these roles and integration processes.

Despite the presence of these factions and the further intensification of conflicts between them during the course of the institutionalization of the labor movement, union leaders from different factions managed to remain under the organizational umbrella of the KCTU. This was managed by leaders skillfully coordinating their differences in movement goals, organizational strategies, and alliance-making, especially compared to party leaders of major factions.[11]

Emergence of Industrial Unionism and Growth in Cohesiveness and Embeddedness

In contrast to embeddedness, which emerged from radical activists' ideological conversions in the early 1990s and the influx of progressive professionals sympathetic with the labor movement into civil society, cohesiveness was built upon the systematic collective efforts of new union leaders during the entire 1990s. In particular, those who built the KCTU in 1995 rapidly consolidated a three-layer structure of union organizations (as illustrated in Figure 4.2) composed of grassroots firm-level unions, industrial union confederations, and a central peak union confederation, which was very similar to the European centralized union structure.

From the early 1990s, the majority of, if not all, labor activists agreed that they needed to build German-style industrial unions to overcome many problems originating from the Japanese style firm-level union structures that dominated the institutional structure built during the developmental era of the 1970s and 1980s. Leaders collectively realized that the labor movement would be in jeopardy in the near future unless they came up with a more solidaristic organizational structure to bargain with both employers and the state. With only fragmented bargaining institutions at

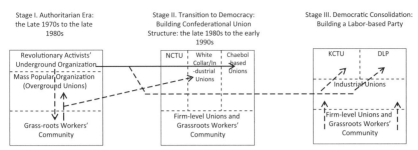

FIGURE 4.2. Organizational Evolution of Labor-Based Organizations from Autocracy to Democracy

the firm level, union leaders thought that they could neither bring broader social reform issues to the bargaining table, nor make collective efforts to react to declining membership or reach unorganized workers.

Although this study is not about the specific union strategy to build industrial unions and its implications and consequences, it is necessary to discuss the emergence and institutionalization process of industrial unions in detail, as it provides critical information on how labor activists have built (or failed to build) cohesiveness and embeddedness in South Korean labor politics during the past few decades. As labor activists established the KCTU and its industrial branch organizations, union structures that preceded the KCTU, such as region-based union confederations and business conglomerate-based confederations, were discouraged or absorbed into the emerging industrial union structure, if not completely dissolved.[12]

Since the early 1990s, most activists' efforts and resources were concentrated on building and consolidating industrial union structures. The institutional impacts of this consolidation have enabled or constrained activists' future goals and agendas. In this section, I initially describe the opportunities that industrial unionism brought, setting aside for later discussion its limitations and negative impacts.

Industrial Unionism as a Movement Strategy

First of all, it is important to point out that industrial unionism was primarily elevated and pursued as a 'movement strategy' by labor activists in South Korean not only to overcome firm-level bargaining, but also to pursue broader 'social reformism.' One of the early proponents of industrial unionism, Im Yŏng-il, a prominent labor scholar in the 1990s and an important strategist for contemporary union movements, recalled in my field interview with him the early development of industrial unionism:

Industrial unionism movements were launched as the NCTU [the confederation of regional union organizations] was dissolved in the mid-1990s. We started discussing its theoretical base in 1993 at the Yŏngnam Labor Institute. We built a team in Seoul, too, publishing a book [on Industrial Unionism]. We first focused on building a metal union in Yŏngnam [south-eastern part of the country] regions. Many union leaders from Pusan, Ch'angwŏn, Ulsan, Kŏje, and Chinju industrial areas collectively joined the institute as members. We succeeded inviting the leadership and members of 'Yŏngnam regional Union Representatives' Congregation.' So, the metal union established its office in Pusan, and then spread its influence and membership to Seoul between 1993 and 1995. The metal union had the most advanced theory and strategy. Most of them were not factional activists but grassroots union leaders.

Industrial unionism was promoted as union activists' primary organizational goal when the NCTU, the first democratic union confederation since democratization, famous for its militant, uncompromising strategies, was dissolved and the KCTU was established by leaders and members from three large groups of union organizations (the NCTU, Congregation of the Industrial Unions, and Hyundai/Daewoo Group Unions). Before and after 1995, union leaders built 16 new industrial-level confederations that ranged from metal, transportation, banking, medical, and other white-collar industries, to public service and teachers' unions.

The most important point regarding the emergence of industrial unions is that the industry-level unions provided not only institutional domains and venues in which union leaders could collectively coordinate and bargain with employers at each industry level,[13] but also material support and organizational spaces for union activists. These union activists were eager not only to wage centralized, coordinated struggles and negotiations beyond firm-level bargaining, but also to be engaged in union-centered political activities. The following two veteran (student-turned-)labor activists (from my field interviews) in the KCTU also found their material and personal support in industrial unions after they quit their regional union-building efforts.

After I came out of a local factory, I was involved in a night-time study group for workers which was organized by a local church and then in activities in a regional union association in Kuro area [an industrial complex area filled with small electronic, manufacturing, and chemical firms in the south-western part of Seoul]. Then, I ended up with going to Hospital Unions in 1993, an association linking a couple of unions of medium and large hospitals. My colleagues said, "well, we know that you cannot take care of your living out of your work here with us [as a local activist]. If you should go, just go." I worked there until 2005. During that time, I got involved in building the first industrial union, Health and Medical Industry Union. I also participated in the first founding members of DLP, serving as a director of Kwangmyŏng city DLP regional organization [a satellite city close to Kuro area of Seoul, another worker-concentrated region].

I was almost about to quit my career as a labor activist [probably because of financial issues]. I happened to be called upon to join the Public Transportation Union Confederation, as a chief of organization department. Then, I was also requested to join the campaign camp for the chief of KCTU by Tan Pyŏng-ho [one of the most renowned worker leaders among the first generation of KCTU and DLP builders], so that I got involved in both KCTU and DLP since then.

Both activists, after their underground activities, remained on as union activists, and kept struggling to solidify industrial unions and the KCTU and eventually to build the DLP, even while witnessing many comrades' departures and betrayals. In such processes, both activists played multiple roles. At the industrial union levels, they were involved in persuading local unions to join the industrial union confederations, leading industry-level wage bargaining with employers' associations, organizing and leading industry-level strikes against hostile legal disputes or lay-off decisions, educating local union activists, and lobbying political parties for favorable legislation. At the KCTU level, they participated in organizing and building the leadership structure every three years through election campaigns, national-level strikes, support of regional-level strikes, and conveying industry-level demands, opinions, and policy agendas to KCTU leadership structures. Most importantly, they were also able to build DLP organizations at local and central levels. This remarkable range of activities were surely not all conducted simultaneously, but they went back and forth depending upon their factions' decisions, their personal decisions, and their political situations.

Industrial Unions and Cohesiveness

The base camp of cohesiveness-building was, therefore, industrial unions, as illustrated in the third sequence of Figure 4.2. Those intellectuals who were determined to remain with the labor movement and their allied workers were able to build their community bases around the industrial union confederations even after they left grassroots unions. They built new networks of activists – networks which linked local and central unions. In this capacity, they reached out to other social movement activists for alliances, and nourished their next organizational projects.

In short, industrial union confederations were not only the upper bargaining units for firm-level unions. They also functioned as organizational bridging units and resource containers for union activists who aimed to play a less direct and more general political and economic game against the state and employers. Figure 4.2 shows how the underground activities waged by radical intellectuals in the 1970s and 1980s led to the establishment of the KCTU national center and industrial unions in the 1990s (the second sequence), and then eventually the foundation of the DLP in the 2000s (the third sequence). Establishing industrial unions was not only an organizational goal for the majority of labor activists who desired Western European-style 'democratic corporatism' and 'welfare states,' but also a career bridge that sequentially and institutionally linked activists' initial efforts to cultivate grassroots unions and the national three-layer structures to their next career project: building a labor-based party.

The sequential two-track strategies of establishing industrial unions and then a labor-based party were also "a coupling strategy to bind policies and organizations" (field interviewee Kim Yu-sŏn). Building the three-layer structure of unions and a labor-based party was an organizational realization of the political zeal of radical intellectuals who went underground in the 1980s to defend workers' rights and organize their interests. By institutionalizing workers' bargaining and political organizations, they hoped to consolidate their intellectual roles as both policy-makers and political organizers who could translate, channel, and implement labor-centered policy agendas not only in the factories but also in congress.

The Founding of the DLP and Changes in Unions' Cohesiveness

The establishment of the DLP in 2000 and its electoral success in the 2004 general election meant that the KCTU gained a political agent that could channel workers' interests and demands. With the presence of the DLP in congress, the KCTU's mode of cohesiveness changed dramatically: the KCTU, as a shareholder, began to treat the DLP as its unilateral policy-crafting partner, while investing less in building policy deliberation ties with politicians in other parties (especially the incumbent Democratic Party). As the bulk of congressmen and their staff were recruited from among KCTU leaders and activists, policy-crafting procedures were easily institutionalized along personnel networks. The switched focus of cohesiveness from the incumbent DP[14] to the social democratic DLP is reflected well in the following remarks of an assistant to a DP congressman who belongs to the Health and Welfare Committee in congress.

The majority of civic associations had resorted to the DP [for lobbying], but once the DLP was founded, they all started contacting the DLP. However, it is possible to make a policy through the [small] DLP, but they need a bigger force to make it pass through the legislative process. Therefore, they could not treat the DP in antagonistic ways. The point is that their contact points were diversified and initial policy-making started with the DLP rather than with the DP … when they worked with the DP, it [the relationship] was established between [a lobbying] organization and a congressman. But, as for the DLP, it was between unions and the policy committee [under the central bureaucracy]. They have much more stable communication structures, as they knew each other already and many of the staff were recruited from there [the unions].

The collaboration of the KCTU and other progressive civic associations with the DLP represents an unprecedented revolution in the history of congressional policy-making processes in South Korea. The KCTU, progressive civic associations, and the DLP brought their social movement-based policy-crafting processes directly into congress. The policy assistant comments:

I remember the case of 'universal health care for cancer patients.' They initially made universal health care as a public issue, and decided to start with cancer patients as those patients were suffering from the biggest [medical] costs. They first created a movement from outside [in civil society]. The DLP joined it, made a bill, and then made a policy suggestion to the government [it was passed eventually]. I think it is a kind of systematic team work. Their activities were exactly fit with each other.

This exemplifies the effective policy-channeling process between labor unions/progressive civic associations and the DLP. Movement organizations with high mobilization capacity also devise policies in alliance with associations with professional knowledge and expertise. Since the KCTU has had its own political agents in congress (since 2000), they did not have to approach the incumbent DP. With cohesiveness with the DLP, the KCTU's crafting, making, passing, and implementation of policy tended to occur not through individual lobbying channels with the DP, but through established informal networks as well as formal policy-discussing committees with the DLP. During this time, the cohesiveness with the incumbent party (the state) was greatly weakened, while the cohesiveness with the labor party became strengthened.[15]

GROWTH IN EMBEDDEDNESS I: UNION-SIDE
STORIES

Embeddedness as a Mobilization Capacity

Over time, the first dimension of embeddedness, 'embeddedness as a mobilization capacity,' emerged during the authoritarian era, grew with cohesiveness during the democratic transition era until the mid-2000s, but then gradually declined since the 2000s for political, structural, and demographic reasons. During the democratization era, which could be extended up until 1997 (when the opposition party leader, Kim Dae-jung, was elected as president), it was almost conventional for union organizations to wage struggles with student and other Minjung movement organizations such as the Korean University Students' Confederation and the National Alliance.[16]

In terms of 'contentious' politics, alliances among labor movements and other civil society organizations (especially Minjung movements) were highly coordinated. Students-turned-activists and leaders of the student movement organizations were densely connected through two layers of social networks: alumni networks and ideological factions. Under these alumni and underground study circles run by several ideological factions, groups of leaders built dense networks of underground and overground organizations in the 1980s. Based on such informal networks, it was not difficult for NCTU leaders to ask leaders of student and Minjung movements to run joint activities such as demonstrations and to organize conventions. One renowned labor leader who served as president of the NCTU recalls, "when I was in charge of Kyŏnggi regional union organization (under the NCTU), we invited every organizational body involved in local, regional political situations"(field interviewee Yang Kyu-hyŏn).[17]

However, despite the seemingly close collaboration between labor and civil society, there were growing concerns within the labor movement about the isolation of labor organizations from democratization forces and reformist civil society after the 1987 Great Workers' Struggle and ensuing strike waves. The two conservative governments (the Rho Tae-woo and Kim Young-sam regimes) severely suppressed labor and other radical Minjung movements by arresting key leaders, while providing more moderate civil society forces with political opportunities such as positions and resources. Especially in the early to mid-1990s, in response to such a mixed (suppression in conjunction with co-optation) strategy, leaders of labor movements were engaged in both defending the NCTU against the state's harsh suppression and building a new, larger inclusive national confederation in an open, legal space which could incorporate all branches and segments of union activities. Simultaneously, this new organizational expansion strategy went along with a 'societal reform initiative', which was proposed as a primary organizational agenda for the new union confederation. It sought to accomplish comprehensive social reform goals beyond the traditional 'bread and butter' issue of wage bargaining.

With the social reform initiative, labor activists within the KCTU mainstream circle at the national center started adopting universal social welfare reforms mainly developed by the RHCS (Regional Health Care Service) and its upper-level industry union, the KHMU (the Korean Health and Medicine Union). During this early period in the mid- to late 1990s, the KCTU national center vigorously embraced other Minjung movements' social reform agendas as their own, and they developed policy units specifically responsible for communicating with other civil society associations. It is at this point that the KCTU started diversifying its organizational goals and strategies in order to pursue hegemonic leadership in labor-linked associational fields.

Figure 4.3 illustrates the levels of embeddedness of labor unions in terms of mobilization capacity and policy capacity over time in South Korea. Embeddedness as a mobilization capacity increased dramatically

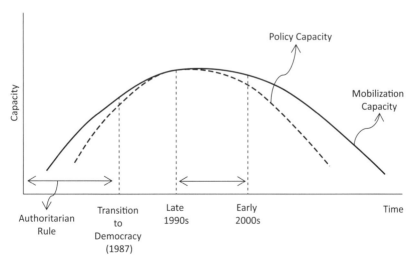

FIGURE 4.3. Trajectories of Mobilization and Policy Capacity of Union Organizations during the Course of Institutionalization in South Korea

from the 1970s to the mid-1990s, with the democratization and labor movements growing together. Embeddedness for contentious mobilization increased first and reached its peak during the 'Great Anti-Labor Law Struggle' under the Kim Young-sam regime. In January 1997, two union confederations, the FKTU and the KCTU, launched a general strike for the first time in late twentieth-century South Korea. The opposition parties and civil society forces also joined the strike, which led the incumbent ruling party to abandon its legislative ambitions. The strength of embeddedness through mobilization capacity reached its highest possible point at this time, as labor-centered solidarity eventually toppled the semi-authoritarian regime, leading to peaceful regime change in the ensuing presidential election – the first in modern Korean history.[18]

For South Korean labor politics, both dimensions of embeddedness (mobilization and policy) hit their ceilings around the late 1990s and the early 2000s.[19] An opportunity for expansionary reforms was open and present between the late 1990s and the mid-2000s (as shown in Figure 4.3) during two reformist regimes. Unions built and sustained durable solidarity with civil society forces during that time, and enjoyed multiple collaboration channels with the incumbent parties and their own creation, the DLP. However, both dimensions of policy capacity plummeted during the 2000s – and especially since the mid-2000s.[20] In many ways, South Korean labor activists were following the same trajectories as their European predecessors who founded their unions in the late nineteenth and early twentieth centuries, and then established social democratic parties in the first half of the twentieth century – at least up until the early 2000s. One decisive difference between them and their European counterparts was that they failed to institutionalize their policy capacities in their relationships with political parties and other civic associations when their mobilization capacity was still influential.

Embeddedness as a Policy Capacity

Embeddedness as a policy capacity or, more briefly, policy embeddedness, followed a similar trajectory of development (and decline) to embeddedness as a mobilization capacity, at least up until the late 1990s. Among labor activists, there emerged a need for policy specialists who were able to analyze wage data, macroeconomic trends, labor laws, and their relevance to the economy and politics; bargaining strategies at the firm, industry, and national levels; and the historical examples and comparative trends of all these issues in other societies. When the NCTU was established in 1990, a small group of policy specialists[21] was formed within the NCTU leadership group: as the core leadership group of the NCTU joined the KCTU, a couple of policy experts such as Kim Yu-sŏn (who later established KLSI) emerged as the key figures of an internal think tank within the KCTU.

Furthermore, within the Korean Health and Medical Workers' Union (KHMU), the earliest industrial union confederation, there emerged a group of labor activists such as Yi Chu-ho, who specialized in industrial union-level bargaining with employers and the government as well as National Health Insurance and related welfare policies. With the launch of the KCTU, some of these different groups of policy specialists joined in the Office of (Labor) Policies within the KCTU national center, while other policy experts in the industrial unions (KHMU and KSIU) continued operating their solidarity networks with other civic associations (via the NCHIU).

Another group within the 'policy circle' of the labor movements was labor scholars who had been actively engaged in strategizing for the labor movement since the late 1980s. This group of scholars primarily resided in universities, state-funded institutes, or non-profit private institutes, but some of them were deeply involved in union activities, especially in the areas of policy-making, strategy-making, and leadership education. In particular, two academic programs, Labor Studies at Korea and Sogang Universities, trained numerous labor scholars who later provided theories, policies, and strategies for the KCTU through their PhD programs. For instance, Im Yŏng-il, a prominent scholar in the area of labor and labor movements, actively participated in not only developing theories of industrial unionism but also, from the early 1990s, educating unionists about the histories and strategies of industrial unionism. He and his colleagues managed a study group that introduced the idea of industrial unionism into Korean labor politics, and he later ran an organizational unit composed of union leaders and supporting policy specialists within his labor institute, the Yŏngnam Institute of Labor Movements. In the Yŏngnam area (a south-eastern industrial area of South Korea), and more specifically the Ulsan (where Hyundai companies are located), Masan, and Ch'angwŏn areas, labor scholars were closely engaged with the production of knowledge regarding labor movements, labor law, employer–employee relationships, and other related labor issues. These labor scholars, who were present both in the unions and outside the unions, were key components of embeddedness as a policy capacity.

How, then, did these two dimensions of embeddedness evolve and change over time during the critical era of democratization and democratic consolidations in the 1990s and the 2000s? One convenient way to observe the mobilization embeddedness and policy embeddedness of unions is to identify unions' solidaristic efforts to hold demonstrations or engage in policy-crafting and lobbying activities among themselves or along with other civic associations. Figures 4.4 and 4.5 present over-time trends of mobilization embeddedness and policy embeddedness using two-mode co-affiliation networks of key labor and civic associations with major mobilization and policy-relevant events from 1991 to 2005.[22] On one hand, the mobilization embeddedness of the NCTU (1990–95)-KCTU (1995–), measured by a centrality score (betweenness centrality),[23] stays near the top with just a couple of exceptions. Intuitively, the findings convincingly show the new militant labor movement organizations represented by the NCTU-KCTU-led civil society as primary, central bridging nodes of policy formulation as well as of mobilization around

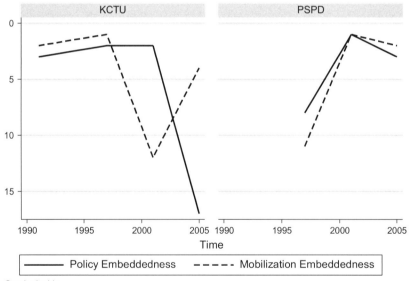

Graphs by idn

FIGURE 4.4. Mobilization Embeddedness: Over-Time Betweenness Centrality Rankings of Key Labor and Civic Organizations in Associational (Co-affiliation) Networks in South Korea: 1991–2005
Notes: KCTU – Korean Confederation of Trade Unions; NCTU before 1995; PSPD – People's Solidarity for Participatory Democracy; founded in 1994.

major demonstrations and organizing efforts during the entire 1990s and the 2000s.

On the other hand, Figure 4.4 also shows that the policy embeddedness of the same NCTU-KCTU started declining in the mid-2000s, as they lost the central positions they had kept during the entire 1990s and early 2000s, as discussed in Figure 4.3. This implies that new labor movements began to lose their role as a headquarters for policy deliberation and lobbying efforts when they reached peak political momentum with the launch of the DLP (in 2004). In Figure 4.4, the KCTU's policy embeddedness plummets from the top position to near twentieth position.[24] On the other hand, the PSPD emerged as the most central actor of the labor–civic solidarity network from its very foundation. It ranked as a top-ten influential association in terms of both mobilization and policy capacity in 1997, three years after its founding. Since then, it has never dropped below the top five. These findings are highly consistent with my qualitative description of its prominent role as both a party and a movement organization. In contrast to the decline of the KCTU in the 2000s, the PSPD's durable central leadership as a movement and policy broker between the state and other minor civic associations was sturdy – at least until the mid-2000s.

GROWTH IN EMBEDDEDNESS II: CIVIL SOCIETY-SIDE STORIES

Embeddedness, by its own definition, needs collaborating partners in other domains and units in civil society. These can range from professional associations, religious institutions, traditional Minjung movements, or student-based movement organizations, to emerging new social movement organizations (NSMOs) in the areas of human rights, peace, women's rights, environment, and cooperative movements. In terms of both mobilization capacity and policy capacity, unions need allies with whom they can exchange ideas and collaborate on common agendas. Therefore, in order to analyze the embeddedness of unions, it is indispensable to consider the growth of the larger 'organizational community' (Aldrich and Ruef 2006; Suchman 1995), or 'organizational fields' (DiMaggio and Powell 1983) in which unions are embedded to a certain degree.

Here, I shift focus to the aforementioned short-lived top-down solidarity of the 1980s. As I discussed above, such solidarities rapidly transformed into the cohesiveness and embeddedness of unions in political parties and civic associations, as radical leftist intellectuals left the factories in the early 1990s. Now I draw attention to those who left the factories in this period and began to establish variegated modes of progressive political and civic associations in the 1990s. Additionally, I will include those who did not go into factories but wanted to engage in civic associational activities in the 1990s.[25]

The emergence of the embeddedness of unions in civil society came slightly earlier than that of cohesiveness in South Korea. This was because the limited democratic rule by the Kim Young-sam regime, which was a coalition government between former authoritarian elites and a center-right segment of the democratization movement, had not extended citizenship rights to the more radical Minjung and labor movements. During this period, radical intellectuals' conversions from revolutionaries to reformists were not uniform but variegated, in contrast to their initial going-underground decisions. Some decided to stay, while others decided to leave – all with different reasons. I will not delve into all those different modes of departure, but will underscore those who switched from labor-centered organizational activities to broader 'citizenship'-based activities. The reason why these departures are critical for assessing the embeddedness of unions in civil society is that they evolved into the most critical alliance points for labor politics over the next couple of decades. The mushrooming foundation of politicized civic associations in the early to mid-1990s was driven primarily by either former labor activists or those who had close ties with labor activists from the 1980s. Therefore, the embeddedness of unions should be judged not only from the union side, but also from the civil society side. While some turned hostile or apathetic about labor movements, those converts generally contributed to extending the scope and depth of labor–civil society cooperation.

For instance, the most influential civic association when it comes to policy agenda-setting and legal monitoring of governance in contemporary Korea, the PSPD (People's Solidarity for Participatory Democracy), was founded in 1994 by three key figures: a human rights lawyer who often defended workers' cases (Pak Wŏn-sun), a former student-turned-labor activist who was once engaged in union-building in a local factory (Kim Ki-sik), and a reformist sociology professor specializing in labor–civil society coalition movements (Cho Hŭi-yŏn). In 1989, another influential civic association in the field of economic justice, the CCEJ (Citizens' Coalition for Economic Justice), was similarly founded by a Presbyterian pastor, Sŏ Kyŏng-sŏk. He had led missionary works and labor rights movements in urban factory areas in the 1970s. In the CCEJ, several key positions at the secretary level were filled by former students-turned-labor activists, such as Ha Sŭng-jang, one of the influential leaders in the civic association movement field since the 1990s. Additionally, the HRMA (Human Rights Movement Association; Inkwŏn undong sarangbang), the most influential human rights association after the transition to democracy, was founded by Sŏ Chun-sik along with a former student-turned-labor activist, Pak Nae-gun. Several key profession-alized activists of these associations were students-turned-union organizers. One of the key leaders of labor–civic solidarity during health care reforms, the NCHIU, Cho Kyŏng-ae, was also a student-turned-labor activist. All of these students-turned-activists switched their careers from student move-ment leadership in elite universities to union organization in the Seoul and Incheon areas in the 1980s. Then they changed their personal trajectories to civic association organization in the 1990s. Thus, in an important sense, the striking growth of civil society in South Korea in the 1990s, especially in the core social movement sectors ranging from the environment to human rights, was to a considerable degree the by-product of the collective or indi-vidual conversions of radical intellectuals from underground to overground activities in the 1990s.

So, what induced these labor activists to change their careers to become founders of emerging civic associations? What impacts did such collective but variegated conversions have on the emerging civil society of South Korea? These two questions are not directly associated with the main re-search question of this study, but they are worth addressing in their own right to further understand the growth of the civil society and labor sectors in South Korea. The following account from Kim Ki-sik about his vision when he "quit" makes an important point regarding the growing skepti-cism about labor-centered revolutionary ideas among activists.

In 1990, I quit going-underground in the factory, because otherwise I was in danger of being captured … In factories, I watched how workers' proper demands for their rights were destroyed and oppressed, and started thinking about how I could make some more tangible achievements for their lives … In any system, both in capitalist and in socialist systems, I realized power becomes concentrated and monopolized, through the process of representation. I thought that people should be able to monitor power, and participate in the creation and management of power. I spent two years struggling with that idea … I searched for people to work with … Prof. Cho Hŭi-yŏn, Lawyer Pak Wŏn-sun, and Activist myself, three created a great synergy … one provided policy, the other offered legal knowledge, and I was in charge of activist networks … this was the most effective format in which each segment respects each other and makes up for each other's weakness.

Kim Ki-sik and his colleagues' vision pointed towards the new state and civil society relationship that was only sprouting at the time of the transition to democracy in the early 1990s. He understood the state as an inevitable evil that concentrates power around its apparatuses, and therefore that needs to be monitored and domesticated by civil society forces. He thought that an expert organization other than unions was needed to play such a role. Progressive lawyers and professors comprised the key organizational units of the PSPD. Its organizational units were paralleled to almost all government agencies. Experts in each area not only monitored and challenged the government's actions and policies, bringing them to judiciaries, but also eventually suggested and lobbied for alternative policies. The PSPD was all but a party organization, lacking only its own candidates.

The most important feature of the PSPD in terms of its place on the ideological spectrum was that it sought to build cooperative relationships with older social movements, especially labor. This is the biggest difference between the PSPD and other politicized associations such as the CCEJ, which were much more hostile to labor movements and other Minjung movements. All three of its leading figures maintained personal and organizational ties with labor organizations and were eager to promote the PSPD's primary policy agendas through more systematic solidarity with emerging labor movement sectors.

Cohesiveness and Embeddedness through a Broker (the PSPD)

The PSPD played a crucial role in opening policy channels to labor unions, which had lacked direct ties to the major political parties during the transition-to-democracy era. The professionals (professors and lawyers) and activists of the PSPD, who had close ties to congress, governments, other civic associations, and unions, played a bridging role in coordinating different interests and positions. The PSPD was able to play such a role because key activists in the association not only knew exactly what should be done in rapidly changing political and civil societies during the transition to democracy but also held social status and capacity based on a core leadership composed of lawyers and professors. They not only mobilized around existing issues in novel ways but also raised new issues regarding democratic governance and social policies, areas which had been neglected by the existing political parties.

First, they launched a novel organizational form, one that is rare in the history of social movement organizations. They formulated a large 'department store'-style structure composed of numerous team-based organizations that nearly matched all areas of government activities.[26] The key activities of each association were considered, discussed, and honed by experts such as lawyers and professors in their specialized field. Next, both activists and experts themselves negotiated with parties and civil society stakeholders, mobilizing public opinion and support from media and the public, and channeling such policies and opinions into policy-relevant departments and committees within the government bureaucracy and congress. The PSPD indeed behaved like both a party and a movement organization. The organizational form (Clemens 1993, 1997), which "mirrors the structure of the government" (Skocpol *et al.* 2000), was carefully designed to conform to, compete against, and transform government and congressional activities. It matched all the forms and domains of state-driven or civil society-driven legal processes relevant to policy-making and policy-crafting. Most importantly, the PSPD organization knew it could not do it all by itself, and therefore it formed coalitions with other influential actors in political and civil societies depending upon the issues at stake. With this unprecedented organizational structure and capacity, the state bureaucracy could not help but recognize the PSPD's presence and incorporate its lobbying and challenging activities into the policy-crafting process. "The government asks the social welfare committee of the PSPD about its opinion for any kind of social welfare-related policy-making or legal change"(Kim 2004, p. 8).

Next, the PSPD brought legal processes into the new field of civil society movements. It was the first to introduce two kinds of lobbying efforts which had not been used by social movement organizations at that time in South Korea: "inside lobbying" and "outside lobbying" (Kollman 1998; see Hong 2007 for their application to PSPD activity) of Korean political parties, including both the ruling and opposition parties, had been at the time largely disconnected from civil society in terms of policy-making. As a result, civil society actors were largely ignorant of policy-crafting processes, and movement leaders mostly constrained themselves to merely challenging or resisting the final products, relying primarily on "contentious politics" (McAdam *et al.* 2001). The PSPD occupied this empty arena in the 1990s when diverse social movement fields and repertoires (Tilly 1978, 1993) erupted, but their demands were not yet properly channeled into official politics. In other words, the PSPD activists and professionals played the role of "brokers" (Gould 1989; Gould and Fernandez 1989), linking grassroots civil society groups with politicians who were uninterested in or incapable of representing such newly emerging needs. Or, in a sense, the PSPD activists first recognized the novel "political opportunity structure" (Hong 2007) that, while about to emerge, was largely invisible to most other social movement leaders and politicians.

Most importantly with regard to labor movements, the PSPD redefined social policy areas at the national level as broad citizens' agendas by integrating variegated civil society organizations of different interests into a solidarity network.[27] Unlike many other civic associations of the time who intentionally maintained their distance from radical labor movements, the PSPD consciously built alliances with unions on case-by-case bases. For instance, while the CCEJ consciously distinguished itself from so-called radical Minjung movements from its very start, the PSPD did not hesitate to form coalitions with the labor movement at critical moments in the state–civil society confrontations of the 1990s. In the 1996–97 Anti-Labor Law Struggle, the PSPD decided to fight against the Kim Young-sam government alongside the two union confederations and other progressive civic associations such as the Korean Women's Associations United (the KWAU) and the Korean Federation of Environmental Movements (the KFEM). After the Kim Dae-jung regime, the PSPD, however, only selectively allied with the labor movement, especially the KCTU. It did not support the KCTU's lonely struggle against labor market reforms, although it played a critical role in passing social policy reforms in alliance with the same KCTU.[28]

Cohesiveness and Embeddedness through a Third Organizational Body

Another important civic movement in the area of social welfare was the NCHIU (National Conference for Health Insurance Unification). In contrast to the PSPD, the NCHIU was an issue-based (health) solidarity network that sought the unification of fragmented health insurance providers. While the PSPD embraced almost all issue areas related to social reform agendas, the NCHIU embraced almost all organizations engaged in the health care integration movement. While the PSPD sought a 'department store' model, the NCHIU pursued a 'combination' model in which all relevant social movement associations would cooperate to achieve a single policy agenda, with each of them playing a different, independent role within its own area. Under the umbrella of the PSPD, professionals, intellectuals, and citizens with different interests and agendas built their own issue units as branches of the PSPD and developed that issue using the 'brand' and structure of the PSPD. However, under the framework of the NCHIU, different organizations convened to promote a common policy agenda and contributed their own share in the form of personnel, money, and expertise. Hence, the NCHIU is a sort of 'consortium' model, in which different shareholders provide their own resources to produce a common final product.

The earliest movement form for health care reform traces back to peasant discontent with unbearably high premium levels in a separate health care plan for agricultural regions dating from 1988. Disgruntled peasants organized grassroots-level organizations in response to the government plan, and in the late 1980s several religious associations from agricultural areas and reformist professional associations joined the reform movement. The following associations participated in the movement: the PPA (Protestant Peasant Association), the CPA (Catholic Peasant Association), the YMCA-Agricultural Branch, the KPDS (Korean Pharmacists for Democratic Society), the CMAP (Christian Medical Association for the Poor), and the CAUP (Catholic Association for the Urban Poor).[29] These groups organized demonstrations, petitions, and, most importantly, movements refusing to pay for premiums. Thanks to such movements, the national average rate of premium collection reached a lowly 43.8 percent (NSIU and HPACA, 2010, p. 57).

In 1988, these diverse associations created the National Association for the Health Care (NAHC), which comprised 48 relevant associations and 40 regional province-level associations. NAHC presented its main agenda as (1) provision of health rights for all (including the poor), (2) opposing privatization of health services, and (3) integration of health insurance providers. They submitted a reform bill including the integration of fragmented health care institutions and premiums increasingly proportional to income to the major parties and requested it be legislated. They succeeded in drawing a consensus among the incumbent party and three opposition parties. However, the bill was blocked by a veto from the president, Roh Tae-woo, after having passed congress. 'Corporatist' solidarity forces[30] were able to persuade President Roh Tae-woo that the 'integrationist' bill would lead to an abrupt increase in premiums for wage earners, which would impose immense financial burdens on the regime.

However, after suffering through some waning periods, peasants' associations, labor unions, civic associations, and professional associations in health fields launched a larger, more comprehensive solidarity consortium, the National Conference for Health Insurance Unification (NCHIU). It aimed to advance three main agendas – the integration of health insurance providers, lower health care costs for patients (the extension of insurance coverage for formerly non-insured items), and a more equitable cost-sharing system. The NCHIU, a cooperative network composed of activists, professionals, and intellectuals drawn from 77 relevant national associations and six regional solidarity associations, had completed building its two organizational hubs – mobilization capacity and policy capacity – by 1994.

It was able to organize national-level strikes and demonstrations for a single, universal policy agenda – health care reform – and had ample intellectual expertise to justify its agendas in the national political arena. By seeking the integration of fragmented health care providers into a single national pillar organization, it was capable of publicizing its ultimate goal as the extension of entitlements to health care to the entire population and achievement of more fair and just imposition of premiums for the socially marginalized. During the democratic consolidation era, after procedural elections were introduced in 1987, it was the most durably organized and well-coordinated solidarity movement bridging different social classes and associations, and is one that has extended its influence and activity down to the present time.

In terms of mobilization capacity, the NCHIU also had one of the most combative union organizations: the NCTU.[31] While the two prongs of the NAHC, peasants and progressive health professionals, did not on their own have sufficient mobilization capacity to threaten the incumbent government, the union organizations' participation in the NCHIU decisively enhanced the mobilization capacity of the network.[32]

In terms of policy capacity, the NAHC, despite its failure to get its bill passed in 1989, kept investing in its policy capacity by developing better arguments to confront corporatist solidarity during the waning period (1989–94). Before 1994, experts and students in progressive professional associations in health fields[33] played a central role in policy-making. Furthermore, once labor unions, especially the KHMU and the RHCS, joined the NCHIU in 1994, the policy capacity of the solidarity network was greatly enhanced. Policy experts in unions had all the necessary data to develop and justify the logic of the integration movement.[34] The policy specialists in the solidarity network prepared issues and agendas with which normal citizens could instantly agree – such as lower premiums, the extension of insurance coverage, and more equitable cost-sharing. They developed programs in which the members of the superior HCSE (the Health Care Service for Employees) could see their interests and feel that their health care coverage would be improved with integration. Based on the upgraded policy capacity, peasants, workers, and the urban self-employed began to find common interests in the integration move-ment.[35] Kyung-Ae Cho (a former executive secretary of the NCHIU) addresses the synergy effects among labor unions, civic associations, and health professionals as follows:

> Material and human resources were provided by unions, while policies by health professionals. Civic associations were in charge of publicizing the agendas. Three parts exactly played their own roles. Each part had its own resources, but needed the other parts to compensate for the resources each part lacked.

In short, the NCHIU successfully strengthened its key institutional struc-tures and capacity by forging solidaristic ties between health profession-als, civic associations, and labor unions. Embeddedness was deepened and widened between former movement leaders, composed of mainly medical professionals, and the newly joining labor leaders. Its core leaders raised public awareness of the integration movement through numerous con-ferences, symposiums and advertisement sessions at universities, regional civil society organizations, industrial unions, and local factories. They approached politicians from both the incumbent and the opposition par-ties with highly sophisticated policy alternatives. This policy-specific em-beddedness of unions in civil society later bore fruits during the latter period of the Y. S. Kim regime and the early phase of the D. J. Kim regime (which will be discussed in detail in the next chapter).

   In addition to solidarity linkages between civic associations and labor unions, the NCHIU developed effective lobbying channels to the existing political parties and bureaucrats. Professionals in health fields within the NCHIU worked closely with labor leaders to pressure both the incum-bent conservative party and the state bureaucrats. For instance, Yong-Ik Kim (the executive commissioner of the NCHIU) entered into the Committee for Health Care Reform established within the government (by the Ministry of Health and Welfare) with Yung-Gil Kwon (the presi-dent of the confederation of white-collar unions), and led debates with the bureaucrats who were in support of the current corporatist system. They also initiated and organized conferences on integration in congress as well as in the government. Due to its comprehensive and potent member associations and their public influence (and growing public discontent with the existing health care system), bureaucrats and politicians had little choice but to listen to the NCHIU's lobbying efforts and respond to the request to establish a reform committee. The leaders of the NCHIU approached congressmen from the incumbent and opposition parties and persuaded them to adopt the integration bill. The NCHIU was the first civic association in modern Korean history that was able not only to develop policy alternatives with highly refined reasoning and data, but also to put pressure on the state and major parties with electoral and non-electoral threats.

This chapter explored two components of the institutionalization processes of labor movements: cohesiveness and embeddedness. So as to explore the early shaping of these alliance/coalition structures, I discussed the historical background of the going-underground projects of radical intellectuals. In particular, I explored how radical intellectuals who went underground during the authoritarian regimes came out to build the KCTU and the DLP in the 1990s during the political opening under the Kim Young-sam and the Kim Dae-jung regimes. I showed how their unique experiences and the resources they built through going-underground activities evolved into the embeddedness and cohesiveness of labor unions in civil and political societies. In the process, I attempted to show how different modes of adaptations made by radical intellectuals regarding their career-building strategies led to different repertoires of organizational forms (Clemens 1993, 1997): some went on to build a centralized union confederation composed of several industrial unions as well as a labor-based party, which were the ultimate realizations of the political visions that had been generated in response to authoritarian suppression. Others departed from their initial paths and chose to build variegated progressive civic associations with allied professionals. Through my descriptions of these processes, I intended to reveal the multiple processes by which a labor-linked associational field is formed over time through divergent actors' organizational strategies and their intended/ unintended consequences.

Next, I turned to the career choices of individual activists and their divergent repertoires, which, in the subsequent section, moved on to consideration of the organizational trajectories of labor movements. That section analyzed two layers of organizational histories. First, it examined the history of the formal agendas of the Korean democratic labor movement. At this level, Korean activists hoped to build industrial unions as the center of an overarching organizational structure, all aimed towards the eventual construction of German-style social corporatism. As well, they sought to found a Brazilian PT-type programmatic labor-based party, which, independent of the existing political parties, could embrace a wide range of labor-friendly social movements.

Then, I explored how two sub-dimensions of embeddedness, mobilization capacity and policy capacity, were developed by labor activists' conscious strategies to seek solidarity with civic associations. I focused upon two civic associations as solidarity partners, the PSPD and the NCHIU, which were built in part by students-turned-labor activists.

These historical analyses of the emergence and institutionalization of labor–civic solidarity structures will enable me to account for the successes and failures of welfare state development in South Korea in the subsequent chapters. With the general over-time trend and transformation of associational fields, I focus on issue-based solidarity networks in the next two sections, which will open a closer investigation on labor–civic solidarity and welfare politics in the 1990s and the 2000s in South Korea.

5

Embeddedness, Cohesiveness, and the Politics of Social Policy Expansion in South Korea

Universal vs. Selective Reforms

INTRODUCTION

In contrast to most rich democracies that enjoyed the post-war Golden Era, developing countries did not experience relatively long periods of durable economic growth under consolidated democracies. Just as the third wave of democratization began in the 1980s and 1990s, neo-liberal market pressures immediately followed in the mid- to late 1990s.

The South Korean case illustrates the simultaneous occurrence of these large-scale political and economic transformations. The depth and scope of such transformations were considerable, and they had an immense impact on citizens' lives. It was a clear moment of 'critical juncture' (Collier and Collier 1991; Pierson 2004) in which new institutional rules and norms radically transformed or even replaced the old ones.

Chapter 5 analyzes how South Korean labor leaders succeeded in promoting universal social policy reforms during these tumultuous changes. The chapter explores how changes in my two main independent variables, unions' embeddedness and their cohesiveness, are associated with welfare state and labor market reforms from the late 1990s to the late 2000s in South Korea. Specifically, this chapter asks: how and why did the leaders of the KCTU (and the DLP) succeed in developing the embeddedness and cohesiveness of their unions? How did they execute their organizational tasks – the formal institutionalization of the labor movement – and what were the consequences of such processes, especially in the field of labor market regulations and the development of social polices? In particular, what mechanisms account for the striking growth of the welfare state in South Korea during the same period? What role did the labor movement and its allies play in building and defending welfare regimes during democratization, and the financial crisis and neo-liberal market reforms that subsequently struck the Korean society and economy?

To answer these questions, this chapter and the next focus on the politics of the KCTU (and partially the FKTU) during the last years of the conservative Kim Young-sam regime (1996–97) and the two reformist regimes, the Kim Dae-jung (December 1998–2003) and Roh Mu-hyun (2003–08) regimes. Specifically, this ten-year period (1998–2008) was critical to the growth and decline of labor movements, and the development and retrenchment of labor market and social policy institutions in South Korea. At the beginning of this period, two unprecedented critical events took place – the financial crisis (November 1997) followed by 'rescue packages' from the IMF, and the first peaceful regime transition through a democratic election with full-blown civil society and labor movements (December 1997). The period ended with a return to another ten-year period of two conservative regimes and the dramatic dismantling of the Democratic Labor Party. This chapter analyzes how unions and related civic associations bargained and negotiated with the state and employers based on their mobilization and policy capacity under the critical 'constraining' or 'opportunity' structures created by the economic crisis and political regime changes during the ten-year period.

I proceed with two analytical strategies: one is a comparison of two reformist regimes, the Kim Dae-jung and Roh Mu-hyun regimes, and the other is a comparison of three major social policy domains: National Health Insurance, National Pension, and labor market regulations (especially regarding lay-off and non-standard/indirect employment). In this way, the chapter expands a single case study (on South Korea) to a comparative case study of two periods (regimes) as well as three policy fields. Through deep historical case studies using union and civic association documents and field interviews with labor and civic leaders, the following discussion will analyze the variations in the politics of coalition between unions, and parties and civic organizations. In this research strategy, I initially treat the KCTU as if it were a unitary actor. However, in analyzing different social policy outcomes in the pension and health care areas, I will inevitably highlight the variations in form and content of (industrial) unions' embeddedness and cohesiveness, across policy domains, with both political parties and relevant civic associations. These case studies will then be used for conducting "contextualized comparisons" (Mahoney and Rueschemeyer 2003) and building an analytical causal framework.

Overall, the chapter advances two arguments: (1) the embedded cohesiveness of unions plays a decisive role in the passage of universal social policy; and (2) the cohesiveness without embeddedness of unions leads to selective social policy reforms, as the state and unions agree to implement policies that narrowly serve unions' organized members' interests rather than those of the wider citizenry, including marginalized outsiders. In the processes of making these arguments, I initially describe how cohesiveness and embeddedness were dramatically institutionalized in the 1990s in South Korea. Next, I will discuss how the emergence of an opportunity/crisis structure in the late 1990s provided both labor and capital with unique opportunities to fundamentally reshape the existing labor market and social policy institutions. Then I will analyze how union and civic leaders successfully (or unsuccessfully) crafted the three different social and labor market policies (National Health Insurance, National Pension, and labor market regulations) under such conditions. In particular, I highlight the role of a wide-ranging labor–agrarian–intellectual solidarity (through the National Conference for Health Insurance Unification, NCHIU) in the passage of the bill that integrated national health insurance societies. Finally, I assess the degree to which the divergences in policy outcomes across different regimes in South Korea are accounted for by the proposed theoretical framework of this book – policy and mobilization capacities of embeddedness and cohesiveness – and then draw the larger implications these findings have for other societies with regard to the politics of expansion of labor market and social policies. The current chapter starts these processes with a discussion of the universal and selective expansion of social and labor market policies under the tripartite committee during the Kim Dae-jung regime.

THE CONSOLIDATION OF COHESIVENESS AND EMBEDDEDNESS: A BACKGROUND HISTORY[1]

A Short Success Story: Cohesiveness with Labor Parties

When analyzing the formal institutionalization processes of labor movements, I earlier deployed the notion of cohesiveness to capture the cooperative relationship between labor unions and labor-based parties/the incumbent political party. As in other such societies, in South Korean labor politics diverse trends and factions of radical intellectuals and labor activists came together, organized legal or covert political organizations, debated within and against each other, built partial or broad solidarity, and, eventually, shattered into factions again after bitter disagreements and power struggles. The cohesiveness of unions and labor-based parties is likely an outcome of such complex processes. Nonetheless, I will not explore in detail such repeated fracturing and reorganizing trajectories among leftist intellectuals in this study.[2] Rather, I will focus mainly on the processes through which union activists construct institutional channels and representative agents to advance workers' interests in the broader political society.

The 1987 Great Workers' Struggle was "a watershed in the history of the South Korean working-class struggle"(Koo 2001, p. 153). I also find that 1987 was a watershed in the history of South Korean radical intellectuals' desire for political power, as they explicitly started presenting themselves as 'revolutionary political fronts' or 'legal representative bodies' of the working class. These political movements emerged just as most radicals thought that their going-underground activities were finally seizing the moment of 'revolutionary fervor.' Between 1987 and 1992, two presidential election years, radicals hastily prepared to build a labor party (Minjungdang, People's Party), which would be ideologically and organizationally independent of existing conservative and liberal parties.

At the time, leftist intellectuals' primary agenda in building a labor-based party was a radical and fundamental transformation of Korean society through a progressive mass party that would treat the interests of the working class as the most central goal. Like the early PT in Brazil, these initial labor party builders did not purport to make it a professionally competitive electoral party. The bulk of radical intellectuals thought they were using the legal, formal electoral system as a vehicle to strengthen the class-consciousness and organizational capacity of the working class. However, by the early 1990s, most union leaders, who were deemed leaders of mass organizations by both radical intellectuals and unionists themselves, desired to build a durable union confederation first, rather than focusing on what they saw as premature utilization of the formal electoral space. Thus, mainstream union leaders fought against first obtaining full citizenship for labor under the harsh suppression by the democratically elected, but still semi-authoritarian, conservative regime (Kim Young-sam regime, 1993–97). Because of these incongruences in leaders' strategies, the early builders of the labor party did not obtain much support from grassroots unions and so could not overcome their own internal limitations, or pre-existing external formal and informal constraints such as the majoritarian small-district electoral system and region-based voting trends, in the early 1990s. As a result, they failed to receive the minimum vote necessary to maintain the party. In short, labor-based, social democratic cohesiveness did not evolve in the early and mid-1990s.

During the latter part of the Kim Young-sam regime (1995–97), the union movement gained the most important momentum since the 1987 Great Workers' Struggle. New democratic union leaders had just completed building a united, centralized organization with the launch of the KCTU (in 1995).[3] In the days after Christmas in 1996, the ruling party passed several anti-labor laws that lifted regulations on mass lay-offs and the use of non-standard labor, while prohibiting pay for specialized union staff. Against the passage, the KCTU and FKTU launched several general strikes during the entire winter of 1997. Although this initial solidarity between the two union confederations drew concessions from the ruling party, union leaders could not systematically coordinate their voices in the negotiation between the ruling and opposition parties, and, therefore, the final compromise was not significantly different from the original.

Labor leaders collectively realized and agreed that they should build an independent labor-based party after the debacle in 1997. Following this experience, union leaders agreed to support an independent presidential candidate representing workers (Kwon Yŏng-gil, the first KCTU president), and the labor campaign organization was converted into a party organization.

As I described earlier, union activists in industrial unions who came up through grassroots union organizing efforts in the 1980s (mostly then in their twenties) became 'party enthusiasts' in their thirties. After successfully building 16 industrial unions and a centralized union confederation, they held both resources and personnel at the local and central levels. They had gained both the political and the social skills (Fligstein 1997; Swidler 1986) that would be necessary to build new organizations at the political center. They had already run three presidential campaigns with their own independent workers' candidates (Paek Ki-wan in 1987; Kwŏn Yŏng-gil in 1992 and 1997). They had just successfully built a new, independent national-level confederation, which was strongly underpinned by other progressive civic associations. Based on the activists' networks and resources accumulated through three campaigns, grassroots union leaders and core leaders at the KCTU national center together discussed their political strategy and eventually forged a consensus to create an independent labor-based party. The majority of the union activists at every level of the KCTU organizations, from grassroots and industrial unions to the national center, actively participated in the early founding processes of the DLP. They indeed provided everything from money to 'bodies,' as key organizers. Many of them ran as DLP candidates for parliamentary elections in 2004. Of a total of 121 DLP candidates, 53 percent were from the KCTU (from interview with Yi Kŭn-wŏn and other KCTU leaders). Only four years after its founding, the DLP received a total 13.1 percent of votes, which became translated into eight seats in the partial proportional representation system of Korean electoral rule. These results demonstrate that, from the late 1990s to the mid-2000s, the KCTU's cohesive ties with the DLP were at their pinnacle, most notably in terms of mobilization capacity.[4]

Embeddedness under an Opportunity Structure

Up until the late 1990s, democratic union movements went hand-in-hand with Minjung movements, especially with 'Chaeya' (movement forces outside formal party politics) and student movements. As many pro-labor or labor-linked civic associations were established in the 1990s, unions' embeddedness became increasingly strong.

Thus, both mobilization capacity and policy capacity as two dimensions of embeddedness were at their peak in the latter part of the 1990s, as discussed in the previous chapter. For mobilization-related embeddedness, the ruling party's attempt to legislate radical neo-liberal reforms in 1996 provided unions and civil society with an ideal 'issue' space for solidarity. The labor law reform was not only a political, regime-level move: all of South Korean capital also coordinated an attempt to transform the labor market structure into a 'flexible' manufacturing system coupled with 'flexible' labor market institutions. Against the attack, unions and civil society formulated a wide range of mobilization networks. The KCTU, founded on three segments of union groups – the former NCTU (the National Council of Trade Unions), composed of metal unions, the former Chaebol-group-based unions, and white-collar-based unions mainly concentrated on the banking and health sectors – was ready to use its militant muscles. The FKTU, formerly a docile corporatist union confederation and a subsidiary partner of the authoritarian regime, was unable to tolerate the degree and scope of the reform, as its core members (especially in the public sector) were expected to be severely hit by the passage of the law. Progressive civil society associations such as the National Alliance and National College Students' Association still had not lost their capacity to wage militant struggles against the semi-authoritarian state. In particular, the ruling conservative party's attempt

to pass two controversial laws – a labor law encroaching upon workers'
rights, and a law on the Agency for National Security Planning (NSP),
reinforcing the NSP's power by allowing its investigation of pro-North
(Korea) activities – simultaneously fueled the political rage of the opposition party, civil society, and unions.

The turmoil in the Korean political economy due to the passage of
these two laws had deep and wide impacts. The several waves of general
strikes in the winter of 1996–97, being supported by civil society forces,
almost paralyzed the economy and political system of the entire nation.

On November 21, 1997, the ruling New Korea Party (NKP) announced
that the government would seek an assistance fund from the IMF to resolve the impending currency crisis. The Asian Financial Crisis issued a
final blow to the NKP. In the ensuing presidential election, the opposition
party, the Democratic Party (or NCNP, the National Congress for New
Politics, from 1995 to 2000), achieved the first peaceful regime change in
modern Korean history.

On December 4, the government and the IMF reached an agreement
about the assistance fund and the relevant reforms of firms, financial sectors, and the labor market. The two peak associations of capital, FKI
(the Federation of Korean Industries) and KEF (the Korea Employers'
Federation), sought a fundamental transformation of labor market institutions through the abrogation of the Labor Standards Act, the introduction of laws allowing mass lay-offs and flexible labor market, and a
reduction in labor costs through substantial cuts in pay and a cap on pay
increase rates of 3 percent for the next five years. The KCTU proposed
the formation of a tripartite committee (among the state, employers, and
unions) to overcome economic crisis and maintain stable employment
on December 3. The candidate of the opposition party, Kim Dae-jung,
after having been elected as the president on December 18, proposed on
December 26 that representatives of labor, capital, and the government
convene to discuss solutions to the economic crisis.

The Kim Dae-jung regime started its governance in an unprecedented
environment in modern Korean history: a collapse, with the Asian Financial
Crisis, of the old accumulation regime based on the state-led financing and
monitoring of a Chaebol-oriented economy, and a collapse of the old authoritarian regime that had governed the country with a coercive state apparatus for the previous half century. It was an unusual combination of
constraint and opportunity for both capital and labor, in which an outside
lender, the IMF, imposed several policy recommendations on the government, a borrower, the ranges and details of which were not initially specified.

The newly elected president had played a central role in the democratization movement. His opposition party career since the late 1960s made him a figure symbolic of support for democracy and human rights. He recruited many radical activists of Minjung movements into the DP (or NCNP) and thereby developed numerous formal and informal ties to civil society organizations. Unions were no exception. Immediately before the 1997 election, the FKTU formed an electoral alliance with the DP led by Kim. Even within the KCTU, Kim had numerous allies who sympathized with his party. Overall, however, while the FKTU was able to construct a fairly high level of cohesiveness with the DP, the bulk of KCTU leaders viewed the DP merely as a liberal reformist party, with which they might form alliances only on a short-term, case-by-case basis.[5]

Employers and their representative organizations were relatively silent and less influential during the first era of the regime. The traditional capital mobilization system based on state-sponsored/ monitored banking, the backbone of the Korean developmental state, had just collapsed, with numerous industrial and commercial banks going bankrupt. The very close linkages among the state, Chaebols, and irresponsible banks were blamed for the crisis. Therefore, employers had to hold their breath and merely observe the policy direction to which the newly elected reformist government[6] was steering. They did not have many connections within the long-time minority party, which had been excluded from power for the last half century.[7] However, they considered the financial crisis and the IMF's intervention in the economy another opportunity to legislate the lay-off law and the law for dispatched workers, both of which were defeated during the 1996–97 Anti-Labor Law Struggle. They thus successfully linked the IMF's request for labor market flexibilization to their long-term policy agenda.

For unions (and civil society), the financial crisis and the launch of the reformist regime were both an obvious crisis and an uncertain opportunity. The IMF requested that the newly elected government accept austerity measures, including high interest rates, dissolution of financial institutions with bad assets, and the lifting of labor market regulations, including allowing mass lay-offs, and that it make more effort to expand social security provisions for the unemployed and economically marginalized. Employers wanted to shed labor force in response to the severe economic downturn and restructuring pressures. Mass lay-offs were impending, and the IMF's first policy recommendation was exactly in line with employers' needs. The newly elected government also considered the lay-off components as a given, non-negotiable component of the impending reforms. Therefore, workers in the metal and banking sectors, key industries underpinning the KCTU, were in deep fear of losing their jobs in a country with little social safety-net provision. Labor, especially leaders of the new union movements, had no choice but to prepare for uncompromising fights against such an implicit agreement between the IMF, the newly elected reformist government, and employers' associations such as the FKI and the KEF. Other leaders of unions and civic associations, however, also saw an opportunity in which the incumbent reformist regime and its leaders might protect them by minimizing the size and impacts of lay-offs (or at least make them quite difficult to implement) and providing employment and income protection policies. The tripartite committee "opened the door (both) to a new welfare state and to a radical revision of the Labor Standards Act by allowing redundancy dismissal and employment adjustment" (Yang 2010, p. 457) The labor movement thus started fermenting deep division within itself regarding reactions to the newly elected government's labor market and social policy reforms.

The three-party bargaining structure indeed opened ample opportunity for the solidarity of unions and civil society in which they could forge both a mobilization-relevant solidarity and a policy-relevant solidarity. Unions and civil society needed each other to defend their rights against the employers' (and the state's) attempts to introduce neo-liberal market reforms, while at the same time maximizing the scope and depth of universal social policy initiatives. Unfortunately, labor leaders had to witness themselves becoming increasingly divided as negotiations and struggles unfolded. They needed both dimensions of embeddedness to achieve the most desirable outcomes for their constituents – moderate labor market reforms and generous social policy programs.

Labor Market Reforms: Between Cooperation and Resistance

The biggest issue of the tripartite committee in seeking to overcome the impending financial crisis and introduce labor market reforms was the enactment of the lay-off law, which was requested by both domestic and international capital. Domestic capital had been eager to legislate it in order to make restructuring easier during economic downturns, and they saw the impending crisis as the best opportunity to pass it. International capital also had a shared interest in the passage of the law, as it hoped to be able to buy Korean firms through mergers and acquisitions, which would lead to a restructuring of such firms, accompanied by lay-offs. Although the IMF told union leaders they had not asked the government to include anything related to lay-offs in the reform package, there was a consensus within the core policy circle around Kim Dae-jung that the lay-off law was the most urgent policy to be dealt with in the tripartite committee, and they argued that it needed to be passed as an agreement signed by all parties, especially the KCTU.

For the KCTU, the lay-off law was labor's line in the sand. The FKTU also initially refused to accept it but, as the FKTU had maintained a strong electoral alliance (cohesiveness) with the new incumbent party since the presidential election, it was expected to back off as long as there was a reasonable level of compensation through other policies. Within the KCTU, however, there existed deep division about the passage of the lay-off law. According to a former KCTU policy strategist:

Especially regarding the lay-off issue, the central leadership and grassroots started showing a big schism. For other issues, such as health care integration, grassroots unions just agreed with the direction posed by the national center, as we kept emphasizing its importance almost for two years. However, regarding the lay-off issue, there was huge disagreement between policy-line experts [at the national center] and rank-and-file leaders and workers at local factories. [For us] the main issue was whether we could make the details of the lay-off law advantageous to us by reinforcing the requirements of the lay-off. However, for the grassroots-level leaders, they were unable to tolerate the agreement made at the tripartite committee. They thought like, "how dare you [the national center of workers' organizations] agree with the law allowing capitalists to fire workers freely?" It was not about whether we could make it more advantageous or not.

On one hand, moderate labor leaders, who were later classified as 'Kungminp'a' (the faction of Nation), ultimately expected that it would be hard not to accept the lay-off law, and therefore focused on maximizing the contents of any compensation package, including more sophisticated devices to limit the actual operation of lay-off law. White-collar workers' unions were the main groups behind this position. On the other hand, the more militant labor leaders and grassroots metal unions were vehemently opposed to any type or level of compromise with the acceptance of the lay-off law. Unions in the large manufacturing industries (especially workers of Hyundai group companies in Ulsan) threatened to strike if the KCTU leaders agreed with anything related to the lay-off law. Thus, for example, white-collar workers, especially in banking industries, were more strategic and realistic, having already accepted their fate – restructuring and mass lay-offs – and they therefore hoped to minimize the scope and degree of the lay-off law and maximize the contents of the retirement packages. In contrast, metal union workers were more fearful of lay-offs because they expected to have no (alternative) future once they lost their jobs. From the very beginning, the KCTU leadership oscillated between unions preferring negotiation and those insisting on resistance.

On February 6, 1998, the committee reached an agreement after a month of agenda-setting and negotiation games. Both the FKTU and the KCTU utilized a potential joint strike as a threat, but on Feb 5, the FKTU (suddenly) announced it would sign the deal. The KCTU, under the pressure that the deal could be made without it, also agreed to sign. The key contents of the deal included (1) the passage of lay-off with constraining conditions such as the limitation of lay-off to situations of merger and acquisition due to continuing administrative difficulty; (2) the legalization of the KTU (Korea Teachers' Union) and KGEU (Korea Government Employees' Union); and (3) several other agendas to be discussed during the second period of the committee such as (eliminating) the prohibition of paying for union staffs, (allowing) unemployed workers' affiliation with unions, reduction in working hours, and unions' participation in management.

However, on Feb 9, the agreement was rejected by the vast majority of representatives in the eighth ad hoc convention of the KCTU (88 approved vs. 184 disapproved).[8] The KCTU leaders all resigned in response to the striking revolt by the grassroots union leaders, who were primarily mobilized in workplaces expecting radical restructuring plans by their firms. Then, an ad hoc committee announced that the agreement was no longer valid. Nevertheless, the KCTU leadership decided not to launch the general strike that they had announced earlier, due to internal conflicts and divisions regarding the agreement.[9]

Overall, all participants, with the exception of the KCTU, were satisfied with the first agreement of the tripartite committee. The new incumbent government had no choice but to draft an agreement, because it did not want to be involved in the sort of conflicts with unions which had ultimately toppled the former regime just a year earlier. Although the KCTU eventually walked away due to its own internal conflicts, the government was able to draw an initial agreement and therefore claim political legitimacy before launching market-oriented reforms. The concession in the final agreement, however, did not actually go beyond what the KCTU initially expected. Employers got what they wanted to get, while postponing other pro-labor agendas to the second committee. "The issues such as allowing teachers' unions and government employees' unions were not directly relevant to capital's interest, while the lay-off law and the law for dispatched workers were the issues that could drastically transform the balance of power between capital and labor"(No 2008, p. 175). The FKTU managed to maintain its docile political relationship with the incumbent party (cohesiveness without embeddedness), while achieving a consensus with the KCTU. However, with the agreement, deep internal strife started to develop between factions within the KCTU.

Even if the KCTU failed to defend labor's key interest in labor market reforms during the first tripartite committee, it nonetheless achieved the expansion of major social policies thanks to its close embeddedness in civil society organizations. Unions were among the central players that determined the structure – in terms of universal entitlements and generosity – of the major social policies advanced at the time, but they were able to do so only through their close collaborations with civil society forces, especially policy-relevant professionals and experts. The following sections discuss how the cohesiveness and embeddedness of labor unions account for the establishment of two universal social policies, national health care and national pensions, as well as for their sustenance or cutback during two reformist regimes in South Korea from the late 1990s to the late 2000s.

LABOR UNIONS AND UNIVERSAL WELFARE STATES

The Brokerage Role of Labor Unions in Civic Associational Networks and in Building Coalitions for Universal Health Care

Figures 5.1 and 5.2 illustrate how the KCTU, its member unions, and allying civic associations were able to build broad labor–civic solidarity during the tumultuous year of 1997, when labor movements were at center-stage of a series of critical events – the Anti-Labor Law Struggle, the Asian Financial Crisis, the fifteenth presidential election, and the tripartite committee. The co-affiliation networks of labor and civic associations reveal how labor unions and civic associations were interconnected within and beyond their own fields, thereby establishing broad-ranging cross-class coalition networks. On the surface, several other civic and popular-sector associations, as well as the KCTU, emerged during the 1990s as central players in civil society, as discussed earlier in Chapter 4. However, the role of new union movements led by the KCTU and its member unions were decisive in bridging different civic associations, which resulted in comprehensive social solidarity across social classes toward universal, expansionary social policy reform.

In Figure 5.1, diverse civic and labor organizations are interconnected through their participation in solidaristic mobilization events in 1997. Approximately three large cliques are formulated: non-ideological centrist or right-leaning civic associations on the left (e.g. YMCA and CCEJ); leftist civic associations and popular-sector associations at the center (e.g. PSPD, KFEM, and Lawyers for Democracy); and labor unions on the right (e.g. KDMU, the National Teachers' Union, and Hyundai Unions). The structural position of the KCTU is within the center group along with other progressive civic associations, while it is simultaneously at the center of other key grassroots labor unions and industrial unions, bridging two large cliques – unions and civic associations. In other words, the KCTU positions itself as a bridging association, which plays the role of a 'broker' by linking two large, mutually exclusive, but internally well-connected sub-groups. The KCTU's "brokerage roles" (Gould and Fernandez 1989) among different sub-groups such as unions, civic associations, popular-sector associations, and peasant associations, which are presented in Figure 5.3,[10] are exceptional in their magnitude compared to those of other top influential civic associations. Importantly, among the KCTU member industrial unions, the KHU (Korean Hospitals Union), which later evolved into the KHMU (Korean Health and Medicine Union), played an even more impressive brokerage role than the KCTU in interconnecting unions and other civic associations in different fields.

Most of the core central mobilization-oriented events that linked unions and civic associations in 1997 occurred in January, when the Anti-Labor Law Struggle reached its peak moment, and labor–civic solidarity was converted into policy-oriented solidarity in the latter part of the year. Figure 5.2 presents the structure of policy-oriented labor–civic networks in 1997, in which associations are more sparsely connected and fragmented than those in mobilization networks in Figure 5.1. The KCTU and the KMU's dominance in their brokerage roles across different fields of civic and labor associations are no less impressive in policy networks in Figure 5.2 than in mobilization networks in Figure 5.2: no other associations played similar bridging roles, with the exception of Lawyers for Democracy and Women's Link (not shown).

Another important point is that the KDMU, the biggest and most powerful union of the time among the KCTU member unions, played

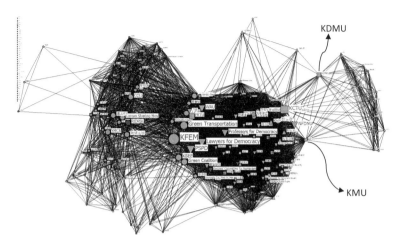

FIGURE 5.1. Civic Mobilization Network in 1997 in South Korea (based on Mobilization-Oriented Events)
Notes: The size of nodes and labels represents the degree centrality of each association: the bigger a node and its label, the higher the degree centrality of the association.
Source: Arranged by Graphic Theoretic Layout.

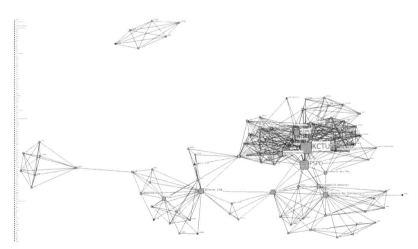

FIGURE 5.2. Civic Policy Network in 1997 in South Korea (based on Policy-Oriented Events)
Notes: The size of nodes and labels represents the degree centrality of each association: the bigger a node and its label, the higher the degree centrality of the association.
Source: Arranged by Graphic Theoretic Layout.

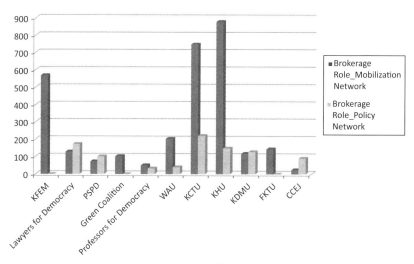

FIGURE 5.3. Number of Brokerage Roles of Key Labor Unions and Civic Associations across Sub-Groups

Note: The *y*-axis is the total count of five brokerage roles (coordinator, gatekeeper, representative, consultant, and liaison) classified by Gould and Fernandez (1989).

Abbreviations: KFEM (Korean Federation of Environment Movements); PSPD (People's Solidarity for Participatory Democracy); WAU (Women's Associations United); KCTU (Korean Confederation of Trade Unions); KHU (Korean Hospitals Union); KDMU (Korean Democratic Metal Union); FKTU (Federation of Korean Trade unions); CCEJ (Citizens' Coalition for Economic Justice).

a significant role in bridging grassroots unions, the KCTU, and other progressive civic associations.[11] While most other influential civic associations (even those ranked at the top in terms of their centrality indices) devoted their organizational resources to their homophilic neighbor organizations in the same field, the KCTU and its core member unions coalesced with wider civil society. In other words, around 1997, a wide-ranging cross-class coalition embracing manual working classes, peasants, urban middle classes, and professionals was formed in South Korean civil society. This coalition eventually served as a core bargaining unit in the tripartite committee, which started with the new Kim Dae-jung regime. The remaining sections of this chapter further investigate how this labor–civic solidarity formed during the course of democratization and militant union-building in the 1990s, and eventually culminated in universal health care reform.

Integration of Health Care Organizations and Labor's Leading Role

In contrast to labor-law reforms, in the field of social policies, labor movements pushed forward their key agendas with a very high level of embedded cohesiveness. The enactment and implementation trajectory of National Health Insurance in South Korea would not have been possible without the unions' (quasi-)embedded cohesiveness. The new, alternative union movements of the 1980s and the 1990s formed a core driving force behind the civil society-wide solidarity advancing the health care reform. Union activists served as key stakeholders in health care reform, not only participating in but also managing a comprehensive solidarity organization over the long term, actively building lobbying channels into political parties and the government bureaucracy.

Workers in the Regional Health Care Service, a sort of public sector organization responsible for region-based members (who are not affiliated with formal organization-based providers), constructed a nationwide union organization in the late 1980s, at the same time establishing its organizational agenda as the integration of fragmented, unevenly scattered health care providers into a unified national organization. The development of this particular labor union was crucial for the subsequent course of health care development in South Korea, as it served as a backbone of the entire 'pro-social rights' group for the next couple of decades. Because of its region-based, non-firm-based identity, the organization's core members were peasants, who were already disgruntled with discrimination against them in health care services when compared to urban, firm-based members. The organization's workers were also discontent with the low levels of wages compared to their counterparts, workers in the Health Care Service for Employees (the HCSE). As a result, the union of the Regional Health Care Service and the Korean Peasants' Association (KPA) shared a common interest in promoting national-level integration of fragmented health care services. Peasants wished to be integrated into a unified, single-pillar plan so as to address their higher premiums and the lower quality of their health care plans (in terms of benefits and coverage of illness). Workers for the Regional Health Care Service viewed their union activities as achieving not only improvements in their working conditions (with an expectation that they would be treated at the same level as workers at the superior counterpart, the HCSE) but also as advancing their vision of universal social citizenship through the democratic union movement.[12] In a sense, the very structure of the region-based health care system provided an opportunity in which a disadvantaged social class in a backward industry, peasants, could be represented by well-trained and nationally organized (but disaffected) semi-bureaucrats (the RHCS union). The strong, unprecedented solidarity behind universal health care started with such an unexpected but politically ideal collaboration.

The two powerful stakeholders (the KPA and the RHCS union) and their representatives joined a solidarity movement, the National Conference for Health Insurance Unification (NCHIU), in 1988 and 1993, respectively.[13] The participation of the union organization of the RHCS in the solidarity network was a decisive momentum-builder for the NCHIU, as it was then a three-party alliance among a popular organization of peasants, a nationally organized union organization (the RHCS) with strong capacity for mobilization, and diverse health care professionals' and intellectuals' organizations that could provide discursive and technical expertise and rationales for the movement.

The NCHIU, established in 1994, emerged as a key player in the making of the health care reform policy just as the KCTU, which was the second momentum-builder for the movement, was launched in 1995. The former policy specialists from the NCTU and the KHMU (the upper-level industrial union with which the RHCS union was affiliated) were all absorbed into the KCTU – indeed, they comprised the core decision-making group – and the KCTU eagerly included health care reform as a central component of 1995 wage bargaining (NCHIU 1994–95, report no. 8, September 12, 1995).[14] This implies that the core KCTU member unions participated in the struggle for health care reform indirectly through a refusal to pay for premiums and through the fights to prevent increases in premiums. Importantly, the central KCTU activists, aiming to overcome the narrow wage-centered, firm-level struggles that had until then dominated the labor movement, launched the 'Social Reform Movement,' or 'Social Reform Unionism,' as the key organizational agenda at the KCTU's foundation.[15] During 1995, the NCHIU devoted its organizational efforts to spreading the rationale behind the integration movement to grassroots union leaders and members. Finally the KCTU set three items as its main organizational agenda: elimination of upper wage limits (set by the government), reform of anti-labor laws, and the integration of health insurance providers with the extension of coverage (NSIU and HPACA 2010, p. 100).

With the KCTU-level involvement in the movement, health care reform became one of the key issues in the tripartite committee in 1997 and 1998. The same leadership group which later failed to defend labor's core interests against labor market reforms sought by employers and the state vigorously pursued solidarity with civil society groups to promote, in particular, more universal and egalitarian social policies (which later served as one reason for the divisions within the labor movement). Overall, with the most powerful movement organization at the time, the KCTU, as one of its core member organizations, the NCHIU overpowered nearly all other organizations and stakeholders in health care policy-making, even the Ministry of Health and Medicine, in its role in the policy-crafting process.

A critical event that built momentum for the reform was the election of Kim Dae-jung, who listed health care reform as one of the top tasks to be accomplished during his term. Although the health care plan became National Health Insurance during the last months of the Kim Young-sam regime in 1997, the key reforms – the integration of fragmented institutions into a single pillar and the extension of universal coverage to the self-employed – were realized during the Kim Dae-jung regime. This was especially thanks to the combined KCTU-civil society pressure group's coordinated efforts to include more progressive and universal elements in the final bill. The high level of embeddedness between unions and civil society groups was further augmented by the cohesive ties between the solidarity network and the newly elected reformist regime. The core leadership of the NCHIU and the KCTU utilized its informal networks within the Kim Dae-jung regime and the conservative opposition party to bring their social policy agendas to the negotiation table, especially in the tripartite committee active in 1997 and 1998. During this critical period, intellectuals in the NCHIU extended and deepened their efforts to lobby legislators in the incumbent and opposition parties,[16] while the leaderships of both the NCHIU and the KCTU attempted to reach and persuade grassroots union leaders.

We [the chief of the NCHIU, Kim Yong-ik, professor of Seoul National University, and the spokesman, Kang Ch'ang-gu, the former chairman of the RHCS union] visited numerous local union gatherings (including Hyundai and Daewoo unions' executive councils) to persuade the necessity of the health care reforms … if union executive councils end at 10:00 or 11:00 pm, we waited until the end and opened information sessions to convince them … eventually large factory unions such as Hyundai and Daewoo agreed to join us." (Kang Ch'ang-gu, a former union president of the RHCS)[17]

The Kim Dae-jung regime launched a final-stage policy-making unit within its welfare department in 1998, and the bill passed congress in 1999. By 2003, 139 pillars of the occupational health care organizations and regionally divided organizations were completely integrated into a single institution, the National Health Insurance Service (the NHIS). With these reforms, premiums were imposed in a more egalitarian way (high-income members pay more) and administrative costs were reduced thanks to the introduction of the single-pillar system. It became possible to run the fiscal structure more effectively, and it also became possible to extend the scope and strengthen the coverage for health-related issues.

In the tripartite committee under the financial crisis, the regime intended to give something to labor, in return for the flexibility of labor market. Just one day before the final due date of the committee when most of the terms were largely settled, the KCTU additionally brought up the health care reform upon the negotiation table [while accepting the laws on the labor market reforms]. The FKTU [which was opposed to the integration] was alarmed, but it also wanted to get some financial remuneration packages to its sub-units. While the FKTU was delighted with the monetary amount of the package, the KCTU simply added one last demand … the consensus of the tripartite committee served as a binding device since then, whenever the opposition group attempted to halt the passage of the bill. The consensus in the committee was a final blow. (Kang Ch'ang-gu)

The solidarity movement pushing the integration of health care organizations points to the importance of embedded cohesiveness in welfare state development. Labor and civil society groups built durable solidarity around their common interests, developing policy expertise as well as a trust network. The solidarity initially started as a mobilization network (in 1988), but increasingly galvanized policy capacity through policy experts' knowledge accumulation and the provision of convincing alternatives over time. The KCTU policy team accomplished this high level of embeddedness (in terms of policy capacity) through their continuous collaboration with experts in civil society, such as Professor Kim Yong-ik's group and the PSPD. In a sense, civil society groups gained their decisive bargaining power through the KCTU,[18] while the KCTU extended labor's hegemony to a policy-relevant field through their alliance with civil society experts. Importantly, within the solidarity movement, three different social classes – peasants, the blue-collar working class, and the white-collar working class (middle class) – all found their own interests, mobilization units, and representatives, which is almost equivalent to the peasant–working class alliance that undergirded the Swedish welfare state (Esping-Andersen 1985, 1990). This solidarity, furthermore, extended the reach of the movement to the most problematic social group, the urban self-employed, who tended to avoid and mislead the tax administration through lower reporting of their income. By doing so, the solidarity increased the coverage of the reform to a nearly perfect universal comprehensiveness.

In short, the "struggle over needs" (Fraser 1990) for health care that emerged among peasants during the early democratization period eventually evolved into a struggle over universal entitlement in which divergent social forces and groups participated and collaborated as part of a comprehensive solidarity network. In that process, the RHCS union and later the KCTU played a decisive role in expanding the struggle of a narrow, disadvantaged class (peasants) into a wide-ranging, cross-class alliance by persuading the general public as well as their members of the need for universal health care. In particular, the RHCS union and its higher confederations achieved this outcome through their membership in the NCHIU, the most well-organized interorganizational solidarity network in the health field. Union organizations were able to maximize their mobilization capacity in a specific policy field through their coalitions with appropriate partners, such as progressive professionals in the health field.

The FKTU's Defense of the Selective Social Policy Regime

In contrast to the KCTU, the FKTU was vehemently opposed to the integration movement, supporting the maintenance of the pre-existing fragmented health insurance corporations.[19] Against the integration movement, the FKTU and its allies kept spreading anti-integration arguments, e.g.: (1) managing people with different income and medical needs under the same insurance system would be inefficient; (2) the gigantic national-level bureaucracy would generate an inflexible, unitary hierarchy that could not respond promptly to changes; (3) wage earners might have to pay higher premiums to sustain non-wage earners and the self-employed; and (4) eventually, the integration of different health care insurance systems would weaken the financial soundness of the entire health care insurance system (Yi 2009).

In contrast, they contended that the corporatist management systems differentiated by members' income and occupation could serve different social groups more effectively, as each corporation could serve homogeneous social groups sharing similar characteristics. In addition, they argued that each corporation could determine its own level of premiums and administrative issues according to members' expenses and affordability. They added that the corporatist management would encourage not only members' democratic participation in decision-making processes, but also competition among different corporatist management systems (insurance societies). They expected that the former would further enhance solidarity among members, while the latter would make the entire system more efficient because it would become much easier to compare and assess insurance corporations.

Despite its rationale for maintaining the corporatist system, the FKTU's stance ultimately reflected the interests of well-protected, standard wage earners, refusing to embrace peasants, non-regular workers, and region-based members, most of whom were self-employed or non-employed. Therefore, the FKTU sought to maintain the status quo, selective corporatist system. Its refusal to pursue the universal system implied that the FKTU was not much interested in defending or embracing the basic health rights of non-unionized civil society forces. Its defending logic based on competition, democratic management, and efficiency reflects only the best-case scenario of rich corporations based on employees of large conglomerates, which cannot be applied to poor insurance societies based on regions and peasants. Ultimately, the FKTU and its member unions did not want to share their rich resources with the more disadvantaged members in society.

The solidarity among KCTU, civil society, and reform-minded politicians in the Kim Dae-jung regime enabled them to isolate the FKTU's opposition. The FKTU and the (semi)authoritarian state had been able to maintain selective corporatist insurance societies for decades, excluding non-unionized social groups in civil society, but had to relinquish the old system and its core member union in the wave of the integration movement. It was the unions of the large conglomerates that changed the center of gravity between the KCTU's UR (universal reform) strategy and the FKTU's SR (selective reform) strategy in the competition to mobilize grassroots unions' support. The unions of Hyundai Automobile Company, Daewoo Ship-Making Company, and other large Chaebol-based manufacturing industries were persuaded by the (aforementioned) NCHIU's joint campaigns that reached grassroots rank-and-file workers and leaders. As these large unions under the influence of the KCTU admitted that their accumulated premiums in the company should be spent to increase the levels of benefits for the entire working class under the integrated scheme, the FKTU's SR strategy could not find significant supporters other than the HCSE union and the old allies from the ancient regime. There were prolonged resistance attempts from the FKTU and corporatist league to halt the integration of insurance societies in the late 1990s and the early 2000s when laws on the financial integration were passed and implemented. However, the financial integration was completed in 2003 and universal reform finally defeated selective reform.

Pension Reform and Labor's Limited Role

In contrast to health care reform, labor activists were not so interested in pension reform[20] during their heyday in the 1990s. At this time few were recipients of pensions, and the core leadership and members of labor movements were still too young to be seriously concerned about their retirement. Because it had been less than a generation since social rights were expanded to aging populations, both leaders and members of Korean labor movements were largely ignorant about the importance of seeking 'risk class' or 'risk'-based solidarity (Baldwin 1990) when their organizational capacity (mobilization and policy) reached its peak. A successful activist and professor, Kim Yŏn-myŏng, who as one of the leaders of the PSPD Social Welfare Unit played a key role in implementing the current form of the National Pension in the late 1990s, retrospectively recalls:

When I first joined Kim Yong-ik's group [the NCHIU], I found that there is no such parallel counterpart [solidarity unit] in the pension area, so I started organizing a movement group [in and around the PSPD] … but to little avail. It was hard to build such a stakeholder interest group … nobody in the KCTU seriously listened to the importance of the pension … Even Korean [existing] pension recipients did not want to expose themselves to the public as a noticeable advocacy group. There was a cultural barrier[21] that made it difficult for them to act for themselves especially in the pension field.

Most importantly, labor unions did not have a sufficient number of experts well versed in the core contents of the existing pension plan, its problems, and possible alternatives that might enhance its solidarity and redistributive effects for the working class, nor did unions have well-organized, policy-based solidarity with other civic associations on this issue.[22]

In contrast to the RHCS union, which served as a key backer of the early establishment of the NCHIU, the union of the NPS (the National Pension Service) was much weaker and less militant from the very beginning (since 1999). While the RHCS union was one of the most militant and well-organized branches of the democratic labor movement (the KCTU), the preceding organization of the NPS union was affiliated with the FKTU for most of the 1990s. Historically, unions in pension fields were severely crushed by government suppression during the democratization era in the late 1980s, and had failed to recover from the damage since then. During the entire 1990s when union movements erupted and grew in other industries, the heads of the pension service were predominantly former military officers who maintained an authoritarian hierarchical system and a subordination culture. Even though the NPS union converted its affiliation from the FKTU to the KCTU in 2003, "its organizational networks were not densely linked to the KCTU center and other unions for the early and mid-2000s"(a chief union officer of the NPS union).[23] During the critical periods for pension reform in the late 1990s and the mid-2000s, when the sustainability as well as the coverage and the replacement rates of the pension emerged as primary public concerns and became the center of a political battle, the union switched its affiliation from the FKTU to the KCTU. It ultimately played little significant role in the pension reform during the tripartite committee and the introduction of retirement pensions in the 2000s. It was not until the late 2000s that the union emerged as a main stakeholder and movement force in the pension reform area.

Since labor initially lacked both embeddedness and cohesiveness in the pensions field, there were no significant movements in civil society other than the PSPD (and their direction was initially unclear) when the Kim Dae-jung regime initiated pension reform as one of its major policy agendas.[24] As the Committee on the National Pension Reform delivered its final suggestions to the Prime Minister's Office (in communication with relevant stakeholders within and outside the committee), the two central unions (the KCTU and the FKTU) and the PSPD formed a policy solidarity network to influence the direction of reforms.[25] As the two unions and an influential civil society organization forged a single, collective voice, the final bill addressed their concerns by establishing a management institution (the National Pension Service) independent of the MOSF (the Ministry of the Strategy and Finance). This institutional reform built a more democratic management system by increasing the number of representatives from affiliates (including unions) in the monitoring committee, mandating the reporting to congress of all management procedures and results, and maintaining strong redistributive components and high replacement rates (60 percent vs. the World Bank's suggested 40 percent).

In sum, the unions' policy networks through the PSPD allowed them to push pension reform to approximate the ILO model, expanding social citizenship (Kim 2009). Activists and experts in the Committee on Social Welfare within the PSPD actively formed alliances with both the KCTU and the FKTU to steer reform towards guaranteed universality, democratic governance, and generosity. Reform efforts were initiated and accomplished in expert communities and networks without active involvement and informed decisions from workers and citizens. A few respected experts in the PSPD, the KCTU, and the incumbent party succeeded in including pension reform, along with health care reform, in the vital package deal of the tripartite committee in 1997–98. The abrupt power shift during the regime transition and financial crisis prevented an opposition group within the incumbent regime (bureaucrats in the Ministry of Finance and Economy), employers' associations, and the conservative opposition party from establishing a significant voice against the reform.

However, despite the presence of the policy networks, the lack of core stake-holders within the unions and a lack of the organized solidarity network linked to grassroots labor that would have been needed to sustain the universality and generosity of the pension scheme created space for market forces and opponents to later reverse the reform efforts during the Rho Mu-hyun regime in the 2000s – which I label 'a great reversal of the reform initiative' in the following section.

AN ANALYTICAL COMPARISON: POLITICS OF COHESIVENESS AND EMBEDDEDNESS IN LABOR MARKET AND WELFARE REFORMS DURING THE TRIPARTITE COMMITTEE

During the tripartite committee periods of the Kim Dae-jung regime, labor–civil society solidarity achieved dramatic and expansionary reforms in health care areas thanks to their embedded cohesiveness. The solidarity network, in which both labor activists and civil society experts were closely involved, held the mobilization and policy capacity needed for effective threats and deliberation, as well as the ties to the state needed for further policy development and passage of the bill in congress. At this time, the mobilization and policy capacity of the NCHIU had grown dramatically in the decade following its founding, and it succeeded in expanding the discourse on the necessity of health care integration to political and civil societies.

The integration of fragmented health care organizations was an impressive outcome of embedded cohesiveness, which almost completely changed the way Korean people thought about managing their health. The 'equal' and 'fair' entitlements all citizens shared greatly increased the popular support for the NHCS, and the relatively low costs resulting from the legally unitary insurer's power (over health service providers and drug companies) have further justified the reform. Moreover, the extension of entitlements (to the self-employed) and the equal treatment of less prestigious classes (peasants) represent the first cases in modern Korean history where citizens subject to different life conditions and risk groups could 'pool' their risks for collective responses and solutions. As will be discussed in the next section, this durable solidarity structure protected national health care from being swayed by the market-oriented reform efforts advanced by large hospitals, their physicians, and conservative bureaucrats and politicians during the Roh Mu-hyun regime and later conservative regimes.

In contrast, unions' interest in pension reform was only lukewarm. The elderly pension recipients were fewer in number and too timid to mobilize themselves. The NPS union was passive and disorganized when compared to its health care counterparts. It was the PSPD that led the entire process of pension reform, and the KCTU and the FKTU followed that outside initiative. The base community of unions was not interested in pension reform, and, as a result, the reforms were coordinated at the policy expert level and between the PSPD and the KCTU national center. Under these conditions, a network, based purely on policy capacity muddled through weak opposition within the regime and from employers, but was able to defend the more universal and generous ILO pension model. It also established a more democratic structure for pension management. The relatively easy process of passing the bill may be partially attributed to the favorable political opportunity structure created by the tripartite committee during the Kim Dae-jung regime. However, since this achievement, the KCTU has rarely invested in institutionalizing its policy unit, especially for pensions. The presence of the KCTU in the coalition was important for pushing the bill through the tripartite committee, but the policy embeddedness was primarily constructed through the PSPD's efforts. As the KCTU also lacked its own pension policy networks linked to the political parties, it had to rely primarily on the PSPD's lobbying and policy-crafting capacity. This weak cohesiveness and shallow embeddedness later left the core principles of the National Pension vulnerable to the retrenchment attempts of the Roh Mu-hyun regime.

In the field of labor market regulation, the state–employer–FKTU solidarity network prevailed in achieving policy gains regarding labor law retrenchment. As opposed to its earlier victory against the state in the 1996–97 Anti-Labor Law Struggle, the KCTU was here completely isolated both from its moderate competitor (FKTU) and from the civil society forces with which the KCTU collaborated for health care and

TABLE 5.1. *Politics of Labor Market and Social Policy Reforms during the Tripartite Committee under the Reformist Kim Dae-jung Regime*

	Labor Market Reforms (Market-Oriented)	The Health Care Reform (Expansionary)	The Pension Reform (Expansionary)
Winning Coalition*	The state–employers–the FKTU	The state–the KCTU–civil society	The state–civil society–the KCTU–the FKTU
Key Player (Initiators)	Employers	The NCHIU (labor-civil society solidarity network)	The PSPD
The Opposition Force	The KCTU (no civil society forces)	The FKTU and Employers	Employers (but Weak)
Cohesiveness with the State (KCTU–Incumbent Party)			
Electoral Mobilization	Weak	Moderate	Weak
Policy-Crafting and Lobbying	Weak	Strong	Moderate (through PSPD)
Embeddedness (KCTU-Civic Ass.)			
Contentious Mobilization	Moderate	Strong	Weak
Policy-Crafting and Lobbying	Weak	Strong	Moderate (through PSPD)
Outcomes	Launch of lay-off law and Act on Dispatched Workers	Launch of a National Health Care Plan through integration	Launch of a national-level independent and democratic pension service

Note: One may think that the state should be the key actor, because it is in the winning coalitions for all policy fields. Note that labor market reforms are 'retrenchment,' while the other two social policy reforms are 'expansionary.' Therefore, the state is always in the winning coalition, but indeed not always in the coalitions for expansionary welfare reforms. Theoretically, in these cases, the state may be deemed a 'pendulum' swayed by core stakeholders of civil society and the market. A more positive interpretation of these completely different actions by the state is that the newly elected Kim Dae-jung regime was an active mediator which helped employers and unions to exchange labor market reforms and social policy reforms through the tripartite committee. This active role of the state as a mediator may open a path for state-centric theory; but in my opinion such an arbitrator role of the state is not identical to the original version in which state bureaucrats act as conscious breeders and implementers of generous and universal social policies, independent of other social forces.

pension reforms. At this time, during the financial crisis, with most of the KCTU's previous allies accepting the lay-off law as an inevitable reform, the KCTU had no choice but to agree to lift key labor market regulations. The decision to accept deregulation (if inevitable) engendered a deep schism in the KCTU for the ensuing decade, which will be described and discussed in more detail in the next chapter. The KCTU threatened the state with a call for a general strike, but without support from the FKTU, civil society organizations, and some of its own member unions, the strike did not materialize. As a result, the state–FKTU–capital solidarity network eventually achieved a policy agenda – the passage of the lay-off law and Act on Dispatched Workers. The former immediately engendered division within union organizations, while the latter resulted in enormous structural impacts that still affect labor markets today and have subsequently plagued labor organizations.

In summary, labor movements had different levels of cohesiveness and embeddedness, depending upon the relevant policy field. Across policy fields, unions developed complex and often divergent relationships with different allies. As a consequence, despite the general tendencies of cohesiveness and embeddedness over time at the national level (which will be discussed in Chapter 9), it was possible to find variations in policy-relevant solidarity with regard to each policy outcome. Overall, labor unions developed different levels of embeddedness and cohesiveness across two policy fields: labor market regulation and social policies. In the latter, they were able to build a wide range of horizontal solidarity and a meaningful number of vertical channels to advance their agenda through the politics of lobbying and pressure. In the former, however, labor movements did not have many choices. They were barely able to add some constraints to the lay-off law.[26]

DISCUSSION AND CONCLUSION

The chapter shows that, depending upon the level of policy-specific organizational embeddedness and cohesiveness, development outcomes widely vary across policy domains of health care, labor market regulation, and pensions. The embeddedness of unions in civil society organizations, especially the KCTU's linkages to the NCHIU, produced substantial influence on the shape of the universal health care system in South Korea at the critical juncture of the late 1990s. Through the NCHIU and its own cohesive channels, the KCTU was able to play a decisive role in the final passage of key health care reform – the integration of health care providers into a single-pillar national system. The role of the KCTU in the NCHIU, and their cooperative relationship in channeling demands through cohesive ties with the political parties and the state, stand as the clearest case of embedded cohesiveness in the politics of the South Korean welfare state. Moreover, this policy-based solidarity has sustained itself over time even in the face of the retrenchment of the 2000s. And even without a high level of cohesiveness (in the 2000s), the embeddedness sustained the existing welfare institutions against neo-liberal privatization forces in the health care field (and continued to do so up till now, in the early 2010s, under the currently incumbent right-wing party); this will be discussed in the next chapter.

The success and duration of the NCHIU and the KCTU's involvement in the solidarity network exemplifies the game in the bottom-right corner (the passages of health care integration and pension reform under the 1997–98 tripartite committee) of Figure 5.4. The KCTU (its member industrial unions) had both mobilization- and policy-related embeddedness in the NCHIU or through the PSPD, while also having deliberation and negotiation channels to the incumbent Democratic Party. The KCTU's strong mobilization capacity in 1997–98, which had just toppled the conservative regime, was clearly recognized by the incumbent regime, and so the state was aware of the costs of ignoring the social policy agendas coordinated by civic associations and unions. In addition, the NCHIU and the PSPD developed sophisticated reform agendas

| | | Cohesiveness (Unions' Linkages to Incumbent Party) | |
		Weak	Medium to Strong
Embeddedness (Unions' Linkages to Larger Associational Field)	Weak	Zero-sum Pure Conflict Game: Dominant Outcome: No Union-driven Reform Exemplary Case:	Corporatism Game: Dominant Outcome: Unions' Selective Reform and State's acceptance Exemplary Case: The FKTU's Resistance to The Integration of Health Care (under the D.J. Kim Regime); The KCTU and FKTU's reluctance to the Universal Extension of Pension Coverage to the Self-Employed (under the D.J. Kim Regime)
	Medium to Strong	Unilateral Union Dominance Game: Dominant Outcome: Union-driven Universal Reform and State's acceptance Exemplary Case: Growth of NCHIU in the 1990s	Dominant Outcome: Unions' Universal Reform and State's acceptance Exemplary Case: The Universal Integration of Health Insurance Providers in 1997-8 (under the D.J. Kim Regime)

FIGURE 5.4. Network-Informed Strategic Actions of the State and Unions in the Combinational Spaces of Cohesiveness and Embeddedness: Expansion Games (South Korean Cases)

that deeply penetrated and persuaded politicians and bureaucrats inside
the state and the incumbent party, and so robbed the state of convincing reasons not to pursue reforms. Moreover, notable was the ability of
the NCHIU to discourage opponents while mobilizing and coordinating
the diverse proponents of the reform – an ability that proved decisive in
building policy-specific embedded cohesiveness and finally achieving the
subsequent integration of the health insurance system. The presence and
role of the NCHIU was critical for maintaining not only "civic coordination" (Weingast 1997) but also 'institutional coordination' in the building of universal social policies in South Korea. In short, the organizational
growth, maturation, and diversification of the NCHIU offers convincing
support for a proposition built upon the two important ideal spaces of
embeddedness and cohesiveness: unions' embedded cohesiveness is an
important determinant for the passage of universal social policy. In an
era of expansion, unions may take into account the interests of civil society as their own, and introduce universal reforms in social policy fields,
restraining their desire to launch selective reforms.

The FKTU's status quo rights under the authoritarian regimes regarding the fragmented corporatist management of insurance societies represent cohesiveness without embeddedness in the upper-right corner of
Figure 5.4. In a situation such as this, unions attempt to maximize their
own, particular interests, as they do not have serious commitments to
unorganized social forces in civil society. The FKTU's support of the pre-
existing corporatist management system of health insurance squarely fits
this scenario, as it refused to share its rich resources with other disadvantaged social groups such as peasants and the urban self-employed.
Typically, without having to incur significant lobbying costs (thanks to
pre-existing channels to the state), unions with cohesiveness (without embeddedness) succeed in defending status quo rights that serve their own
interests, with the state being supportive of such limited reform. However,
the newly elected reformist regime that had just ended the authoritarian
party's four-decade domination was more attentive to the KCTU and
NCHIU's lobbying efforts. Therefore, the FKTU's resistance to the integration movement failed eventually due to its incomplete cohesiveness.
In the field of pension reform, moderate (in terms of policy capacity) to
weak (in terms of mobilization capacity) levels of unions' embeddedness
contributed to the passage of pension reforms in an incomplete form in
terms of universality. While the KCTU and FKTU were generally uninterested in promoting pension reforms, compared to the progressive professionals in the PSPD, both displayed discontent regarding the extension of

coverage to the urban self-employed, whose incomes were not well documented. As a result, the coverage of the National Pension was universally extended to the entire citizenry only in a weak sense, as there remained a significant number of (poor) urban populations who were incapable of contributing to the pension fund and who were therefore excluded from the distribution of pensions in the future. Both the FKTU and the KCTU were silent about providing egalitarian safety nets to such marginalized populations in the late 1990s, when the social reformism of the KCTU was at its peak. Although it may be hard to judge this tendency as a clear example of SR strategy, the case illustrates how unions can resort to their self-interest when they are not deeply embedded in civil society in terms of their policy and mobilization capacities.

To summarize, this case study of the development and retrenchment of social and labor market policies in South Korea during the eras of democratization and globalization reveals that the success of labor politics hinges on the establishment of a wide-ranging, solidaristic leadership that can closely knit together diverse organizational and policy resources inside and outside of labor unions. Such a leadership promotes policy-specific solidarity both horizontally with civic associations and vertically with the state. I have shown that such a solidarity network and its structure cannot be built quickly by one or a few organizations and their leaders, but instead is historically shaped and structured over time by many different organizations and activists. In particular, the NCHIU example illustrates how such horizontal solidarity operates during favorable and unfavorable times, utilizing political opportunities at one time to promote universal health care and effectively resisting reactionary neo-liberal reforms at other times (the latter will be discussed in the next chapter).

The case study also demonstrates that effective labor–civic solidarity requires both components: mobilization capacity and policy capacity. This requirement is revealed in the comparison between the outcomes in health care and pension policies. In both fields, the role of policy experts was critical: for health care reform, experts in the NCHIU built policy and mobilization capacity, while in pension reform, experts in the PSPD took over policy-crafting without mobilization capacity. Additionally, the KCTU provided an organizational umbrella for health care reform, by offering resources for both mobilization- and policy-related solidarity, but was inactive on pensions. While the PSPD provided policy expertise and access to political parties, the KCTU grassroots unions were indifferent to the details of pension policies. Allies were able to supplement the KCTU's lack of policy expertise on some important details, but were unable to overcome the lack of mobilization capacity. In this example, the KCTU–PSPD solidarity was limited, because the PSPD played a brokerage role for the KCTU, while the latter was not ready to fully embrace and utilize policy-relevant expertise and lobbying capacity from the PSPD. The solidarity networks were most successful when unions and their civic allies accounted for both aspects of embeddedness – mobilization and policy.

The sub-national comparison of the FKTU and the KCTU cases in the 1990s provides a vantage point from which to evaluate existing theories of the welfare state. One may contend that it is active state bureaucrats using their capacities (Heclo 1974; Weir *et al.* 1988) that drives expansionary reforms during both authoritarian and democratic eras. However, the EC approach distinguishes itself from state-centric theory (and power resource theory) by considering the embeddedness dimension. Without embeddedness, the FKTU was content with selective expansionary schemes serving its members' interests during the developmental era. The FKTU traditionally had denser ties with state bureaucrats because it had been a subsidiary partner of the authoritarian state. State bureaucrats (especially from the MFE, Ministry of Finance and Economy), being lobbied by the FKTU, consistently attempted to block integration reform. Therefore, the integration reform case in South Korea in the late 1990s sets a limit on the applicability of state-centric theory for expansionary reforms. Without embeddedness, state bureaucrats may serve as defenders of the inherited policy legacy, as theorized by the state-centric approach. However, embedded unions, under the new KCTU umbrella, actively pursued more universal reform projects embracing all citizens, mainly through congressional institutions.[27] Even within the government bureaucracy, the newly empowered MOHW (Ministry of Health and Welfare), in solidarity with labor unions and progressive civil society organizations, was able to make its voice heard against the traditional conservative leadership of the MFE (Kim, J. 2001; Yang 2004). Therefore, it is unions' embeddedness that creates differences between the state-centric approach and the EC approach.

More importantly, my analyses show that even the KCTU and its sub-unit organizations, such as industrial unions, had widely different levels of embeddedness depending upon the policy field. In the field of health care, pre-existing labor–civic solidarity made inroads in the subsequent phases of universal reform, despite the strong presence of anti-unification forces rooted in the past corporatist system. The absence of such solidarity in the field of pensions, however, led to both unions' implicit ignorance of coverage for marginalized urban populations, leaving universal coverage an incomplete mission.[28]

This politics of embeddedness also resolves the long-term debate between state-centric theory and power resource theory regarding the issue of which actor matters more for welfare state expansion. As both the state and unions are present as key actors in Table 5.1 and Figure 5.4, it is not difficult for either theory to find its own cases and explanations under the two cells of '(medium to) strong cohesiveness.' Indeed, power resource theorists have not had to pay attention to this embeddedness dimension, because their primary positive cases in Northern Europe have enjoyed high levels of union density (exceptionally encompassing unions) (Huber and Stephens 2001; Korpi and Palme 2003; Thelen 2014) or leftist party-led political coalitions under proportional representation electoral systems (Iversen and Soskice 2009; Persson and Tabellini 2003) that replaced the role of civil society or labor–civic solidarity. However, for developing countries in which unions rarely reach half of all wage earners and have not had sufficient time to accumulate institutional resources through democratic political mechanisms, traditional power resource theory loses its explanatory power because of its inattention to the historical evolution of civil society as an active promoter of the welfare state along with unions during democratization eras. The comparison of the FKTU and the KCTU at the confederation level, and another comparison of the divergent roles of KCTU-affiliated industrial unions, demonstrate that unions' embeddedness plays a decisive role in determining the universality and generosity of coverage and benefits of existing social policies. The core difference of the EC approach from power resource theory is its explicit operationalization of historically constituted labor–civic solidarity (or unions' embeddedness) as an analytical dimension of the politics of social policy-making.

Overall, South Korean labor leaders succeeded in establishing a democratic national confederation supported by large militant unions and policy experts at the national center and within the industrial unions. They also established a labor-based party that embraced multiple social classes that supported leftists' social democratic vision, thereby pursuing two dimensions of cohesiveness – cohesiveness with the incumbent party (the state) and cohesiveness with a labor-based party – simultaneously. The embeddedness and cohesiveness of labor politics vigorously created and mobilized progressive policies and public opinion aimed at an egalitarian transformation of Korean state and society, advancing their vision by protecting workers and citizens from the risks generated by market forces. However, this case study shows that it was only in the late 1990s that South Korean labor politics built its strongest embedded cohesiveness and, consequentially, could advance universal social policies.

In the 2000s, when labor activists devoted their energies to building cohesiveness with their own labor-based party, the DLP, both dimensions of solidarity declined. The tragedy of South Korean labor politics is that one dimension of embeddedness – union-centered expertise networks and their policy capacity – waned quickly, while the other dimension of mobilization also gradually declined, as the KCTU became increasingly un-disciplined due to its internal factional divisions and strife. The following chapters (6 and 8) attempt to analyze the consequences of this decline in the problematic 2000s, when a supposedly pro-labor government and its neo-liberal market reforms fundamentally shattered the Korean economy and society.

6

The Politics of Retrenchment under Market Reforms

South Korea's state, economy, and civil society all faced fundamental transformations after the 1997 financial crisis and the ensuing structural reforms imposed by the IMF. The traditional developmental state suffered its own demise with the bust of its state-directed financial sectors. Firms had to launch mass lay-offs to survive the unprecedented economic downturn. Unions and other civic associations, which had collaborated against the military and the authoritarian regimes (and successors) since the 1970s, witnessed the sudden collapse of the old regime. Yet, simultaneously, they faced the market-oriented reforms introduced by the newly elected reformist government, a former ally during the democratization era. Overall, the solidarity of the democratization struggles abruptly ended, just as a new solidarity focused on 'anti-neo-liberalism' congealed in civil society.

This chapter analyzes the social policy reforms during the neo-liberal reform era of the 2000s. During the period, retrenchment drives on social and labor market policies started with the second reformist regime, the Rho Mu-hyun regime (2003–07), and became further intensified under the two conservative regimes, the Lee Myung-bak (2008–12) and Park Geun-hye (2013–17) regimes.

What happened to two solidarity linkages, cohesiveness and embeddedness, between labor movements and political/civil societies during this time? How did they affect the retrenchment of the welfare state and labor market institutions? Why and how did labor movements and civil society manage to sustain or fail to defend the main pillars of the universal welfare state that were built during the Kim Dae-jung regime? How were

143

some union–civic solidarity movements able to survive during the harsh retrenchment era, while others failed to do so?

In particular, the chapter explores why such militant labor movements had no choice but to watch the intensified neo-liberal rules and norms during the reformist Rho Mu-hyun regime that should have been labor-friendly in its nature. It delves into what role cohesive and embedded ties played in defending the welfare state during the Rho regime.

This chapter pursues additional, specific research questions regarding the structure of solidarity and the retrenchment of welfare policies during the conservative regimes. Did unions react to the governing conservatives' (more coordinated and sophisticated) retrenchment efforts in the same way that they had to the earlier reformist regimes' attempt at retrenchment? To what extent and how did they forge alliances with other civil society actors to enhance their mobilization and policy capacities and respond to the conservative government's neo-liberal reforms?

Using in-depth field interviews as well as archival case studies of the mobilization and channeling processes of social policies in South Korea during the 2000s and following, the chapter advances two arguments about the politics of retrenchment: (1) the embeddedness of unions in civic associations (even without cohesiveness) is sufficient to defeat retrenchment efforts by the state (and employers), but unions need both mobilization- and policy-wise solidarity with civic associations; and (2) when unions lack both embeddedness and cohesiveness, or even when unions lack embeddedness (but have cohesiveness), they will be vulnerable to radical market reforms significantly affecting their core interests and rights.

In the following, I initially describe the trajectory of unions' embeddedness and cohesiveness in the 2000s, before analyzing the retrenchment drives of reformist and conservative governments in two policy domains: health care and pensions. I show how unions' varied levels and strengths of cohesiveness and embeddedness enabled or hindered them in responding to privatization efforts. In the conclusion, I discuss the degree to which the proposed theoretical framework accounts for observed variations in the retrenchment of social policies.

THE SURVIVAL AND DECLINE OF EMBEDDEDNESS UNDER RETRENCHMENT DRIVES

Decline in Embeddedness

Labor unions' embeddedness in South Korea had reached its highest point in the late 1990s or the early 2000s, but abruptly started declining from that point. Such a dramatic turn originates from three factors: internal divisions, changing coalitional politics in civil society, and the institutionalization of social movement sectors.

First, the KCTU was deeply divided regarding the usefulness of the tripartite committee: one faction (Kungminp'a) supported participating in the tripartite committee, while the other (Hyŏnjangp'a) was vehemently opposed to it. It first started with the participation in the tripartite committee during the Kim Dae-jung regime in 1997–98. The first KCTU leadership eventually resigned. The second and the third KCTU regimes, led by Yi Kab-yong (1998–2001) and Tan Pyŏng-ho (2001–04), both of whom were famous for their uncompromising militant leadership in the history of Korean labor movements, were deeply skeptical about the Kim Dae-jung and Rho Mu-hyun regimes' stance between capital and labor, and were therefore reluctant to participate in the tripartite committee run by the government. Both leaderships were classified as leftist within the labor movements, and some (if not all) of the grassroots base of those two leaderships tended to view cooperation with the reformist governments (cohesiveness) and even with civil society (embeddedness) as a sort of 'reformism' that might enervate workers' capacity for struggles against capitalists, and their agency.[1]

The Rho regime's harsh repression of strikes by the truck drivers' and railway unions during its early incumbency in 2003 further intensified such skepticism and discontent about the regime. The KCTU was internally divided, and the faction favoring participation in the tripartite committee formed the fourth leadership in 2004. From then, the KCTU started taking part in a labor relations committee discussing multiple unions' unified bargaining at a factory level, prohibition of payment for union staff, and extension of supplemental employment, all of which were supposed to encroach seriously upon labor's rights. The FKTU was content to draw up an agreement to postpone the first two issues for three years, while accepting the extension of supplemental employment for key public facilities, and the further lifting of regulation for lay-off.[2] This FKTU-Rho regime's agreement further intensified divisions and factional strife within the KCTU, as the KCTU regime formed by the pro-participation faction was able neither to defend the KCTU's core interests nor to receive compensation packages in return. After all, both the third regime's anti-participation strategy and the fourth regime's pro-participation strategy "turned out to be ineffective" (No 2008). The KCTU had to witness the serious retrenchment of labor's rights, while it was unable to launch comprehensive solidarity due to its internal division.

Second, the PSPD began to build its own solidarity network. Although it maintained ties with labor regarding some social policies, it also launched its own initiatives independent of labor regarding other reform areas, and strategically marshalled its resources according to the impending importance of each issue. The two most controversial movements led by the PSPD (regarding its relationship with the labor movement) were 'Solidarity for the General Election' and 'Movement for the Rights of Minority Stockholders,' both of which the PSPD launched in 2000. The KCTU and the DLP (founded in 2000) were uncomfortable with the civic associations' collective intervention in the general election. The DLP suspected that the PSPD-led monitoring and evaluation of candidates would ultimately help the Democratic Party (the incumbent party of the time). The KCTU activists were also skeptical about the ultimate direction of the 'minority stockholder' movement, predicting that it would only reinforce capitalist norms by rationalizing the ownership structure of the Chaebols, which would not change anything regarding labor's rights. Such tensions between the two organizations only increased during the 2000s, as the PSPD emerged as one of the most politically influential civic associations, able not only to steer the direction of policies but also to mobilize public opinion in civil society and media through its superior policy capacity compared to other players. For instance, in the field of policy suggestion through congress, the PSPD overwhelmed all other non-governmental associations, proposing 13 bills with 260 other civic associations compared to five bills by the KCTU and four bills by the FKTU (Hong 2007, p. 116). In contrast to the 1990s, when the KCTU and the PSPD were in collaborative relations, they entered into a 'competitive collaboration' relationship in the 2000s (Hong 2007; Ŭn 2001, 2005b).

Third, many leaders in progressive civic associations were recruited to the government agency and the incumbent reformist party, thereby weakening the solidarity network in which labor was embedded. The constant incorporation of politicized civil society leaders into the existing party system, especially the DP, significantly reduced the embeddedness of the unions. A renowned policy specialist in the KCTU center laments, "There were few civil society allies to collaborate. They all left for political parties." During the reformist Rho regime, many civic leaders determined to participate in the regime as advisors to presidents and politicians, as chief executives or in elected positions in municipal governments, or as candidates for national or local congresses. Such co-optation of civic leaders continued through the following conservative regimes. The DP kept providing civic leaders with positions in proportional representation slots: for instance, the two founders of the PSPD, Pak Wŏn-sun and Kim Ki-sik, became a mayor of Seoul in 2011 and a congressman of the DP in 2012, respectively. Naturally, their networks and reputations were uprooted and transplanted to the institutionalized parties along with them, while many civic associations lost their renowned leaders (thereby losing personal leadership and the leaders' reputations). Although this might have improved the cohesiveness of unions with the incumbent party, it also implied that the KCTU had lost its policy brokers who not only solidified labor–civic networks but also linked unions and parties, or unions and bureaucrats, from unions' perspectives.[3]

Fourth, with the launch of the DLP, labor movements tended to put more focus upon building alliance with the DLP rather than with the incumbent reformist party, which increasingly turned away from labor and civil society since the second year (2004) of the regime. Especially, many 'policy folks' moved to the National Assembly, primarily as legislative assistants of the newly elected representatives.[4] Consequently, labor-centered (social democratic) cohesiveness was greatly enhanced thanks to the resources that became available through ten seats in congress, but labor-centered embeddedness, especially policy capacity, suddenly atrophied, as there were increasingly fewer experts who could sustain and cultivate labor–civic policy networks.

The unions' (KCTU's) embeddedness unexpectedly started declining when they should have been tasting the fruits of their endeavors during the several previous decades. The early 2000s was a critical moment for the democratic labor movement and its leaders. They had begun witnessing the positive outcomes of their efforts to build a centralized union confederation and a labor-based party. They had toppled the formerly omnipotent developmental state with their labor–civil society solidarity just a couple years earlier (in the 1996–97 general strike against labor law reforms), succeeded in passing several important pieces of social policy legislation in collaboration with civil society and allies in the incumbent party in the 1997–98 tripartite committee (although they had to watch the passage of lay-off law), and witnessed the launch of a labor-based party in 2000 and finally its electoral success in 2004. At the very moment of such success, unions' embeddedness in civil society was collapsing for several structural and political reasons: the growing negative effects of their internal division, and their allies' differentiation and co-optation into the incumbent party and bureaucracy. After the heated struggles of the 1990s, it was about the time to start institutionalizing their core capacities, especially policy capacity, but the KCTU lost the moment in the pitfall of factional conflicts. As a consequence, the labor movement lost its best chance to consolidate and further expand the Korean welfare state at its critical moment.

Decline in Cohesiveness (with the State/Incumbent Party)

Many leaders of labor unions were excited about the second reformist regime. Many of them remembered the moments when the president, Rho Mu-hyun, a former human rights and labor rights lawyer and then a lawmaker, delivered speeches soliciting reform of labor rights in front of thousands of workers in the Ulsan, Masan, and Ch'angwŏn industrial areas in the late 1980s. Initially, the Rho regime showed its willingness to collaborate with unions by filling key positions on the cabinet and Blue House (presidential) staff with pro-labor intellectuals and labor activists.[5] At that time, union leaders found themselves holding the closest ties to the president. Cohesiveness, if it could be redefined merely by the distance through human resource networks between labor leaders and the president, the leader of the incumbent party, was at its highest level under the Rho regime in 2003 since the transition to democracy. Indeed, the Rho regime showed its pro-labor tendency by listening to unions' requests (for wage increases and the withdrawal of its privatization plan) when truck drivers' and railway unions waged strikes for the first couple of months after the regime's inauguration. However, when the NTU (the National Teachers' Union) halted the regime's plan to introduce an electronic system for students' personal records, the regime (and the president) started turning against labor unions.[6] "The president and union leaders knew each other very well, because of their relationships tracing back to the turbulent 1980s. Truck drivers' unions and their leaders had a direct contact line to the presidential office. Because they knew too well, it was neither necessary to intermediate them, nor possible to recover their relationship [when they turned their backs on each other] through any kind of mediation"(Kim Yŏng-dae). "There was no connection between the two since the 2003 government–labor debacle" (Pak T'ae-ju, an industrial relations policy advisor to President Roh in 2003).

After the impeachment of President Rho by the opposition parties (and labor's silence during that time) with the majority in congress[7] and the incumbent party's overwhelming success in the general election (winning the majority, 152 seats out of 299), the regime stopped collaborating with the unions almost completely. Many of the 108 newly elected legislators out of the total 152 of the incumbent party were former bureaucrats who collaborated well with President Rho for the first year of his presidency, but few of them were experts in labor and welfare issues. There were few lawmakers like Yi Sŏng-jae (DP), who played decisive roles in representing and channeling labor and civil society's demands for health care and pension reforms during the Kim Dae-jung regime.

The regime went on to launch four major reform agendas (reform of private school law, national security law, media law, and a law for clarifying past cases of human rights encroachment), none of which had anything to do with workers' lives or the rights which were rapidly deteriorating in the context of growing inequality and poverty in the 2000s. Moreover, the incumbent reformist party virtually failed to enact those four reform agendas, blocked by staunch opposition from the GNP, and did not have any further capacity to wage other reform projects in the latter part of Rho's presidency.

Cohesive ties between labor unions (especially the KCTU) and the state were almost absent after 2005. The key labor-friendly intellectuals who participated in the regime had to quit after a year or so. While the KCTU successfully launched a labor-based party with ten seats in congress, it also lost its allies in and channels to the incumbent party, which increasingly isolated itself from its core allies in civil society. Consequently, during this time, unions, in spite of their great success in establishing a labor-based party, did not have any influence on the key policy-crafting processes within the incumbent reformist party – a huge difference from the situation during the Kim Dae-jung regime. KCTU leaders were completely ignorant of and isolated from what was going on within the regime regarding its neo-liberal turns, while the regime was indifferent to the unions' interests and concerns. With its increasing unilateral alliance with the DLP, the KCTU completely closed its lobbying channels to the conservative party, which had remained open during the health care integration movement. This strikingly divergent development of three dimensions of cohesiveness – social democratic cohesiveness, non-ideological cohesiveness with diverse parties, and cohesiveness with the state – was costly. The KCTU closely allied itself with its own creation, the DLP, for policy production and mobilization, but the establishment of an 'alternative cohesiveness' was not necessarily effective in launching and moving forward important policy agendas without collaboration with the incumbent party.

From 2006, the KCTU started actively participating in the tripartite committee, but the regime was already collaborating with the FKTU to achieve its own agendas – the extension of replacement employment for key public firms and the lifting of regulations for lay-offs. From the perspective of the KCTU, the Rho regime was no different from the Kim Dae-jung regime in the sense that both aimed to introduce and extend labor market flexibility. It was worse than the Kim Dae-jung regime, however, in that it almost completely shut down conversation channels with unions; labor did not have any informal or institutionalized channels to have conversations with the Rho regime while the regime started introducing key privatization moves in the areas of health care and pensions, thereby encroaching upon the fundamental framework of the Korean welfare state. The (corporatistic) cohesive ties between the reformist regime and the FKTU were as stable as those during earlier authoritarian regimes, while the KCTU was losing its channels to the regime.[8]

Overall, with its declining embeddedness, the KCTU could neither effectively threaten the regime, with its contentious mobilization capacity nor persuade it, due to its lack of cohesive ties. In both labor market institutions and social policy fields, the dramatic neo-liberal turn of the supposedly most labor-friendly regime was unstoppable. The only exception was the consistent presence and role of Solidarity for Health Rights (SHR) and the KHMU in the health policy field.

Health Solidarity Networks and Politics of Retrenchment during the Rho Regime (2003–2007)

The Rho Mu-hyun regime started with a minority in congress, but emerged as the majority incumbent party after the 2004 general election with 152 seats (out of the total 299 seats). In addition, the DLP entered the congress for the first time as a labor-based progressive party with ten seats. Many believed that the Rho Mu-hyun regime was the first progressive regime of which the core leadership was primarily composed of the student movement generation of the late 1970s and early 1980s. Above all, the president himself was a renowned lawyer and a congressman in the field of labor and human rights in the 1980s and the 1990s. Indeed, Rho included in his shadow cabinet and first cabinet a significant number of pro-labor intellectuals and leaders, raising the level of expectation for pro-labor reforms.

However, the Rho regime is also deemed the one that launched key privatization moves in the field of social welfare, especially in the largest two social policy domains, pension and health care. The regime intended to introduce 'for-profit hospitals' in free-trade zones, and also allowed private insurance companies to pay for the health care premiums and expenses not covered by public health insurance. In the area of pensions, the regime reduced replacement rates from 60 percent to 40 percent, ultimately switching from the ILO model to the World Bank model, thereby allowing private pension plans to extend their shares in the pension market. In addition, it introduced the retirement pension, management of which became wide open to private pension companies.[9]

The Rho regime also betrayed nearly every wish-list of the labor movement by normalizing flexible labor market institutions and laws: it introduced an act on non-standard employees, which ended up legally justifying the use of non-standard workers on a short-term, two-year basis. In contrast, it did not make any efforts to stop the violation of basic labor rights in indirect-contract and supplemental employment. The regime came up with more than 1,000 arrests and indictments of labor leaders by strictly imposing legal guidelines and principles, which was unprecedented even in the previous authoritarian regimes (No 2008).

Many labor leaders were deeply embarrassed and disturbed by this neo-liberal turn of the Rho regime, which nearly everyone had expected to be 'labor-friendly.' Many believed that the launch of the new reformist regime based on Minjung movement tradition and the entrance of a labor-based party into the congress would offer the best opportunity for labor and labor movements to promote pro-labor social and labor market policies. As a labor leader regretfully testifies, it turned out to be a "disaster" for Korean labor movements. A scholar who had been involved in the PSPD movement laments by saying, "an inexperienced doctor killed a patient."

Although the KCTU's cohesive ties and embedded ties were both declining, there were significant variations in embeddedness and cohesiveness across policies. In the field of health care, the core element of the NCHIU, which was formed in 1988 and played a crucial role in the integration movement, was still operating as a comprehensive solidarity network bridging unions, civil society intellectuals, physicians, and other associations in the health and medicine field (under the name of 'Health Solidarity') until 2002. The solidarity network converted itself into two organizations hoping for more effective and comprehensive reform movements in health fields: one was the Health Rights Network (the HRN), established in 2003, a new organization with new 'citizen-based' membership and renewed agendas focusing on patients' rights; the other was Solidarity for Health Rights (SHR), which sought the enhancement of insurance benefits (such as raising benefits up to 80 percent of total health care costs) and the defense of the public health care plan against privatization (of service providers). Most associations in the NCHIU rejoined these networks aiming at influencing candidates' platforms in the general election in 2004.

As the solidarity network held its own paid professional personnel sent from several member associations, and institutionalized organizational routines and bases for nearly two decades, it was able to respond promptly to any retrenchment moves by employers, conservative politicians, or bureaucrats – at least in terms of analyzing policies, their details and contents, and their implications and impacts. Consequently, the KCTU, although it was losing its key policy folks, was able to sustain unions' embeddedness thanks to the Health Rights Network in the 2000s, and the critical role of its two member unions (the Korean Social Insurance Union and the Korean Health and Medicine Union) in the solidarity network. Through its participation in the network, as addressed earlier in the chapter, unions were able to tap in to specialized expert networks for health care issues, which were willing to share their policy-relevant resources with the unions, while the HRN obtained mobilization networks that could promptly activate thousands of protestors and potentially a much bigger number of the electorate through the union organizations.

The associational network data presented earlier in Chapter 4 convincingly show the significant role of the KCTU and its allying associations such as the KFMA and KHMU. In the betweenness centrality ranking (of integrated events) in Appendix D (Table D.2), the KFMA was ranked at 18, with the KHMU being listed at 88 (not shown). Although the HRN was not included in the top 100 associations for mobilization-oriented embeddedness, it was ranked at 47 for policy-oriented embeddedness (in terms of betweenness centrality). In the ranking of mobilization-based embeddedness, the KHMU (formerly the KHU) soars up to 15 (in Table D.3), supporting my earlier argument in Chapter 4 that unions in the health field provide critical resources for threat and punishment measures, compared to other civic associations in the same policy field. These associations are core organizational actors, which helped achieve the universal integration of health care societies in the late 1990s (as discussed in Chapter 5).

Figure 6.1 presents only between-group linkages (between health-welfare associations and other associations) in mobilization networks. It shows that a couple of key civic organizations in the health fields play broker roles by linking core central associations such as the KCTU and the PSPD at the center (large rectangles) and other minor politically neutral, livelihood-issue-oriented associations. The KFMA and the KHMU, as expected, play prominent mobilization roles in labor–civic solidarity in the health field. The figure also shows that People's Medical Solidarity and Rights for the Disabled are new bridging associations that emerged in the mobilization-oriented health networks in the 2000s.

This tendency of the 'health-field civic network' is even more salient in the policy-oriented network in Figure 6.2. Core health- and welfare-related civic networks surprisingly form close and dense links to other issue-based non-political civic associations as well as popular political civic associations (such as PSPD). The KFMA, the inheritor of the NCHIU, plays an especially major bridging role in linking not only other welfare-related civic associations and labor unions but also progressive civic associations. As I described in Chapter 4, in the health care field, this sort of consortium organizational form has played a leading role in mobilizing resources, coordinating different interests,

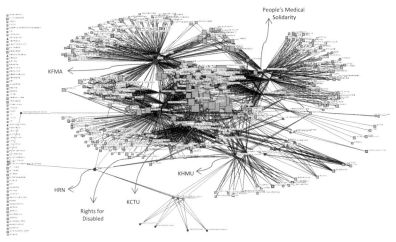

FIGURE 6.1. South Korean Health Field Networks in 2005 (based on Mobilization-Oriented Events)

Note: In order to operationalize intergroup ties between health and non-health associations, I built three categories: (1) health-related civic associations, (2) welfare-related civic associations, and (3) all others. Circles are health-related civic associations and unions, while rectangles are non-health related associations and triangles are welfare associations mostly for the disabled and the poor. Figures 6.1 and 6.2 are arranged by 'graphic theoretical layout' procedure available in UCINET. The size of a node indicates the degree centrality of the association: the bigger the size, the higher the degree centrality.

Source: Arranged by Graphic Theoretic Layout.

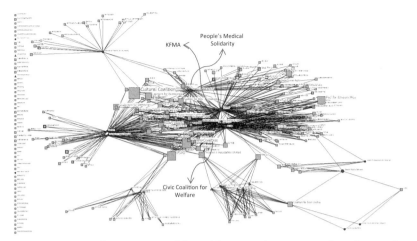

FIGURE 6.2. South Korean Health Field Networks in 2005 (based on Policy-Oriented Events)
Source: Arranged by Graphic Theoretic Layout.

and lobbying political parties, with labor unions taking part in health-related agendas as member associations. The other primary actors in the health and welfare fields are associations representing the disabled and socially marginalized (such as the poor and migrant workers, mostly located at the upper-right corner in Figure 6.2) and general civic welfare/international welfare associations, such as the Civic Coalition for Welfare, mainly formed by intellectuals and religious organizations (mostly located at the center-right in Figure 6.2). These associations are closely connected to the health field, reinforcing their legitimacy and reputation. Therefore, it is not surprising that the universal health care project promoted by the NCHIU in the 1990s was further defended by the KFMA and Health Rights Network in the 2000s. The coalition drew wide support from numerous issue-based associations serving the socially marginalized.

The solidarity had enabled an unusual alliance to be maintained between health professionals of these associations and unions through the notion of 'health rights for all.' Based on these two groups (health professionals and unions), progressive professors and graduate students in health fields played the role of 'bridging activists' who connected diverse actors and coordinated their resources and information. In contrast to the KCTU national center, the DLP, and other civic associations, all of which suffered significant decline in their organizational capacities during the Rho regime, the solidarity network around the KFMA, the HRN, and the KHMU enjoyed the highest level of organizational capacity in terms of knowledge production and lobbying efforts during the same period.

After the integration, so many important policy agendas were brought in and discussed [between the regime and civil society] during the Rho regime. We had a lot of resources to mobilize and a lot of access points to important information through our networks within and outside the Rho regime. (Kim Ch'ang-bo)[10]

Therefore, the solidarity network provided the unions with quasi-cohesiveness as well as strong embeddedness. Although the cohesive ties with the incumbent party were not through institutionalized ties to the existing political parties, the network had sufficiently diverse and reliable allies and their own personnel within the regime. Thanks to such horizontal and vertical solidaristic ties, it was able not only to fight against the neo-liberal turn of the regime in quite an effective way, but also to increase the benefits of national health care significantly for key diseases. The discussion on introducing profit-oriented hospitals in free-trade zones was brought on to the table, but could not go further as it was blocked by strong protests led by the solidarity network. Although the network was unable to universally increase the levels of health care benefits up to 80 percent (from 60 percent) for all illness by increasing the premiums, government subsidies, and employers' matching benefits, it played a critical role in improving insurance coverage of high-cost diseases. It also succeeded in enhancing coverage and benefits for the socially marginalized. The reform included reducing patients' payment down to 20 percent for 103 chronic diseases, 10 percent for cancer and heart and brain vessel diseases, and zero for natural birth, infant hospitalization, and clinic for children under six years old. The disabled and citizens in the bottom social strata also started receiving medical benefits from the government. Although the network was unable to block the introduction of 'supplementary indemnity insurance' provided by private insurance companies, it managed to halt the further discussion of profit-oriented hospitals outside the current health care system.

Overall, during the Rho regime, at least in the health fields, there were more successful universal reforms that were beneficial for the lower classes and marginalized than there were retrenchment attempts. This strong resistance based on the solidarity network kept operating even under the conservative Lee regime (2008–13), successfully blocking further legislative attempts seeking (or for) profit-oriented hospitals.

Retrenchment on the National Pension during the
Rho Regime

Pension reforms followed a completely different trajectory to that of
health care reforms. While the social welfare branch of the PSPD succeeded in extending the coverage of the pension to the self-employed,
defending the core parameters of the scheme in the late 1990s through
the package deals in the tripartite committee, during the retrenchment era
of the 2000s there was no such a parallel organization as the NCHIU-
KFMA in the pensions field. When neo-liberal bureaucrats, in alliance
with the private insurance companies, attempted to reduce benefit levels
to 40 percent, the unions, both the KCTU and FKTU, did not adamantly
protest against it. When the core decision-makers in the presidential
office, deeply influenced by bureaucrats in the Ministry of Finance, introduced the retirement pension (equivalent to the 401k in the US) and private insurance companies took over this new market, the unions did not
understand the implications of the plan, because of the lack of knowledge
and expertise within and around them.[11]

By law, the KCTU and the FKTU folks, as representatives of pension recipients,
are supposed to participate in the decision-making processes of the pension
reforms. They were just sitting there, but only without knowing what was going
on. They were neither experts nor enthusiastic activists who wanted to understand and advocate it. (Professor in the PSPD social welfare unit)

Furthermore, in the field of pensions, conservative economists, business
professors, and specialized bureaucrats dominated the discussion on the
financial projections and management plans of pension funds in the future. The social work and social policy professors within the PSPD were
unable to match experts on the government side, especially regarding
the financial projection issue, which was a key battleground in the deter-
mination of the pension premium and the amount of benefits for current
affiliates. In 2003, bureaucrats and their allies, including the conservative
media, kept spreading the results of their financial projection that the
National Pension would be depleted in the year 2070 if the current contribution and benefit levels were maintained. Although the KCTU and
the PSPD policy folks rejected their projection, they did not have a convincing blueprint based on alternative projections that they could put
forward with confidence. "There was no single professor in the entire
country specializing in insurance projection who was willing to work
with us to defend the existing pension scheme"(a professor in the PSPD
social welfare unit) After all, in the pensions field, the KCTU-PSPD

alliance did not have sufficient 'knowledge capacity' or 'policy networks' to compete against the solidarity among bureaucrats, private insurance companies, and conservative economists.

Importantly, the PSPD and the unions (both the KCTU and the FKTU), although they largely appeared to be on the same page, had different thoughts on pension reforms, despite their frequent collaborations since the 1996–97 Anti-Labor Law Struggle.

There were two strategies [under discussion within the PSPD] for pension reform. One was to introduce [or increase] the basic pension [for the lower classes and the uncovered], while the other was to increase the replacement rates for the middle class [who were the existing eligible recipient] within the current pension scheme. Whereas the former would be supported by women's associations and non-standard employees, the latter would be supported by the KCTU and the FKTU regular workers … but many political leaders were skeptical about the plausibility of the idea of increasing the premiums because of the political burdens of tax-increase … after all, the KCTU suggested that the solidarity network launch a movement to set up a Maginot line to defend a 45 percent replacement rate [without increasing any premium]. We [the civil society forces within the solidarity network] discussed whether to accept the idea, and declined. They did it on their own for a month … [but to no avail]. (Professor in the PSPD Social Welfare unit)

In a sense, the KCTU, whose membership was composed of regular workers with stable employment records in large conglomerates or public firms, was reluctant to embrace the basic pension (for all elderly populations) in the current pension scheme, as the basic pension's universal coverage might not necessarily be to the advantage of the KCTU's standard workers. However, intellectuals in the PSPD desired, through the basic pension, to expand coverage to formerly uncovered, marginalized populations – a possibility that was not considered in the 1999 reforms. The unions wished to protect their (working-age) members' future benefits by defending the replacement rates of the National Pension, as opposed to introducing the basic pension, while PSPD intellectuals thought that it was more urgent to help the elderly poor of the current generation, even at the cost of the National Pension. Therefore, there were unignorable divergences in interests between two organizations that ought to have worked together towards a common goal. Within the Rho regime, reformist politicians and intellectuals, including President Rho himself, were convinced by the argument, promoted by bureaucrats in the Ministry of Finance and Economy, that the National Pension needed to be reformed before it was depleted and that other alternative, supplementary measures such as basic and private pensions should be introduced.

As politicians (including the president) refused to raise social security taxes, the question was not whether to cut the National Pension but by how much it should be cut. Reformists in the regime, including Yu Si-min and Kim Yong-ik, promoted the introduction of the basic pension (with means testing) in exchange for the retrenchment of the National Pension, reasoning that the current older populations suffering from poverty needed to be taken care of first.

However, why couldn't unions and their allies defend the 60 percent replacement rate, while still introducing the basic pension? Unions were unable to defeat the retrenchment of the National Pension, instead witnessing the passage of the basic pension. In the field of pensions, the KCTU had neither a strong specialized union organization such as the KHMU nor strong solidarity between expert organizations and unions such as the NCHIU (the HRN). Although NPS union staffers ran to the congress and staged demonstrations, they were not supported by any other unions, either those under the KHMU or other public sector unions. Even the KCTU national center was indifferent to the NPS union's lonely struggle.[12] As grassroots union members were indifferent to their retirement schemes and often hostile to the National Pension because of the rumor that the fund would be depleted by 2070, it was difficult to mobilize union-based popular protests against the retrenchment move by the regime. In the end, in 2007, the pension reforms (lower replacement rates for the National Pension and the introduction of retirement pensions run by private firms) were executed as the regime hoped, without meaningfully strong resistance from unions and civil society. One last striking point of the analyses in Figures 6.1 and 6.2 is that not a single association in the field of pensions in 2005, including the NPS union, was listed among the 1,744 associations. This result implies that the NPS union did not participate in a single solidaristic event in 2005. This is mainly because there had been few events regarding pension reforms in the form of joint organizational activities such as demonstrations, petitions, and press conferences until the reformist government launched retrenchment in pensions in 2007. This inactivity of the NPS union in civic associational networks in the mid-2000s is in accordance with my field interview data with key organizational leaders in and around the NPS.[13]

Without embeddedness in terms of both mobilization and policy capacity, the KCTU-PSPD solidarity network was incapable of stopping the neo-liberal reform of pensions. Put differently, the KCTU-PSPD solidarity of the 1990s was substantially non-operational in the pensions field in 2007, as summarized in Table 6.1.

TABLE 6.1. *Politics of Market-Oriented Reforms of Social Policies during the Reformist Rho Mu-hyun Regime*

	Health Care Reform	Pensions Reform
Initiative	The state, employers	The state, employers
Key Player	The NCHIU (labor–civil society solidarity network)	Employers (private insurance companies)
Cohesiveness with the State (KCTU)		
Electoral Mobilization	Weak	Weak
Policy-Crafting: Deliberation and Negotiation	Moderate	Weak
Embeddedness (KCTU)		
Contentious Mobilization	Moderate	Weak
Policy-Crafting: Lobbying	Strong	Weak
Outcomes	Privatization halted: discussion on privatization of health care, but postponed Extension of eligibility and coverage: higher benefits for some serious illnesses	Privatization introduced: replacement rates lowered/introduction of (the US 401k-type) retirement plan run by private investment firms Basic universal pension (means-testing) introduced

With declining embeddedness, the KCTU could not build a durable solidarity network to fight against the retrenchment of existing labor market regulations. Especially, as the KCTU lost its specialized policy personnel in the 2000s, its capacity to respond to the state's retrenchment action was greatly weakened following the mid-2000s. Consequently, when the KCTU returned to the tripartite committee, it did not have as much policy capacity as in the late 1990s. Even worse, as it was divided along the lines of participation vs. non-participation in the tripartite committee, it was unable to mobilize effectively a general strike against the agreement between the state and the FKTU. The regime was well aware of the KCTU's internal divisions and weakening leadership, and therefore was able to launch the pro-business lifting of several labor market regulations.

In addition, the KCTU–PSPD relationship kept weakening in the 2000s, as the PSPD continued to develop its own hegemony between the state and civil society, drawing its attention to the rationalization of the governance institutions of the firms and the state, while staying away from 'labor market issues' such as lay-offs and non-standard workers' rights. Many other civic associations which were formerly favorable to the KCTU became increasingly reluctant to support repeated strikes by the KCTU. These moves away from the KCTU by the PSPD and other civic associations left many radical grassroots union members and leaders considering solidarity activity with the PSPD as 'reformism' and 'opportunism' in a derogatory sense. In the end, the KCTU was left alone again in the 2006 tripartite committee. While the FKTU and the Rho regime passed their agreement on labor market reforms, the KCTU had to watch it helplessly without any significant resistance.

VARIATIONS IN EMBEDDEDNESS AND DIVERGENT POLITICS OF RETRENCHMENT UNDER THE CONSERVATIVE REGIMES

The victory of conservative parties in the presidential elections in 2007 and 2012 meant that privatization agendas in social policy fields would be pursued as unified, coherent government policy. Under the reformist Rho regime, bureaucrats in the MFE (Ministry of Finance and Economy) first introduced privatization ideas such as allowing hospitals for foreigners in free-tax zones, supported by foreign capital (on Cheju Island), enrolling such hospitals as profit-oriented corporations and allowing them to serve native Koreans, and then permitting foreign capital-based hospitals to invest in domestic corporations. The conservative Lee regime continued to push the privatization plans initiated by the earlier reformist government. President Lee had not only defeated his opponents by a big margin (more than 5 million votes), but he had also gained a safe majority in congress, which constituted an ideal political environment for privatization. Members of the Ministry of Finance and Economy, already the strongest policy unit within the government under the reformist government eras, started serving as the primary proponents of privatization in the health and pensions policy areas. The Lee regime announced several supplementary policies allowing medical corporations to issue bonds, merge among themselves, utilize management services, etc., in addition to legalizing the entire agenda of launching profit-oriented hospitals. In 2009, the government also announced that it would discuss plans to allow Korean citizens to run profit-oriented hospitals, to issue visas for foreign customers of medical services, and to allow domestic insurance companies to serve foreigners and exchange patients with foreign medical institutions. The Park regime also reneged on its own election promises – the introduction of the basic pension for the entire elderly population – and succeeded in making the benefits of the basic pension contingent upon the length of subscription to the National Pension (so that the entitlement criteria became non-universal).

The important difference between the two policy domains, pensions and health care, however, was that while the increasing privatization of health provision was delayed by severe protests and resistance from labor–civic solidarity networks, the withdrawal of the universal basic pension was pursued with only minor pushback. Labor–civic solidarity deepened and became more sophisticated in one policy domain, as unions and their allies responded effectively to the strategies and actions of the state and businesses, but not in the other policy domain. Overall, this section analyzes the successes and failures of labor–civic solidarity in responding to the renewed market reform drives of these two conservative regimes.

Privatization of Health Care as the Government's New Industrial Policy

The plans to introduce privatized health care, although it had started its legislative life during the recent two conservative regimes, first emerged from the Kim Dae-jung regime – the same regime that had integrated health care insurance. The logics of these plans expanded during the next reformist Rho regime. Table 6.2 illustrates how and when each element of the neo-liberal market vision for the health care industry emerged historically and how they have developed, since the early 2000s, as realistic alternatives to public health care institutions. Again, most of these privatization plans were first formulated under the two reformist regimes but then deepened during the recent conservative regimes.

Bureaucrats in the Ministry of Finance and Economy, sponsored by large hospitals (SNU, Yonsei, Samsung, and Hyundai) and private insurance companies, aggressively promoted these plans, describing them as new industrial policies that would create markets and profits for Korean firms in the future. They pushed these plans at the end of the Kim Dae-jung regime, when the reformist president was a lame duck. The Rho regime wholeheartedly embraced this privatization plan for health care as its main governance agenda. The ideas were subsequently refined as a concrete policy agenda during the conservative Lee regime. The ultimate goals of all these reforms were deemed by critics to be "weakening public health insurance systems, which may result in the strengthening of private insurers' roles in health care industries" (Sin 2010).[14] Government officials from the Ministry of Finance and Economy and the Ministry of Health and Welfare confirmed that the government aimed to be responsible for the basic needs of citizens while letting the market be in charge of newly emerging demands for health care (HRN 2010).[15]

Incidences of Success in the Defensive Movements of Labor–Civic Solidarity

A series of privatization attempts targeting health care institutions ignited the relaunch of the health solidarity network. This 'defense'-oriented movement was further galvanized by the conservative Lee regime's announcement during its electoral campaign that it would seek the abrogation of a "Health Insurance Mandate for Health Care Service Providers."[16] During the two conservative regimes, there were two important moments when the government attempted to launch at least one of the major privatization plans (shown in Table 6.2): (1) an attempted repeal of the health insurance mandate with Lee's inauguration (2008); and (2) the attempt to pass the law for profit-oriented hospitals in Cheju Island (2009). Solidarity for Health Rights (SHR),[17] run jointly by unions and relevant civic associations, responded to each of these moves relentlessly and effectively, reactivating all of its policy and mobilization capacities.

First, against the Lee regime's attempt to eliminate the health insurance mandate, it launched a national campaign to show Michael Moore's *Sicko* (2007), which revealed the bare realities of an American-style private health care system – unequal service delivery at extremely high costs. Union members and local civic associations actively participated in the campaign during all of April, which then joined up with a 'Candlelight Demonstration' against importing US beef, protests which swept across South Korean streets for several months in spring and summer 2008.

TABLE 6.2. *Development of Privatization of Health Care (Ideas and Laws) in South Korea*

Contents of Privatization Drives	Kim Dae-jung Regime (1998–2002)	Rho Mu-hyun Regime (2003–2007)	Lee Myung-bak Regime (2008–2012)	Park Geun-hye Regime (2013–present)
Overall private health insurance policy	Task force report for activating private health insurance (2002) (representatives of private insurance companies requested the transfer of individual disease information)	Plans for developing medical industry (2004) Plans for enhancing the competitiveness of medical services (2005)	Announced a plan for 'Global Healthcare' (2009) Announced a plan for 'U-Health' (2009) to incorporate medical and IT industries	Declared intention to repeal any obstacles that deter advancement of medical industries
Repeal of (national) health insurance mandate for health care service providers	Korean Medical Association (KMA) filed a suit at the Constitutional Court (2002)		Introduced as one of the Lee's campaign agendas (2007) Announced: not to be sought further (2008) KMA filed the second suit at the Constitutional Court (2012)	
Introduction of 'supplementary indemnity insurance'	Idea was discussed in task force (2002) led by Ministry of Finance and Economy	Law introduced and legislated (2007)	First insurance product launched for sale (2008)	First private insurance product for the elderly (older than 70) for sale

(continued)

TABLE 6.2. (*continued*)

Contents of Privatization Drives	Kim Dae-jung Regime (1998–2002)	Rho Mu-hyun Regime (2003–2007)	Lee Myung-bak Regime (2008–2012)	Park Geun-hye Regime (2013–present)
Profit-oriented hospitals in special free-economy district	Proposed by Ministry of Finance and Economy (2002)	Announced the legislation (2004) (including foreign capital's participation) The law passed in congress in December 2004 Opening of medical service markets and implementation of the special law in Cheju Island (2005)	Announced plans allowing Korean citizens to run profit-oriented hospitals, issuing visas for foreign customers for medical services, and for domestic insurance companies to serve foreigners and exchange patients with foreign medical institutions (2009)	
Allowing medical institutions to be engaged in profit-oriented activities		The idea was first introduced along with the 2005 plan	The idea was expanded with additional policies such as activating MSOs (management service organizations) for hospitals, running child-companies, issue bonds, receive foreign patients, etc. Passed a law allowing hospitals or a third agency to entice and introduce patients (2009) Allowing diagnosis and treatment using remote-controlled medical devices for the disabled and elderly	Allowing child-companies to sell remote-controlled medical devices Allowing the corporate pharmacies to run chain systems

Source: Summarized and tabulated by the author, based on HRN 2010.

SHR cleverly juxtaposed 'anti-mad-cow disease' with 'anti-privatization of health care,' a framing which allowed the public to perceive that importing both American beef and American market-oriented health care could be hazardous to people's health. The entire nation's participation in mass demonstrations led to the government canceling (in May 2008) its announcement of the elimination of the health insurance mandate. This victory was primarily due to the threatening power of mass participation in the Candlelight Demonstration, and not necessarily to the capacities of SHR in itself. Nevertheless, without SHR's previous preparation for mobilization and its cautious development of strategies and tactics to 'frame' anti-privatization mottos in conjunction with growing concerns about US beef, it would have been impossible to ride on the power of the Candlelight Demonstration in 2008.

Although during the mass demonstration against the import of beef from the US in May 2008, the Lee regime declared it would not seek the repeal of the mandate; the regime's privatization plans were multi-layered and multi-dimensional. In the midst of the Candlelight Demonstration, the governor of Cheju Island (who was a member of the incumbent GNP) announced that they would seek 'profit-oriented hospitals.'[18] The SHR fought against this privatization effort with its full capacity: it held press conferences; it launched anti-privatization campaigns on the internet; it started collecting funds to respond to the privatization plans; it participated in the Candlelight Demonstration to publicize its rationale for opposition; it held a conference in congress with the three opposition parties; it put an advertisement in a newspaper (along with the Public Transportation and Service Union); it sent its expert activists to panel discussions organized by major broadcast media; and, finally, it dispatched a group of activists who cycled the entire Cheju Island carrying mottos opposing profit-oriented hospitals (HRN 2010, pp. 2–4). A poll was conducted by the governor's office, which announced that it would not pursue the plan if citizens of the Cheju Island disagreed. The majority answered 'no' and the governor declared that he would abandon the plan.

The small victory illustrates how effective SHR was in defeating the government's privatization plans. As with the integration movement, the three constituents of SHR organically cooperated by supplementing each of the other's weaker dimensions: professionals in health fields developed the logics of the arguments against privatization, primarily refuting the myth of an efficient market mechanism, while highlighting not only the unequal distribution and lack of physicians, but also the potential inequities in access to those facilities that might be generated by the profit-oriented hospitals. Activists from civic associations developed and deployed diverse repertoires of action, utilizing the logics developed by the professionals. The KHMU provided the resources needed for mobilization capacity by participating in the major defensive actions of the solidarity networks. The industrial union circulated anti-privatization arguments to its member unions and collected key resources for campaigns and advertisements. Most importantly, it sent large numbers of union members to public demonstrations. SHR managed to defeat the ongoing privatization attempts represented by the series of legislation efforts by the government up until 2010, when the incumbent party was severely defeated at every level of municipal election.[19]

The durable solidarity network against neo-liberal market reforms in health fields, therefore, is illuminating. Compared to the KCTU national center and metal union model, the health solidarity networks kept renewing their cohesiveness and embeddedness in terms of both policy and mobilization capacities. The health solidarity network convincingly shows that labor movements can only succeed as a part of the broader civic associational community. Labor and civic associations have effectively compensated for each other's weaknesses. The KHMU was happy to play a coordinating role among numerous civic and professional stakeholders in the health fields, but it rarely pushed its own agendas (SR strategy)[20] at the cost of the solidarity network.

Figure 6.3 illustrates the mechanism through which so many stakeholders and civic associations have been able to coordinate their different

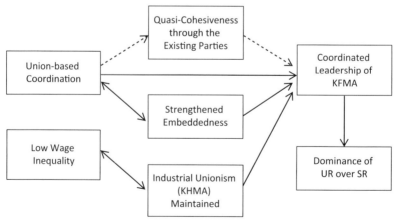

FIGURE 6.3. Embeddedness, Coordination, and Dominance of Universal Reform Strategy in the Health Care Field

interests and goals in defending and expanding National Health Insurance and other health policies. Differences due to their heterogeneous base communities were periodically discussed in the representatives' consortium meetings, and the solidarity network came up with 'minimalist' consensuses as its primary agenda. Such coordination was possible because the solidarity network shared a common, core theme: defending and expanding people's health rights. The fundamental consensus on basic rights and related issues made it possible for different organizational actors to remain in the network and solve collective action problems. Unions acknowledged that civic associations provided expertise unions could not match and channeled the voices of unorganized citizens that unions could not otherwise reach. Civic associations expanded and deepened their civic bases by mobilizing diverse groups of patients and consumers of health products. Civic associations also admitted that unions offered strong mobilization capacities that civic movements could not match. Both unions and associations conceded that PSPD lawyers and professors provided valuable knowledge regarding legal processes. Some physicians and pharmacists, if not all, accepted the necessity of maintaining the public health insurance system to protect small hospitals' profits as well as patients' universal coverage and rights. The network developed cohesive deliberation and lobbying channels with both the DLP (and its various fragments) and the main opposition party, regardless of factional and ideological differences. Therefore, it did not panic when the DLP split and lost influence. Since 2010, the network has worked closely with progressive lawmakers in the opposition party to defend National Health Insurance against privatization moves by the government. It has also worked to send its promising leaders to the national congress and the city government of Seoul, developing, in the process, new sources of cohesiveness. It is not a coincidence that the solidarity network was successful in both expanding National Health Insurance and defending it against privatization moves.

Retrenchment on Pensions

Since the replacement rate was retrenched to 40 percent from 60 percent in 2007 under the Rho regime, the biggest issue in the pensions field was the introduction of a basic pension for the entire elderly population. It was originally proposed by the DLP and the GNP during the Rho regime and then introduced as a basic old-age allowance with means testing. However, in the 2012 presidential election, the conservative candidate

Park promised to introduce one of the most innovative and generous social policy reforms on offer, proposing to introduce about US$200 per month of basic pension for the entire elderly population. However, the Park regime, once it took the office, broke its word and decided to introduce an alternative basic pension plan in which the amount of the basic pension would vary according to the period of affiliation to the National Pension, which meant that some long-term affiliates of the National Pension could be disadvantaged in their entitlement to the basic pension.

The KCTU, the PSPD, and the opposition DP all refused to accept the government bill, and they determined to defeat it using all possible tactics. The NPS (National Pension Service) union, which had fought a lonely fight against retrenchment (the lowered replacement rate)in 2007, was at the center of this movement, where it attempted to build new sources of embeddedness with which unions could mobilize broader solidarity against the government bill.

Compared to its lonely struggle and defeat in 2007, this time the NPS enhanced its mobilization and policy capacities in several respects. First, it was able to receive support from the KCTU national center, which designated defending public firms against privatization and the National Pension against the distorted basic pension bill as key organizational goals. Second, it received organizational support from its own upper industrial union structure, the Public Transportation and Service Union. Third, the NPS deepened its policy-wise embedded ties with progressive professionals in the PSPD social welfare unit. Most importantly, in 2013, 22 labor and civic associations formed a solidarity association, Actions for Pension, to fight against the bill. The content and structure of the consortium were very similar to those of SHR. Unions were at the heart of the consortium (comprising nearly half of the 22 associations),[21] providing key resources and personnel, and other progressive civic associations joined them, contributing their own expertise based on their respective strengths. The unions' embeddedness in terms of their solidaristic ties with other civic associations "greatly improved" and "public opinion and citizens' awareness of the issue were not comparable [to those of the 2007 retrenchment case]"(Pak Jun-u).

In 2014, unions were in much more favorable conditions to oppose retrenchment. Scholarly and popular discourse arguing for the strong need for social welfare expansion spread and permeated public discourse in early 2010, such as with 'universal free school lunch' movements during municipal elections. Intellectuals formed several civic associations to advocate for expanded public provision of social welfare, such as the

Welfare State Society or "The Welfare State I Build." The KCTU national center also acknowledged the importance of building the welfare state as its primary organizational goal. Both conservative and reformist parties started copying and revising the former DLP's social policy platforms. In all, unions had more diverse and deeper grounds for embeddedness, and, indeed, they consciously forged alliances with other civil society actors so as not to repeat their painful defeat of 2007. In this sense, the KCTU national center no longer remained aloof from the pensions field, and instead pursued strong efforts to build policy and mobilization capacities around the proposed pension reforms. For instance, the KCTU and the NPSU recently developed and launched a policy agenda, the '1045' campaign, which refers to a 10 percent replacement rate for the basic pension and a 45 percent replacement rate for the National Pension (a demand which would require a significant increase in the basic pension, with only a moderate increase from the current 40 percent replacement rate in the National Pension).

However, even as the unions' embeddedness in the pensions field was on the rise, the depth and scope of their embeddedness were not at the level necessary to defeat the sophisticated retrenchment drives of the government and the incumbent conservative party in 2014. The capacity of unions to draw solidaristic mobilization from other unions and civic associations, as well as the NPS union's own internal mobilization capacity, were insufficient to send threatening signals to the government. The KCTU national center, despite its best efforts to reallocate resources to support the NPSU in its struggle, was already considerably weakened in terms of its mobilization capacity and therefore unable to draw other unions into the defensive movement. The main branches of the KPTSU – the public transportation unions – were not able to offer much help after having exhausted their resources in their struggle against the privatization drive by the government in 2013. As a result, while the NPSU was not as isolated as in 2007, it could not expect decisive labor support such as national- or industry-level coordinated strikes. Furthermore, the organizational solidarity built through Actions for Pension was limited to unions and former Minjung movement associations such as the KWAU and the NPA. The Old Age Union, which was listed in the solidarity consortium, had only just been formed in 2012–13 as an association composed of dozens of unemployed older people. While SHR had patients' associations and other customers' associations which directly anchored their interests in public health care, the pensions consortium did not have a single 'stakeholder organization' that could directly represent the program recipients: the elderly.²² Although some demonstrations and petitions occurred inside and outside of the congressional building, they did not go beyond conventional protests, failing to reach the intensity at which the incumbent party might become worried about losing the next election: both parties must have felt that the costs would not be severe even if they compromised and passed the law.

In terms of policy-wise solidarity, the unions did not develop strong alliances with relevant experts. With the PSPD, the only civic association that is capable of providing professional expertise in the pensions field, few economists or business professors or researchers have joined the Action for Pension consortium as yet. This is again in sharp contrast to SHR, a consortium in which numerous physicians and professors from diverse health research backgrounds participated and provided valuable knowledge and arguments to counter the privatization drive, as described in the previous section. Importantly, then, most associations and unions that were participating in the solidarity over pensions were not able to provide expertise in the pension field. They loaned their names and good will, but they did not have much of substance to offer. Thus, despite their enhanced embeddedness, the depth of policy capacity and the strength of mobilization capacity were not impressive enough to fight against the sophisticated plans proposed by the government. On the contrary, the majority of the opposition party, the NPADP (formerly the DP), was persuaded by the government plan and agreed to pass the bill in 2014.

In short, despite some improvement, unions in the pensions field lacked both the mobilization and the policy capacities needed to fight against privatization and defend existing social policy institutions. Ultimately, what mattered as a difference between the two cases was mobilization capacity. "We have developed some policy capacity within (the NPSU)." The president of the NPS union succinctly summarizes the most critical element in its defensive struggle against the retrenchment efforts. "But we still don't have such a strong mobilization capacity yet ... and what is most important in the labor movement is just one thing, solidarity"(Pak Jun-u). The case of the NPS union and its allies' struggle against pension reforms in the 2000s and 2010s convincingly demonstrates how important the depth and scope of the embeddedness of unions is for the politics of retrenchment. The historically shallow depth of the NPS's embeddedness (see Chapter 5), which dates back to the era of the Great Labor Struggle in the late 1980s, has constrained the NPS' capacity to reach other civil society actors and convince them of the importance of the National Pension in the critical retrenchment period of the 2000s. The solidarity partners of the NPS were almost entirely absent in 2007 due to the shallow embeddedness of unions in the pensions field. A couple of social welfare professors in the PSPD were not enough to broker connections between the NPS and broader political and civic associations, and the NPS union itself did not have its own policy and mobilization capacities to break through the ice of the pensions field. While the number of partner organizations increased from only a couple to 22 in the Action for Pension alliance, the scope is still not impressive when compared to the 88 associations of SHR (not to mention the depth of knowledge and trust accumulated from SHR's historical solidarity activities during the last two decades). As the reformist regime easily passed its retrenchment attempt in 2007, the conservative regime did not face significant difficulty in passing the basic pension bill (a bill which encroaches upon the National Pension system).

In sum, despite the continuous decline in the cohesive and embedded ties of the KCTU national center during the retrenchment era of the 2000s, some industrial unions retained durable organizational strength in terms of their resources and influences. Health and medical sector unions in particular successfully maintained their embeddedness in associational fields, which enabled them to defend their core interests against the conservative regime's retrenchment efforts. The core forces of the former NCHIU have also sustained (as SHR) vitality through renewed structures and networks, even given the different organizational settings of the 2000s (after their success in passing the integration bill), and so they effectively fought the neo-liberal reform attempts by both the reformist Rho Mu-hyun and the conservative Lee Myung-bak regimes. As most core professionals, civic association leaders, and unions of the NCHIU returned to SHR, the labor–civic solidarity network maintained its durable embeddedness (as described in Table 6.3).

However, the NPS union, which switched its affiliation from the FKTU to the KCTU in the early 2000s, was incapable of defending the pension scheme throughout the 2000s. Due to its extremely low embeddedness, it failed to build a society-wide solidarity network to defend the pensions system against the retrenchment drives of the reformist regime in 2007. And despite subsequent direct organizational support and resource allocations from the KCTU national center, it has not been able to fully develop a strong mobilization and policy capacity in alliance with other civic associations (as denoted as weak embeddedness in Table 6.3). As a consequence, its resistance, in 2014, to the introduction of the universal basic pension as a Trojan horse encroaching upon the National Pension

TABLE 6.3. *Politics of Neo-Liberal Reforms during the Two Conservative Regimes (2008–2014)*

	Health Care Reform	Pensions Reform
Initiative	The state, employers	The state, employers (and private insurance companies)
Key defender	The NCHIU/SHR (labor–civil society solidarity network)	NPS union and PSPD
Cohesiveness (KCTU or its member unions)		
Electoral mobilization	Moderate	Weak
Policy-crafting: deliberation, negotiation and channeling	Moderate	Weak
Embeddedness (KCTU or its member unions)		
Contentious mobilization	Strong	Weak to moderate (no grassroots resistance)
Policy-crafting: lobbying	Strong	Weak to moderate
Outcomes	Successful resistance	Radical retrenchment

was not strong enough to stall the government's disguised retrenchment of the National Pension.

DISCUSSION AND CONCLUSION

This chapter has demonstrated that the embeddedness of unions in civil society plays a crucial role in defending core components of the welfare state against market-oriented retrenchment efforts initiated by the state (and businesses). SHR (formerly the NCHIU), a consortium organization of unions, peasants, and professional and civic associations in the health policy field, fully utilized its mobilization and policy capacities to defend existing health care institutions. Under the reformist Rho regime, SHR had allies within the presidential office and the Ministry of Health and Welfare, as well as a broad and substantial policy and mobilization network that had developed during the integration movement. Although the

| | | *Cohesiveness* (Unions' Linkages to Incumbent Party) | |
		Weak	Medium to Strong
	Weak	**Zero-sum Pure Conflict Game:** **Outcome: State's Radical Reform Drive & Unions' Militancy** Reforms on Labor Market Institutions in 1997-8 and in 2005; Market-oriented Pension Reform in 2007 (under the Rho Regime)	**Unilateral State Dominance Game:** **Outcome: State's Radical Reform Drive & Unions' Restraint** FKTU's docile acquiescence to the Rho Regime's retrenchments on the National Pension and Labor Market Regulations
Embeddedness (Unions' Linkages to Larger Associational Field)		**Unilateral Union Dominance Game:** **Outcome: State's Radical Reform & Unions' Militancy** Reforms on Labor Market Institutions in 1996-7 (Anti-Labor Law Struggle) Attempts to Introduce Profit-Oriented Hospitals Failed (under the Rho and Lee Regimes, in 2005 and in 2008 respectively)	**Standard Assurance Game:** **Outcome: State's Moderate Reform & Unions' Restraint** Privatization of Health Care System Raised but Buried under the Rho Regime
	Medium to Strong		

FIGURE 6.4. Network-Informed Strategic Actions of the State and Unions in the Combinational Spaces of Cohesiveness and Embeddedness: South Korean Retrenchment Cases

idea of privatization in health care first emerged under the Rho regime from bureaucrats in the MFE (Ministry of Finance and Economy), SHR successfully defended the spread and realization of such ideas during the Rho regime. This moderate or unrealized reform under the Rho regime could be classified as the MR-R (moderate reform-restraint) outcome under embedded cohesiveness in Figure 6.4. Even politicians and bureaucrats within the regime supporting retrenchment restrained their voices with the fear of being punished, and well-organized resistance groups put considerable pressure on the regime.

To abbreviate, in contrast to the complete absence of the NPS union in the pensions field, several 'shareholder-style' umbrella organizations such as the KFMA and Health Rights Network (both of which are the product of the NCHIU in the late 1990s and early 2000s) remain as central actors, not only embracing other unions (e.g. KHMU) but also linking numerous civic associations in the health care field. This difference in the configurations of associational communities between pensions and health care must have contributed to the markedly different movement outcomes against neo-liberal reforms.

The health care solidarity network durably survived over time, even in the face of neo-liberal privatization attacks during the two conservative regimes. The attempts at privatization in the health care system were further intensified and took on a more refined form under the conservative Lee regime, and the SHR had to develop its own logics to critique those proposals and promulgate alternatives. The privatization forces filed lawsuits, lobbied conservative legislators and municipal governors to consider special laws on profit-oriented hospitals, and painted a rosy picture of the efficient market-oriented medical system that would follow from their plans. Most efforts to launch privatization, however, were blocked by the SHR's organized and coordinated demonstrations and public awareness campaigns. These successful defenses of universal welfare programs under the Lee regime (along with the defeat of labor law reform in 1996) exemplify the union dominance game in the bottom-left corner in Figure 6.4.

In the field of pensions, the 1997–98 universal reforms under the tripartite committee did not last long, and eventually led to the retrenchment of the pension scheme in 2007 under the Rho regime and then another retrenchment under the Park regime in the course of the introduction of the basic pension in 2014. During the second reformist regime, under President Rho Mu-hyun, there was no solidarity network between unions and civil society associations (no embeddedness), and so the pension plan introduced earlier was vulnerable to modification efforts in the replacement rate (from 60 percent to 40 percent) that enabled market forces to take over the expanded room for intervention. The KCTU did not have a member union that could operate as a leading force, such as the RHCS Union in health care, nor did they develop a serious expertise unit in pensions at the national center or within the industrial unions. As the KCTU national center's embeddedness and cohesiveness waned in the 2000s due to its internal divisions and its loosening relationships with key civic associations and the incumbent reformist party, the neoliberal advocates (advocates of 'sound budget') in the government and incumbent party were able to accomplish the retrenchment/privatization projects without much difficulty.

The retrenchment of the pensions system from 1997 to 2007, therefore, can be illustrated as a move from the lower-right corner (standard assurance game) to the upper-right corner (unilateral state dominance game) or even to the upper-left corner in Figure 6.4. At first glance, the move is due to the weakening or lack of union embeddedness, represented by the loosened solidarity between the KCTU and the PSPD, but the more important underlying factor and implication is that policy-related embeddedness cannot be sustained over time without mobilization-related embeddedness. While the two organizations (KCTU and PSPD) collaborated "symbolically" (Ŭn 2005a) at the central administration level, they rarely developed deeper collaborative ties by, for instance, sharing organizational resources either with each other or with other civic or popular-sector associations, which is in stark contrast to the durable embeddedness of the KHMU within the SHR in terms of both policy and mobilization capacities.

The indifference among the KCTU grassroots to the expansion or retrenchment of the National Pension prevented 'civic coordination' from evolving to defend against neo-liberal market reforms of the pension system. Because the KCTU did not have strong cohesive ties to the incumbent Rho regime in the 2000s, it could even be moved to the upper-left cell in Figure 6.4, where unions have neither cohesiveness nor embeddedness. With the lack of both embeddedness and cohesiveness, the Rho regime was dominated by 'budgetary conservatives' composed of economists and bureaucrats from the Ministry of Finance, representing the interests of private insurance companies such as Samsung and Hyundai, which led to the radical retrenchment in pensions. In short, the pensions case shows that, without embeddedness, the existence of cohesiveness may not hold firmly against neo-liberal privatization forces. Such cohesiveness could become a pure conflict game, or else result in non-resistance and impotence among anti-privatization movement forces.

In summary, the case of retrenchment in the National Pension supports the theoretical argument advanced earlier (in Chapter 3) that unions isolated from both the state and civil society (low cohesiveness and low embeddedness) will be unable to defend their core rights (labor market institutions) and assets (wage and social benefits). However, the FKTU's silence regarding the Rho regime's cutbacks of the National Pension and labor market regulations greatly fits with the upper-right cell (state dominance game), supporting the argument that unions disconnected from civil society but well connected with the incumbent party may be exploited by the state. Without their embedded ties to civil society, unions will acquiesce even to severe market reforms by the state. Unions with durable solidarity with civic associations but without direct lobbying channels to the state may moderate the state's retrenchment drive, as unions may be able to punish the state with their strong mobilization capacity. The state may withdraw their initial retrenchment efforts by making concessions or even by abandoning privatization in advance. The halted efforts of privatization in the health care system under the Rho regime could be interpreted as a case of high embeddedness and moderate (to high) cohesiveness, in which unions with both strong mobilization-wise embeddedness and fairly well-developed communication channels with the state effectively coordinate their actions with the state for a 'moderate reform and restraint' solution.

Overall, the politics of labor–civic solidarity during the market-oriented reform era of the 2000s reveal distinct stories across various policy domains and different layers of union organization. First, the KCTU national center dramatically lost both embedded and cohesive ties after the tripartite committee in 1998, and, throughout the 2000s, it continued to decline with respect to its influence on civil and political organizations. As a result, the KCTU failed to defeat the retrenchment of the National Pension and other key labor market regulations. However, at the lower levels of union organization, labor–civic solidarity operated effectively in defending existing social policies. The industrial union for health and medicine workers (the KHMU) provided both policy and mobilization capacity for a long-lasting solidarity network between unions and civic associations (the HRN and SHR), thereby successfully defending the core elements of the National Health Insurance program against the coordinated attempts of conservative regimes to advance privatization.

The politics of retrenchment in South Korea in the 2000s and after provides rich stories of labor–civic solidarity and its consequences. Their markedly different trajectory across two policy fields, health care and pensions, conveys an important lesson to students of the welfare state, by posing an important challenge to what previous welfare state scholarship had taken for granted: first, what matters in defending an existing social policy institution is not simply the power of unions or leftist parties, as conventional power resource theory predicts (Huber and Stephens 2001; Korpi and Palme 2003), but how unions are embedded in an issue-based, historically constituted, civic community. Moreover, cohesive ties, in the form of either social democratic cohesiveness or cohesiveness with the state, are neither an effective nor a reliable tool to defend existing social policies from market-oriented reform pressure, in sharp contrast to the prediction of power resource theory. Second, it may not be policies themselves that shape relevant advocacy groups (Pierson 1996; Skocpol 1992), at least during the early phase of policy-making and consolidation. The real story may be that social movement forces that once crafted a specific social policy through their policy and mobilization capacities eventually institutionalize themselves around the same policy, and then continue to defend it within and outside the state. Furthermore, the presence of this social movement force is critical for the survival of a social policy during its early phase, when it is vulnerable to retrenchment pressure.

Power resource theory has some validity in the South Korean case, as the most generous and universal policy expansion occurred in 1997–98, when unions reached a peak point in their mobilization capacity, as discussed in the previous chapter. Even without a leftist party, Kim Dae-jung's reform-oriented centrist party was an appropriate agent to pass universal reforms in pensions and health care, thanks to the bargaining power of the KCTU. However, under the (same reformist) Rho regime in the 2000s, conventional power resource theory cannot account for two sharply contrasting outcomes of retrenchment in two policy fields. In particular, the two contrasting outcomes of retrenchment politics occurred after the impeached president had returned with the incumbent reformist party (the Open Uri Party, which became shortly spilt from DP) and a newly emerging DLP in congress until 2007, and the conservative party (GNP) had returned to the power, also with a majority in congress since 2008. I propose that it is the presence or absence of labor–civic solidarity, especially unions' embeddedness in associational community that explains the two contrasting outcomes within the same political environment. Especially, the organic combination of unions' capacities for threats/punishment through their mobilization capacities and professionals' policy knowledge networks created a highly effective 'consortium organization' that coordinated different interests among participants and lobbied different political parties and the state with a unified voice.

This challenge to power resource theory naturally leads to the second point challenging the state-centric approach. Participant organizations in the consortium were deeply embedded in the health care field, grassroots communities, patient groups, and professional societies through their historical participation in the integration movement of health care societies during the democratization era. Therefore, once the integration movement generated a successful outcome – the passage of universal health care for all citizens – it quickly turned into a guardian organization of its own product. The biggest difference between the fate of National Health Insurance and that of the National Pension was again the presence of a guardian force in civil society: the KHMU, as a member of SHR, played a significant role in defending the original structure against attempts to privatize health care by both reformist and conservative regimes, but the NPS did not succeed – even under the reformist regime. If one observes only the period after 2007, one may claim that one policy created its own constituency to defend itself, while the other did not. However, a true story is that one policy field was born from a labor–civic solidarity that had historically evolved along democratization movements and the birth of civil society, while the other was not. In short, it is social movements that shape policies and their advocates, rather than policies that shape their own constituents – at least for the early phase of social policy-making. Therefore, Pierson's 'new politics' thesis (1996) during the retrenchment era at least exaggerates the role of new social groups and expanded state capacities (Skocpol 1992, p. 58) created by social programs, while unduly discounting the roles of "social movements and labor organizations that expanded social programs in the first place" (p. 147). Power resource theory may put too much emphasis on partisan politics by attributing the role of social coordination to political parties (Korpi and Palme 2003), as Pierson asserts, but state-centric theory and the 'new politics' thesis put too much emphasis on the discontinuity between old bearers of a social policy and a newly created constituency of the policy. In the South Korean case, at least for the last three decades of the politics of expansion and retrenchment, the same SMOs that achieved universal health care remained influential defenders of their own policy, and have kept reinventing movement strategies and constituents to protect universal health care. The EC approach claims to study historically emerging agents of civil society through social movements to find the source of 'social coordination' to build an encompassing solidarity rather than focusing on parties, employers, or policy (the state) itself.

PART III

7

Market-Oriented Reforms of the Welfare State and Union Responses in Brazil and Argentina

The neo-liberal welfare state reforms initiated by the state and employers in the 1990s in Latin America and the 2000s in East Asia presented new challenges for labor leaders and leftist/center-left reformist politicians. The integration of global financial and production markets generated new realities in developing countries. Employers were able to threaten unions with the option to move to countries providing cheaper labor and with little or no union power. Governments, in their race to the bottom, also kept persuading unions to relinquish their prerogatives hard-won through several decades of struggle. Inside workplaces, employers were eager to introduce more flexible manufacturing systems in terms of pay scales and incentives, work hours, and work organizations. Outside the assembly line, employers and the state sought not only to curb generous social benefits but also to partially or wholly privatize social safety-net programs such as pensions and health care.

Facing these unprecedented pressures, union leaders in democratized developing countries have witnessed the continuous waning of their existing organizational resources built through struggles for democratization, and have faced difficulties cultivating new resources in increasingly heterogeneous organizational communities. With the advent of democratization, however, union leaders also increased their access to political influence and so were able to express their concerns in policy-making processes. In short, the sources of their cohesiveness and embeddedness were continuously changing. Leaders had to adapt their organizations to complex, changing environments, on one hand, while, on the other, preserving internal union coherence and coordination, an increasingly fragile task due to newly introduced union democracy.

In these circumstances, why do some unions cooperate with or remain silent about market-oriented reforms of the public sector and of
social policies, while others remain militantly opposed? What accounts
for these wide variations in union–state relationships? This and the
next chapters examine these longstanding questions by investigating, in
four recently democratized countries that underwent extensive market
reforms,[1] how major labor union confederations formulated their organizational strategies alongside a changing broader civil society landscape.
Based on the theoretical models I developed earlier (in Chapter 3), in
which union linkages with the state and civil society determine preference
ordering for each actor and so their eventual actions, this chapter investigates why unions (more specifically, union confederations) cooperate
with or militantly oppose the state given pressure for market-oriented
reforms. With these two concepts of solidaristic linkages – cohesiveness
(unions' ties to incumbent political parties) and embeddedness (unions'
ties to civil society) – I empirically apply the models of Chapter 3 to the
behaviors of major union confederations facing market reforms in four
country cases (Argentina, Brazil, South Korea, and Taiwan) in the current
and next chapters.

The two Latin American countries entered the 1990s with deep economic crises, which arrived in these two countries just after democratization movements led by both labor unions and popular-sector associations
became well consolidated. Both countries suffered serious debt and currency crises accompanied by unprecedented levels of inflation, which
went above 2000 percent in 1990. The crises led neo-liberal economists
to introduce stabilization plans in 1990 in Argentina and in 1994 in
Brazil, which subsequently opened the way for market-oriented reforms
in public sector firms and social policies, as international agencies such
as the IMF and the World Bank (emerging from a Washington consensus)
recommended. However, under these common grounds, unions and civil
society in these countries responded to market reform pressures in stunningly different ways: Brazilian unions, primarily led by the CUT, drew
moderate reforms and concession packages from the centrist government,
while Argentine unions, under the Peronist government, remained silent
about radical privatization and retrenchment in social policies. What
accounts for these markedly different reactions by unions and different
policy outcomes implemented by the state?

In the 2000s, in both countries, leftist governments enjoyed decade-
long incumbencies with impressive expansions of the welfare state. While,
in Argentina, the Kirchners re-nationalized privatized pension funds, in

Brazil, the PT leaders Luis Ignácio da Silva and Dilma Rousseff dramatically expanded several (conditional) cash transfer programs for children and poor elderly citizens, but failed to make necessary adjustments to public pensions due to the strong resistance of labor–civic solidarity. How did unions contribute to such expansionary reforms and what kinds of social policy regimes were created as a result of the state–union interactions in these two countries? What roles did labor–civic solidarity play in Argentina and Brazil during the tumultuous retrenchment and expansion periods, and how did different forms of labor–civic solidarity emerge in these countries?

BRAZIL: THE DEVELOPMENT OF STATE–UNION COORDINATION

This section explores how Brazilian unions responded to the state's reforms contingent upon their ties to the incumbent party and civil society during two political periods: (1) the presidency of Fernando Henrique Cardoso (1995–2002),and (2) the regime of Luis Ignácio da Silva (2003–11) and his successor Dilma Rousseff (2011–present). Before I delve into the 1990s and after, it is worthwhile to visit the earlier authoritarian and democratization periods during the 1970s and 1980s, in order to highlight the unique origin of Brazilian labor–civic solidarity.

With the onset of democratization in Brazil in the 1980s, new independent labor movements emerged from the popular sector. During the *abertura* (political opening) period, the major union central organizations – Central Única dos Trabalhadores (CUT) in 1983, Central Geral dos Trabalhadores (CGT) in 1986, and the Força Sindical (FS) 1991 – were formed with diverse origins and social backgrounds. While the CUT was deeply embedded in the oppositional popular sector (civil society) along with the Workers' Party (PT) and the Landless Workers' Movement (MST) in the ABC region of São Paulo, the other two unions were more closely involved in centrist parties such as the PMDB (the Party of the Brazilian Democratic Movement) and the PSDB (the Brazilian Social Democracy Party), with weak engagement with other civil society groups. The biggest difference between the Brazilian labor movement and the others in our study is that Brazilian union organizations both worked autonomously from each other and forged coalitions for national protests, assemblies, and days of commemoration during the *abertura*, thereby developing a high level of coordination among themselves as well as with other civil society actors. Brazilian unions, especially their leftist wings led by the CUT, developed high levels of embeddedness in terms of both depth and width.

Their community origins enabled them to be engaged with informal civic associations from their founding onward, while their philosophy of seeking 'citizens' unions' allowed them to build a wide range of coalitions with diverse social movement organizations encompassing landless peasants and the urban poor. During the harsh authoritarian repression era, many intellectuals, peasant movement leaders, and labor leaders went underground to be engaged in clandestine organizational activities in local progressive churches. They were deeply influenced by liberation theology and reform-oriented priests. Before the CUT-PT alliance evolved, there existed "an ecclesiastical community that was very connected to the progressive Church":

> In 1977, I arrived in São Paulo and we could not demonstrate or meet, so the place where I lived ended up with soldiers going there, to know what we were doing, and there was a group of young people who met every Saturday at the end of the day to organize the Church youth, so my militancy was not in a political party, nor in the union – it was in the Church at that time.
>   (Adi dos Santos, the current president of the CUT-SP)
>
> I was inside the history of our re-democratization and actively participating in it. And the only place for reflection during the dictatorship was inside the church.
>   (Remigio Todeschini)

Labor leaders first evolved from this amalgamation of different social movements in Brazil during the authoritarian era.[2] Adi dos Santos, the current president of the CUT-SP, nicely summarizes how new labor leaders, along with popular classes consisting of peasants, neighborhood activists, and oppositional intellectuals, forged their social movement-based union activities: "We did the social work outside the factory, and within it, gave support to union actions." Rosane da Silva backs this up by saying, "It was not only activities at union headquarters, we did many things, and we went to the neighborhoods to talk to people." Eventually, Brazilian unions and civil society forces played critical roles in bringing down the military dictatorship in the mid- and late 1980s after the Diretas Já (the mass civil unrest in 1984 that demanded direct presidential elections). From the democratization movement, unions were aware of their role as a representative of the entire social class that "fight for other (unorganized) workers, not just for themselves"(Renato Zulato, the Director of Finance and Administration, the CUT-SP).

In alliance with community-oriented popular-sector movements and the MST,[3] the CUT first focused on traditional social-movement union organizing and strikes by workers in heavy manufacturing industries in the 1980s. The young (at the time) union leaders encouraged more direct confrontations, demonstrations, and strikes, while rejecting traditional, corporatistic state–union relationships. The new unionism of the 1980s saw more direct relationships being pursued between unions and labor-based parties, which facilitated the growth of the Workers' Party (the PT). In a sense, the CUT's high embeddedness reaches back to its social movement origins in the 1980s, as just discussed, but it also may be attributed to its continuing renovation of its idea of 'social class' as an encompassing, fluid solidaristic category by the creation of the idea of 'citizens' unions' under the leadership of Gilmar Carneiro.

What is a 'citizens' union'? It's a way of speaking about class struggle in a less aggressive way, so what are you? You're a woman, working hard to be a [good] mother, you need transportation, you want to study, you want a good salary, you're in certain working conditions, want to make a career, but at the same time, you have transit in the street, safety in the street, leisure – it goes to leisure, to family, right? So we started to see the worker not only as a job, salary, working conditions, and the worker's relation with the business, we started to see the worker [as one with] a choice in sexuality, as one with a certain color of skin, so this made … with the unions, it created a citizens' movement, the word 'citizenship' in this recent period.
(Paulo Salvador)

This interview suggests that new Brazilian union leaders (of CUT) have collectively overcome the old leftist idea of the centrality of the working class to embrace larger and broader concerns of citizens in which different social identities and interests can continuously emerge and form a new category of solidarity depending upon impending issues and conjunctures. The CUT leaders understood "the support of the social movements" as "the support from society in their struggles," which eventually would bring in "public agents transforming [society]" (Regina Costa). This social movement origin and its solidaristic and flexible idea of social class are two crucial differences between the CUT and the Argentine CGT (which will be discussed in the next section). Although both were deeply rooted in neighborhood-level informal linkages, the CUT deemed itself a part of a solidarity network with the larger popular sector, while the CGT limited itself to a Peronist patronage clique. In contrast to Argentine CGT leaders, the bulk of the CUT leaders expressed their support for solidarity vigorously when I asked, "how would you evaluate the efforts of CUT in building partnerships or linkages of solidarity with other civil society organizations, other unions, other centers, or political parties?"

The following answer by Renato Zulato was repeated over and over again by many other CUT leaders:

Well, the CUT has ... because we see ourselves not only as fighting in defense of workers but of society in general. So we have always sought to listen to central leadership, to hear opinions, and where there is consensus and points of convergence, we act together. And the CUT in political parties stands with the leftist parties. We have relations with the PT, PC do B Communist Party of Brazil]... and with social movements too. The housing movement, the health movement – we conduct activities together... we had events together with the people from the health movement fighting for maintenance and strengthening of the SUS [*Sistema Único de Saúde*, Unified Health System]. So these are areas that are on CUT's agenda, because we understand that our agenda is not only a union one, right? It's a mission that has to be in connection.

This flexible and more inclusive notion of 'class struggle' enabled many women union leaders to pursue their own agendas within the framework of the CUT. They highlighted women's rights within union movements by bringing minority identities into the central realm of union politics. They claimed that "a left-wing organization, a class entity, if it does not address issues of women, young people and blacks, it is making a false speech to workers ... women live in different conditions, so there is a need to think about social policies to end the discrimination that we are exposed to"(Rosane da Silva). The CUT base supported this 'women's' agenda with an approval of 90 percent. Furthermore, the CUT has recently approached labor issues as a broad human rights issue, which has resulted in the extension of its coalition partners to associations fighting against child labor and torture as well as associations fighting for the rights of people with disabilities, those in forced labor, and LGBT (Lesbian, Gay, Bisexual and Transgender) people. "We fight a lot for the constitutional right of people who are disadvantaged" (Expedito Solaney).

During the 1990s and the 2000s, Brazil's political elite sought to restructure market, labor, and trade institutions. The onset of democratization saw various kinds of protests and oppositional labor mobilization, including but not limited to strikes (Boito 1991; French 1992; Murillo 2001; Seidman 1994). In particular, among the three largest union movements (CUT, Força Sindical, and CGT), Força Sindical sought the most pragmatic relationship with the government.[4] A leader of Força Sindical distinguishes its position from other militant unions by saying that "the capital/work relation must happen through a partnership of compromise." José Gaspar, the current Executive Counselor of the

Força Sindical, succinctly distinguishes its pragmatic position (from that of the CUT) by saying that:

we developed a concept called "Unionism with Results," invented by Luiz Antonio Medeiros, that is, not pointless striking, but striking to get results, and not striking to overthrow the government, because at that time we were living through a democratic transition, in the Figueiredo government.

In general, the 1990s witnessed a more pragmatic tendency among Brazil's unions.[5] The unions turned their focus away from traditional forms of militancy – protests, strikes, and other forms of agitation – toward negotiations with the Cardoso government. Because Força Sindical was strongly connected to the PSDB of Cardoso, union leadership could more easily approach the Cardoso government (high cohesiveness). During this period the rank-and-file members and the leadership of all three central union organizations began to strategize with the state. Over time (in the 1990s and 2000s), the CUT became more pragmatic, creating further opportunities for their union leadership to enter the state at the local municipal levels. In this sense, both union organizations moved toward the center and approximated the values and approaches of one another. In the 1990s, the majority faction of the CUT also approved a sweeping negotiation plan with the Carodoso government and organized a calendar for mobilization, which set the tone for its strategic approach to the government for the decade to come (CUT 2003a).

However, despite these pragmatic moves, Brazilian unions, especially the CUT, exhibited strong, militant resistance to the Cardoso regime's neo-liberal reforms. The national Strike for the Maintenance of Rights, held June 21, 1996, signaled a critically important collaboration among the CUT, the CGT, and the FS against the neo-liberal politics of President Fernando Henrique Cardoso. Their demands included access to work, decent salaries, retirement, agrarian reform, and the maintenance of worker's rights. Nearly 12 million workers went on strike in Brazil. These unions' politically oriented militant reactions to state repression demonstrate not only the strong mobilization capacity of Brazil's unions but also their high level of embeddedness in civil society. To resist the Cardoso regime's neo-liberal reforms, the CUT organized wide ranging labor–civic solidarity consisting of the MST, the UNE (National Union of Students), opposition political parties, other civic associations, and other union confederations. For example, in 1998, the CUT, along with the CGT and several opposition parties, organized large-scale demonstrations against pension reform being considered in the House of Representatives.

These waves of general strikes and demonstrations between 1995 and 1998 discouraged the Cardoso government from pursuing the radical privatization of public services and social policy institutions. The final bill introduced only minor modifications to the existing pension programs, while preserving the old schemes for teachers and public employees. The Cardoso government's gradual efforts to withdraw from initial retrenchment reforms approximates game 3 in Appendix C.1, embeddedness without cohesiveness. However, in general, unions and the state also became more intertwined with one another, which may suggest that the Brazilian state–union relationship was already shifting from high embeddedness/low cohesiveness to high embeddedness/medium cohesiveness during the mid- to late 1990s. This shift began at the local municipal level with participatory governance movements. In 1995, in the ABC region, leaders of 17 unions organized the Forum of Citizenship (Fórum da Cidadania) with mayors of municipal governments, businessmen, and religious youth groups ("the Pastoral Worker and Youth," which is linked to the Catholic Church). Composed of more than 100 organizational entities, the forum questioned the neo-liberal economic policies of the Cardoso regime and established a negotiation committee (Memoria dos Metalurgicos do ABC). In 1998, the president of the metallurgists' union, Luiz Marinho; the Minister of the Supreme Federal Court, Sepúlveda Pertence; the attorney Márcio Thomas Bastos, former president of the Order of the Lawyers of Brazil; and Vicente Paulo da Silva, president of CUT at the national level, all gathered together at the CUT office to discuss the theme of 'justice and citizenship.' Meetings such as these opened dialogue and interaction between the unions and the state even under Cardoso. During this period, the teachers' union had already developed "a particularly influential lobbying force" (Huber and Stephens 2012, p. 171). By the end of the 1990s, nearly all of Brazil's union confederations were building different degrees and repertoires of cohesive relationships with the state.

The primary difference between the CUT and the Força Sindical was that while the former utilized cohesive lobbying ties on the basis of strong, embedded mobilization capacity, the latter primarily relied on its cohesive ties with the government. Therefore, it was the CUT that spearheaded negotiations with the Cardoso regime in the 1990s and eventually gained concessions from the government, and these tendencies persisted during the subsequent PT regimes.

During the early years of the da Silva (2003–11) administration, the government initiated substantial economic reforms in terms of both general social policy and, more specifically, extension of welfare state options for the public. The Lula 2000s brought further reforms, most notably the legalization of central unions. During this period, the main Brazilian union confederations, deploying their mobilization and lobbying capacities, had great influence on the presidential electoral fortunes of both Luis Ignácio da Silva and his successor Dilma Rousseff (Boito and Marcelino 2011). Trade union confederations obtained greater levels of dialogue, easier entry, and expanded permanence in national politics, while also maintaining their room for contestation, protests, and strikes directed against the reforms of the federal government. Under several factors favorable to the labor movement (including a return to economic growth, an expansion of available jobs, the implementation of democracy, and the decline in neo-liberalism indicated by the new left-wing and center-left governments in Latin America; Marcelino 2008), increased PT incumbency at the local municipal levels and Lula's presidency at the national level provided labor with an unprecedented level of embedded cohesiveness. Union leaders, closely linked to neighborhood and community political groups, also became deeply involved in the policy-making and implementation process through participatory governance movements. The CUT's most important achievement under the Lula regime was its success in passing the minimum wage law through its constant negotiations with the regime. It "has been a bone in the throat for Brazilian bourgeois and a great victory for workers, as the minimum wage increased by 76 percent from the Lula to the Dilma regime" (Julio Turra, the current executive director of the CUT).[6] Such an achievement was possible not only because the Lula government opened the door for discussion and negotiation, but also because the CUT headquarters had a strong policy capacity, underpinned by the active participation of its policy experts in DIEESE (Departamento Intersindical de Estatística e Estudos Socioeconômicos; Inter-Union Department of Statistics and Socioeconomic Studies) in the negotiation process.

I will say that now the union movement has a space – I don't know if it existed before, but it does now, and DIEESE is serving as a shield to support and subsidize the union movement, as well as other institutional actors.

(Leandro Horie, technical board of DIEESE)

Regarding units of data analysis, legal advice, and political training:

We [industrial unions] can use DIEESE as an analyst of more economical and political [matters], right? … We also have DIAP, which is the Intersyndical Parliamentary Studies Department … This [consulting DIEESE] is very common [in union activities].

(Regina Costa)

In short, DIEESE was created to provide policy-related expert advice to industrial unions as well as confederations. "It was just an institute in São Paulo that researched 'prices',"(Regina Costa) but it later evolved as an impartial, inter-union policy institute that provided educational training as well as economic and political policy-related advice and consulting to union centers regardless of their political positions. It also created a 'work-science' faculty within the institute, which provide educational degree programs to union leaders. Several union leaders whom I interviewed either had finished or were attending the program. Today, DIEESE has technical experts with different political views from center-left to center-right, and therefore function as a 'unions' academy' in which different points of views on union and social policies are discussed, debated, and coordinated: "DIEESE is a school for the chief to learn how to live with differences"(João Cayres).

In brief, the Brazilian CUT (and Força Sindical in the 2000s) fit squarely into the medium to high cohesiveness/high embeddedness model. As shown above, the unions readily mobilized against unfavorable conditions and state policies during the 1980s and part of the 1990s, exemplifying a typical strong embeddedness. Additionally, union leaders were also able to carve out spaces within the government through participation in political office in the 1990s and the 2000s, increasing their cohesive linkages with the state. Beginning with the Cardoso presidency and carried through the Lula presidency to the Rousseff regime, the state and labor increasingly established close communication channels.[7] Such institutions have permitted expanded dialogue between both parties, enabling coordination for moderate market reforms.

Simultaneously, however, Brazil's embedded unions have not simply followed the restraint requests of the PT government, but have rather staunchly maintained their autonomy and voice (including potential militancy) on behalf of the rights of working classes, such that they could continue to exert influence on the state's social and labor market policies while maintaining a credible level of threat. Clemente Ganz, the director of DIEESE, supports this assessment, saying:

CUT did some strong movements at the time of privatization during Fernando Henrique Cardoso], and protested against the government of Dilma [Rousseff]. Despite the fact that they supported the election of Dilma, it organized national level protests and mobilizations against Leilão de Libra [Auctions of Brazil's petroleum mines in 2013]. So it protested against a policy of a government that it helped elect ... [Also, they] protested against the government of Fernando Henrique, who they did not support.

The other important leader of the CUT also testifies, "Autonomy has been always maintained. CUT has done strikes against the PT government several times, the strike of Banco do Brasil, for example"(Gilmar Carneiro, former secretary-general of CUT, leader of Bankers' Union). Another leader of the CUT summarizes the relationship between the CUT and the PT as follows:

Maybe it [independence of the CUT from the PT] was not so explicit in the '80s, or even in the '90s, but now as the PT took over power, it becomes more obvious that the union center [CUT] has an independence of the PT. I think that, in the 1980s and the 1990s, as the party led the opposition, a lot of people in common [across the two organizations], being mixed up [in their roles] … But since the party took over power, this [independence] has been made more explicit. The party does not run our center, it does not dictate who will be the president or influence the administration of the center.

For instance, the CUT initially resisted the pension reforms proposed by the Lula regime in 2003, mobilizing mass protests in June of that year, including nearly 70,000 protestors in Brasilia. The demonstration was supported even by some public sector unions, as well as civil society associations not formerly linked closely to the CUT – the National Union of Internal Revenue Service and National Association of Tax Auditors.[8] In 2008, the CUT also resisted the government's plan to increase the retirement age.

Under the Dilma regime, which did not have such a close relationship with unions compared to its predecessor the Lula regime, unions and their allies adamantly protested against the government's pension reform bill, which aimed to increase the minimum length of contribution. Under the new rule, those who were newly entering the job market would have to contribute about 12 more years than current retirees (SINDUSP 2012). Although the majority of the CUT supported the reform (CUT 2013), a more radical leftist wing of the CUT ("CUT Pode Mais"; CUT Can Do More), in alliance with other unions and civic associations, marched against the reform project.[9] As a consequence, the Dilma regime decided not to pursue pension reform further. Public sector workers, for the most part, secured their previous rights and replacement rates.

In all, the embedded cohesiveness of labor unions under the Lula and Dilma regimes did not necessarily mean just peaceful coordination but allowed for a full range of threats, demonstrations, and negotiations (especially under Dilma). It is important to note, however, that threats rarely led to full-blown general strikes as under the Cardoso regime. Rather, they were accompanied by continuous conversation and restraint.

Therefore, in Brazil, Chilean- or Argentine-style sweeping radical reforms of the public sector never occurred. Instead, the government implemented modest adjustments to excessive privileges through careful negotiations.

It is difficult to discuss Argentine labor politics without referring to Peronism, as Peronist ideology deeply penetrated into early union movements and its influence is still lingering today (James 1988; Levitsky 2003b; McGuire 1997). Unions were deeply involved in the creation of Peronism from 1945 to 1983 and, as Carlos Holobica, a Peronist government official, recalls, "labor unions were responsible for keeping Peronism alive ... as the institutional Peronism." Both union leaders and grassroots union members have been deeply "committed to the popular essence of the Peronist ideology."[10] During the era of harsh repression by military dictatorship, unions and their informal soccer clubs were clandestine informal 'guilds' in which Peronists hid and solidified their organizational networks. Roberto Digón, a former union leader and a congressman of the PJ, explains Perionist intellectuals' choice of the time as follows:

I wasn't planning on being a trade union leader, I just wanted to be a youth leader, a political leader, but, well ... since we couldn't express ourselves and we were politically banned, I think many of us affiliated to trade unions to express our ideas ... We didn't want to use the name CGT, '62,' because of the detained colleagues. So we worked and set it ['25': a Peronist union faction which is distinct from '62') up province by province, event by event, and we did very well in the rest of the country because people participated a lot, they were scared, sure, because everyone was scared ... in 1980 ... we could see the dictatorship was increasingly weaker... and then we just confirmed it with the strikes we started to make in 1981 and the protest of March 30 in 1982.

Oraldo Britos recalls the routines of the time as follows:

The routine involved secret meetings at night that rotated among various locations, with the lights off, so only the puffs of smoke from our cigarettes could be seen. Nine or ten local union leaders helped to normalize or standardize the CGT after a soccer tournament featuring teams from local unions.

In a sense, Peronist political movements were deeply embedded in unions, which were also deeply embedded in soccer clubs. In such clandestine cliques, Peronists built their daily, micro-level, historical roots of 'clientelism' in which Peronist political leaders, union members, and local communities exchange social benefits and political support. One renowned union leader who became a congressional representative (of the PJ) succinctly summarizes the relationship:

Peronism is to help the patient, the one who needs the medication, and to be in what is called 'fundamental' 'social' and 'daily'... Peronism is your companion. Peronism is the interest of the other, it is the interest of sharing and integrating with the companion ... Peronism is the people, the humble, the poor, the worker, the school, the first aid, the plaza ... organized community ... That relationship should be permanent.

In other words, this deeply ingrained historical trust relationship between unions and the PJ emerged in the middle of the twentieth century with Peron, became solidified as personal, emotional, and material attachment to the local poor by solving their livelihood issues (Auyero 1999, 2000). These historically institutionalized Peronist networks played different roles in state–society relations and transformation of the public sector in the 1990s and the 2000s. They engendered both the strongest cohesiveness without embeddedness in terms of scope, and the strongest "clique-based embeddedness" (Lee 2016) in terms of depth. The former represents the durable corporatistic alliance between the PJ and the majority of the CGT, which enabled the PJ to launch one of the most radical market reforms. The latter enabled the PJ to sustain its local patronage networks during the market-oriented reforms. However, some radical Peronists' deep attachment to the working class also produced a new labor movement centering upon labor–civic solidarity, if minor in its size and influence.

The recent history of Argentine state-initiated market reforms of public sector and social policies, as well as the union responses to these efforts, can be divided into two broad periods: first, controlled conflict between the state and major segments of organized labor while Carlos Menem's government pursued market reforms during the 1990s, followed by economic crisis and mass protest at the turn of the century, and, second, the resurgence of strong public sector involvement and the reversal of some market reforms under the governments of Néstor Kirchner and Cristina Fernández de Kirchner during the 2000s, accompanied by new forms of engagement between labor and the state.

President Carlos Menem's radical neo-liberal reform of the public sector and social welfare programs, especially pensions, in the 1990s, along with a striking transformation of the PJ, led to immediate political and electoral success with huge controversy. Menem's reform strategy fundamentally transformed the Argentine economy from a protected market with a large public sector to a more market-oriented open economy. Menem and the PJ's neo-liberal reform projects of the public sector were all the more striking because the PJ was a representative left-wing, labor-based party that had played a central role in creating modern Argentina's relatively generous welfare programs (Brooks 2008; Levitsky 2003a).[11] After a period of economic crisis under the de la Rua administration (1999–2001), however, the PJ returned to power with Néstor Kirchner, a little known leftist Peronist from the Santa Cruz province. The Kirchners introduced extensive social policy reforms and labor reforms, not only revamping the PJ's traditional strongholds (the urban poor and organized labor), but also drawing in the unemployed and new social movements around their platforms. They renegotiated with the IMF for more favorable debt terms, renationalized partially privatized pensions, cancelled flexible labor market measures (such as lay-offs), recentralized wage-bargaining institutions, and achieved budget surplus during their first term (2003–07). Such labor-friendly policies were accompanied by relatively high inflation (Etchemendy and Garay 2011) and lingering debt crises. How was it possible that these completely different reform initiatives came from the same PJ party? How did unions and civil society respond to Menem's market reforms, and then contribute to the emergence of the Kirchners?

In response to Menem's market-oriented reforms, organized labor developed different patterns of relationships with the state and civil society. Initially, many union leaders did not recognize the devastating impacts of privatization on their own organizations and lives, or a significant number of them were too deeply committed to the PJ to criticize Menem's radical market reforms. Many of them did not change their positions until discontented grassroots members deserted unions that were deeply connected to the PJ. A Peronist government official interprets the union leaders' acquiescence of the time as follows:

I tell you, for example, just to name a case, the Railway Union … It had almost 100,000 affiliates before Menem's period. They became 5,000 [after Menem]. I can't believe [the leader] knew this was going to happen. I think that he believed something different, and when he realized it, it was too late to get out. I think the same thing happened in other cases [of union politics], but a significant number were too committed to a policy that was against their interests.

The unexpected conformism of Argentinian union leaders during the Menem era is in sharp contrast to Brazilian unions' more militant responses to the government's (even moderate) market reform moves. Most of them thought that, "as there was a Peronist government, they have to be the guarantors of its policy before the people"(a dissident union leader against the CGT).

The two main tendencies are represented by two union confederations, the CGT (Confederación General de Trabajo) and the CTA (Central de los Trabajadores Argentinos), each with a distinct philosophy of state–society relations. The CGT has been the major union confederation in the country for more than half a century, with roots going back to the formative alliance between Peronism and the working classes. It represents the cohesiveness without embeddedness of Argentine labor movements, as I described earlier. It has its own internal (but closed) informal social networks consisting of numerous Peronist soccer clubs and neighborhood organizations. As Argentina has much weaker civil society (Lee 2007, 2012) than its Latin American counterpart Brazil, the CGT's solidaristic ties with other civic associations have been relatively sparse.[12]

Even if smaller in scope and relatively recent, the second tendency, the emergence of the CTA, began to develop in 1991 when a group of unions disaffiliated from the CGT to form the CTA. The newly-formed CTA criticized the CGT's conciliatory stance over neo-liberal reforms under Menem, as well as the CGT's privileging of core sector workers. The CTA established itself as a formal alternative labor confederation in 1997, one characterized by a stronger stance for social solidarity.

The CGT has historically maintained close ties with the Peronist Justicialist Party and its party machine,[13] with union leaders often occupying posts within the party structure and the state (Godio 1987), thereby building durable cohesiveness between unions and the state. Under Menem's government, however, the CGT found itself in a difficult position. Even though Menem had run on a populist platform, garnering support from labor, once elected he began to implement comprehensive market-oriented reforms, reforms that would weaken both labor and social policies. Menem's shift was not entirely unexpected given the macroeconomic context, fears of hyperinflation, and his background as one of the *renovadores* in the PJ party, a group of individuals calling for a re-examination of unions' historically powerful role in shaping the party agenda (see, e.g., Gordillo *et al.* 1987). Nonetheless, it dealt a major political blow to organized labor. His harsh austerity and aggressive retrenchment drives led to deep liberalization of the Argentine economy, including radical privatization and the shrinking of the public sector. Widespread lay-offs following the privatization of public enterprises and the government's hostile stance toward labor protections further weakened the labor movement.

The CGT initially divided into three factions, with CGT San Martín maintaining official support for Menem, CGT Azopardo forming the opposition, and a third group remaining independent (Murillo 2000). Despite the occurrence of sector-specific strikes and episodic mobilization in various parts of the country, more than three years of Menem's term in office went by before CGT leaders held their first general strike in November 1992. When the strike was held, it focused primarily on wages, was not supported by pro-Menem CGT factions, and received little attention from the government. In 1992 the CGT reunified, yet the previous events had been divisive and the public sector and teachers' unions – unions that formed the core of the opposition to Menem – set off to create an alternate confederation. When the oppositional unions organized general strikes in August 1994, the mainstream CGT did not participate. The CGT limited its general strike activity, especially during Menem's first term in office. The arrangement represents an excellent example of retrenchment game 2 (in Chapter 3), with high cohesiveness with the state administration and low embeddedness in civil society. Without strong ties to civil society actors, the mainstream CGT remained loyal to its traditional political partners, at least in the short term, and so tolerated radical, pro-market reforms.[14]

Yet with changes in the labor landscape under Menem, labor's strategies and identities shifted. One group, the MTA (Movimiento de los Trabajadores Argentinos), favored combining disruptive politics with negotiation, while retaining ties to the CGT and striving to change the direction of the confederation. The CTA, comprised of the dissident unions that split off from the CGT after pursuing an oppositional strategy, built their agenda around issues like unemployment and economic reforms, critiquing the neo-liberal economic model and advocating strengthening the public sector. This round of labor fragmentation led to the creation of an alternative confederation with a different orientation toward civil society, an expanded repertoire of contentious actions, and an explicit goal of increased autonomy from the state, business, and political parties (Arellano and De Gennaro 2002; Rauber 1997). One of the founders of the CTA describes why and how he and his group had to depart from the CGT:

The traitor was Menem, but ... the CGT was subordinate to the government ... all leaders [of the CGT] said that as there was a Peronist government, [they] would be the guarantors of what people want ... but it was the opposite: leaders have to defend people against the government, wherever one has voted ... We began to convene a Workers' Congress, we are not the CGT ... we toured the country and made a Labor Congress.

This stance reflects some union leaders' different preferences, seeking embeddedness over cohesiveness when facing radical market reforms. For them, "it is the government that should be 'guarantor' of what people wanted and leaders [of unions] must defend the people against the government" (one of the CTA founders). In Burgess' loyalty dilemma (2004), the CTA leaders chose to defend the interests of grassroots union members and wider civil society over their political allies.

In the mid-1990s, leading up to and following Menem's re-election, there was a momentary shift in labor politics, representing a weakening of the high cohesiveness/low embeddedness model. In 1994, the CTA and the MTA – supported by the leftist CCC (Corriente Clasista y Combativa), retirees' organizations, and social movement groups – organized a federal protest (the Marcha Federal) during which thousands of people converged on the capital from around the country to criticize Menem's economic model. After the government introduced initiatives to implement labor flexibilization, the CGT, CTA, and MTA came together for major nationwide general strikes in August, September, and December of 1996. They mounted a major challenge to Menem's policies despite the prohibition of strike activity in the capital and a heavy police presence in other parts of the country. This time, the government responded with restraint and some CGT labor leaders acquired a seat at the table to negotiate the course of labor flexibilization. The majority of the oppositional groups in the CTA and MTA, however, remained mobilized and continued to strike, distancing themselves once again from the CGT and organizing a national march for employment in 1997 and further instances of mobilization throughout the late 1990s.

The CTA more closely represents retrenchment game 3 (in Chapter 3), with low cohesiveness and high embeddedness. This group of unions, composed of a core base of public sector employees and teachers and closely associated with Catholic-based leftist priests and intellectuals, set off to construct an alternative identity for organized labor. They favored a more confrontational strategy or combining mobilization with other strategies, which is very similar to the approach of Brazilian CUT.[15] They even briefly considered allying with opposition party candidates because of strained ties with the Justicialist Party during Menem's government, but largely abandoned such efforts, identifying as *peronistas* but not *menemistas*. To strengthen its membership base, the CTA allowed individual members to affiliate and included non-union civil society groups within its organizational structure, which greatly increased its embeddedness. During its general strikes, CTA leaders explicitly called for broader community involvement and social mobilization. One of its leaders clearly summarizes its community-linked unionism as follows:

> The factories in which we had much representation, meaning that within our jobs we had well-organized workers and the Union was strong and against privatization ... where a majority had the possibility to go discuss issues with the community. And if the community agreed and we were organized, the companies restrained [their privatization plans]. Where we were a minority or a community did not accompany us, meaning workers inside did not have to strengthen its power and the community did not accompany or the union was not committed [to the community], it was privatized.

As a result, the CTA managed to form broad-based coalitions, bringing unions together with feminist groups, informal-sector employees, and the unemployed. The confederation embraced the use of social movement tactics, as well as neighborhood associations and local institutions, to articulate its demands. For example, the teachers' unions within the CTA linked their particular demands to the universal demands for stronger public schools and the right to education, thereby generating public support at the community level. The CTA also has ties with the academic sector, research centers, and intellectuals (Palomino 2005, Rauber 1997). For instance, the CTA reached out to professional think tank communities such as FLACSO-Argentina (Latin American Faculty of Social Science in Argentina), providing them with financial support while receiving appropriate policy advice. The CTA also built close relationships with public universities, encouraging its members to receive further education and training. Furthermore, the CTA built close alliances with other civic associations, including human rights groups, immigrant groups, and indigenous groups, many of which were mobilized behind electing the Kirchners' FPV (Frente Para la Victoria; The Front for Victory)-PJ.[16]

Following Argentina's turn-of-the-century economic crisis, which was accompanied by unemployment, political instability, and social protest that once again involved a broader range of labor factions linked to civil society, Néstor Kirchner was elected on a neo-Peronist platform in 2003. His election marked a renewed era of strong alliances between organized labor and a reinvented Peronist Justicialist Party. During the run-up to the election, Kirchner was supported primarily by the CTA, the more leftist segment of the labor movement, and received only lukewarm support from the mainstream CGT. However, upon his election he sought to incorporate both the old and the new political actors who had emerged in 2001–02, connecting them to party structures and the state. During this period, the government also pushed through minimum wage increases, supported collective bargaining, and invested in public works, in addition to implementing social security reforms that extended access to informal-sector workers and the unemployed (Levitsky and Murillo 2008). Two policy changes in particular were monumental expansionary reforms that earned unions' support: first, the renationalization of private pension funds in 2008 by the Cristina Kirchner regime, and, second, the extension of non-contributory pensions to an additional 500,000 elderly people in 2003 (Huber and Stephens 2012, p. 188). The CTA actively participated in shaping these expansionary, universalist social policy reforms.[17] In this context, the CGT and CTA experienced some convergence in their relationships with the incumbent party, though not in their primary identities, strategies, and practices.

In sum, given the absence of radical market reforms, the relationship between organized labor and the state during the Kirchner period is dualistic over time. Initially, during the campaign, the Kirchners emerged with the social movement union, the CTA, forming typical embedded cohesiveness between the state and unions as well as between unions and civil society. However, having taken over power, they courted the CGT, and eventually rejuvenated the traditional PJ machine by providing unions and their leaders with labor-friendly policies and positions in the state. The incumbent PJ under the Kirchners, therefore, enjoyed relationships not only with corporatistic top-down partners backed up by the CGT but also with more resilient social movement-based partners, the CTA. Based on such cohesiveness (with the CGT) or embedded cohesiveness (with the CTA), the Kirchners were able to introduce bold expansionary social policy reforms in unemployment benefits, pensions, and family allowance policies.[18]

COMPARISON: THE PAST, CURRENT, AND FUTURE OF LABOR–CIVIC SOLIDARITY IN LATIN AMERICA

Two major unions in Brazil and Argentina, the CUT and the CGT respectively, faced similar market-oriented reform pressures, responded to them in markedly different ways, and drew widely different responses from the state. I traced back these unions' different engagement with society during the authoritarian eras, which later evolved into different relationships with their political allies. While the CUT, originating from community-oriented popular-sector social movements, formed durable alliances with peasants and other civic associations against the state, the CGT were content to remain in the Peronist clique, failing to reach out to non-Peronist social forces. The CUT's stance – autonomy from the state – was not limited to right-wing or centrist governments, but applied to its own creation, the PT incumbency. The Argentine CGT, however, tolerated Menem's market reforms, which resulted in grassroots unions' increasing grievance. Because of their different levels of embeddedness, the CUT was able to mobilize a much wider range of coalitions for its demonstrations in the 1990s compared to its Argentine counterpart, the CGT, thereby exerting greater pressure on the state. As a result, the CUT, even under the centrist Cardoso regime, was able to draw concessions from the state, while the CGT had to helplessly witness Menem's radical departure from its own social base.

To abbreviate, my model and case studies in this chapter demonstrate that union cohesiveness without corresponding embeddedness may encourage the state to take advantage of union–party solidarity, as illustrated in the CGT case. They also show that successful resistance to neo-liberal market reforms requires unions' strong embeddedness in civil society, as shown in the CUT case. While the Brazilian and Argenine cases in the 1990s offer intriguingly contrasting examples of state–union interactions in the era of market reforms, their stories in the 2000s provide a surprising convergence. Latin American leftists' takeover of state power drove countries in the region to jockey to introduce more generous social assistance programs for the poor. During this era, it may be an exaggeration to argue that such moves in both countries were solely promoted by labor–civic networks and their political representatives in power, but it is undeniable that the CUT and its broad civic alliance was essential for sending the PT and its leaders to the presidential office and the congress. Based on such cohesive ties, the CUT initiated bottom-up policy reform in the form of the minimum wage policy, for which the DIEESE, the inter-union policy think tank, played a decisive role. In Argentina, the CTA, if still meager in its size and influence, emerged as an alternative Peronist union both seeking negotiation and utilizing militancy against its state ally. The CUT and CTA examples demonstrate that, for unions to achieve an optimal outcome – moderate reform and restraint – they need institutional coordination mechanisms with the state beyond mere partisan linkages, backed by strong mobilizational ties to civil society. I defer an ultimate comparison of these two Latin American countries with two East Asian counterparts to the next chapter, which starts with a comparative analysis of South Korean and Taiwanese unions' responses to market reforms.

8

Market-Oriented Reforms of the Welfare State and Union Responses in Taiwan and South Korea

Market reforms arrived in East Asia during the mid-1990s. Although it appears that they were implemented mostly during or after the 1997 Asian Financial Crisis, South Korean and Taiwanese firms, which were competing in global markets, desired to introduce more flexible labor market institutions in the early to mid-1990s. These firms desired reforms such as irregular and indirect employment, dispatch, and easy lay-offs. In contrast to Latin American counterparts, however, the welfare states in both countries were under expansionary modes in the 1990s. Facing growing deindustrialization, aging populations, and increasing welfare demands from unions and civil society, both countries were unable to rely on firm-level provision of welfare and a traditional family support system. In both countries, expansionary social policy reforms emerged as one of the key electoral issues and political parties jockeyed to introduce more generous transfer programs to attract votes. As shown earlier in Figure 1.1, these two countries not only expanded major social insurance programs such as health care and pensions to (nearly) the entire population in the 1990s, but also introduced numerous assistance-oriented transfer programs such as basic (minimum) income, basic pensions, and child care subsidies, among others. As a result, social security expenditure skyrocketed in South Korea, if to a lesser degree in Taiwan.

Despite these expansions around transfer programs, the principles and ideologies of market reform started permeating deeply into state bureaucracies and political parties in both countries, as I discussed in Chapter 6. Market reform forces attempted to change the core parameters of social insurance systems by lowering replacement rates, introducing individualized accounts and partial privatization (for pensions). How did unions and their civil society allies respond to these varied retrenchment attempts in the two countries in the 1990s and the 2000s? How did union and civic leaders manage (or fail) to solidify their institutional engagement with the state and political parties? How did their historical institutionalization processes from the authoritarian era affect their responses to the state-driven market reforms in these two East Asian new democracies?

Labor movements in South Korea and Taiwan developed their organizational strengths primarily in the 1980s with increasingly militant strategies. In both countries, new labor leaders emerged from grassroots workplaces, independent of existing corporatist, docile unions, which had been created and sponsored by authoritarian states. However, their origins and early organizational forms differed as widely as those of their Latin American counterparts. In South Korea, thousands of student activists armored with revolutionary socialist ideologies, most of whom became radicalized after the massacre of citizens by the military government in Kwang-ju in 1980, permeated into workers' communities in major industrial cities. Such radicalized underground activities created a completely different lineage of labor movements in the 1980s, independent of the pre-existing formal oppositional parties and their leaders. New labor leaders initially envisioned revolutionary paths, and then moderated themselves to more reformist, social democratic paths. Therefore, in a sense, labor movements were independent of democratization movements in South Korea, even if they reinforced each other.

Alternatively, in Taiwan, oppositional party movements and labor movements emerged from the same root, the Dangwai ('outside the party') movement. Labor leaders learned their goals and strategies from the DPP leaders' democratization movements, and therefore were linked to the DPP not only ideologically but also organizationally through personal networks. Furthermore, very few Taiwanese intellectuals depicted revolutionary paths during their struggles and even the most radical groups limited themselves to 'sympathetic helpers' outside the factories. For these reasons, Taiwanese labor leaders and oppositional party leaders, if they had factions, rarely spent their energies building separate, independent labor parties, but remained united under the DPP umbrella. These different origins and organizational forms employed by labor activists led to different outcomes of social policy reform during the growth and retrenchment eras in South Korea and Taiwan.

TAIWAN'S ORGANIZED LABOR: FROM PARTY
PUPPETS TO AGENTS OF CHANGE

Competing Union–Party Relationships: Corporatisms from Above and from Below

The two main union confederations in Taiwan, the CFL (Chinese Federation of Labor) and the TCTU (Taiwan Confederation of Trade Unions), built different relationships with the state and civil society. The CFL shared its core agendas and personnel with the authoritarian government for several decades. Established in 1948 under the authoritarian KMT regime, the CFL was the subsidiary organ for state corporatism. As it was also a part of the KMT's strategy for controlling labor unions and the workplace, the CFL was highly connected to the incumbent party by nature, while completely disconnected from broader civil society organizations. The KMT in the late 1940s brought to Taiwan repressive labor legislation from China, effectively demobilizing labor and eliminating workplaces as rallying points for any form of opposition. There were no true autonomous unions at the time, and the KMT infiltrated and dominated the workplace (Hsiao 1992). When workers began to voice their discontent in the late 1980s, therefore, the CFL failed to champion workers' demands and became a target of protest for many factory workers (Ho 2006). Overall, because of its extremely high cohesiveness with the KMT regime and low embeddedness with civil society, the CFL has never displayed serious opposition to the government or employers.

Unions outside of the system are rather different from unions inside the system, we're a union within the system, so it's more moderate. Those outside of the system are more radical, but the results aren't necessarily better … The ones who collide [with employers and the state] more, actually they want to obtain their own interests and power, but they are not resolving the problem. In the recent ten years, this has become more of a backstage method, through other methods such as institutional channels. More effective methods [than militancy] can be used to resolve labor issues.

(CFL union leader)

However, the same leader also admits that unions with cohesiveness only do not gain much from the state, either: "it is limited, the only thing you can do is give suggestions to the government under their policies, but it doesn't really impact much." In other words, the CFL had access to the state bureaucracy and its decision-making process, which led its policy experts to make suggestions on crafting major labor market and social policy positions. However, the CFL did not have other options by which the state could be forced to move closer to unions' positions. It quietly delivered its preference to the KMT and then swallowed what it got without explicit resistance for several decades.

In contrast to the CFL, the TCTU was a product of autonomous labor unions and the other anti-KMT forces that emerged simultaneously with the DPP during the democratization movement. The DPP stemmed from the Dangwai political movement in the 1970s, which was the predecessor to many of the social and political movements in civil society at the time, such as the environmental movement and the student movement. From the beginning, labor leaders were also an important part of the axis of the Dangwai, as the TCTU and autonomous groups emerged from such similar roots: namely, the anti-KMT political movement. Mao Chengfei, an honorary chair of Taoyuan County Confederation of Trade Unions, recalls:

At that time [the 1980s], countermovements and street demonstrations were prevalent. They were against the military's intervention in party affairs and the re-election of the parliament. Many of us [union leaders] participated in them … we learned from the DPP. We were very sympathetic [with the DPP leaders], and they [the DPP] also realized that they should cooperate and ally with the labor movement. At that time, many labor movement cadre members were very much in touch with their [DPP] movements.

During this period, a group of intellectuals from the Dangwai movement formed a legal-assistance/consulting association for unions, which later evolved into the Taiwanese Labor Front (TLF). As workers of the time "didn't understand how to form a union, we came in contact with them" (Cheng-fei Mao). "They (also) carefully organized an anti-nuclear demonstration, and came to our union cadres to do education on nuclear issues." In 1986, the DPP was officially established, and workers finally had an anti-KMT opposition party. In short, the DPP and the TCTU mainstream forces developed a close, cohesive relationship through their joint activities during the democratization era of the 1980s.[1] The TCTU maintained its organizational structure (unapproved as a union confederation), and finally became official when the DPP took over state power in 2000.

Around the same time, the deepening influence of globalization and market reforms occurring in China brought significant external threats for Taiwanese workers. Plant closures affected many workers in the late 1980s, particularly in labor-intensive industries, as labor costs were cheaper overseas or in China (Huang 2002). In this context, motivated by threats from outside and growing internal grievances in factories, as well as by KMT's unwillingness to legally recognize independent unions, aggrieved workers began reacting to their repressive working conditions. With these far-reaching systemic changes, and without strong local linkages to a supportive regime, the workers turned to more militant forms of action. From 1988–90, there was a surge in strikes and labor protests across the nation.

The KMT state made some concessions by lifting labor regulations in the late 1980s and early 1990s, but they simultaneously cracked down on social protests from 1989 to 1991. The solidaristic ties between independent unions and civil society were not strong enough then to warrant full state concessions and to guard against coercive repression by the state. Eventually, state repression and the threat of capital flight by employers effectively curbed these protests. Only two major strikes occurred after the crackdown. Faced with external threats and effective state repression, organized labor was forced to halt its militant action and seek out other strategies for achieving their demands. As a result, the confrontation between the KMT state and independent unions in the late 1980s and early 1990s initially looked similar to embeddedness without cohesiveness, but the relationship returned to authoritarian repression by the state and acquiescence by the unions.

Having learned from state repression during the wave of protests, labor activists shifted their strategy to one of legislative defense in response to new state actions (a combination of repression and concession), gradually giving up on grassroots union organizing (Ho 2003). Labor unions forged political partnerships with the DPP at various locations and coalesced with the party for lobbying opportunities. Labor activists started pressuring mayors and local magistrates to form local federations. With the KMT's refusal to recognize independent unions and the increasing power of the opposition in local politics, the rise of labor activists' demands for autonomous federations paralleled the DPP's rise to power (Ho 2006). Overall, in the 1990s and 2000s, pro-DPP independent unions gradually transitioned from weak cohesiveness and moderate embeddedness to exemplary high cohesiveness and moderate embeddedness.

In 2000, the DPP took power and the TCTU was officially recognized. As central and local elections became more competitive in Taiwan, and as representatives became more responsive to civic issues, electoral campaigns became a platform for workers to make demands (Lee 2006). Since both parties' candidates could take seats in the legislature, winning local and presidential elections, these confederations refocused on labor issues, and their rhetoric shifted from the 'anti-political party' sentiments of the past to new 'pro-lobbying' sentiments.[2] Both confederations responded to regime changes by adopting more proactive strategies for institutional engagement. The KMT and the DPP also both tried to absorb labor activists into local labor affairs councils, which could then serve as nodes of communication for various labor organizations. As a result, both the CFL and the TCTU exhibited cohesiveness with incumbent parties, as the confederations became part of the institutionalized political process.[3]

The state–union relationships in Taiwan under the democratization and market reform eras can be summarized by three exemplary modes: (1) a hierarchical corporatism between the KMT state and CFL before and after the democratic transition, with high cohesiveness and low embeddedness (game 2 in Appendix C. 1); (2) moderate conflict between the KMT state and moderately embedded independent unions that resulted in a combination of concession and repression (a case partially similar to game 3 in Appendix C.1); and (3) increasingly convergent state–union relationships that led to the state's moderate reform and unions' restraint under low pressure for reforms (a deviant case from the four ideal game types).

Intellectuals' Changing Roles in Taiwanese Labor Movements

One of the distinctive features of Taiwanese labor movements is their policy orientation. Many progressive intellectuals in the lineage of labor movements identified their roles in the web of 'policy networks,' in a way that was distinctively different from South Korean labor leaders' 'militant' orientations. The emergence and persistence of the TLF in the political and civil society in Taiwan, therefore, deserve attention. In spite of the absence of an influential labor-based party, it is critical to understand the role of the TLF as a significant policy think tank.

> We help workers in factories organize unions … As organizers, we help organizations to be formed. Our goal and strategy are different from others who often become a part of the organization they build. Workers need to be independent, and unions need their own lives. Workers should be able to make decisions on their own. We only help, but do not intervene further to make unions manage their lives. We serve as union consultants.
>
> (Former secretary-general, TLF)

The TLF's organizational goals and identity were surprisingly modest but effective. As the TLF confined its role to 'midwifery,' it has been able to maintain its organizational structure and identity for nearly three decades. By providing workers with legal advice and policy information, the

TLF played the role of broker between the DPP, unions, and other civil society organizations. TLF intellectuals working in the central and local TLF offices discussed with union leaders (1) how to organize unions, (2) how to respond to employers' and the government's repressive or compromising actions, and (3) how to propose labor and social policies and negotiate them with the government. The TLF shifted its goals and identity from those of a '(self-limiting) union organizer' to those of a 'policy-relevant advisor or promoter' for unions and workers, especially during the 2000s. The transformation of the TLF's identity was driven by the fulfillment of its own original goal. As unions were established in many mid- to large-sized firms in the 1980s and 1990s, and as unions built their own institutional capacity, it became increasingly difficult for the TLF to sustain its organizational missions. This shift in the TLF's involvement in labor politics reflects the changing characteristics of the embeddedness of Taiwanese unions in civil society. Leftist intellectuals self-limited their influence on workers by identifying their role as that of helpers rather than that of leaders, the role which South Korean intellectuals assumed through their going-underground movements. Ironically, this less aggressive engagement in union organizations allowed them to explore, much earlier, new 'bridging' roles between unions and the larger intellectual and civil society – something which was never clearly institutionalized in South Korean labor movements. A former secretary-general of TLF addresses the transformation of its organizational identity as follows:

They would think, "TLF, you are still doing organizing works. Why are you trying to factionalize us?" This is a natural phenomenon. So, after the mid-1990s, the TLF has been transforming its roles from organizing to leading policy discourse.

During the gestation periods for union politics, the TLF's role in cultivating linkages for mobilization capacity was limited, which did not help the overall level of embeddedness. However, during the consolidation periods, the TLF was able to occupy the "structural holes" (Burt 1992) among emerging democratic institutions, especially among unions, parties, and civil society. Its shift of identity to being a policy advisor and a policy mobilizer for unions helped independent unions (later the TCTU) build channels through which to discuss and negotiate policy-relevant issues with the DPP and state bureaucrats. Indeed, the TLF played a key role in enacting the annuity system under the Chen Shui-bian regime, the employment and unemployment insurance act, and gender equality in employment. Following this, they worked hard to push forward National

Health Insurance and a civic surveillance alliance, as well as representative workers' participation, which would directly import the German 'workers' council' model (an effort, however, which eventually failed; Han and Chiu 2000). Furthermore, they mobilized and built connections with professionals such as lawyers and professors, similar to those of the PSPD in South Korea.

> We are of the 'coalition system.' We are composed of many different alliances and coalitions. I have a colleague who is a part of the social housing promotion alliance. I am also in charge of the health insurance alliance. TLF is also a part of the anti-nuclear plant movement. We have worked with judicial reform groups, and have been a part of the anti-death penalty movement.
>
> (Former secretary-general, TLF)

In short, the TLF successfully found a niche in the rapidly developing policy deliberation space or "policy network" (Knoke *et al.* 1996; Laumann *et al.* 1977, 1985) between the state and civil society, such that they were able to play a key role in compensating, through 'policy-bridging' activities, for the relative decline of embeddedness of unions (the TCTU) in civil society.

TLF leaders also created the TLSA (Taiwan Labor and Social Policy Research Association), which was similar to the KLSI in South Korea or DIEESE in Brazil:

> We are an organization that deals mostly with policies … From a policy perspective, labor groups rarely start from a policy standpoint, labor groups are mostly 'firefighters,' they go wherever there is a problem. As for union groups, they only pay attention to issues related to themselves … we hope we can play the role of the comprehensive policy improver.
>
> (Feng-yi Zhang)

The TLSA closely coalesced with the TCTU, TLF, Taiwan Alliance for Advancement of Youth Rights and Welfare, Taiwan Occupational Safety and Health Link, Taiwan Federation of Financial Unions, etc.

While the bridging role of the TLF in the state–society policy network was impressive and the TCTU closely collaborated with the TLF in institutional policy-making, the TCTU's embeddedness continued to decline, especially in terms of its mobilization capacity. The abrupt decline of the mobilization capacity of the TCTU is mainly attributable to its (too) close relationship with the DPP. Upon its establishment in 2000, the TCTU was the biggest active union organization in Taiwan, and as of the 2010s it still had 280,000 members. However, before it was able to solidify and institutionalize its organizational structure by disciplining its own

leaders and members with core organizational goals and routines, the
TCTU was exposed to the strong co-optation forces of the new, incumbent DPP patronage system. The early core leaders of the TCTU pursued
their personal political interests by seeking positions in the DPP, hoping
to become legislators.

While, with its moderate embedded cohesiveness in the early 2000s,
the TCTU succeeded in amending the Labor Standard Act, decreasing
the working hours (to 84 work hours per two weeks), and participating
in passing the labor pensions and other important labor reforms (the
Employment Insurance Act and the Act on the Gender Equality in
Employment), it had to witness its gradual decline in embeddedness,
and especially its mobilization capacity. After 2004, as many of the
TCTU's most important leaders were absorbed by the DPP, it increasingly became a confederation of routinized annual meetings, without
a centralized disciplinary organization generating concrete policy
and strategic mobilization against the state and employers. Especially
the core public sector unions of the TCTU almost ceased function-
ing, after the 2000s, as politically significant mobilizers, and many
local union leaders (of firm-level unions and province-level TCUs)
under the TCTU now admit that they do not have sufficient capacity
to mobilize grassroots workers. "The TCTU had a large impact on
the state until the early 2000s. [Since then] its influence on the state
labor policies went downhill. The Labor Bureau started ignoring the
TCTU" (county-level TCU director). The bulk of interviewees (out
of 21) responded that the TCTU has lost its influence significantly.
With the DPP in power at both the local and national levels, TCUs
and the TCTU did not dare to openly challenge their political allies'
decisions, which is in sharp contrast to the situation of the KCTU in
South Korea and the CUT in Brazil.

Many intellectuals outside and inside the TCTU, especially those who
were more left-leaning, recognized that the historical bonding between the
DPP and the TCTU had been detrimental to the influence of the TCTU,
because of the DPP's unclear positions regarding workers' issues. For instance, a professor involved in DPP-lineage informal think tanks com-
plains that, "DPP didn't embody its mass class foundation … the class
foundation of DPP should be the workers. Its feet are with the workers
but its head is still with the capitalist class." The criticism leads to skepticism about the utility of the cohesive ties between them: "They understand that even during the eight years of the DPP's ruling, the DPP didn't

always protect the interests of the workers. So, they also need to keep a certain distance away from the DPP." Indeed, a high-ranked TCTU leader supports these claims by saying, "the DPP and KMT are both right-sided ... I seldom see a party that would actively stand by the working-class side." A TCTU insider commented that:

Many members of the TCTU who come from state owned companies started to claim that it is useless to keep a good relationship with any of the parties as the parties still only consider their own interests. Our committee discussed that no party is trustworthy. So, they were preparing for the establishment of their own party of labor.

The influence of the TCTU on the state and civil society reached its peak during the first term of the DPP incumbency (in the early 2000s), when the TCTU played a crucial role in building key labor market and social policy institutions such as 84-hour work (over two weeks) and unemployment insurance.[4] Since then, the TCTU has become increasingly similar to the CFL in its relationships with the mainstream political parties. It rapidly became a part of the existing political institutions without further strengthening its own organizational base and alliances. In alliance with the TLF and the DPP, it was able to build important institutional channels and policy capacities (in terms of cohesiveness and embeddedness), but it gradually lost its mobilization capacity, as the TCTU's leaders increasingly lost connection to grassroots unions and civil society allies. The following lament by a high-rank TCTU official sums up Taiwanese unions' situation:

The TCTU cares about all workers in a broader view, so unemployment and poverty are main concerns of the TCTU. [But our] member unions don't care too much about these issues. I always feel powerless every time when I need to persuade them to promote these kinds of policies. So the workers in Taiwan were not united together. Everybody stood by his own interest. Sometimes during the meetings, they would ask me why it matters to them ... the workers complain about why they should participate in such activities that don't mean anything to them ... I said there is no direct connection ... but it might matter a lot to your friends or your children ... we should ensure our descendants have better jobs to support the future retirement mechanism.

Overall, I summarize two contrasting trends in Taiwanese labor politics. On one hand, the TCTU, its leadership as a centralized confederation, has been declining in the 2000s due to its member unions' firm-based bargaining structures and increasing skepticism about the headquarters' relationship with the DPP.[5] On the other hand, in spite of the TCTU's declining significance, unions and their coalitional politics in the form of policy-networks in wider civil society kept extending their solidarity and deepening their vertical channels with political parties in the late 2000s and after, creating more tensions and new opportunities in their relationships with political parties.

SOUTH KOREA: UNIONS' CONTRASTING RESPONSES
TO THE STATE'S NEW LABOR POLICIES

Competition between Unions during Democratization

In recent decades, the two major union confederations in South Korea, FKTU (Federation of Korean Trade Unions) and KCTU (Korean Confederation of Trade Unions), have developed divergent relationships with the state and civil society.[6] State–union interactions in South Korea illuminate three forms of market reform effort and related union responses: (1) severe conflicts between the state and unions after the transition to democracy in the late 1980s, with low cohesiveness and low embeddedness (game 1 in Appendix C.1; KCTU elements before its founding); (2) state concessions after a series of union protests during the 1997 general strike, evincing low cohesiveness and high embeddedness (game 3 in Appendix C.1; KCTU along with FKTU); and (3) unions' sacrifice following the state's reform initiative in the 2000s under two reformist governments, characterized by high cohesiveness and low embeddedness (game 2 in Appendix C.1; FKTU).

The two union confederations have markedly different origins and ideological stances. The FKTU cooperated with the ruling authoritarian parties under state corporatism throughout the 1970s and the 1980s: it participated in the partially centralized wage-bargaining pact with KEF (Korean Employers' Federation) until 1996, when, for the first time, the ruling conservative party lost the presidential election. After 1997, the FKTU started taking part in another reformist, state-driven wage-bargaining pact, and it was organizationally and electorally aligned with the incumbent Democratic Party on the centrist reform party side. In general, the FKTU switched its stance according to convenience regardless of the ideological alignment of the government, while it failed to develop close relationships with emerging civic and political associations until the late 1990s.

In contrast, the KCTU originated from strong anti-authoritarian, anti-capitalist leftist social movements active during the harsh authoritarian era (as discussed in Chapter 4). Its antecedent organization was established in 1990, when labor movements were at their peak, democratic elections were restored, and the Great Labor Struggle (in 1987) opened a wave of union organizing efforts and strikes demanding higher wages and better working conditions. When, during collective bargaining with the KEF in 1993, the FKTU agreed to wage restraint at a 4.5 percent level, many unions in major conglomerates walked away from the FKTU[7] and joined several alternative labor organizations, which later became the KCTU. They mobilized wide-ranging anti-corporatist movements and succeeded in persuading large conglomerate, manufacturing-based unions such as those at Hyundai and Kia to turn their backs on the FKTU.

The non-cooperative and militant union strategies and organizing efforts led by these new union leaders reflect the constant struggles between unions and the state under the conditions of weak cohesiveness and weak embeddedness. Although militant labor movements emerged from the democratization movement, labor did not necessarily coordinate its organizing and struggles with the larger civil society and middle class-based social movement organizations in the 1980s. An assertive labor movement had not yet established its own parties, nor did it enjoy systematic channels with existing political parties. The state, with the support of large conglomerate businesses, kept actively undermining labor's rights, with unions vehemently resisting such actions. As a result, the state and unions pursued more confrontational strategies with no incentive to cooperate or withdraw (as implied in game 1 in Appendix C.1).

The two union confederations' contrasting behaviors converged in the mid-1990s. On the one hand, the KCTU, after its founding in 1995, pursued social reformism in alliance with other reformist social movement associations (thereby strengthening its embeddedness in civil society). On the other hand, the FKTU changed its stance from its traditional corporatist relationship with the government and businesses to a more reformist position – a move made mainly to compete with the newly ascendant KCTU.[8] The leadership of the FKTU became more sensitive to the pressure from grassroots unions for a more reformist stance, while the shift in political regime from a conservative to a centrist party compelled them to align with the new government.[9] And regarding their explicit goals and platforms, the two confederations increasingly converged in the late 1990s.[10]

The narrowing gap between the two confederations led them to cooperate for the first time in a 1997 general strike targeting a new, market-oriented attempt at labor reform by the ruling conservative party. In the bill, the government included (1) a law allowing massive lay-offs and (2) a law facilitating non-standard, temporary, flexible employment (including substitute dispatch workers). In early 1997, both labor organizations jointly waged mass, solidaristic strikes that lasted for two months. Four hundred thousand workers from 531 local unions under the KCTU and 420,000 workers from 1,648 unions under the FKTU participated in the strike (KLI 2010). The ruling party and the leading opposition party agreed to revoke the planned labor reform bill and pass a new, revised bill as a conciliatory measure. This brief victory achieved by the 1997 general strike illustrates an extensive game that occurred under conditions of low cohesiveness and high embeddedness. The state's initially radical reform aspiration triggered mass resistance from the allied labor confederations, here supported by wider civil society organizations (mainly on the side of KCTU), and their response drew substantive concessions from the state.

The founding of the KCTU and the subsequent joint general strike waged by the two confederations entirely realigned the terrain of labor politics in South Korea. First, the FKTU, formerly under the influence of the ruling conservative government, realigned itself with the reformist centrist position, especially the Democratic Party, which situated the FKTU under high cohesiveness and low embeddedness again (after earlier corporatistic relationships with the authoritarian regimes), even under a democratic reformist incumbent. Second, the KCTU, after its partial victory during the general strike in 1997, realized that it could not tolerate the neo-liberal tendencies of the two primarily center-right or centrist political parties. In contrast to the FKTU, the KCTU accelerated its social democratic political and economic agenda through the establishment of a labor-based party and the founding of industry- or sector-based union confederations (as described in Chapters 4 and 5).

These new political movements placed the two union confederations, which seemed to be converging around 1997, on vastly different trajectories in the 2000s. The ruling party and businesses continued excluding the KCTU from the bargaining table and policy-making process, and the KCTU extended its collaboration network to include progressive civic associations such as People's Solidarity for Participatory Democracy (PSPD) and other progressive professional associations – groups focused on broader social reform rather than just wage and work issues. Over time, while the FKTU solidified its cohesiveness with the ruling reformist party (without embeddedness), the KCTU further reinforced its embeddedness (without cohesiveness) significantly during the late 1990s and the early 2000s.

The beginning of the reformist regime and the simultaneous financial crisis in the late 1990s placed the two branches of the labor movement in difficult situations. The reformist regime attempted to introduce two reform drives: one a neo-liberal labor market reform recommended by the IMF, and the other a social welfare reform driven by labor-civic solidarity. The regime encouraged both the FKTU and the KCTU to participate in the government-led tripartite committee to deal with labor market reforms, such as easing lay-offs and the use of substitute workers. In return, the government offered the legalization of a key KCTU union, the National Teachers' Union, the legal recognition of the unemployed as union members, and the delay of plural unionism and no-pay policy for union officials. The reformist Kim regime persuaded the two labor organizations to accept the deal, and both the FKTU and the KCTU initially signed the deal including 110 different elements regarding labor law reforms. However, the KCTU had to withdraw its initial agreement due to mass resistance from grassroots union members, primarily those in manufacturing industries. In 1998, the KCTU pursued two general strikes against the passage of the bill and the regime's delay in implementing remuneration policies. In 1999, the KCTU walked away from the three-party committee, and after that point remained antagonistic towards the first reformist regime.[11]

The same story was repeated under the second reformist regime. The president, Moo-Hyun Rho, formerly a labor rights and human rights lawyer, attempted not only to introduce another labor law change regarding non-standard workers, but also to launch free trade agreements with the US and the EU. The regime deployed the same strategy as the Kim regime, which utilized the FKTU as a close ally at the tripartite negotiation table so as to press the KCTU to accept the reform agendas. The KCTU was unable to remain at the negotiation table as a result of resistance from grassroots union members (No 2008). This time, in contrast to 1997, many allies in civil society maintained distance from the KCTU, as they had close ties with the reformist regime. Therefore, the KCTU had to struggle largely alone against the reformist state, finding itself isolated from the rest of progressive civil

society (denoted in Table 8.2 as 'y' implying 'weakened, moderate embeddedness'), and therefore it was unable to extract significant concessions from the incumbent reformist party.

In these circumstances, the FKTU remained at the bargaining table as
the sole negotiating partner for the reformist regimes as well as for the
two recent conservative regimes. It did not necessarily return to its traditional corporatistic relationship with the government, but rather strove
to maintain a moderate, reformist position between the state, civil society, and the KCTU. The FKTU's realignment with the former oppositional party and other reformist civic associations, however, should be
considered a significant change in the terrain of labor politics in South
Korea. The FKTU, due to its low mobilization capacity, rarely played
a significant role in contentious politics after the 1997 general strike,
but it has served as the primary policy think tank of the moderate labor
movements.

Structural Changes and Declining Labor–Civic
Solidarity in South Korea

Why, then, did the KCTU, one of the most successful examples of social movement unionism in the world in the 1990s along with the CUT
in Brazil, suffer such an abrupt decline in the 2000s? How could the
impressive emergence of strong embeddedness and cohesiveness turn
into a sudden decline in the 2000s and after? Aside from the dramatic
collapse of labor activists' collective project of a labor-based party (and
their strategic mistakes),[12] what are the fundamental structural changes
that reshaped the terrain of labor movements and contributed to these
declines?

Since the 1990s, union movements have been fundamentally challenged
by deep structural changes in the global capitalist economy. These include technological developments rendering labor redundant, intensified
competition among workers as a result of new personnel management
systems, the spread and normalization of firm-based bargaining systems
(leading to increased inequality among workers in firm-based wage and
welfare benefits), and the normalization of lay-offs and nonstandard/
indirect/subcontract employment. These structural and institutional
changes, occurring on a global scale, have greatly increased inequality
within labor in South Korea, which has in turn fundamentally weakened
solidarity within and among unions in South Korea, as in almost every

other country with the exception of a couple of countries in Northern Europe and Scandinavia. Wage inequality has dramatically increased in South Korea since 1996, after having decreased up until 1995 (3.618). In 2010, South Korean wage inequality measured by a decile ratio (decile 9/decile 1 = 4.854) was the third highest among OECD countries, with only Mexico and the United States above it.[13] Importantly, the strong and militant union movements which developed around large manufacturing industries in the 1980s and 1990s in South Korea greatly contributed to the 'split' characteristics of the labor market. During the heyday of the militant labor movement in the late 1980s and the early 1990s, about 85 percent of workers in large factories (those with more than 500 workers) were organized by unions, while less than 9 percent of workers at smaller firms were unionized (Chŏng 2013). In these large firms, where unions were staunchly opposed to flexible labor management systems such as contract workers, firms had strong incentives to turn to subcontract workers outside the firm.

I consider the strategic choices made by large manufacturing unions in the late 1990s and early 2000s a critical turning point in Korean labor politics, especially regarding unions' collaboration with the KCTU national center, the state, and employers. Immediately after the KCTU assented to the state's new laws on lay-offs and dispatched workers in February 1998, grassroots unions faced the announcement by employers of mass lay-offs. For example, in 1998 Hyundai Auto Company announced several types of employment adjustments for 12,000 workers, including several thousand immediate lay-offs and forced unpaid leave. Unions eventually accepted the lay-offs without meaningful changes after 36 days of strike and negotiations. More than 100 core union leaders were included in the plan. At this time, metal unions and the KCTU national center attempted to aid the most consequential and representative confrontations between the state/capital and unions by waging solidaristic strikes. During the mass lay-offs in the late 1990s – at the same time as the financial crisis – the KCTU and metal unions failed to demand and establish 'employment-security institutions' such as unemployment insurance and assistance in training and job search, which led to the establishment of a "flexible labor market without social safety nets" (Chang *et al.* 2011) in the 2000s and after. Workers who were laid off had to leave their jobs with only a one-time payment of 'retirement money' and so without any guarantee of re-employment or any assistance from the state or firms in nearby industries. Although the KCTU succeeded in achieving welfare reforms in health insurance and pensions, those reforms, although universal in their coverage, did not mean much for those who lost their regular jobs or who could not afford insurance premiums due to immediate income loss. As a result of these painful experiences, workers and union leaders learned to focus on maximizing income during their employment (Pak 2014) while defending their own employment status as long as possible. The focus on these more immediate and defensive strategies reduced their appetite for larger solidaristic activities beyond firm-level unions, let alone solidarity with non-standard workers within their own factories. This implicit switch from UR strategies to SR strategies among large manufacturing unions was further reinforced by the employers' divide-and-rule strategies with regard to standard and non-standard workers in the 2000s.

After the financial crisis and mass lay-offs of 1998, and facing strong resistance from unions, employers in large manufacturing firms (e.g. Hyundai Automobile Company) chose to pursue a two-track strategy: one track was to guarantee high levels of wage and employment protection for unionized regular workers in core tasks, and the other track was to maximize the use of non-standard, subcontract labor for non-core tasks. As a result, the strong labor organizations focusing on male workers in large manufacturing firms managed to defend the interests of their existing members, but they allowed employers to develop indirect/non-standard/subcontract employment practices even in the presence of – and possibly with the implicit agreement of – the unions. The unions of regular workers discreetly preferred that firms utilize non-standard workers rather than lay-offs to adjust to market fluctuations due to economic cycles. At the firm level, "they rarely made efforts to organize increasing non-standard workers who even worked together on the same assembly line"(director of a local institute for labor education). A labor leader, now a lawmaker at a local assembly, cuttingly criticizes the behavior of the unions at large conglomerates: "They have plugged and sucked the same straws as those which were put by employers [on non-standard workers]. They were domesticated by the leftovers offered by capitalists."

In the 2000s, large unions in South Korean manufacturing industries increasingly relinquished their broader role as social movement organizations, a role that so surprised and impressed the world in the 1980s and 1990s. As firm-level bargaining systems became deeply institutionalized (while industrial union-level bargaining failed to develop between employers and unions, despite the KCTU activists' persistent efforts for two decades, the most militant social reformist unions and their members were domesticated by generous wage increases, stable employment protection, and profit-sharing programs provided by globally competitive Chaebol companies. A high-ranking union leader at Hyundai Automobile Company said, "Union officials increasingly became the messenger of union members who were subject to materialism with 300–400 percent wage increases since the 1990s."

As a consequence, since the 2000s, unions of globally successful large manufacturing firms have begun to control their voices on social reform issues as well as the collective agendas of the labor movement, including issues such as enhancing the rights of non-standard labor. For instance, while smaller unions in small to mid-sized firms have actively participated in industry-level wage bargaining, most unions from large conglomerates refuse to waive their bargaining rights to the upper-level (industrial) metal union. As a KCTU high-ranked strategist complained, officials of these unions "do not care about the bargaining of industrial unions and pretend to respond to the requests from the national confederation [the KCTU] for reforms for non-standard workers and regional-level solidaristic movements – they do so only when they have extra time once they have finished with [firm-level] bargaining." These changes have affected both grassroots workers and their leaders at the factory level. Another KCTU strategist lamented, "Standard and non-standard workers are identical. Once their problems regarding wage, employment, and working conditions are resolved, then they go back to their factory and shut the door. Nobody is going to come out beyond the factory wall for social solidarity."

KCTU increasingly has become an organization for the interests of male workers in large, factory-based unions. More accurately, though, a stronger claim is that the KCTU national center has increasingly lost agenda-setting control over the established unions representing regular male workers in large manufacturing industries. Although they superficially announce support for unorganized, non-standard workers' labor rights and social insurance entitlements,[14] the core member unions of the KCTU rarely give up their share of the resources in negotiation with employers and the state to enhance non-standard workers' wages and benefits. A high-ranked KCTU official adamantly said:

If one is going to give her flesh to others, that 'other' should not be 'the other,' but a part of 'us.' In order to share their own prerogatives with non-standard labor, regular workers should have a belief that all workers belong to the same solidarity ... in the end, while it is necessary to decrease benefits for one or increase benefits for the other, it is now impossible to let them [regular workers] accept decrease in what they already have.

Another official from the KCTU national center, who is in charge of collective action such as strikes and demonstrations, reported bitterly, "in the past, member unions blamed the KCTU national center for its inactive, less militant tendencies. Now, if I request them to participate in the militant struggles [waged by the national center] in a meeting of chiefs of grassroots organizational units, nobody talks. Nobody wants to contribute." This embarrassing collective action problem at the KCTU national center, where few member unions are willing to offer mobilization capacity, succinctly illustrates how weak the leadership of the labor's national center has become since the early 2000s.

The impacts of structural changes and increasing labor market inequality on South Korean labor movements are twofold. One is the gradual defection of workers in large factories in the globally competitive manufacturing sectors from both militant labor struggles and social reform agendas, culminating in unions embracing a SR strategy based on their implicit "alliance with their employers" (Lee *et al.* 2011; Swenson 1991a, 1991b). The other follows from the first: as large manufacturing unions drop out of the KCTU's national-level mobilization strategies and policies, the KCTU has lost the core organizational base through which it could exert meaningful influence on the state and civil society actors.[15]

In summary, the continuous waning of the embeddedness and cohesiveness of the KCTU in the 2000s, which resulted in an eventual halt and retreat in South Korean welfare state development after the late 2000s, is attributable to three factors: the shallow embeddedness of earlier going-underground activities, ideological factionalism in labor politics, and broader structural changes in economic processes such as increasing wage and job security differentials within labor. Although these issues are South Korea-specific, they emerge as important causes of variations in labor–civic solidarity when compared to the other three cases. In addition, the South Korean case also suggests that while embeddedness and cohesiveness may operate at different levels in different domains, as displayed in health care and pensions politics, at the highest level of organizational politics South Korean labor unions lost their status as the locus of civic solidarity and partisan politics after the 2000s. The KCTU's shallow embeddedness in local civic communities, intensified factional strife, and poor mechanisms of coordination with labor activists, as well as, most importantly, the departures of large manufacturing industry unions from social solidarity mobilization, meant that the decline of the KCTU occurred from all directions – from the bottom, outside, and inside. While the shallow embeddedness of the going-underground activities of radical intellectuals continued to limit the KCTU's embeddedness in local communities and civic organizations, intensified factional strife and the consequential split of the DLP enervated the KCTU's mobilization capacity from within, as factionalism spread deep into grassroots union politics. In particular, the implicit conversion of large manufacturing unions from a UR to an SR strategy in the 2000s was critical in the overall weakening of the KCTU, as it lost the major motors of its mobilization capacity. Although labor–civic solidarity remained durable in the health care field, the overall decline of the KCTU's embeddedness and cohesiveness weakened the influence of labor unions in nearly all other policy realms – a weakening that allowed both reformist and conservative regimes to implement market-oriented reforms in key social and labor market policies.

A COMPARISON: PAST, CURRENT, AND FUTURE EMBEDDED COHESIVENESS IN EAST ASIA

South Korean and Taiwanese unions showed markedly different responses to market reforms in the 1990s. A more surprising finding is not just such different responses in the 1990s, but also a dramatic reversal in the next decade in South Korea and a gradual improvement in unions' institutional lobbying power in Taiwan. Two South Korean union confederations waged nationwide joint strikes in 1996–97, which eventually resulted in the first peaceful, democratic change of political power in South Korean history, and passage of universal social policy reforms during the tripartite committee. The unions' stunning and potent militancy linked to numerous civic and popular associations, however, witnessed equally stunning decline in the 2000s, which opened a path toward retrenchment in key social insurance schemes. The KCTU's deep and wide linkages to civil society and their linkages to political parties, which made great strides in the early 2000s, became shredded. As I discussed earlier, in Chapter 4, the KCTU's policy and mobilization capacities declined after the mid-2000s, and its policy capacity declined precipitously. Therefore, the KCTU's confederational-level achievements were limited to universal

social policy reforms in the late 1990s. After the split of the DLP, it was
unable to find political representation due to its staunch refusal to negotiate with both reformist and conservative parties. As a result, the KCTU,
due to a lack in both policy embeddedness and cohesive lobbying channels, was hardly able to draw any pre-bargained policy outcomes from
the incumbent parties after the mid-2000s.

However, in Taiwan, while their mobilization capacity was much
weaker than that of their South Korean counterparts, union leaders
and civic leaders have cautiously built their policy capacity and networks through key think tank organizations around the TCTU and the
DPP. The TLF, which historically converted its role from one of union
organizer to one of policy think tank, has been at the center of this
institutional development. The TCTU, despite its weakening organizational resources, maintained its cohesive ties with both parties, with
stronger weight on the DPP. Such consistent policy-oriented linkages of
the TCTU and the TLF to the DPP gradually became institutionalized
without creating the serious factional cleavages typical of South Korean
labor movements.

To abbreviate, South Korean militant labor movements built a strong
national confederation buttressed by industrial unions and a labor-based
party in an unprecedentedly short time-frame, and then failed to transform such militancy into institutionalized policy networks during two
reformist regimes. The labor–civic networks around the KCTU became
considerably weakened in the late 2000s (with the exception of the health
solidarity network, which survived because of the KHMU and KFMA).
This was due to, first, factional strife within the DLP and KCTU and,
second, increasing inequality in wage and job security among workers
(and the consequential departure from KCTU influence of large manufacturing unions). Accordingly, the universal social policy schemes achieved
by labor–civic solidarity in the 1990s suffered gradual or radical retrenchments in the 2000s, as I described in detail in Chapters 5 and 6. The
KCTU did not have any influence on the enactment of new social policy
schemes during two conservative regimes either.

However, Taiwanese labor-civic networks, while their initial mobilization and policy capacities were incomparable to those in South
Korea, gradually institutionalized themselves in the web of policy
fields between the DPP and civic associations. While the KCTU leaders
devoted their energy to building the DLP, which led to an implosion due
to factional strife, the Taiwanese unions and their civic allies fully utilized the existing party system to promote labor's interests. Such efforts

prevented the KMT and the DPP from introducing radical privatization of state firms and launching privatization of pensions, including individualized accounts, while succeeding in implementing unemployment insurance and reduction in working hours.

In short, South Korean labor movements achieved too little with their considerable mobilization capacity, while Taiwanese labor movements obtained quite a lot with relatively meager resources and influence.[16] I attribute these relative differences in their roles in social policy outcomes to too-abrupt decline in the embeddedness of unions in associational networks in South Korea, and relatively successful institutionalization of policy capacity among unions, civic associations, and political parties in Taiwan.

Nevertheless, it is important to point out that the core frameworks of universal social insurance programs built upon strong embeddedness in South Korea and Taiwan survived and persisted across radical market reform attempts in the 2000s and after – something which cannot be captured by comparative analyses of the two union confederations, the KCTU and TCTU. The single-pillar systems of National Health Insurance and National Pension have been intact throughout the 2000s in South Korea. In Taiwan, the main stories of gradual social policy reform did not fundamentally change the fragmented insurance systems along sectoral lines or the transfer-centered vote-buying efforts of two parties, which will be further discussed in the next chapter. In South Korea, at the critical juncture of the late 1990s, major universal social insurance programs were enacted and implemented by strong labor–civic networks despite the presence of strongly entrenched corporatistic interest groups (e.g. FKTU). In Taiwan, the gradual improvements to labor's institutional lobbying power helped the introduction of several key social policies, but were hardly enough for universal reforms and integration of fragmented social policies.

Furthermore, the legacy of militant unionism, despite having significantly declined, along with failing to institutionalize its policy wings, has not completely disappeared in South Korea. In contrast, unions' mobilization capacity is still meager in Taiwan. My theoretical frameworks predict that, if the state attempts to make radical retrenchments to existing insurance schemes via privatization or to cut social transfers from its budget in the future, the KTCU and TCTU institutional trajectories and legacies may result in completely different outcomes from the ones I have discussed. These unions may want to learn from each other's history of mistakes and achievements in the twenty-first century.

SUMMARY AND DISCUSSION: CAUSAL
EXPLANATIONS OF LABOR COOPERATION AND
RESISTANCE: CONFEDERATIONAL-LEVEL ANALYSIS

Revisiting Alternative Explanations

I here take into account several alternative economic and structural factors along with the data presented in Table 8.1. With respect to demographic structure and interest group politics by the elderly, an aging population is not closely associated with the development or retrenchment of the welfare state in these four countries. The harshest retrenchment occurred in Argentina while the share of Argentina's population that was elderly was the highest among the four countries. The other major retrenchment in old-age pensions occurred in South Korea, when the aging of the population grew rapidly in the late 2000s. Voters in their sixties or seventies, who had enjoyed the benefits of rapid economic development under authoritarian regimes during the developmental era, have been the most consistent advocates of the conservative party in the 2000s and since in South Korea, therefore making this demographic group the most persistent opponent to the expansion of the welfare state.[17] As a result, aging appears associated with neither the politics of retrenchment nor the politics of expansion at least in these four countries, which is in sharp discordance with the predictions of industrialization theory (Pampel and Williamson 1989). In the sense that retrenchments occurred and diffused in much faster and more drastic ways in these countries than in Pierson's (1994) rich democracy cases, the theories of blame avoidance or policy legacy do not work properly here, either.

Next, regarding the role of economic openness and economic crises, note that the levels of debt shown in Table 8.1 are approximately the same across the two Latin American countries and the two East Asian countries. The levels of trade openness were also similar within each region. Over time, increases in debt and trade were parallel within each region, too. Similarly, even economic crises occurred about the same time, in the early 1990s in Latin America, causing extremely high inflation in the two Latin American countries. However, despite these within-region similarities, retrenchment outcomes widely differ within each region. Argentina and South Korea suffered radical retrenchment in pensions and labor market institutions in the 1990s and the 2000s, respectively, while Brazil and Taiwan did not. In both Argentina and

TABLE 8.1. *Basic Economic, Demographic, and Social Spending Data for Four Countries: 1990s and 2000s*

	Argentina		Brazil		South Korea		Taiwan	
	1995	2005	1995	2005	1995	2005	1995	2005
GDP per capita, PPP (US$)[a]	9,616	10,819	7,724	8,505	15,761	22,783	15,067	26,657
Age structure (65 years and over)	9.6	10.6	5	6	5.9	8.6	–	9.6
Total Debt (Domestic + Foreign, % of GDP)	33.8	70.3	39.6	60.3	10.2	30	12	38.5
Inflation (annual %)	3 (2070 in 1990)	9	93 (2700 in 1990)	7	7	1	–	2
Gini	0.49	0.50	0.59	0.56	0.32 (1998)		0.32 (1998)	
Social expenditure (% of GDP)	16.9	15.2 (18.1 in 2010)	15.5	18.0 (21.2 in 2010)	3.3	6.5 (9.4 in 2009)	9.5	10.1 (9.7 in 2010)

Sources: World Bank (2011); total debt data drawn from UNCTAD 2008; social expenditure drawn from ILO 2014–15.
Note [a]: PPP = purchasing power parity.

South Korea, supposedly labor-friendly regimes betrayed their supporters by introducing radical market-oriented reforms. In short, both economic openness and economic crisis factors do not account for varied
outcomes of state–union interactions regarding social and labor market
policies.

Then, do economic crises affect unions and their cooperatives negatively, so potentially serving as an alternative third factor that causes
declines in both labor–civic solidarity and the welfare state? Based on
the case studies of eight union confederations and their varied levels of
embeddedness in civil society, I find mixed evidence: economic crises and
globalization did not significantly affect labor organizations and their
surrounding civic communities in Brazil and Taiwan. In Brazil, unions,
especially new union movements around the CUT, largely preserved
their organizational resources and their social movement connections
throughout the 1990s and the 2000s. In Taiwan, new union movements
around the TCTU also moderately increased their linkages to civil society groups during the corresponding periods. However, under similar
economic crises, Argentine labor organizations became divided and some
factions bolted in response to the neo-liberal turn of their former partisan allies (the PJ), building a new confederation, the CTA. Therefore,
some may argue that Argentine labor movements were weakened due
to Menem's neo-liberal turn, but others may find that labor movements
began to cut cohesive ties with the PJ, cultivating broader solidarity with
civil society after the 1990s. Similarly, in South Korea, economic crises
led labor movements to be divided along factional lines. Also, neo-liberal reforms on labor standards and laws introduced new arrangements
and contracts between capital and labor, thereby dramatically increasing
heterogeneity and inequality among the working classes. Factional strife
within labor movements and structural reforms at the firm and industrial levels jointly affected labor movements in South Korea in deeply
negative ways. These changes inevitably led to decline in labor's embeddedness in civil society. Therefore, economic crises and globalization do
not account for variations within and across cases in uniform ways. As
for cross-sectional comparisons, they do not explain much. However,
regarding over-time variations in Argentina and South Korea, economic
crises played some role in retrenching not only the welfare state, but also
labor's embeddedness.

Nevertheless, I showed in Chapter 6 that some (industrial) unions
and their allies in civil society built durable labor–civic solidarity that
survived reformist and conservative regimes' neo-liberal reform drives

in the health care sector in South Korea. The KCTU industrial unions' renewed civil society orientation and Argentinian Peronists' resurgence using labor–civic solidarity (around the CTA) suggest that such negative impacts of economic crises and globalization are neither unitary nor omnipotent. Then, how do the primary factors of this study – cohesiveness and embeddedness – perform in accounting for the retrenchment outcomes?

Mechanisms and Causal Influence of the EC Approach

Tables 8.2 and 8.3 summarize variations in our two causal factors, unions' embeddedness and their cohesiveness, and the outcome variable, unions' response to market reforms, across the eight major union confederations in the four countries over two decades, the 1990s and the 2000s, respectively.[18] I have added three other potential competing extraneous factors: the presence or absence of severe economic crisis (or pressure for market-oriented reforms), coordination between union confederations, and coherence within each union confederation.[19] Unions' cohesiveness has two dimensions: alliance with the incumbent party and alliance with leftist parties. Note that the second dimension does not drastically change over time, as it is a relatively stable relationship between unions and leftist parties, while the first dimension of cohesiveness varies over time depending upon the altering partisanship of the state under competitive democratic elections. In the following summary discussion, the first dimension will be mainly utilized to examine the causal impacts of cohesiveness (with its relationship to embeddedness) on market reform outcomes. The last two columns summarize variations in our outcome variable(s): unions' actions – militancy (M) or restraint (R) – in response to the state's actions –radical reform (RR) or moderate reform (MR) of existing social policy and labor market institutions. On the union side, 'restraint' implicitly includes 'exit/silence' due to internal incapacity and divisions. On the state side, 'no reform' could be an option (as illustrated in Figure C.1 in Appendix C), but was not considered as an option in this chapter, because all countries were exposed to economic crises and pressure for market-oriented reforms (as illustrated in factor 1 in Tables 8.2 and 8.3) and developing countries often do not have other options than conforming to such pressure to a certain degree. As the state primarily responds to leading or majority union confederations' actions, we fill the state's action row selectively only for the columns of the major union confederations of the time.

TABLE 8.2. *Causal Combinations: Determinants of State–Union Interactions in the 1990s (Time of Economic Crisis) at Confederation Level*

	Argentina		Brazil		South Korea		Taiwan	
	CGT	CTA	Força Sindical	CUT	FKTU	KCTU	CFL	TCTU
Factor 1: Economic crisis/pressure for market reforms	Y	Y	Y	Y	Y	Y	y[c]	y[c]
Factor 2: Solidarity (coordination) between confederations	N	N	Y	Y	N	N	N	N[b]
Factor 3: Coherence of a confederation	N	Y	Y	Y	N	Y	N	Y
Factor 4: Embeddedness (alliance with civil society)	N	Y	N	Y	N	Y	N	Y
Factor 5.1: Cohesiveness I (alliance with incumbent party)	Y	N	Y	y	Y	n	Y	N
Factor 5.2: Cohesiveness II (alliance with leftist party)	Y	N	N	Y	N	N	N	N
General Outcome 1: Union militancy/restraint (or exit/division)[a]	R	M	R	r	R	M	R	M
General Outcome 2: State: moderate reform (over radical reform)	RR			MR		RR→ Concession	MR	

Note [a]: These union actions are responses to the state's market reforms (originating from Factor 1) such as retrenchment of the welfare state or labor market flexibilization.

Note [b]: TCTU was established in 1997, but was not recognized by the government until 2000.

Note [c]: Lower-case letters imply 'moderate' degrees of presence instead of 'strong.'

Abbreviations: CGT (General Confederation of Labor); CTA (Argentine Workers' Central Union); CUT (Unified Workers' Central); FKTU (Federation of Korean Trade unions); KCTU (Korean Confederation of Trade Unions); CFL (Chinese Federation of Labor); TCTU (Taiwanese Confederation of Trade Unions).

TABLE 8.3. *Causal Combinations: Determinants of State–Union Interactions in the 2000s (Time of Growth) at Confederation Level*

	Argentina		Brazil		S.Korea		Taiwan	
	CGT	CTA	Força Sindical	CUT	FKTU	KCTU	CFL	TCTU
Factor 1: Economic crisis/pressure for market reforms	Y	Y	Y	Y	Y	Y	y[c]	y[c]
Factor 2: Solidarity (coordination) between confederations	Y	Y	Y	Y	N	N	y	y
Factor 3: Coherence of a confederation	Y	Y	Y	Y	N	N	N	N
Factor 4: Embeddedness (alliance with civil society)	N	Y	Y	Y	N	y	N	y
Factor 5-1: Cohesiveness I (alliance with incumbent party)	N	y	Y	Y	Y	N	y	Y
Factor 5-2: Cohesiveness II (alliance with leftist party)	Y	Y	N	Y	N	Y	N	N
General Outcome 1: Union militancy/restraint (or exit/division)[a]	R	r	R	r	R	M	R	R
General Outcome 2: State: moderate reform (over radical reform)	MR[b]			MR	RR			MR

Note [a]: These union actions are responses to the state's market reforms (originating from Factor 1) such as retrenchment of welfare states or labor market flexibilization.

Note [b]: In Argentina, there was a reversal of market reforms following the 1999–2002 crisis. Therefore, this MR is actually a reverse transition from RR to the status quo, or even a positive expansion of social policies.

Note [c]: Lower-case letters imply 'moderate' degrees of presence instead of 'strong.' Abbreviations: CGT (General Confederation of Labor); CTA (Argentine Workers' Central Union); CUT (Unified Workers' Central); FKTU (Federation of Korean Trade unions); KCTU (Korean Confederation of Trade Unions); CFL (Chinese Federation of Labor); TCTU (Taiwanese Confederation of Trade Unions).

First, cases of 'cohesiveness I' without embeddedness, which illustrates the second case (Appendix C.1), led to cooperation (restraint) with the government (R in Outcome 1) and radical reform by the state (RR in Outcome 2). In the 1990s, the CGT in Argentina, Força Sindical in Brazil, the FKTU in South Korea, and the CFL in Taiwan all chose restraint over militancy when reacting to state-initiated labor-repressive policies (South Korea and Taiwan) or market reforms (Argentina and Brazil). In the 2000s, the FKTU in South Korea and the CFL in Taiwan opted to cooperate with the current governments. In all cases, the common components that drove the state's and unions' decisions were unions' incapacity to mobilize a wide-ranging political alliance in civil society and their very close loyalty to the state. While the former, low embeddedness, led the state to be less concerned about electoral punishments and disruptions resulting from contentious politics, the latter, high cohesiveness, allowed unions to disregard their restraint costs (in the short term). This 'disarticulated cohesiveness' eventually allowed the state to launch radical reforms in Argentina in the 1990s and South Korea in the 2000s, but not in Taiwan.[20] An important point is that 'cohesiveness II', 'alliance with leftist parties,' does not account for variations in market reforms, as unions with 'cohesiveness I' chose restraint, regardless of their ties to leftist parties. In other words, when the incumbent party initiated radical reforms, unions without embeddedness opted to tolerate them regardless of their alliance with leftist parties.

All cases of embeddedness without cohesiveness, discussed in the third case (game 3) in Appendix C.1, resulted in union militancy. In the 1990s, the CTA in Argentina, the KCTU in South Korea, and the growing anti-CFL labor organizations as a part of the Dangwai movement (the TCTU since 1997) in Taiwan followed this path. In the 1990s, the CTA, KCTU, and TCTU maintained their solidaristic ties to the larger civil society groups, all of which originate from their collaborative struggles against authoritarian regimes. Such embeddedness gave these unions ample capacity to punish the state's repressive or anti-labor reform moves, while their low cohesiveness meant that restraint costs were higher than militancy costs. Being intimidated by unions' strong capacity to mobilize large segments of civil society, the state had to withdraw its initial radical reform aspirations and propose a revised bill (in South Korea in 1997), or establish a conciliatory bargaining institution (in Taiwan in 1987). As they increasingly lost their ties to civil society groups in the 2000s, however, both the KCTU and the TCTU never regained such influence and mass mobilization momentum. The TCTU, reinforcing its ties with the DPP, succeeded in participating in institutional politics (Lee 2011) along with the TLF. But the KCTU maintained its recalcitrant position and behavior through the 2000s, refusing to align with the incumbent reformist parties. Among the eight union confederations, the KCTU was the only one that never cooperated with the state (with the exception of the 1997–98 tripartite committee), while maintaining its unilateral solidarity with leftist parties during the 2000s (which turned out to be a disaster, with the implosion of the DLP). As a result, the KCTU neither succumbed to state-led radical market reforms nor was able to draw more moderate reforms on its own in the 2000s and after. However, the TCTU managed to defend existing (if fragmented) social policy schemes, while introducing new social transfer programs through its collaboration with the DPP and the TLF.

Long-term embedded cohesiveness, the most ideal case for unions, has been realized only in Brazil (it was also realized briefly during the tripartite committee era in South Korea in the late 1990s: see Chapter 5). The CUT in Brazil, seeking strong bottom-up grassroots social movement unionism, has maintained strong ties to both civil society and the PT from its founding era in the early 1980s. The CUT maintained its influence even under Cardoso's regime in the 1990s (moderate cohesiveness, denoted as 'y' under factor 5), which makes the CUT in the 1990s an intermediate case between embeddedness without cohesiveness and embedded cohesiveness. The CUT eventually achieved the ultimate embedded cohesiveness as the PT took power in 2003. Throughout the 1990s and early 2000s, the CUT experienced internal conflicts and tensions with the PT due to factional strife, but thanks to the CUT's long-held formal and informal coordination institutions with the PT under embedded cohesiveness, both the incumbent PT and the CUT were able to achieve an optimal outcome (MR-R path, Figure C.1 in Appendix C.1). The CUT cautiously restrained their capacity for contentious politics during the PT government, but they adamantly fought against the PT's reform agendas to push them in union-friendly directions. The CUT, with its strong mobilization capacity alongside other popular-sector actors, effectively defended the existing pensions scheme against both Lula's and Dilma's pension reform bills in 2003 and 2012, respectively. The CUT also played a decisive role in legislating minimum wage law through its policy-relevant lobbying capacity.[21]

It is hard to regard the Argentine state–labor relationship in the 2000s as another case for embedded cohesiveness, because the CGT remained a corporatist union without much effort to connect to civic associations. Even though the Argentine case does not quite match the Brazilian case, the new PJ leadership under the Kirchners was able to build alliances with the traditional partner, the CGT, and the newly emerging social movement union, the CTA. The CTA often returned to its militant, non-conciliatory stance, but its organizational ties with the first Kirchner regime during the electoral campaign enabled the CTA and the PJ to co-ordinate their actions under the umbrella of the *peronistas*.[22] With both the CGT and the CTA's collaboration, the Kirchners were able to launch their ambitious universalist social policy agenda in the 2000s and after.

In short, the embedded cohesiveness approach squarely accounts for variations in unions' actions. Cohesiveness without embeddedness led to radical reform by the state and union restraint, with the exception of Taiwan in the 1990s, while embeddedness without cohesiveness resulted in unions' militancy and concessions by the state in each case. Embedded cohesiveness engendered moderate reform by the state along with union restraint in three instances: CUT (Brazil) in the 1990s and the 2000s, and KCTU briefly in the late 1990s. As for the state's actions, cohesiveness without embeddedness permitted radical reform efforts in Argentina in the 1990s and in South Korea in the 1990s and the 2000s. Embeddedness without cohesiveness initially allowed radical reforms in some countries such as South Korea in the 1990, but ended up with concessions by the state. In other countries, unions with very strong embeddedness drew moderate reforms from the state even without strong cohesiveness, as the CVT did in 1990s' Brazil. Finally, embedded cohesiveness led to moderate reforms in Brazil in the 2000s.

One caveat is the role of the 'coherence of the confederation,' which captures the degree to which a confederation is internally unified and its leadership is underpinned by grassroots unions' consensual loyalty. Even if I initially did not theorize the role of this variable as part of the core components of our theoretical claim, it plays a role in driving unions' militancy as a combinational variable with unions' linkages to civil society. With the exception of the KCTU in the 2000s in South Korea, all other labor–civil society solidarity that led to unions' militancy had 'coherence' as a pre-condition. However, the role of coherence is not clear enough in explaining the MR-R outcomes: for the CUT case in Brazil, coherence, union–civil society linkage, and union–incumbent party linkage were all present, but for other cases, coherence was not necessarily a part of the explanatory combinations.

Overall, during the 1980s and the 1990s, new labor movements emerged that challenged the docility of unions under the umbrella of state-led authoritarian corporatism in all four countries during their transitions to democracy. These new labor groups sought to confront existing state–labor relationships with stronger militancy and encompassing solidarity with civil society groups. Such challenges may be considered collective transitions in labor movements from cohesiveness without embeddedness to embeddedness without cohesiveness during the 1990s. These movements bore fruit in two Latin American countries, where they successfully transitioned to embedded cohesiveness as leftist parties won their electoral competitions in the 2000s. In contrast to Latin America, however, such challenges have slowly dwindled in the two East Asian cases, especially in South Korea, thereby allowing the state to introduce radical retrenchments of social policies and labor market institutions during the 2000s.

9

Associational Networks and the Welfare State in Argentina, Brazil, South Korea, and Taiwan

INTRODUCTION

This chapter[1] extends the study's focus to a comparison among all four democratized, developing societies. As previewed earlier in Chapter 1, the chapter attempts to answer the core research questions animating this study: what factors explain the markedly divergent trajectories of development (and retrenchment) in social policies in these countries? Why did labor politics in some countries successfully defend the welfare state in the era of market fundamentalism, while others were vulnerable to market-oriented reforms? Why did some unions and their allies succeed in building more a universal welfare state, while others failed to do so? How does the South Korean case fare in comparison to other cases, and how much explanatory power does the EC approach have beyond the South Korean case?

In order to answer these questions, the chapter conducts a country-level cross-national case comparison based on the theoretical model developed in Chapter 3. The embedded cohesiveness approach, built upon "the configuration of civil society perspective" (Collier and Collier 1991; Rueschemeyer *et al.* 1992; Sandbrook *et al.* 2007) and social movement perspectives (Amenta *et al.* 2011; Andrews 2004), is expected to account effectively for the variations in social policy outcomes between these countries. As in the previous chapters, this chapter will again highlight two network-based variables, embeddedness and cohesiveness.[2] Then, utilizing co-affiliation networks built upon several waves of World Values Surveys and evidence from comparative case studies of Argentina, Brazil, South Korea, and Taiwan, I investigate the structures of civic networks and their role in steering the political choices of party and union elites regarding the retrenchment or expansion of the welfare state in each country.[3]

In particular, the current chapter focuses on how to measure embeddedness and cohesiveness empirically and how to utilize such data in accounting for the cross-national and over-time variations in the structures of associational networks and welfare state outcomes. I begin by utilizing network analysis of co-membership data (Borgatti *et al.* 2002; Breiger 1974). While the previous chapter explored how each union confederation responded to the state's market reform initiatives differently depending upon its political and civic ties, the current chapter focuses on country-level associational structures centering upon parties and unions. Then, I build a causal framework to explain the effects of organizational configurations of formal and informal civic spheres on the politics of welfare states. Detailed comparative/historical case studies in combination with the results from formal network analysis, which I call 'network-informed case studies,' will jointly account for the politics of social protection in the four recently democratized developing countries.

Overall, the chapter will demonstrate that the differently configured coalitions and interorganizational structures between labor unions and wider civil society organizations shape the varying degrees of universality and generosity of social policies in these four countries.

In discussing the positive cases – namely, Brazil, South Korea in the 1990s, and Argentina and Taiwan in the 2000s – I highlight the importance of the social embeddedness of formal politics in associational fields for promoting welfare policies. In discussing the negative cases – namely, Argentina in the 1990s and South Korea in the 2000s – I explore how leaders of formal organizations (both parties and unions) disarticulated from civil society eventually pursue either the radical retrenchment or the unexpected but fragmented and limited expansion of the welfare state and how unions succumb to such unexpected moves. The chapter concludes with current and future prospects for welfare state developments in these countries.

In the following sections, I will conduct two case studies; one comparing Brazil and Argentina and the other comparing Taiwan and South Korea. Such within-region comparison will extend to a cross-region comparison in the third section, in which I will compare two embedded cohesiveness cases, Brazil and South Korea, with two disarticulated cohesiveness cases, Argentina and Taiwan. In conclusion, I will demonstrate that elites in the formal sector make markedly different political choices when confronting economic crises and democratic competitions depending upon their organizational connections in formal and informal civic networks.

Brazil, with its impressive record of growing the welfare state and reduction in poverty, is the most exemplary case of participatory democracy in recent decades. Most importantly, in contrast to other countries in Latin America, it has successfully resisted market reform pressure on both the public sector and social policies. I argue that the political success story of Brazil in the 1990s and the 2000s could be an outcome of the strong cohesiveness and strong embeddedness of the formal sector. Table 9.1[4] and Figure 9.1 show that unions, parties, and professional associations are not only densely connected to each other (column A) but also deeply embedded in informal civic associations, such as churches, cultural gatherings and

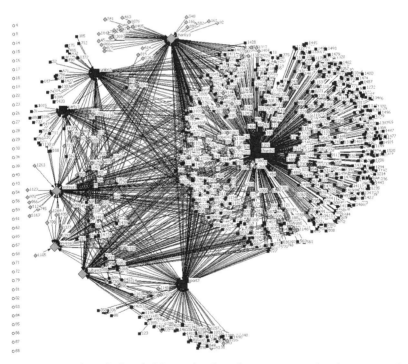

FIGURE 9.1. Associational Networks based on Co-membership Data for Brazil: 2005

Note: See Appendix B for the measurement of network ties.

TABLE 9.1. *Cohesiveness and Embeddedness of the Formal Sector in Four Developing Countries: 1995 and 2005*

Country	Year	Total N	N in Formal Sector (Column A)	N in Informal Civic Sector (Column B)	N of Co-membership Ties within Formal Sector (Column C)	N of Co-membership Ties between Sectors (Column D)	Stock of Social Capital I (A+B)/Total N	Stock of Social Capital II (B/Total N)	Cohesiveness of Formal Sector (C/A)	Embeddedness of Formal Sector (D/A)
Argentina	1995	1079	94	312	17	119	0.38	0.29	0.18	1.27
	2005	1002	62	284	11	60	0.35	0.28	0.18	0.97
Brazil	1995	1149	234	542	93	480	0.68	0.47	0.40	2.05
	2005	1500	262	943	80	511	0.80	0.63	0.31	1.95
South Korea	1995	1249	120	432	10	136	0.44	0.35	0.08	1.13
	2005	1200	45	418	21	111	0.39	0.35	0.47	2.47
Taiwan	1995	780	104	135	9	80	0.31	0.17	0.09	0.77
	2005	1227	84	257	21	91	0.28	0.21	0.25	1.08

clubs, environmental associations, and charity associations (columns D and D/A).

Table 9.1 shows that formal-sector associations in Brazil are noticeably denser and better linked to other associations than those in other countries as determined by either size or linkages. In 1995 the cohesiveness and embeddedness of formal-sector associations (C/A and D/A) were nearly twice as large as those of Argentina. Tables 9.2 and 9.3 also show that labor unions' cohesiveness and embeddedness decreased slightly from 1995 to 2005 but that political parties' linkages with formal and informal civic associations have been stable with a slight upward trend. Compared to Argentina, Brazil's union and party linkages within the formal sector are not impressively higher,[5] but their connections to informal civic lives are vast: Brazilian formal organizations' embeddedness in the informal civic sphere is roughly 2 to 2.5 times higher than that of the Argentine formal sector (see column B in Table 9.2 and column D in Table 9.3).

Furthermore, Brazilian political parties have maintained a very different structure of organizational linkages with unions and other informal civic organizations, compared with their Argentine counterparts. In Table 9.2, both parties' and unions' linkages within and outside the formal civic sector are the highest among the four countries in 1995, and the second highest in 2005. Both left and non-left have maintained relatively close linkages to unions within the formal sector. In Table 9.3, unions' ties to leftist parties, one of the key dimensions of cohesiveness in this study, are not noticeably greater in Brazil than those in Argentina. However, as compared with parties and unions in Argentina, the Brazilian parties and unions' embeddedness in the informal civic sphere has remained much higher. Within Brazil, these differences in the strength of party–union linkages between the left and non-left parties (column C in Table 9.2) are not noticeably large (0.26 versus 0.31 in 2005), but the leftist partisans moderately increased their embeddedness in the wider non-formal civic community (1.47 compared with 1.70).

Based on the strong embeddedness of the formal sector in informal civic organizations, both centrist parties and labor-based parties have been relatively committed to the demands of the poor and the working classes. Party and union leaders embedded in citizens' everyday lives through religious and cultural activities are less likely to conform to radical neoliberal reform paths, as Argentinian and other Latin American organizational leaders did. Indeed, Brazilian unions vehemently resisted the Collor and Cardoso regimes' retrenchment attempts, while negotiating with the

TABLE 9.2. *Parties' Interorganizational Ties within and outside the Formal Sector in Four Developing Countries: 1995 and 2005*

Country	Year	Party's Ties[a] within Formal Sector/ N of Party Members (Column A)	Party's Ties[b] outside Formal Sector/ N of Party Members (Column B)	Party–Union Ties/N of Party Members (Column C)	Party's Ties outside Formal Civic Sector/N of Party Members (Column D)
Argentina	1995	0.32	0.85	0.20 (PJ) / 0.11 (non-PJ)	0.87 (PJ) / 0.84 (non-PJ)
	2005	0.33	0.63	0 (PJ) / 0.36 (non-PJ)	0.50 (PJ) / 0.43 (non-PJ)
Brazil	1995	0.51	1.46	0.34 (Left)[c] / 0.21 (non-Left)	1.47 (Left) / 1.45 (non-Left)
	2005	0.56	1.53	0.26 (Left)[c] / 0.31 (non-Left)	1.70 (Left) / 1.28 (non-Left)
South Korea	1995	0.23	1.00	No partisanship information available for South Korea	
	2005	1.00	2.08		
Taiwan	1995	0.23	0.92	0.18 (KMT) / 0.22 (non-KMT)	0.53 (KMT) / 1.67 (non-KMT)
	2005	0.38	0.95	0.46 (KMT) / 0.13 (non-KMT)	0.54 (KMT) / 1.63 (non-KMT)

Note [a]: Party's ties include co-membership values (1) between party and union and (2) between party and professional association.

Note [b]: Party's ties include co-membership values between party and union and all other informal civic associations.

Note [c]: As coalitional politics are very common in Brazil, I used 'leftist parties' rather than 'PT'. In the leftist parties, PT (Workers' Party), PDT (Democratic Labor Party), PTB (Brazilian Labor Party), PV (Green Party), and PSOL (Socialist Liberal Party) were included (among those listed in the questionnaire). PMDB participated in the coalition (With the Strength of the People) for Dilma Rousseff in the 2010 presidential election, but was not classified as a leftist party in this study, as it is clearly a catch-all party with a wide-ranging ideological spectrum from right to left.

TABLE 9.3. *Unions' Interorganizational Ties within and outside the Formal Sector in Four Developing Countries: 1995 and 2005*[a]

Country	Year	Measures of Cohesiveness			Embeddedness
		Union's Ties[b] within Formal Sector/N of Union Members (Column A)	Unions' Ties with Leftist Parties/N of Union Members (Column B)	Unions' Ties with non-Leftist Parties/N of Union Members (Column C)	Union's Ties outside Formal Sector/ N of Union Members (Column D)
Argentina	1995	0.58	*0.16*[c]	0.10	1.37
	2005	0.57	*0.07*[c]	0.29	0.57
Brazil	1995	0.65	0.10	*0.10*[d]	1.44
	2005	0.45	*0.09*[d]	0.07	1.33
South Korea	1995	0.25	No partisanship information available		1.13
	2005	0.83			2.00
Taiwan	1995	0.12	No labor party	*0.07*[e]	0.55
	2005	0.50		*0.18*[e]	0.68

Note [a]: The interpretation of these results requires some caveats, as they are based on a very small degree of co-membership between unions and leftist (or non-leftist) parties.

Note [b]: Union's ties include co-membership values (1) between union and party and (2) between union and professional association.

Note [c]: For both decades, the incumbent party in Argentina was the PJ, with the exception of the Fernando de la Rúa regime (1999–2001).

Note [d]: For the 1990s and the 2000s in Brazil, the incumbent parties were the PSDB (1990s) and the PT (2000s). For the coverage of 'leftist parties,' see Table 9.2, note c.

Note [e]: In Taiwan there is no labor party. Unionists were co-affiliated with both KMT and DPP. The incumbent parties were KMT in the 1990s, and DPP in the 2000s (2000–08).

Lula regime for more moderate reform (see Chapter 7 for confederation-level details).

It is important to point out that recent policy adoption and implementation processes in Brazil are fundamentally different from market reforms in the rest of Latin America. As the PT illustrates, many party and union leaders in Brazil came out of local, municipal-level community politics.[6] As participatory budgeting movements in Porto Alegre and other Brazilian cities signify, local community politics at the state and municipal levels educate participatory publics and leaders, some of whom eventually rise to the top of national-level politics. They refuse to accept the idea that elite politicians mediate and represent the demands of unions or social movements in conventional representative democracy. They desire to eliminate the dichotomy of government versus movements and thus to build the government from below via social movements. The refusal to permit a dichotomy between governments and movements allowed the PT to develop modes of close "organizational communication between politicians, party organs, and grassroots organizations." (Guidry 2003, p. 104) This open communication mode initiated by community-oriented union and party leaders has enabled the CUT and the PT to represent broader social bases beyond labor unions, as discussed in Chapter 7, and indeed has led wider publics of diverse class origin to support the labor-based party's local and central governance. The CUT and the PT's local and central leaders have occupied the "bridging position"(Mische 2008) between the formal sector and the informal civic sphere. For instance, "the CUT participates in the National Council of Women's Rights, the National Youth Council, the National Health Council, and the National Council of Disabled People" (Rosane da Silva). The PT government provided an important institutional space in which diverse social forces contend, debate, and coordinate their different interests, and the CUT has played central bridging roles in these different fields of social policies. The Health Council is composed of 50 percent civil society actors, 25 percent workers' representatives, and 25 percent health service providers. Social movement leaders arising from a 'pathology society', e.g. those patients and their family members who suffer from incurable diseases (cancer, leukemia, AIDS, leprosy, etc.) or representatives of the associations of Down's Syndrome, diabetes, and autism, played key roles in these health councils, according to Regina Costa (general secretary of the National Confederation of Workers in Social Security). They were ideal examples of the 'embedded' or 'bridging' leaders whom I discussed earlier, in Chapter 3. They eventually became involved in public health boards and councils as representatives of civil society and played decisive roles in shaping drug policies and health care plans. Also, there are civic and union leaders who are better linked to these grassroots associations and their needs, due to their social movement origins. Such a structural position based on its origins in social movement and its communal leadership made it possible for PT municipal and federal candidates to succeed not only in electoral politics but also in participatory institutional governance. Brazilian union and civic leaders, therefore, were able to collaborate again in these institutional spaces to create more universal and redistributive social policies.

This grassroots institutional and movement-based mobilization of publics and leaders and the consequent political trust between formal party organizations and informal grassroots organizations also played decisive roles in federal-level welfare politics. Under economic pressures (regarding the budget and debt crises) similar to Argentina's, Brazilian political leaders were reluctant to turn to economic technocrats. Both Cardoso (1994–2002) and Lula (2002–10) took the radical privatization path off the table, turning to more moderate reform paths by changing entitlement criteria, as the PT, the CUT, and their allied civil society movement activists staunchly opposed any privatization plan (Hunter 2010). Eventually, the CUT and its allies successfully defended the pensions system without resorting to radical retrenchment.

Furthermore, they (the PT policy-makers) introduced Bolsa Familia, an innovative cash transfer program conditional upon a child's regular school attendance and participation in vaccination programs, nutrition programs, and vocational training courses (Hall 2008; Lomeli 2008), by unifying several pre-existing family allowance schemes. In a society like Brazil, in which extreme poverty and inequality are prevalent and existing social insurance programs favor workers in the core industries and public sectors, implementing an effective social assistance program is as important as defending an existing social insurance program. Bolsa Familia has been so effective in fighting poverty that the World Bank praised it as the most efficiently targeted CCT (conditional cash transfer) scheme in Latin America. The universal delivery criteria and performance of the benefits are indicative of the commitment of embedded PT leaders to serving the poor in the urban and rural informal sector: 73 percent of the benefits are delivered to the poorest 20 percent of the population, and 94 percent are given to the lowest two quintiles (Hall 2008). This Brazilian CCT case is impressively comparable to the Argentine case, in which a CCT program has been implemented on a similarly large scale, but the handouts in Argentina were delivered to loyal voters primarily through patronage party brokers' personalized, clientelistic social networks (Calvo and Murillo 2013; De La O 2011), with the result that only 32 percent of the handouts reached the poorest 20 percent. In short, Brazilian embedded formal-sector leaders are more likely to deliver their social policy benefits to a wider range of constituents beyond their partisan loyalists.

These efforts are well translated into impressive increases in social spending measures: social assistance spending increased from 1.43 percent of GDP in 2000 to 2.49 percent in 2010 (Cerutti *et al.* 2014). Total federal social spending per person increased from US$726 in 1995 to

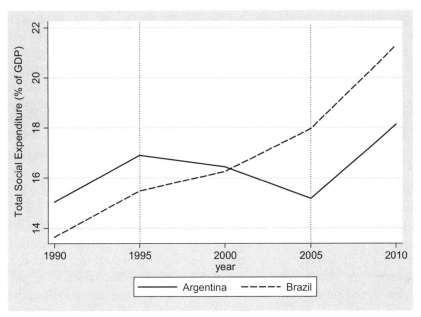

FIGURE 9.2. Total Social Expenditure in Argentina and Brazil: 1990–2010
Source: ILO 2014–15.

$1,642 in 2010, which represents a 172 percent increase. During the same period, total social spending as a percentage of GDP also increased from 13.65 percent in 1995 to 21.29 percent, as shown in Figure 9.2. Bolsa Familia, BPC (the Benefício de Prestação Continuada: Unconditional Cash Transfer program) and the minimum wage policy played decisive roles in reducing deep and widespread poverty problems in Brazil. During the Lula regime, the share of population living in poverty decreased from 35.8 percent (61 million) in 2003 to 21.4 percent (40 million) in 2009 (Higgins 2012).

Overall, Brazilian party leaders have maintained relatively stable inter-organizational linkages within the formal sector and with the informal civic sector, and, despite the pressures from recurring debt and balance-of-payment crises, they not only resisted neo-liberal market-oriented reform pressures on their social insurance system but also successfully extended their universal poverty alleviation program to eligible populations on an unprecedented scale.

The Brazilian case in the 1990s and the 2000s suggests that the embedded cohesiveness of participatory mobilization is critical for deterring and moderating retrenchment pressures on social policies under economic crisis. Party and union leaders embedded in social movement and community associations did not choose to jump on the bandwagon of successful market-oriented reform paths in neighboring countries, but carefully created and utilized room for maneuver among market forces composed of international and domestic capital, labor unions and popular movement organizations, constituents with different interests, and other stakeholders.

* * *

The case of Argentina is emblematic of relatively strong cohesiveness and weak embeddedness of the formal sector. President Carlos Menem's radical neo-liberal reform of public sector and social welfare programs, especially concerning pensions, in the 1990s, along with a striking transformation of the PJ, led to political and electoral success. Menem's reform strategy fundamentally transformed the Argentine economy from a protected market with a large public sector to a more market-oriented open economy. Menem and the PJ's neo-liberal reform projects of the public sector were all the more striking because the PJ was a representative left-wing, labor-based party that had played a central role in creating modern Argentina's relatively generous welfare programs (Brooks 2008; Levitsky 2003b).

A central argument of this study is that the relatively strong cohesiveness and weak embeddedness of formal-sector associations allowed Menem and the PJ to implement such radical neo-liberal reform of the public sector. In 1995, about the time when Menem had just embarked upon pension reform,[7] labor unions still maintained fairly close relationships with political parties, as shown in Table 9.2 (columns A and B). The linkages of Argentina's parties with unions and professional associations were moderately strong compared with the situation in other countries. At the same time, however, the political parties' linkages to non-formal civic organizations in Argentina were much weaker than those in other countries.

The disarticulated formal sector – characterized by weak ties between the formal sector and the informal civic sphere, in contrast to stable, relatively durable ties within the formal sector – gave Menem and the PJ sufficient room to cultivate new electoral coalitions around newly emerging service sectors and those elements of the poor urban sectors that were still loyal to the PJ.[8] Some union leaders of the CGT (General Confederation of Labor) also remained with Menem as the PJ's constituents and clients, receiving the right to create and run their own health care programs (Madrid 2003; Murillo 2001). Some unions' support for Menem, his finance technocrats, and the PJ played a critical role in the passage of pension privatization in the legislature, although the majority of unions remained opposed to the reform drive (Roberts 2006).

As a result of a decade of radical market-based reforms, however, many union organizations increasingly cut their ties with the PJ.[9] In other words, the formerly labor-based PJ's strong cohesiveness in the formal sector and weak embeddedness in informal civic associations eventually weakened its own cohesive ties with traditional allies – unions – in the formal sector. This gradual erosion of the PJ's organizational base within the formal sector was driven mainly by union leaders who could not sustain grassroots-level anger about Menem's retrenchment drive. Menem's technocrats and the PJ legislators kept revising the compromised restructuring proposals by cutting (and eventually eliminating) the guaranteed minimum pension amount, lowering replacement rates, and setting an upper limit on pension benefits (Haggard and Kaufman 2008). Increasingly more union organizations and members became

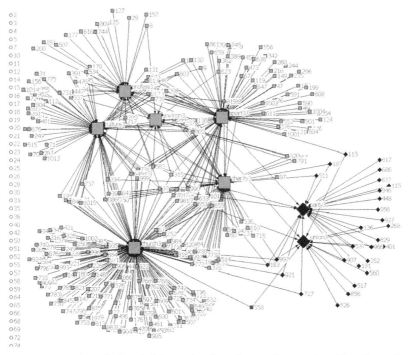

FIGURE 9.3. Associational Networks based on Co-membership Data for Argentina: 2005
Note: See Appendix B for the measurement of network ties.

disenchanted with and enraged by Menem's continued retrenchment moves in times of repeated economic crises.

In the end, the PJ's radical market reforms based on its cohesiveness led to a dismantling of its traditional mass labor party structure, which had been built on close interorganizational networks between the PJ and labor unions. There was a dramatic breakdown of longtime traditions – of union members' participation in the PJ's political activities, of PJ leaders' political careers as union members (Levitsky 2003a), and of union leaders' connections with the informal civic sphere. As a result, labor unions' embeddedness plummeted for a decade, scoring 0.57 in 2005, the lowest among the four case countries (see column D in Table 9.3).[10]

More specifically, Table 9.2 shows that, in 1995, 20 percent of PJ members had ties with labor unions and professional associations, but in 2005, strikingly, none of the PJ members kept ties with other formal-sector associations, while 36 percent of non–PJ Party members[11] were co-affiliated with unions in 2005. In short, after more than a decade of neo-liberal reform, union leaders and members not only cut ties with the PJ but also no longer maintained close ties with informal civic associations. This tendency is also obvious in Table 9.3, which shows that unions' ties with leftist parties (the PJ) and other non-formal civic associations in Argentina also plummeted over time. One possible explanation for this reduced union embeddedness may be that the unions' weakened ties with the PJ also led them to lose their mediating position between the PJ and the informal civic sphere. Overall, the Argentine partisan embeddedness shown in Table 9.2, regardless of partisanship, is noticeably lower than that of other countries, especially Brazil. These characteristics of Argentine formal and informal civic spheres are clearly illustrated in Figure 9.3, in which both union and party are sparsely connected to other non-formal civic associations.[12]

These changes in associational structure were well reflected in changes in social spending measures in Argentina: it suffered a significant decline in its social security budget, which decreased from 16.91 percent (of GDP) in 1995 to 15.18 percent in 2005, as illustrated in Figure 9.2.[13] Redistributive government transfers targeting the lower classes and the poor remained stagnant below 1 percent of GDP during this time, in sharp contrast to Brazil's impressive expansion of redistributive social assistance programs. In addition to its harsh stabilization and austerity measures in the financial sector, the Menem regime introduced a partial privatization of pensions in which private individualized accounts coexisted with the public system (Madrid 2003).

With the pensions reform and decreased social benefits, Argentina was able to cut its budget deficit significantly during the 1990s, but it had to witness dramatic increases in both income inequality and poverty.[14] Argentina had to wait until the Kirchners took over power to witness its own version of expansionary social policy reforms – in the latter part of the 2000s.

To sum up, the departure of a labor-based party from its traditional base of support, as indicated by radical retrenchment of state sectors and state-funded social programs, could be attributed more generally to the lack of social embeddedness of Argentine political parties, especially the PJ. This over-time departure of the PJ from the existing brokerage relationship with unions also led to precipitous decline in union embeddedness in informal civil society (see columns B and D in Table 9.3). As I described earlier, the major unions (CGT), being disarticulated from (weak) civil society, mostly conformed to such radical reforms, while a minority of them (the CTA elements) bolted from of the majority. This Argentine case illustrates how a loosely linked political organization could easily detach itself from both formal-sector allies and its community-based solidarity. The transformative move toward market reforms by the Menemist PJ in initial alliance with unions eventually led to its alienation from its traditional allies, the unions, and consequently, to the demise of labor-based social solidarity.

Argenine labor movements, especially led by the CTA, realigned themselves under the Kirchnerism following the 2003 presidential election and succeeded in building a sort of labor–civic solidarity. This coordination among labor unions and their allies, mainly led by new social movement unionism (as discussed in Chapter 8), contributed to the Kirchners' consecutive electoral successes and the expansion of universal social policies in the 2000s and after.[15]

CASE STUDIES II: TAIWAN VERSUS SOUTH KOREA

Universal and Fragmented Expansion of the Welfare State

In contrast to Latin American economies, plagued with chronic debt and foreign currency crises accompanied by extremely high inflation, the two East Asian developing countries, which had achieved high economic growth and sound, balanced budgets, had a sufficient degree of freedom to expand social safety nets even when confronting the economic crises of the late 1990s. While Latin American countries suffered the pressures of the politics of retrenchment across the entire region, East Asian countries relished the politics of expansion for social policies.

Taiwan and South Korea appear to have followed very similar trajectories in their welfare state development. After the transition to democracy in the late 1980s, both countries achieved the dramatic expansion of their social policy regimes. Not only did they reshape health insurance to cover nearly the entire population, but they also introduced many other major social welfare schemes such as unemployment insurance and old-age allowances in the 1990s and the 2000s. As much previous scholarship points out (Haggard and Kaufman 2008; Wong 2004), this rapid expansion of welfare regimes in the two countries is mainly attributable to consolidated democratic competition.

I contend, however, that the two countries also developed increasingly different structures of civic spheres after the transition to democracy and that these differences drove them to follow increasingly divergent paths

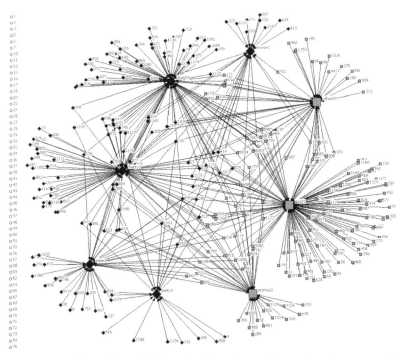

FIGURE 9.4. Associational Networks based on Co-membership Data for Taiwan: 2005

Note: See Appendix B for the measurement of network ties.

of welfare state development, paths not easily detectable on the basis of spending measures.[16] I again focus on the different configurations of their formal sectors, and find that the Taiwanese formal sector has come increasingly close to the Argentine one, if to a lesser degree, while the structure of the South Korean formal sector may have been increasingly comparable to the Brazilian one up until the mid-2000s. During the time, the basic frameworks of major social insurance programs, in terms of coverage, contribution, and distribution systems, were largely determined in the processes of state–society interactions and political competitions in both countries. How, then, have different configurations of labor–civic networks shaped the different trajectories of social policy development?

The connectivity of Taiwanese civic spheres was initially character-ized by the weak cohesiveness and weak embeddedness of the formal sphere in 1995, even if both dimensions of connectivity became some-what stronger over time. Table 9.2 shows that the cohesiveness within the formal sector of both unions and parties in Taiwan was the lowest among the four countries in 1995, but Taiwanese parties and unions rap-idly strengthened their interorganizational ties within the formal sector over the course of a decade, while remaining disconnected from the in-formal civic sphere. Figure 9.4 shows that parties in Taiwan have some visible connections with unions but are barely connected with other non-formal civic associations. Epitomizing the disarticulated cohesiveness in Taiwanese politics was the conversion in the mid-1990s of the Taiwanese ruling party, the KMT, from an anti-welfare conservative force to a pro-welfare centrist party.

The KMT, despite its half-century-long rule, did not develop strong or-ganizational bases in grassroots civil society (see columns D in Table 9.2). This low embeddedness, however, also allowed it to transform itself quickly into a centrist party, often supporting social policy provisions against the interests of its traditional supporters, such as employers. In contrast to the KMT, non-KMT parties, of which the main party is the DPP, show a fairly high level of embeddedness (even higher than that of Brazilian leftist parties). Given that unions' overall embeddedness is very low in Taiwan (see column D in Table 9.3), it is the DPP that has played a leading role in Taiwanese political and civil society.

Confronting growing electoral challenges from the opposition DPP, backed up by a coalition of civil society groups (Wong 2004) advocating ambitious universal health care, pension, and guaranteed income policies, the KMT eventually pushed for progressive social policy reforms, launching National Health Insurance in 1995 and unemployment insurance for all workers in 1999, as pre-emptive policy initiatives just before the legislative elections in 1996 and 2000.[17] As the DPP prioritized (non-contributory) old-age pensions as its main platform (Fell 2005), expanding its electoral base to the rural areas that were traditional KMT strongholds, the main-stream faction of the KMT determined to respond to this electoral challenge by advocating correspondingly radical but transfer-based welfare reforms. During the late 1990s and early 2000s, in short, South Korea promoted a single-pillar, contribution-based universal pension scheme, while Taiwan advanced fragmented, allowance-based pension plans (Choi 2008).

In contrast to the Taiwanese social welfare revolution (over health care and employment insurance) led by the conservative government, or to the compromise solution (over pensions) between a weak reformist government and a strong conservative legislature, nearly all other major 'universal' social policies in South Korea were introduced by incumbent reformist policy-makers, in alliance with strong pro-welfare "advocacy coalitions" (Kwon 2003; Sabatier 1986) drawn from civil society groups. For instance, while, in Taiwan, the KMT policy-makers initiated and final-ized universal health care reform from the very inception of the policy-crafting process, dominating legislative efforts from other party (the DPP) or civil society groups (Wong 2004), in South Korea, national health care reform in 1999 was an outcome of decade-long conflicts and negotiations between labor, capital, parties, and relevant social forces (as described in Chapters 4 and 5), since peasant groups had protested against unequal benefits and administrative structures in 1988. Both national labor and peasant confederations, and civil society groups consisting of 77 organi-zations (NCHIU, National Conference for Health Insurance Unification) set as their primary goal the reform of the segmented corporatist struc-tures of health care administrations into a unitary universal structure; bipartisan efforts (agreements) responding to this pressure passed the bill unanimously in the middle of financial crisis in 1997.

The growth of pro-welfare civil society forces in South Korea coin-cided exactly with the decline of contentious politics and the growth of the cohesiveness and embeddedness of the formal institutional sphere. After the turbulent eruptions of democratization, labor strikes, and di-verse social movements in the 1980s and early 1990s, South Korean associational fields began, in the mid-1990s, to experience the rapid insti-tutionalization of movement organizations and agendas. Both unions and political parties suffered significant declines in their membership, but, simultaneously, key leaders of such formal organizations started building close ties with other main actors in formal and informal civic spheres.

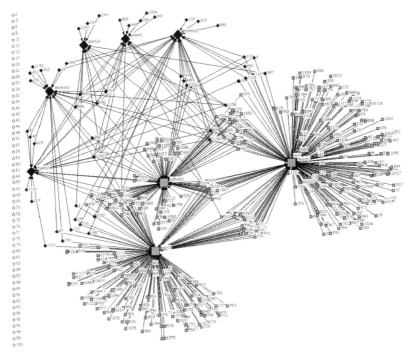

FIGURE 9.5. Associational Networks based on Co-membership Data for South Korea: 2005

Note: See Appendix B for the measurement of network ties.

While Table 9.1 shows a significant decrease in the membership counts for the formal sector,[18] Table 9.2 shows that leaders of both parties and unions dramatically increased their ties within the formal sector (0.25 to 0.83 for unions and 0.23 to 1 for parties) and with informal civic organizations outside the formal sector (1.13 to 2 for unions and 1 to 2.08 for parties). Parties and unions increased their share of personnel resources through co-membership ties, and also become more closely connected with community-level informal civic organizations, as illustrated in Figure 9.5.[19] Within a decade, both the cohesiveness and the embeddedness of the South Korean formal sector surpassed those of Brazil, which was ranked at the top among the four case countries in 1995.

In particular, during this period, labor–civic solidarity succeeded in pressuring the new democratic (D. J. Kim) regime to introduce the universal integration of health insurance societies and the universal extension of pension coverage to the urban poor and self-employed, the processes of which were analyzed in detail in previous chapters. In addition, the introduction of a government-guaranteed basic income, which is known as the minimum living standard guarantee (MLSG), is another good example of civil society-driven welfare reforms. It is stipulated as a citizen's basic right rather than as the state's selective assistance to the needy. Among civil society groups, the role of People's Solidarity for Participatory Democracy (PSPD) was decisive in putting national guaranteed income on the table during and after the financial crisis.[20] The PSPD formed a strong advocacy coalition composed of 26 influential civic associations, including the KCTU, CCEJ, and KWAU, and then kept up pressure upon both the ruling reformist party and the opposition conservative party for the adoption of a national minimum living standard (Kwon 2003, 2007). An important distinction between the PSPD-led advocacy coalition and other pressure groups was that it had allies not only in the ruling party but also in the government bureaucracy and the opposition conservative party. The coalition ignited competition between the two parties by promoting a legislative petition that allied it with a representative of the opposition conservative party, while keeping up the pressure on allies in the ruling party to pass actual legislation. After the law was proposed, while it was passing through the standing committee of the National Assembly, and under intense scrutiny and debate from different ministries within the government for follow-up enforcement regulations, the coalition continued to play a significant role in maintaining the original spirit and content of the regulations during each step of the legislative and implementation process.

The most illustrative examples of the difference in the policy mobilization and crafting processes between the two countries until the mid-2000s are the politics of health care and old-age pensions. Both Taiwan's health care and its old-age pensions basically consist of three different sub-systems that can hardly be called a unitary national scheme: one for state and public sector employees, one for subscribers to pre-existing labor insurance in established firms, and another for formerly uncovered populations, mostly nonemployed, unemployed, and self-employed people.[21] When it comes to the pensions system, its fragmented nature is less likely to generate effective solidaristic risk pooling and redistribution effects. This fragmented structure results in "uneven levels of benefit to different segments of the population" (Ramesh 2004, p. 14). The fragmented structure (of the pensions) was the product of a political compromise between the DPP government and the KMT-dominated legislature. On one hand, the KMT wanted neither to endorse the incumbent DPP's long-held platform (old-age pension) nor to be depicted as an anti-welfare force by opposing the quasi-cash transfer program for the formerly uninsured in the informal sector. On the other hand, without strong support from civil society encompassing both the working and the middle class, but with strong opposition from its significant financial supporters (small business), the incumbent DPP government did not have enough capacity to pass the original universal scheme through the hostile legislature at any point in the 2000s. This is how three different pillars of pension schemes eventually came to coexist in a fragmented form under the name of the National Pension. The KMT's two completely different platforms on social welfare depending upon their incumbency suggest that its policy orientation is based completely on electoral needs and tactics. The Taiwanese health care system is also fragmented, if less so than its pensions counterpart. Most importantly, health care for employees in firms with fewer than five employees is still based on voluntary coverage, while there still exist "special cash benefit systems for civil servants, farmers, public sector employees, and teachers" (USA Social Security Administration 2014, p. 223). Since its inception in 1995 by the KMT, Taiwanese labor unions and civil society have not made much effort to resolve the fragmented system of health care.

However, in South Korea, an old-age pension program was introduced as a single-pillar scheme with strong redistributive income transfer components from corporate employees in the formal sectors to non-employed or self-employed citizens in the rural and urban informal sectors.[22] The integration of the formerly fragmented health insurance was also an enduring and consistent effort to build a national single-pillar system under which the self-employed and non-employees, as well as public and private sector workers, would be covered by the same conditions of service and benefits.[23] Even some segments of labor unions and middle-class NGOs were initially strongly opposed to these single-pillar redistributive systems in pension and health care systems, but the newly elected reformist government succeeded in implementing the progressive single-pillar schemes with strong support from the more progressive elements within unions and civil society groups.

In Taiwan, both main parties, the KMT and the DPP, showed strong interest in expanding the social policy regime in the 1990s. Their mutual competition was initially driven by the DPP's ambitious cash transfer programs, designed to compete with the KMT's vote buying (Fell 2005), which was later matched by the KMT's pre-emptive reform initiatives. As a result, a large part of the Taiwanese social welfare schemes consists of direct cash transfers targeted toward specific groups, rather than

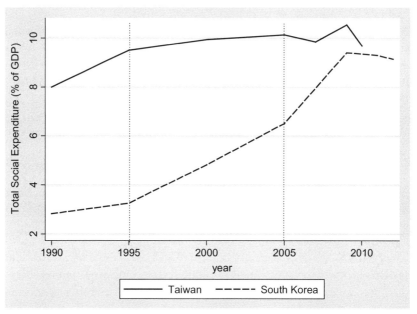

FIGURE 9.6. Total Social Expenditure in South Korea and Taiwan: 1990–2011
Source: ILO 2014–15.

universal programs that embrace different segments of the population under a unitary redistributive scheme.[24]

These institutional differences are not clearly reflected in Figure 9.6, which shows the two countries' overall social expenditure since 1990. But the trends in the figure clearly distinguish Taiwan from South Korea: the former had its 'social policy revolution from above' when the KMT was in power during the authoritarian era and the early transition to democracy, while the latter achieved 'social policy revolution from below' when labor–civic solidarity aggressively pushed forward its agenda between the mid-1990s and the late 2000s. In South Korea, when the conservative regime regained its incumbency in the late 2000s, the rapid expansion of the welfare state was halted or at least suppressed.

SUMMARY AND DISCUSSION: EMBEDDED COHESIVENESS VS. DISARTICULATED COHESIVENESS

In this section, I move beyond comparison within regions. I initially define the Argentine and Taiwanese cases in the 1990s and South Korean case

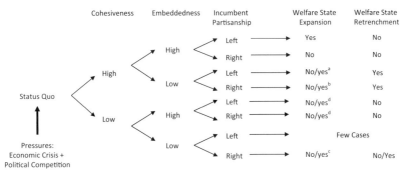

FIGURE 9.7. Disarticulated Cohesiveness, Embedded Cohesiveness, and Partisan Leaders' Preferences for the Welfare State

Notes [a, b,] and [c]: 'yes' only when economic crisis is not imminent and previous growth records are impressive. However, expansionary reform is likely to be limited to a certain client population of the incumbent party.

Note [d]: 'yes' only when unions have a very high level of embeddedness.

in the 2000s as examples of disarticulated cohesiveness, while classifying the Brazilian case (in the 1990s and the 2000s) and the South Korean case (in the late 1990s) as examples of embedded cohesiveness or embeddedness without cohesiveness.[25] In this classification across regions, I formulate a causal path tree that accounts for divergent outcomes of welfare politics, contingent upon the level of cohesiveness and embeddedness, and the partisanship of incumbent governments (Figure 9.7). I then focus on the structural positions of labor unions in associational communities and their consequences for welfare politics in terms of changes over time for both independent and dependent variables (see Figure 9.8 and Table 9.4).[26]

Figure 9.7 proposes causal pathways using two main explanatory factors and an additional variable (partisan incumbency), as well as expansion or retrenchment outcomes for welfare states in four developing countries in the 1990s and the 2000s. All four countries are exposed to initial pressures originating from globalization and democratization. Severe financial crisis and fierce political competition (after transition to democracy) put similar pressures on elites and leaders of formal politics in these countries; nonetheless, they have followed different trajectories, depending upon their organizational capacity as determined by their various modes of linkage.

In theory, with unions' low cohesiveness (with incumbent parties) and low embeddedness, I would assume that there would be little

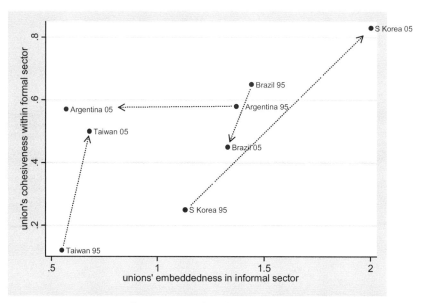

FIGURE 9.8. Unions' Cohesiveness within the Formal Sector and Embeddedness in the Informal Civic Sphere in Four Countries: 1995–2005

interorganizational capacity to push forward radical (expansionary) reform projects. Therefore, no action for expansionary reform will be taken for the rest of the trees.[27] In the case of retrenchment pressure, low cohesiveness and low embeddedness may allow the incumbent right-wing party to introduce radical market-oriented reforms. As discussed in Chapter 8, high embeddedness, even without cohesiveness, is a sufficient condition to prevent partisan government from launching market-oriented reforms. Even in the case of a right-wing incumbent party introducing radical market reform, unions' high embeddedness may lead the state to withdraw its initial action and introduce a revised, conciliatory bill, which was the case in 1996–97 Great Labor Struggle in South Korea.

Depending upon the level of embeddedness, strong cohesiveness would be expected to diverge toward different outcomes. With both high embeddedness and medium to high cohesiveness, under leftist or reformist governments inheriting good growth records and a sound budget situation, unions and allying civil society forces will launch expansionary programs (e.g. South Korea in the late 1990s and Brazil in the 2000s).[28] Even in the event that they inherit an economic crisis (over budget, currency, or debt) from a previous regime, they would not retrench the existing welfare state, as happened in Brazil. Being

TABLE 9.4. *Over-Time Changes in Cohesiveness, Embeddedness, and the Welfare State: 1995–2005*

Country	Change in union cohesiveness	Change in union embeddedness	Change in ratio (cohesiveness /embeddedness)	Change in welfare state (pensions)	Unexpected (non-partisan) changes in welfare state
Argentina	Little (-.01)	Strongly negative (-.80)	Strongly positive (.58)	Radical retrenchment	Yes
Brazil	Weakly negative (-.20)	Weakly negative (-.11)	Weakly negative (-.11)	Moderate adjustment	No
South Korea	Strongly positive (.58)	Strongly positive (.87)	Weakly positive (.20)	Expansion (universal)	No
Taiwan	Weakly positive (.38)	Weakly positive (0.13)	Strongly positive (.50)	Expansion (transfer–based, fragmented)	Yes

surrounded by cohesive formal-sector organizations embedded in supporting civic associations, even a right-wing or center-right government – such as the recent M. B. Lee regime in South Korea (2008–13; its efforts toward privatization in national health care), the recent Ma Ying-jeou regime in Taiwan (2008–16; its pension reform efforts), or the Cardoso regime in Brazil (1995–2002; its pension reform efforts) – would not be able to push radical neo-liberal reform programs, although neither would it be able to launch any new generous welfare programs.

Over-time changes in cohesiveness and embeddedness, as shown in Figure 9.8 and Table 9.4, lend credence to this scenario.[29] Figure 9.8 shows that, with Brazil maintaining its strong case as an example of embedded cohesiveness without noticeable changes over time in either cohesiveness or embeddedness, South Korean labor unions' upward move during the late 1990s and the early 2000s in both dimensions toward another instance of embedded cohesiveness is impressive (while its abrupt decline in the next decade is no less impressive). Consequently, while the few (or only weak negative) changes in Brazil have led to virtually no change in major social policy areas (or moderate adjustment), a very strong positive change brought in universal expansion of major social policy schemes in South Korea (see Table 9.4).

In Table 9.4, the summary columns of over-time changes in cohesiveness and embeddedness suggest that unions' embeddedness has a stronger explanatory power than their cohesiveness.[30] Unions' cohesiveness explains variations between the East Asian countries and the Latin American countries. However, it does not explain variations within a region: little change is associated with differential outcomes, retrenchment in Argentina, and persistence of the welfare state in Brazil. By contrast, changes in embeddedness effectively account for subtle qualitative differences in changes in welfare states. I conceptualize these over-time tendencies not only as a greater incorporation of unions into social democratic politics but also as a greater engagement of unions in community or civil society-based informal solidarity. Strong political trust built upon the durable linkage of unions (union leaders) with other formal-sector associations is embedded in informal civic lives in Brazil and South Korea.

To sum up, the politics of embeddedness or embedded cohesiveness is associated with protecting the welfare sector, even under severe economic crisis or ambitiously expanding universal social policies under reformist governments. In both Brazil and South Korea, the clear commitment of unions and their allying reformist parties or progressive civic associations to guaranteeing citizens' general welfare and living conditions against destructive market competition remained stable (Brazil) or strengthened over time (South Korea, if only until the mid-2000s), and they were underpinned by organizational linkages within the formal sector and between the formal and informal civic spheres in both countries. The leaders of cohesively linked (labor-based) formal organizations, being deeply embedded in the informal civic sphere, have aggressively chan-neled demands for more universal and generous social protections from the wider class and community bases, including the middle and working classes.

These two cases of embeddedness (or embedded cohesiveness) offer convincing support to the predictions made in Chapter 3 for retrench-ment games 3 and 4 and expansion games 3 and 4 (Appendix C.1 and C.2). With strong embeddedness, labor–civic solidarity may succeed in threatening or persuading the state under neo-liberal market reform pres-sures not to introduce radical reforms, as the Cardoso and Lula regimes' moderate adjustments to neo-liberalism illustrate. In addition, when unions are well-connected both to the incumbent party and to progres-sive informal civic associations, labor–civic solidarity is likely to promote universal welfare reforms that embrace a wide range of wage earners and the self-employed, as South Korean pension and health care reforms dem-onstrate. The durable support and leadership of South Korean unions (especially the KHU and the KHMU under the KCTU) in pursuit of uni-versal reforms in the late 1990s (see Chapter 5) is in great contrast with Taiwanese unions' passive and conciliatory stance regarding the KMT and DPP's welfare reforms: Taiwanese unions rarely pursued universal expansionary reforms as their core organizational agenda during the ex-pansionary reform eras of the 1990s and the 2000s. With respect to the National Health Insurance reform in 1995 introduced by the KMT, few unions, at the time and even later on, questioned the limited coverage issue (of employees in firms with five or more employees only) or the fragmented nature of the system along private vs. public sector or indus-trial vs. agricultural sector lines. In a similar vein, regarding the pensions program, Taiwanese unions rarely questioned the fragmented system and its limited potential to support redistribution.

With the high cohesiveness and low embeddedness path shown in Figure 9.7, which I have labeled 'disarticulated cohesiveness,' parti-san governments become non-partisan in the traditional sense, as they have room to maneuver strategically depending upon their judgments of the potential gains to come from transformative politics. The dis-articulated cohesiveness, however, may become unstable over time.

A labor-based populist party's betrayal of its own traditional partner (as in the case of the unions in Argentina) and a former conservative authoritarian party's passive revolution through pre-emptive welfare enactments (as in Taiwan) drove unions to float without apparent political allies in these countries in the 1990s. In Argentina, labor's linkages with informal civic associations sharply decreased (see Figure 9.8) as they became alienated from the PJ and therefore lost their mediating position between the PJ and informal civic community. In Taiwan, the realignment of labor unions with non-traditional allies was accompanied by underdevelopment of ties with informal sectors especially on the KMT side, relative to consolidated unions' linkages within the formal sector (with the KMT). As a result, labor unions' ratio of linkages with formal associations to linkages with informal associations (columns C and D in Table 9.2) have dramatically increased in these two countries ($0.58/1.37 = 0.42$ in 1995 to $0.57/0.57 = 1.00$ in 2005 in Argentina; $0.12/0.55 = 0.22$ in 1995 to $0.50/0.68 = 0.74$ in 2005 in Taiwan). The relative over-growth of cohesiveness in Taiwan or the dwindling embeddedness in Argentina are not comparable to the small changes in Brazil ($0.65/1.44 = 0.45$ to $0.45/1.33 = 0.34$) and South Korea ($0.25/1.13 = 0.22$ to $0.83/2.00 = 0.42$). I define these tendencies toward disarticulated cohesiveness not only as a greater incorporation (co-optation) of unions into formal-sector machine politics (especially regarding the KMT-CFL alliance in Taiwan) but also as a greater disarticulation of unions from community-based informal solidarity (especially for the CGT-PJ alliance in Argentina). The third and last columns of Table 9.4 illustrate that disarticulated cohesiveness may lead to cross-partisan moves – neo-liberal retrenchment reform by formerly labor-based parties and pre-emptive reform in favor of generous social policies by formerly authoritarian right-wing parties. Their directions for either expansionary reform or retrenchment tend to be steered by external pressures or growth records.

The two cases of disarticulated cohesiveness also lend credence to the predictions made for 'cohesiveness without embeddedness' in Chapter 3 – especially for proposition 2. On one hand, when unions are not well tied to civil society groups, maintaining historical alliances with their political partner, they may conform to the incumbent party's retrenchment drive, as the Argentine unions did with their close ties to the Menem regime. On the other hand, cohesiveness without embeddedness may encourage unions to cooperate with co-optation reforms by the (semi-)authoritarian state (if they do not necessarily initiate selective reforms in collaboration with their incumbent political ally).[31] The KMT's pre-emptive welfare reforms in the late 1990s well illustrate this scenario.

After the Heyday: Reversals and Limits of Labor–Civic Solidarity

Since the mid-2000s, however, there has been an unignorable reversal in the trends of embeddedness and cohesiveness in East Asia, as illustrated in Figure 9.9: in South Korea, labor unions' cohesiveness and embeddedness have suffered stunning declines since the mid-2000s, since the second half of the Rho regime. The trends are in great accordance with earlier findings on the dramatic breakdown of labor–civic networks and the consequential sharp decline of embeddedness and cohesiveness in South Korea (in Chapters 6 and 8). In South Korea, unions' ties with political parties and informal civic associations declined precipitously, with the breakdown of the DLP and declining KCTU influence in civil society. The small number of active unionists decreased their solidaristic efforts with political and civil society forces during the decade (from

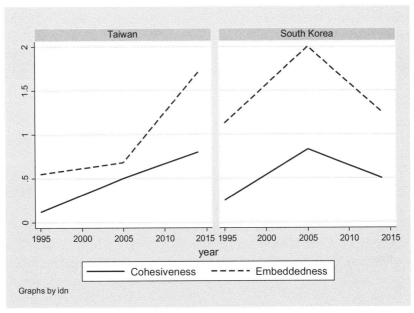

FIGURE 9.9. Unions' Cohesiveness within the Formal Sector and Embeddedness in the Informal Civic Sphere in Taiwan and South Korea: 1995–2014
Note: Refer to Appendix B for the source and calculation of the data. Data for 2014 are unavailable for Argentina and Brazil.

0.83 to 0.5 for cohesive ties and from 2.00 to 1.25 for embedded ties), which I attribute to severe factional strife and the dramatic increase in inequality within labor. During this time, unions of large manufacturing firms retreated to their factories, relinquishing their 1990s' social union-ism, while the KCTU national center kept losing its leadership and most industrial unions were malfunctioning. Then, under the two terms of con-servative regimes (including the latter term of the reformist M. H. Rho regime), institutional expansions of the South Korean welfare state halted (in health care) or suffered substantial retrenchments under neo-liberal market reform drives (in pensions).

In Taiwan, however, labor unions steadily grew their alliances with political parties and civic associations, eventually outpacing their Korean counterparts in the 2010s. In contrast to the unexpected meltdown of labor politics in South Korea, Taiwanese labor leaders continuously extended and strengthened their ties not only with political parties, but also with informal civic associations. By 2014, Taiwanese unions' co-hesiveness had increased from 0.5 (in 2005) to 0.8, while their embed-dedness had jumped up to 1.71 (from 0.68 in 2005). Thanks to these dramatic reversals in cohesiveness and embeddedness in these two coun-tries, recent politics of retrenchment regarding pension reforms in the two countries have also been reversed. In South Korea, unions and their allies were mostly silent about the lowered replacement rate (from 60 percent to 40 percent) in 2007 and distortion of the National Pension via the introduction of the basic pension in 2014. However, in Taiwan, recent similar pension reform attempts by the KMT (Ma regime) toward an introduction of individualized pension accounts of a more fragmented nature faced unprecedented resistance organized by unions and their allies.[32]

One critical difference between Taiwan and South Korea is that the Taiwanese party (the DPP) and union leaders (the TCTU and the TLF) cautiously maintained their policy networks and capacity under their strong partisan institutions throughout the 2000s and up to the mid-2010s, while South Korean leftist labor leaders were unable to discipline and contain their inherent factionalism and increasing internal heteroge-neities under a broad but disciplined partisan umbrella. While in Taiwan younger generations of civic and political leaders keep emerging, provid-ing new input and energy for pursuing the politics of social policies, the formerly more radical and well-mobilized labor–civic networks in South Korea are rapidly aging, unable to institutionalize or reproduce them-selves in the fields of social policies.

Both countries face rapid deindustrialization (due to China's emergence as a new industrial powerhouse) and increasing labor market flexibilization/deregulation. Increasingly irregular and precarious labor among younger populations, in combination with declining fertility and an aging population structure, will put both countries under great strain in their social policy budgeting. Therefore, the future of labor politics in these countries hinges upon the organizational capacities of workers in increasingly irregular and precarious positions. In other words, whether these new underclass populations can emerge as the core of new social solidarity through embeddedness and cohesiveness, with regular workers' unions and civil society associations, will determine the direction of welfare politics in both countries.

While South Korea, an exemplary case of embeddedness in East Asia, failed to sustain its universal social policy reform drive, its Latin American counterpart, Brazil, has tested the limit of labor–civic solidarity: a deteriorating Brazilian economy in the second term of the Dilma Rousseff's regime put Brazilian embedded cohesiveness to a serious test. The federal government's revenues have plummeted since 2010, and increasing government spending (primarily due to pensions and social assistance programs) has surpassed revenues since 2013. In combination with the balance-of-payment crisis and corruption scandals involving the PT and its coalition partners, Brazilian politics and the economy look worse than ever in 2015 and 2016.

Can Brazilian embedded cohesiveness readjust its expansionary efforts under the economic crisis, or is it too strong to control itself or to be checked by a third body (e.g. the opposition parties)? Pensions are not only constitutionally protected but also shielded by public sector unions, the stronghold of the CUT. Whenever cuts in the program have been pursued (by the Cardoso and Lula regimes), labor–civic solidarity successfully defeated them. Bolsa Familia was the most successful cash transfer program in reducing poverty, and Rousseff's additional spending on transfer programs such as BPC is expected to reduce poverty further. The embedded cohesiveness of the CUT-PT social movements has contributed to expansionary social policy reforms in Brazil for the last two decades, as discussed in the previous two chapters. It survived the neo-liberal reform pressures that plagued its neighboring countries in the 1990s and the early 2000s. However, it now faces a similar challenge to that experienced by a couple of Southern European countries after the 2008 financial crisis: how long can it sustain its overspending under economic crisis? Can the embedded cohesiveness constrain its own government or push it to the limit? The answer will again depend on how and to what degree labor–civic solidarity can discipline its own creation, the incumbent PT.

CONCLUSION: EMBEDDED COHESIVENESS AND THE POLITICS OF SOCIAL PROTECTION IN THE GLOBAL MARKET

This chapter brought the configuration of associational networks into the discussion of welfare politics in developing countries and formulated concepts of embedded cohesiveness and disarticulated cohesiveness, aiming to account for the politics of both retrenchment and expansion in welfare state development in four developing economies under consolidated democracy. It suggests that the development of an explanatory model of the politics of welfare states in developing countries should go beyond traditional theories of the welfare state developed mainly on the examples of advanced industrial countries. It contends that the origins and sources of politics of social protection need to be extended to informal civic space and configurations within and outside formal-sector politics beyond narrow phenomena of electoral competitions and alliances. Especially, the strength of political linkage and trust between leaders of formal organizations and citizens of informal civic associations, or simply the embeddedness of the formal sector (especially unions), along with cohesiveness, emerge as the significant explanatory factors for variations in the politics of social policies in (democratized) developing countries.

When an analytical framework is able to focus on this larger, deeper process of political trust-building based on interorganizational ties rather than mere political competitions, it can effectively account for politics of both expansion and retrenchment in social policies. When leaders of the formal sector build entrenched solidarity across different classes and sectors (embedded cohesiveness), a reformist government facing economic crisis may conduct essential but moderate structural reforms, based on supportive constituents. Or, based on such support, a reformist government with a good track record of growth may be able to launch a more ambitious universal social policy that extends its coverage to nontraditional supporters. In such a civic community, leaders of the formal sector will be loyal to their old constituents even in a time of crisis.

However, when leaders of the formal sector are not committed to their constituents through grassroots-level connections, they may opt to discard their traditional positions and ideological commitments and switch to opposite platforms that might enhance their chances for electoral survival. This opportunistic gamble is likely feasible when severe economic crisis and electoral competition put the leaders in jeopardy of losing ground in the near future. I argued that the politics of welfare state retrenchment by a labor-based or a reformist party is an exemplary case of this opportunistic transformism. I also demonstrated that other opportunism is feasible under an authoritarian regime or its descendent, under the pressure of democratization. With a good track record of economic growth, the conservative party may introduce expansionary reforms to cultivate new electoral bases even without embeddedness. This politics of disarticulated cohesiveness, therefore, is a reservoir for state-centric theory. Under both partisan governments, the lack of embeddedness provides state elites with unique space in which the incumbent party leaders take advantage of crises and newly emerging orders resulting from globalization and democratization. Partisan politicians and state bureaucrats may build an elite coalition to exploit such a space, in which leftist politicians rely on neo-liberal economists or right-wing politicians recruit social democratic policy-makers. The former happened under Menem's regime in Argentina, while the latter occurred under the KMT in Taiwan. An important point is that this seemingly state-driven or state-centered maneuvering of economic environments and political realignment processes is only possible under the condition of high cohesiveness and low embeddedness. State-centric theory, therefore, may be subsumed as a case of the EC approach. I further discuss the implication of the intersection between state-centric theory and the EC approach in the Conclusion.

The central argument of this study is consonant with the "configuration of civil society" argument promoted by Rueschemeyer *et al.* (1992) and Collier and Collier (1991), and it further refines their central tenets. They commonly argued that a well-developed civil society is conducive to democracy because it provides the working classes with better opportunities to increase their organizational power. Recently, and in line with these previous studies, Sandbrook and colleagues took into account this role of growing civil society as one of the key factors promoting social democracy in the global periphery. They make an important point that dense civil society not only offers a favorable condition for self-organization on the part of the subordinate class but also "reduces the transaction costs of coordinating interests" and "increases the chances that the better argument will prevail"(Sandbrook *et al.* 2007, p. 184). The analysis and evidence of this study improve on these arguments in several respects. I have not only visually presented the divergent configurations of civil society across different societies, but I have also provided additional causal processes using the notion of "embeddedness"(Gran-ovetter 1985), represented by organizational ties between formal and informal civic associations. While Sandbrook and colleagues (rightly) emphasized the emergence of communicative reason (in Habermas's sense) in densely linked civil society, I have focused on the structure of or-ganizational embeddedness in civic associational networks, highlighting the strategic choices of formal-sector elites regarding the expansion or retrenchment of the public sector, contingent upon their having socially embedded relationships of trust with informal civic spheres. I believe that in future studies, it would be valuable to incorporate the communicative, cognitive aspects of civil society and public spheres and the organiza-tional, structural aspects of civil society into a single explanatory frame-work that could account for democracy and welfare state development in developing societies.

Many students of welfare state development in developing countries point out that social welfare programs in those states are often devised for the privileged working class in the formal sector, to the exclusion of a large segment of the population in the urban and rural informal sectors (Haggard and Kaufman 2008; Lee 2005; Rudra 2008; Sandbrook *et al.* 2007). Trade unions' alliances with populist regimes in Latin America made them skep-tical about the role of labor unions in promoting universal social policies in developing societies. I have showed that, in societies in which unions are deeply embedded in informal civic associations, labor unions still play a meaningful role in resisting retrenchment or in sponsoring more generous and comprehensive social policies. I conclude that union embeddedness is essential for preventing the working class from being seduced by the se-lective co-optation strategy of a populist regime.

I also contend that reformist political projects based on embedded co-hesiveness are relatively immune to the pressures of globalization, which directly refutes the argument that globalization foils traditional social democratic projects to build more generous and comprehensive welfare states by weakening essential state-centered activities such as the impos-ition of higher taxes and the protection of labor rights. The comparative case studies and evidence presented in this chapter show that globaliza-tion does not explain variations in the outcome – that is, the (universal) expansion and retrenchment of existing welfare states. Argentina and Brazil, sharing similar debt crises and long histories of exposure to for-eign capital, showed significantly different reactions to common struc-tural reform pressures from neo-liberal market forces. In Brazil, both the Cardoso regime and the Lula regime were initially constrained by economic crisis, but through their second terms, market-oriented reform pressure did not lead to the radical transformation of Brazilian social policy institutions. Taiwan and South Korea – both sharing export-led industrial structures, similar positions in the world economy, and high levels of capital openness – showed somewhat different trajectories of welfare state development. Importantly, globalization itself did not frustrate or constrain any efforts of national governments to expand or protect existing welfare states, with the exception of Argentina. Rather, as the South Korean and Brazilian cases illustrate, cohesively embedded reformist leaders utilized the pressures of international market forces as an opportunity to expand existing social welfare schemes to formerly uncovered, vulnerable populations.

Also, globalization may increase the middle classes' demands for more comprehensive social insurance systems, as they become increasingly threatened by and vulnerable to the increasing volatility of financial situations. The middle classes in Taiwan and South Korea, who increasingly became pro-welfare forces regardless of political partisanship, also support this scenario. In a sense, the impact of globalization on the politics of social protection may be also contingent upon the degree and mode of the social embeddedness of formal politics. With stronger embeddedness, the pressures of globalization may urge leaders of the formal sector to protect or expand welfare states to defend their traditional constituents. However, with weak embeddedness, globalization may provide disarticulated formal-sector leaders not only with incentives but also with justifications for departing from their existing constituents. In short, globalization may strengthen partisan loyalty, but it may also facilitate complete realignments or prolonged chaotic transformative coalitions among politicians or within machine politics regardless of voters' desires.

Recently, there have been many scholarly efforts to explore the conditions and prospects of social democracy in the global periphery, as left-wing or center-left governments take power after decades of dominance by neo-liberalism in political and economic arenas. For this study, however, I intentionally chose country cases that are not yet deemed social democracies. All of the cases have recently emerged from intense authoritarian regimes and have experienced only about two decades of peaceful democratic electoral cycles; indeed, they are still in the process of consolidating democratic institutions to enhance transparency and accountability. All four cases still have powerful coalitions of conservative blocs left over from their respective authoritarian ancient regimes. The influence of big businesses (South Korea), agrarian landlord classes and foreign capital (Argentina and Brazil), and corrupt machine politics (Taiwan and Argentina) still looms over the prospects of democracy. A key ingredient of social democracy – long-term incumbency of left-wing governments (Huber and Stephens 2001) – is not yet in sight in these countries, as even center-left incumbency is often halted or limited by strong right-wing alliances (South Korea and Taiwan) or its own transformation (Argentina). Nevertheless, I find that exploring these countries under democratic consolidation is as fruitful as exploring any other exemplary cases of welfare states, because these cases offer living examples of struggles for equality through democratic competition. They provide valuable lessons from stories of frustrations as a result of betrayal, lack of capacity, and strategic mistakes, and of ongoing hope for new politics and reforms. I believe that the notion of embedded cohesiveness contributes to the understanding of these divergent stories of the politics of social protection and has the potential to account for more stories from other places and other times.[33]

Conclusion

MAIN ARGUMENTS AND IMPLICATIONS

The 'embedded cohesiveness approach' promoted in this book aims to achieve four theoretical goals: first, to build a theory of labor–civil society solidarity and labor–political party solidarity so as to account for divergent welfare state and labor market reform outcomes; second, to develop the theoretical sub-dimensions of labor–civic solidarity (embeddedness) and union–party solidarity (cohesiveness) by developing the notions of policy and mobilization capacities; third, to systematically explain how the state and labor unions strategically interact with regard to retrenchment and expansion agendas; and finally, to delineate the eight 'mechanisms' through which the embeddedness and cohesiveness of labor unions leads to divergent social and labor policy outcomes. With these theoretical modeling efforts, I proposed a theory of both 'the politics of welfare state expansion' and 'the politics of welfare state retrenchment' in which labor–civic solidarity and union–party solidarity jointly account for either universal reforms (UR) or selective reforms (SR) during expansion eras, as well as for either moderate reforms (MR) or radical reforms (RR) during retrenchment eras.

From the very beginning of this book, I have highlighted the importance of linkages between labor and civic organizations as a vital defense or a sponsor of welfare policies in democratized developing countries. The goal of theorizing such linkages was ultimately to fill the 'black box' between social movements in civil society and policy-making within state institutions. Furthermore, I have explored how leaders of labor and civic organizations mobilize and institutionalize divergent repertoires of social solidarity in pursuit of social policy agendas, as well as how they channel their policy agendas into state institutions through lobbying and contentious politics. In examining those processes, I emphasized two symbiotic compensation relationships: the provision of mobilization capacity from labor organizations to the civic sector and the provision of policy capacity from the civic to the labor sectors. These compensation mechanisms matter because the two essential ingredients of labor politics – mobilization capacity for 'the politics of threat and pressures' and policy capacity for 'the politics of lobbying and persuasion' – can hardly be built and developed by one social class or its isolated labor organization.

My case studies and the evidence from my field work offer substantial support for my theoretical claims: (1) Unions with neither cohesive nor embedded ties are incapable of either defending existing redistributive schemes or launching new expansionary social policy reforms. (2) Cohesive unions, without embedded ties to civic associations and community organizations, are more likely to pursue selective reforms that serve their own narrow interests with support from the state, as they are not committed to the interests of non-organized civil society forces. During periods of retrenchment, unions with cohesiveness but without embeddedness will coalesce with the government and are therefore more likely to accept the state's radical reform drives. (3) During the course of neo-liberal market reforms, embedded unions, when they do not possess cohesive ties to the incumbent political party, will either draw concessions after radical retrenchment reforms by the state or induce moderate reforms with their strong mobilization and threat capacities. In addition, embedded unions may be able to pressure the state to accept universal reforms, when they have the highest level of embeddedness. (4) Finally, embedded unions that also attain (moderate levels of) cohesive linkages to incumbent political parties are most likely to attain universal social policy reform, as they are more likely to embrace broader civil society partners' interests as their own. Furthermore, during retrenchment eras, embedded and cohesive unions are most likely to restrict the state to moderate reforms through their lobbying and punishment capacities. These arguments are summarized as causal flows in Figure 10.1, where the going-underground activities of radical intellectuals, and their interactions with informal (civil) society before and during democratization movements, ignite the causal processes, and eventually result in different welfare state outcomes depending upon the degrees and patterns of embeddedness and cohesiveness.

As I argued earlier, the existing welfare state literature neglects both the second (cohesiveness without embeddedness) and the third (embeddedness without cohesiveness) cases that account for wider variations in welfare state outcomes during both expansion and retrenchment phases.

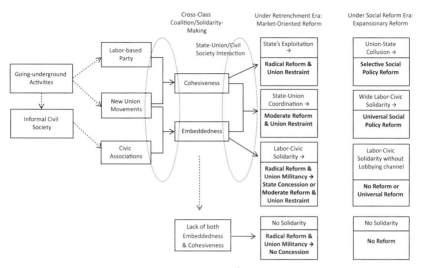

FIGURE 10.1. Causal Argument

My case study of South Korean welfare state development and my subsequent comparative studies of four country cases lend substantial credence to these arguments.

IMPLICATIONS OF THE SOUTH KOREAN CASE

Applying the EC approach, this book conducted a deep case study of South Korean labor politics during the two decades following the transition to democracy in 1987. I focused on how labor leaders and their allies succeeded (or failed) in building and defending universal welfare policies. The rapid developments of the labor movement, their brief success, and their dramatic decline provided rich material that substantially confirmed the EC approach. Chapter 4 described how South Korean labor leaders constructed embeddedness and cohesiveness from scratch – from the authoritarian era to the era of democratic consolidation. Chapter 5 presented how South Korea's new labor-civic solidarity emerged and subsequently succeeded in launching and implementing universal social policy reforms under the reformist regimes. Chapter 6 investigated the neo-liberal reforms conducted by the reformist Rho regime and subsequent conservative regimes, focusing in particular on how labor–civic solidarity sustained or failed to defend the social policies built in the late 1990s. My in-depth case study shows that South Korea offers not only convincing empirical support for the hypotheses of this study, but also ample theoretical and practical implications for scholars of labor and social movements, the welfare state, and more generally, comparative political economy.

First, the success story of the NCHIU (later the KFMA and SHR) in the integration of health care institutions highlights the importance of policy and mobilization capacities in the formation of embeddedness and cohesiveness. Labor activists and health professionals exchanged their capacities for threats/punishment (labor) and for expert policy knowledge (professionals), thereby creating a remarkably effective 'consortium organization' that crosscut the realms of civil society and actively developed lobbying channels to state institutions. As it is very difficult to develop both mobilization and policy capacity in a single organizational unit, it is critical to make provision for resource exchanges and sharing through organizational coalition mechanisms – either ad hoc or long-term consortium units.

Particularly under the neo-liberal privatization moves of the 2000s and after, SHR professionals' policy capacity proved critical in formulating defensive logics to protect universal health care, while the KCTU-affiliated industrial unions' organizational capacity was crucial in providing mobilization resources and networks for public campaigning, demonstrations, and media attention. The labor–civic solidarity networks built in the 1990s survived into the tumultuous 2000s, when they played a crucial role in defending the universal health care system even under two conservative regimes. The key figures and the networks formed during the original integration movement have aged together, all while renewing the solidarity network around new issues in the health fields and simultaneously entering into electoral politics through proportional representatives. As a result, while the KFMA network may have reached its organizational limit, its core leaders were all able to continue their work within and around the health fields. The KFMA's persistence is attributable to its embedded nature, which has evolved since the 1980s. This long-term survival of a movement network and its continued role in defending its crowning achievement imply that a social movement may institutionalize itself around the very policies that it creates, and then further survive to defend those policies during retrenchment eras, in contrast to the 'new politics' argument that social policies will be defended by new social groups created by social programs themselves (Pierson 1996).

However, even in the same country case, unions' and their allies' responses to neo-liberal pension reforms were different – further illustrating the importance of embedded cohesiveness in explaining policy outcomes. In the pensions field, the labor–civic solidarity that promoted the expansionary reforms during the tripartite committee in 1998 turned out to be shallow and ad hoc. In contrast to health care fields, unions in the pensions field were traditionally weak and did not have densely developed historical ties to civic associations. Other than social work professors within the PSPD, there were few professional groups available to defend the pensions against the reformist regime's retrenchment drive. Especially thanks to grassroots manufacturing unions' lack of interest in the retrenchment of their own pensions, as well as the KCTU's own declining significance in South Korean civil society, the KCTU national center did not have sufficient mobilization capacity to defend the core component (high replacement rate) of the National Pension scheme. Thus, the politics of both health care and pensions in South Korea illustrate the vital importance of embeddedness in explaining variations in social policy outcomes.

Further, this striking contrast between two policy domains during the retrenchment conjunctures in the same country suggests that not only the scope but also the depth of embeddedness matters. In a certain policy domain, embeddedness with deep historical origins and roots in either professional communities (South Korea) or regional communities (Brazil) meant that actors could anchor themselves in policy institutions, such that movement leaders become institutional advocates of the policy within the state. Such policies could then survive retrenchment thanks not only to their community/civil society-based defenders but also to their institutional supporters. In other policy domains, however, embeddedness is formed as a result of movement leaders' ad hoc tactics and strategies and so lacks deep roots in professional societies or community organizations. Even though such efforts may succeed in promoting expansionary reforms under a temporary opportunity structure, they are very likely to suffer severe retrenchment when the state turns to neo-liberal reforms, as such embeddedness may not be durable enough to sustain continued attacks on the social policy program and so may fail to draw sufficiently large and sustained opposition to retrenchment efforts.

The South Korean case, thanks to its dramatic social policy growth and decline during a relatively short time span, not only provided negative and positive cases of embeddedness and cohesiveness; it also offered rich stories of the deep underlying dynamics of upward and downward changes in labor–civic solidarity and union–party alliances. These empirically powerful stories of social solidarity and political coalitions in South Korean labor politics become even more productive through systematic comparisons with other exemplary country cases.

IMPLICATIONS OF COMPARATIVE CASE STUDIES
AND THREE RESEARCH QUESTIONS POSED
EARLIER

Again using the EC approach, I then conducted comparative case studies of associational networks and welfare state developments in four countries in the second set of empirical analyses (Chapters 7, 8, and 9). In discussing the implications of the findings of the comparative case studies, I revisit the three research questions I posed earlier in Chapter 1. First, I inquired into the 'durability' of the traditional leftist party–union nexus in the era of globalization (Clark and Lipset 2001; Howell *et al.* 1992; Kitschelt 1994): *Is a close labor party–union relationship still conducive to defending the welfare state and workers' rights – especially under the market reform era?* A leftist party may not want to maintain such a durable linkage, primarily because of the party's motive toward strategic exploitation of incapacity to launch political challenges on the part of unions. Globalization, especially financial openness and the concomitant economic crises prevalent in developing countries, puts incumbent labor parties in a unique position in which the government is under pressure to launch substantial market reforms against its traditional social base (Levitsky 2003b). Particularly in developing countries in which labor-based parties have rarely captured a large, dominant portion of the blue-collar population, labor parties have not always been able to champion redistributive social policies and the protection of workers' rights. They typically needed a wider social base and coalition partners to survive in competitive elections, and therefore they had to propose policies that could attract different socio-economic groups. Labor parties or reformist parties, facing such pressures to transform their platforms (Kitschelt 1994) and especially with their traditional allies not strong enough to challenge reforms, may implement radical market initiatives to achieve more visible economic gains in the short-term; to attempt to impress diverse social groups, even businesses and the self-employed; and eventually to build a wide-ranging electoral coalition to protect their incumbency.

Based on our second model (proposition 2 in Chapter 3), I reasoned that an incumbent reformist or labor-based party may launch radical, market-oriented reforms of social policies because it expects unions to tolerate the costs of reform due to a history of solidarity, or to bear such costs, if unwillingly, due to their low mobilization capacity. Incumbent labor or reformist party leaders in Argentina (in the 1990s) and South Korea (in the 2000s), who in both cases were disarticulated from civic associations, indeed implemented state-driven, radical neo-liberal market reforms. In both countries, unions restrained their militancy or were incapable of resisting despite the state's radical reforms of the public sector. The first research question and corresponding cases, therefore, reflect the recent dilemmas faced by union leaders in many rich democracies as well as in developing countries in which unions have built durable policy channels with political parties but lack solidarity with civil society groups. The EC approach predicts that the more loyal unions remain to the incumbent labor party (without embeddedness), the more exploitative reforms the incumbent may initiate.

What, then, have unions done in response to this changing relationship between unions and labor-based parties? This question led me to the second question: *why and how did some unions successfully defend their rights under these changing and challenging circumstances?* My comparative case studies demonstrated that embeddedness without cohesiveness led to unions' militancy all the time: the CTA in Argentina, the KCTU in South Korea, and the TCTU in Taiwan in the 1990s all built strong solidarity with civil society groups, which enabled them to resist the state's market-oriented reforms. My analysis suggests that the politics of embeddedness through social movement unionism in multi-organizational fields has served as an effective alternative strategy for unions in the era of globalization and industrial transformation. More importantly, 'broadening their social bases' also implies expanding unions' agendas to community-wide health, environmental, social, and human rights issues – issues that extend beyond traditional bread-and-butter issues (Almeida 2008; Rose 2000; Seidman 1994; Voss and Sherman 2000). The EC approach suggests that, when unions are deeply embedded in civil society and remain defiant towards the state, they may be able to mobilize a broader or 'encompassing' solidarity against radical reforms of the welfare state, which may eventually reverse the state's attacks on labor's rights. In such cases, unions represent, in addition to the interests of blue-collar workers, the broader 'civic solidarity' protesting the state's encroachment on citizens' rights. In these situations, citizens may successfully "coordinate their reactions" (Weingast 1997, p. 251) around embedded unions and eventually draw concessions from the state based on their capacity to retaliate against the state's radical reforms or rebuff of universal reform. In contrast to the encompassing unions of Western Europe, unions of developing societies lack the ability to not only represent a significant portion of wage earners but also exert strong bargaining power on employers and the state. Therefore, if they are to respond effectively to market-oriented reforms or pressure the state to introduce universal social policy reforms, it is essential for unions to build broader coalitions beyond the labor sector, embracing diverse civil society issues.

The third question was *how the state and labor coordinate their actions regarding the degree and content of market reforms.* In this case, I sought to examine the conditions and elements that enable the two parties to reach a consensus around the state's moderation of reforms and unions' restraint in response. The EC approach and its empirical analyses showed great predictive validity in the 1990s and the early 2000s by demonstrating that union and party leaders in Brazil and South Korea, who were deeply embedded in community or civic associations, launched moderate neo-liberal reforms and redistributive social assistance reforms (Brazil) or expansionary universal social policy reforms (South Korea). My model and case studies (on Brazilian unions) suggest that such union-friendly outcomes need a high level of deliberation and communication between the two actors, in addition to the unions' linkages to both the state and civil society.

How, then, can the state and unions assure each other that they will stay, in the long run, within such boundaries, which requires a highly sophisticated understanding of the consequences and necessary boundaries of the other party's actions as well as their own? I conclude that the state and unions may need formal and informal communication mechanisms, as the Brazilian CUT (under the Lula and Dilma regimes), the Argentine CTA (under the Kirchners' regimes), and the South Korean KCTU (under the tripartite committee of the D. J. Kim regime) illustrate. When they share institutionalized channels, or at least informal channels that can carry a history of deep communication and cooperation, each actor can better predict the other actor's capacity for punishment, the long-term costs of opportunistic behaviors, and the potential rewards from cooperation (Axelrod 1984). In that sense, when there exist mechanisms for "institutionalized coordination" (Ostrom 1990), the state and unions may more effectively signal to or "enlighten" (Wright 2000) the other player about the consequences of opportunism, inform the other player of the range of their bargaining terms, and convince the other player of the path toward the most optimal outcome that they can co-achieve under a given structure of cohesiveness and embeddedness.

Overall, this study has explored the divergent trajectories of state–labor interactions regarding neo-liberal market reforms. Although more data are needed to test the generalizability of the framework, the key findings based on four intriguing countries may have considerable implications for other societies under similar pressures for neo-liberal reforms. The model and empirical findings suggest that the success of labor politics in developing countries hinges not only on their ability to persuade and assure (or punish when necessary) their bargaining partner, the state, but also on unions' capacity to build solidaristic ties with civil society, through a history of co-mobilization over common agendas and policies. Under the notion of embedded cohesiveness, I have highlighted the importance of 'civic coordination,' as well as 'institutional coordination,' in defending labor rights under the pressure of globalization.

THEORIES OF THE WELFARE STATE REVISITED WITH THE EC APPROACH

Serious challenges to the laborist approach to social politics started with Baldwin's (1990) seminal work on the class bases of the European welfare states. He issued the sharp challenge that, "the welfare state was shaped by an interplay among the interests of many different groups whose concerns cannot invariably be fitted into the binary logic of the laborist interpretation: working-class pressure confronting middle-class resistance," and then further argued that, "the unique features of the Nordic welfare states were determined by the interests of the politically emergent agrarian middle classes neither to be excluded from the benefits of social policy, nor to bear more of the costs than could be displaced to their urban opponents" (p. 289). His argument and convincing documentation encouraged many, especially scholars in the varieties of capitalism (VoC) school, to discount the laborist approach, and further build a new 'employer-centered' account of the development of the welfare state, in which workers and employers co-investing in specific skills are expected to have strong preferences for social protection (Hall and Soskice 2001; Iversen and Soskice 2009).

While the VoC scholars actively promoted Baldwin's non-laborist, middle-class-centered approach, replacing the role of the middle class with employers, I propose that there is an alternative path in line with Baldwin's earlier insight. Baldwin never completely dumped the role of "pressure from below" by workers (1990, pp. 288–99). Instead, he emphasized that workers' pressure alone was not enough to bring in solidaristic measures through expansionary reforms for redistributive regimes: workers needed the middle classes, 'the haves.' He asserts that building universal welfare states was not possible until the privileged discovered that their interest could be realigned with the disadvantaged by "reallocating risk." Baldwin then assured readers that it would be either the agrarian or the urban middle classes, allied with workers, who ultimately achieved redistributive social policies. In other words, Baldwin's argument should not be treated as a complete rejection of the role of working classes but as an emphasis on the indispensable role of middle classes in forging a cross-class alliance in favor of redistributive policies. In his argument, the working classes could not, on their own, complete their goal of achieving redistribution through the state power; they needed an alliance with the middle classes.

Esping-Andersen (1985, 1990) highlights the role of solidarity between the working class and agrarian classes or between the working class and the white-collar middle class in building universal welfare states in Nordic countries. He also made similar arguments to Baldwin's by suggesting that, "the role of the farmers in coalition formation and hence in welfare state development is clear. In the Nordic countries, the necessary conditions obtained for a broad red-green alliance for a full employment welfare state in return for farm-price subsidies" (1990, p. 30). He further implies that, in continental Europe, labor-intensive agriculture led to the absence of such independent farmers' political organizations, thereby allowing conservative alliances to fold farmers into their "reactionary" camp, while isolating unions and left-wing parties. He further adds that the capacity of the social democratic alliance to incorporate the newly emerging white-collar middle classes into "universal social policy schemes" was decisive in maintaining the generous welfare states in Nordic countries (1990, p. 31).[1] For both Baldwin and Esping-Andersen, therefore, the presence of a unified, mobilized working class is a necessary but not sufficient condition for social policy expansions. Depending upon the changing population structure, the working class need an ally – either peasants or the middle classes – to promote and sustain 'universal' welfare states.[2] An important point that was dismissed by many critiques of power resource (PR) theory is that, without the meaningful presence of the working class, neither peasants nor middle classes were capable of promoting a universal welfare state. Methodologically, one needs a combinational explanation, and practically, workers need a cross-class coalition. Even if both celebrated works did not completely dump the role of working classes, it is regrettable that the next generation of scholarship used these arguments to justify their critique of the laborist approach for its 'exaggeration of working-class capacity' in building welfare states.

Like power resource scholarship, the EC approach begins with the role of labor organizations such as unions and leftist parties. However, it radically extends the scope and depth of the analysis of the social bases of labor organizations to encompass civil society by taking into account the roles of embedded ties of unions in informal civil society. This conceptual expansion of the power resources of the working class to civil society organizations through the notion of embeddedness takes into account labor's broader alliance with other social groups and workers' deeper solidarity with broader social constituencies, which has recently been echoed in Kathleen Thelen's (2014) argument regarding "coalitional realignments" of unions to build encompassing solidarity.[3] Or, even if not reaching the level of 'alliance' with other social forces, embeddedness captures the capacity of unions to wage mobilization or policy-oriented collaborations with non-working-class groups. Further, the EC approach highlights the 'synergy effects' that emerge through organizational or informal linkages between unions and other civic associations. This path was not taken by VoC scholars nor further developed by the founders of power resource theory. With this "relational approach" (Diani 2003; Emirbayer 1997), the EC framework shifts the focus from which class matters (between working classes and middle classes) to what kinds of solidarity matter and how (labor–civic) solidarity functions to build a more generous welfare state. I believe that this relational approach is a meaningful extension of the formerly narrow definition of working class power resources that has been confined to "the levels of trade union organizations, share of votes, and parliamentary and cabinet seats held by left or labor parties"(Esping-Andersen 1990, p. 16). In this way, the EC approach takes a third path in which modes of 'collaboration' and 'coordination' between classes receive more attention than the power, reflected through formal political office, of a specific social class.

Overall, the EC approach shares the fundamental impulse behind all 'politics against market' approaches (including the power resource approach) (Esping-Andersen 1985; Korpi 1983; Stephens 1979) working in the Polanyian tradition that has proliferated and dominated welfare state scholarship in the late twentieth century. The idea was that the working-class movement deploys democratic political mechanisms to "decommodify" (Esping-Andersen 1990) wage earners' labor and to expand the social safety net in order to defend workers' and their families' basic rights against the risks of unemployment, sickness, injury, and retirement. The EC approach is similar to the PR approach, in that it starts with labor unions as the ultimate organizational power base of the working class, and simultaneously puts its primary focus on the relationship between unions and (leftist) political parties (Huber and Stephens 2001, 2012). However, the EC approach introduces a new dimension that has been neglected (or vaguely noticed but poorly theorized) in the PR approach – unions' embeddedness in civil society and its complex interaction with unions' cohesive ties with political parties.

   The EC approach brings further theoretical sophistication to this labor–civic solidarity by distinguishing between policy and mobilization capacities as its sub-dimensions. With this new set of factors, the EC approach reveals two additional possible political spaces that were not conceptualized in the PR approach: embeddedness without cohesiveness and cohesiveness without embeddedness. Theoretically and empirically, I showed that this EC approach greatly expands the permutations of 'politics against market' during the retrenchment and expansion movements of political economy: four modes of the EC approach under a retrenchment drive by the state effectively account for the state's and unions' actions (radical or moderate reforms by the state vs. militancy or restraint by unions); another four modes of the EC approach under expansion opportunities also successfully explain the state's and unions' actions (universal or selective reforms by unions vs. acceptance or rejection by the state). Through the development of these additional dimensions, I aimed to expand the concept of 'politics against market' to encompass those larger civil society projects not confined to a narrow social democratic partisan politics – the focus of Esping-Andersen's (1985) original formulation.

   The contribution of the EC approach to welfare state scholarship becomes even more evident when the recent significant challenge of the VoC approach to 'laborist' scholarship is taken into account. VoC scholars consider unions' embeddedness in their theoretical framework, but they direct their attention only to labor–business collaboration by systemizing unions' embeddedness in quasi-market institutions such as banks' governance structures and employers' associations. It regards unions' embeddedness in market institutions as endogenous variables ultimately determined by employers' needs for 'skill specificity' (Estevez-Abe *et al.* 2001; Hall and Soskice 2001; Iversen and Soskice 2001). From the perspective of the EC approach, the VoC school considers unions only as a part of the many institutions comprising a 'coordinated market.' VoC scholarship hardly takes into account unions' embeddedness in civil society and its significance in promoting or defending (universal) social policies.

   In the four countries studied here, what mattered for the politics of welfare expansion or retrenchment was whether labor and civil society were able to build a wide range of solidarity among themselves and with allied political parties, as well as whether they effectively utilized the newly opening political opportunity structures that became available alongside democratization and globalization. In those societies, unions were rarely embedded in market institutions but were closely aligned with democratization and civil society forces. Although in some highly advanced developing societies with globally competitive industrial sectors, such as South Korea, some unions for large manufacturing companies broke their traditional ties with other social reformist unions and progressive civil society forces (as described in Chapter 8), the most important expansionary welfare reforms occurred before this switch from UR (universal reform) to SR (selective reform) strategies (Chapter 5). After their switch, those unions rarely joined the previous solidarity behind expansionary reforms, even when existing social policy schemes were under serious attacks by market reform forces (Chapter 6).

In East Asian and Latin American countries, some unions have been among the most reactionary forces opposing expansionary universal social policy reforms, as shown by the FKTU's vehement efforts to stop the integration of health care societies (South Korea), or persistent resistance to the unification of the health care system in the late 1980s in Brazil by unions in INAMPS (the National Social Security Medical Assistance Institute) (McGuire 2010, p. 177). Particularly in Latin America, at least during the 1990s and the 2000s, unions rarely built alliances with employers regarding social policy reforms. In all the countries analyzed in this study, employers were not the initial proponents of the universal welfare state but were consistent sponsors of market-oriented reforms of existing social policies. Universal welfare programs were never employers' 'first-order preference,' and employers conformed to the pressure imposed by labor–civic solidarity and its allied state only when they found that there was no other choice, as Korpi (2006) convincingly points out in his critique of the VoC school.

The cross-class alliances between employers and unions (Pontusson and Swenson 1996; Swenson 1991a, 1991b), an important theoretical element of the larger VoC approach, and employers' needs for skill specificity and 'wage flexibility' (Pontusson and Swenson 1996) under such alliances, may have played some role in advancing the public provision of social welfare in rich democracies. However, in many developing societies, cross-class alliances between employers and unions occurred either during the authoritarian regimes in the context of 'authoritarian corporatism' or during the expansion era in the context of selective reforms (SR), in which unions were rarely interested in the provision of universal social protection for the wider civil society.

In short, the four ideal-type spaces and relevant pathways developed in the EC approach challenge existing theories of the welfare state in several ways. The power resource approach, which turned out to be most useful for explaining variations among welfare states in developing and developed countries (Haggard and Kaufmann 2008; Huber and Stephens

2001;Korpi 2006), cannot predict important outcomes produced by embeddedness. In particular, existing PRT cannot explain instances of embeddedness without cohesiveness or cohesiveness without embeddedness, simply because it does not take into account labor–civic solidarity as a consequential dimension. As a result, the PR approach can neither account for why labor-based parties often betray their supporting base, unions, during the retrenchment phase, nor explain how or when unions succeed in defending their core rights against state-driven radical retrenchment attempts. Furthermore, the PR approach is not sufficiently refined even when it accounts for the expansion of welfare states. Because it neglects the embeddedness dimension, the PR approach fails to explain why unions end up choosing selective reforms over universal social policy reforms, often resorting instead to ad hoc explanations like a history of authoritarianism. As PRT primarily focuses on the traditional social democratic alliance between unions and labor-based parties, assuming a priori normative superiority, it cannot account for complex situations in which unions coalesce with other social forces to pursue universal reforms (as Baldwin pointed out), or turn their back on them and collude with the state (and/or employers) for selective reforms.

In the earlier theoretical discussion in Chapter 2, I discounted the applicability of VoC theory in accounting for the development and retrenchment of the welfare state in developing countries, simply because it is difficult to find fertile ground for the VoC school's 'skill needs' and 'institutional arrangement' arguments in most developing societies. Developing country cases can be merely utilized in their framework as instances of 'negative cases,' in which lack of skill investment is coupled with lack of consensual politics and lack of the market institutions needed for a coordinated market economy (Schneider and Soskice 2009). Similarly, Pierson's 'politics of blame avoidance' theory does not hold well in developing countries simply because retrenchment attempts in the form of privatization have occurred so often and remain as viable threats.

However, I did not explicitly refute the utility of the state-centric approach, because some of my cases are indeed explained by the state elites' active roles. In Chapter 9, I juxtaposed disarticulated cohesiveness and embedded cohesiveness, while suggesting that the former, a combination of strong cohesiveness and weak embeddedness, could provide a space in which partisan and bureaucratic elites are unleashed from civil society-based institutional constraints, thereby launching radical versions of retrenchment or expansionary reforms of the welfare state. The active role of partisan elites and their allying strategists and practitioners in the bureaucracy in shaping the welfare state in developing societies are twofold: on one hand, disarticulated politicians and "a growing cadre of internationally oriented bureaucrats" (Babb 2001) in many developing societies desire to introduce market-oriented institutions in their economy by privatizing existing social policies and state institutions; and, on the other hand, disarticulated former authoritarian politicians seek to co-opt unions by pre-emptively introducing leftist welfare agendas. In both cases, state bureaucrats overwhelm civil society in terms of their policy capacity, while in rapidly changing economic and political environments civil society actors, including union leaders, have not developed specific positions and logics regarding a specific social policy. Unexpected directions of reforms, therefore, are primarily driven by the coalitions between opportunistic political elites and emerging policy experts.

The EC approach interprets this adoption of either a neo-liberal or a progressive reform model by state elites as a special case of weak embeddedness under certain partisanship, in which state elites find an opportunity to transform the existing political and economic terrains toward new institutional orders that may prolong their incumbency.[4] Therefore, I do not contend that the EC approach completely guards against state-centric theory. Rather, the EC approach may offer a larger theoretical umbrella in which previously competing theories of the welfare state, such as power resource theory and state-centric theory, are subsumed as specific cases. The degree of embeddedness and cohesiveness provides different scope conditions for state actors of different origins. In this EC space, autonomous state actors (especially under disarticulated cohesiveness) may (or may not) launch radical versions of market-oriented or expansionary social policy reforms, depending upon their ideological orientations or on larger structural transformation (such as increasing inequality or economic crisis). Although the EC approach does not necessarily offer explanations as to why autonomous state officials adopt a specific version of market-oriented policies or ideas, it provides for when and under what conditions bureaucrats are able to pursue their policy goals without constraints set by civil society actors.

SOCIAL MOVEMENTS AND WELFARE STATES

This study draws from social movement perspectives in order to explain the two layers of coalition/alliance-making processes and their impact on welfare states: institutional politics and contentious politics. For the former, I developed the notion of policy capacity and for the latter the notion of mobilization capacity. These sub-dimensions of embeddedness (and cohesiveness) enabled me to explore deeper organizational coalition processes between unions and civic associations beyond the mere observation of the structure of interorganizational networks. With these concepts, I aimed to capture how unions and civic associations communicate with each other in order to co-produce agendas, co-mobilize wide and deep ranges of human and material resources, and effectively aggregate and channel demands into state institutions. Through my deep case study of South Korean labor politics, I demonstrated that unions' policy and mobilization capacities were critical in disseminating and legitimizing unions' or allying civic associations' agendas among broader publics. For instance, the 'social legitimation process' of a specific social policy agenda, driven by policy and mobilization capacities, enables union and civic leaders to persuade the general public as well as their own members – in this case, in the health care integration movement. This persuasion process eventually played a decisive role in influencing the legislation and implementation of unions' and civic leaders' policy agenda (during the tripartite committee in 1997–98).

The notions of embeddedness and cohesiveness advance our knowledge by further specifying how social movements matter in shaping policies. The EC approach implies that one dimension of social movement mobilization without the other (between embeddedness and cohesiveness) is insufficient and may even bring in 'undesirable' or 'no' consequences in the final outcomes of policy-shaping or policy-defending processes. For example, while embeddedness mostly captures the 'movement infrastructure' that enables unions to expand their base and forge alliances (thereby strengthening public legitimacy and experts' knowledge support), cohesiveness involves unions' loyalty to the state as well as unions' lobbying capacity through insider negotiation channels. This study demonstrates that cultivating broader social bases through embedded interorganizational networks and promoting movement agendas through cohesive channels are both essential ingredients in successful policy outcomes. Without the former – embeddedness – movement agendas fail to achieve broad, universal reforms, satisfying only the narrow interests of core movement adherents. In cases of retrenchment, furthermore, the absence of wide-range social solidarity may lead to significant setbacks for unions. Without the latter – cohesiveness – movement organizations may fail to achieve substantively meaningful enactment and implementation of their agendas, as they succeed only in influencing initial agenda-setting. Highlighting both embeddedness and cohesiveness, therefore, will enrich recent social movement scholars' efforts to account for movement outcomes. By considering both social processes of interorganizational mobilization and political processes of participation in decision-making, contemporary social movement scholarship may better grasp its latest agenda – the influence of social movements on formal politics and policy outcomes (Amenta 2006; Andrews 2004; Ganz 2000; McCammon *et al.* 2008; Soule and King 2006).

The two main variables of this study, embeddedness and cohesiveness, interact with changing external conditions. I brought in the notion of 'opportunity structures' from social movement literature to account for the impact of these exogenous conditions, but I also assumed that these impacts do not operate in a simple, unilateral manner. For instance, I considered 'economic crisis' or 'globalization' as an opportunity for unions with embedded cohesiveness, as they can utilize the conjuncture to strengthen their social legitimacy and political bargaining power. Yet the same economic crisis may be exploited as an excuse for radical market-oriented reforms by an incumbent party allying with core-sector unions (in cases of cohesiveness without embeddedness). In short, external economic pressures or concurrent internal economic crisis work as a double-edged sword depending upon the structure of associational networks.

While much social movement literature explores "the conditions under which movements matter politically" (Amenta *et al.* 2011, p. 295), the EC approach treats these conditions as the sources/ingredients of movements, rather than their enabling conditions. In other words, political opportunity structure has been considered only as an ingredient of cohesiveness. While previous literature of political opportunity structure considered the incumbency of a political party favorable to a specific social movement agenda as an opportunity, the EC approach treats it as a potential ingredient of cohesiveness and so as internal to the structure of social movements themselves. The incumbency of a political party can be an appropriate lobbying channel only when unions construct close communication and negotiation channels with the party. Therefore, in my approach such cohesiveness is not an enabling condition but a potential source of a partnership. However, even a close collaborative relationship may be relegated to a subordinate corporatistic relationship if unions lack accompanying embeddedness. Therefore, a political opportunity structure is no external structure but merely one of the lobbying channels through which unions may effectively build 'coordination institutions.' Depending upon leaders' capacity for interpretation, strategy-making, and execution, an opportunity structure could enable movement actors to fully utilize it, or it could create conditions under which leaders destroy their existing solidarity. This last contingency, where outcomes depend upon actors' capacity and decisions, leads to the final important point of this section.

The EC approach emphasizes one important component that has not received sufficient attention from social movement scholars: embedded movement leaders' 'coordination skills.' This refers to leaders' capacity to coordinate the diverse interests of different social forces while simultaneously negotiating with the state, thereby maximizing payoffs for their own unions as well as for broader civil society forces. The same structural conditions and resources do not necessarily guarantee the same outcomes. They depend upon union leaders' social and institutional coordination skills, by which they are able to identify the best strategies and actions while cautiously considering their coalition and bargaining partners' interests. With respect to this coordination capacity, what matters is union leadership's ability to envision how a wide range of civil society forces could benefit from unions and their coalitional capacity, as well as what impact a specific social policy will have on the state and society in general. Based on such comprehensive visions, union leadership or civic leadership (embracing union leadership) may be able to bargain with the state more effectively and prudently without resorting to unnecessary quid pro quo politics. In such processes, union and civic leadership needs to be able to: (1) objectively assess their capacity to mobilize internal and external organizational resources; (2) persuade grassroots leaders and members of interorganizational networks of the benefits of a specific social policy agenda; (3) devise persuasive messages and logics to deliver to the general public as well as party and state leaders; and, finally, (4) bargain with both parties and the state, informing them of the potential consequences of courses of action (benefits and costs of subsequent decisions by each party). In other words, union or civic leadership needs a form of 'social skills' – "the ability to motivate cooperation in other actors" (Fligstein 1997, p. 398), with which the core leadership can not only galvanize positive visions and energies from other leaders, rank-and-file members, and sympathizers, but also forge a consensus durable enough to survive the next, more arduous stage of bargaining and the ensuing reactions from skeptics and outsiders, as well as the policy's own adherents. This last realm of decision-making process for relatively open outcomes poses an important set of challenges to the existing literature on social movements, in which structural conditions and their unilateral effects are still predominantly prioritized. The next generation of social movement scholarship needs to explore this more open and contingent leadership dimension (Ahlquist and Levi 2013) – the capacity and skills of social movement leaders to configure the most appropriate actions based on a mixture of certain and uncertain information about themselves and other players. Exploring this dimension will be critical not only for understanding how social movements matter in explaining social policies, but also for theorizing how leaders' coordination skills matter for social movement success and failure outcomes in general.

IMPLICATIONS OF THE EC APPROACH FOR
BROADER LITERATURE

The meso-level analytical strategy of the EC approach greatly advances our understanding of how micro-level norms of reciprocity (in grass-roots civic associations) and civic engagement networks, which have been highly celebrated by Tocquevillians (Putnam 1993; Paxton 2002), evolve into macro-level 'responsible' government. It effectively accounts for two black-box problems that remained unresolved in two significant previous fields of research: one is the gap between grassroots-level civic efficacy and macro-level governance in the social capital scholarship; and the other is the gap between the 'instrumental self-interests' of narrowly defined social classes and the emergence of cross-class solidarity mechanisms glossed over in the larger coalitional politics, democratization, and welfare state literature (Baldwin 1990; Collier and Collier 1991; Esping-Andersen 1990; Rueschemeyer *et al.* 1992).

First, Tocquevillians construct their core theoretical principles – norms of reciprocity and cooperation – at the level of grassroots, informal civil society, which, they argue, can lead to better governance at the macro-level. The empty black box between grassroots horizontal reciprocity and a well-functioning responsible government remains unaddressed, while regional or national variations in the qualities of governments are vaguely accounted for by 'two social equilibria' – one a happy Tocquevillian equilibrium in which trust, reciprocity, and voluntary participation become social norms that sustain participatory governance, and the other a Hobbesian equilibrium in which amoral familialism, vertical clientelism, and opportunism are coupled with authoritarian, hierarchical government (Putnam 1993, pp. 163–80). The EC approach shares many key notions with the Tocquevillian view of civil society – the importance of norms of reciprocity and networks of civic engagement typically abound in informal civic associations. But the EC approach immediately departs from the Tocquevillian static, 'two social equilibria' approach, as represented by Northern and Southern Italy in Putnam's seminal study. To overcome this black box, the EC approach introduces and operationalizes two 'meso-level dynamic mechanisms' into the overly simplistic Tocquevillian model: embeddedness and cohesiveness. With these variables, the norm of reciprocity and the networks of civic engagement discussed by Putnam at the individual level are scaled up to the level of organizations – unions, political parties, professional associations, and variegated informal civic associations. Using this approach, we can analyze the norms of reciprocity through the exchange of policy and mobilization capacity between unions and other civic associations. I explored how these compensatory exchanges occurred in two different forms of solidarity configuration in South Korean health and pensions fields, and the impact such reciprocity had on social policy outcomes (Chapters 4 to 6). The networks of civic engagement, which were expected by Putnam to "cut across social cleavages" (1993, p. 175), were converted into the notion of embeddedness, representing cross-class solidarity and wider cooperation at the organizational level. These organizational-level analyses eventually allowed me to draw inter-associational co-membership networks and reveal how such network structures translate into divergent welfare state outcomes (Chapters 7, 8, and 9). Unions' embeddedness captures their deep trust relationships with members of grassroots community-level associations as well as with experts and professionals in issue-targeting, politicized professional associations.

Second, the EC approach fills the gap between self-interested class actors and the emergence of cross-class solidarity. The power resource school in the Barrington Moore (1966) tradition tends to focus on the balance of class power and 'class constellation' thesis (Rueschemeyer *et al.* 1992), in which the working class is treated as a key driving force of democracy, the landed aristocracy is the most reactionary force against democracy, and the middle classes are deemed 'ambivalent.' For these scholars, what matters in democratization is the relative strength of different classes, and the working class is treated as an 'inherently democratic' force as it continues to seek inclusion of its class interests in the representative process. Such a favorable assumption about the role of the working class is further reinforced in the power resource school's welfare state analysis: the working class, even if not the sole driver of universal welfare states, emerges again as the core component of social democratic alliance, where it is taken to play the decisive role in achieving redistributive regimes (Esping-Andersen 1985, 1990; Huber and Stephens 2001; Korpi 1983; Korpi and Palme 2003; Stephens 1979). Although the EC approach, like the power resource school, provisionally accepts the importance of the configuration of civil society in general, it does not necessarily agree with the implicit assumption of the power resource approach that the working class inherently seeks universal welfare states. Rather, according to the EC approach, unions may do so when they are deeply embedded in civil society. However, when unions are not embedded in civil society, the institutional characteristics of the welfare state are not necessarily universalistic but become particularistic, as shown in the cases of cohesiveness without embeddedness. I analyzed such tendencies in South Korean large conglomerate unions since the 2000s, and further compared such cases in Taiwan and Argentina with other cases of embeddedness in Brazil and South Korea in Chapters 7, 8 and 9 for both expansion and retrenchment eras.

Furthermore, the EC approach shifts focus from the relative strength of the working class compared to that of other classes to the relational strength of the working class organization through working-class linkages to other class (or non-class community-level) actors. In this 'relational turn,' one using a social capital/social network approach (Coleman 1988; Laumann *et al.* 1977; Emirbayer 1997), the EC approach redefined 'class coalition' as 'network-based solidarity' among representative class-based organizations. The EC approach is in a sharp contrast to earlier approaches to social solidarity, in which solidarity was conceived as a pooling of common components of 'risks' in which late joiners can claim their membership (Baldwin 1990). The EC approach does not start with strictly defined pre-existing risks or inherent class interests. Instead, the scope and categories of risks and interests can be constantly negotiated and redefined during the course of the evolution or devolution of embeddedness and cohesiveness.

In other words, the strength and scope of class coalitions, in the EC approach, will be determined by the degree of effective mobilization and policy-crafting processes led by leaders of unions and civic associations. Both risks and class interests can be constantly renegotiated between organizational leaderships regarding their conflicting components, and so they are ultimately determined by the degree to which organizational leaders persuade and convince other organizational leaders, as well as their own social bases. Through these processes, one social class or its representative may perceive other groups' interests as their own, or at least as not conflicting with theirs. In short, universal social policy is constructed by organizational activists' and leaders' constant negotiations of boundaries of interests and risks with many leaders of civil society and political parties. I illustrated these meso-level processes of dismantling and reconstruction of existing interests and risk categories through my examination of new labor–civic solidarity in the integration movement for health care during the NCHIU's organizational activities in the 1990s

South Korea (Chapters 4 and 5). With this case, I highlighted the import-ance of the historical formation of a 'social coordination' process, which originated from a decade-long organizational collaboration network be-tween progressive health professionals and union leaders. The unprece-dented persuasion efforts of South Korean professional intellectuals and their allied union leaders, which compelled large manufacturing industry workers (who were already in the privileged, existing occupation-based health care system) to switch to an integrated, universalistic system, illus-trates how the encapsulation of 'others' interests' in a solidarity can be reshaped, sustained, and institutionalized through a social movement process. Such a successful articulation process was possible thanks to the idea of promoting workers' interests by linking them to the broader pub-lic's interests under a newly integrated institutional umbrella. I demon-strated that social solidarity can be newly constituted by providing potential beneficiaries with a convincing alternative vision that promises to satisfy larger and more universal group interests, and that such a con-vincing policy vision is the product of an effective collaboration between union and civic leaders.

Finally, the EC approach enables scholars of the state and civil society to direct their attention to the contestatory, interactive spaces between the state and civil society where new political entrepreneurs from labor move-ments with strong policy and mobilization capacity engage in lobbying and negotiation with the incumbent political party and the state. Depending upon social conditions and the capacity of civil society actors, there could be a specific group of social and political actors who, having forged under-ground activities during harsh authoritarian regimes, then entered the poli-tics of lobbying and bargaining with the state as leaders of social movement organizations, both during and after the transition to democracy. These are the civic and political leaders who waged underground struggles, experi-enced both violent and non-violent clashes between the state and civil soci-ety, and then occupied policy fields with the resources derived from civil society. The same actors then actively mobilized social movement organ-izations to occupy state institutions in the new electoral spaces of a more passive, democratic state, a position from which they eventually executed the expansion of social policies as partisan incumbents. We may label these political leaders 'embedded mobilizers/negotiators' in the sense that they are distinctly positioned to confront, persuade, bargain with, and punish both party leaders and state bureaucrats, both through their expertise in the relevant policy areas and through the power of the social bases that they built throughout the democratization processes.

Such political forces and actors emerged in many developing societies during the eras of harsh authoritarian repression and transition to democracy in the 1980s and the 1990s, after which they then succeeded, during the 2000s, in occupying state institutions. Particularly in Brazil, the same leaders were also decisive in establishing participatory governance structures at every level of government institutions. We find that these embedded mobilizers/negotiators best illustrate the 'ethical life' Hegel envisioned in his framework of state–society interactions. Drawing from their lifeworld experiences during the eras of consolidation of democracy, they identified and articulated the needs of workers and citizens before then playing crucial roles in institutionally crystalizing those needs through labor–civic solidarity and labor–party alliances. This study suggests that further analyzing the strategies and networks these intellectuals created in forging social and political coalitions could prove fruitful for understanding variations in welfare state development and retrenchment in developing countries.

In all, this study shows that social movement processes matter for welfare state outcomes. By revealing concrete, meso-level 'solidarity-making' processes, I was able to build a social network-based, society-centered theory of welfare state development (and retrenchment), one which focused on union leaders' concrete organizational strategies and their ability to build solidarity with other social groups in civil society. By taking into account this embeddedness dimension, my investigation reveals that the conventional power resource dimension, 'union–leftist party alliance,' needs to be re-evaluated in the larger civil society or community mobilization context. Furthermore, by understanding this embeddedness of unions in civil society, we may be able to find an alternative pathway to universal welfare states without resorting to the corporatisic embeddedness of unions in businesses. Indeed, there must exist a moment of creative coordination of interests among social forces in the process of social movements driving universal social policies (not selective or particularistic social policies). Most contemporary research on welfare states has simply ignored such moments, only to observe their institutionalized outcomes. Scholars of welfare states, who got lost in the long-running debate between 'politics against market' and 'politics for market,' should instead focus their attention on 'politics embedded in civil society.'

Appendix A

Profiles of Labor and Civic Activists from Field Interviews (N = 143)

A.1. South Korea (N = 56)

Name	ID	Role & Affiliation	Age	Gender	Going-Under-ground Activity	Party Involvement	Civic Involvement
(Yi Kŭn-wŏn)	K1	Current KCTU chief officer of Political Committee	Mid-50s	M	Yes	Yes, Founding Committee of the DLP	None
(Yi Pyŏng-nyŏl)	K2	Current KHMU (KCTU) Chief Officer of Political Committee	Mid-50s	M	Yes	Yes, ran as a candidate for DLP	None
(Yi Kwang-ho)	K3	Participated in NCTU/former editor of KCTU official bulletin/current editor of "Redian" (leftist web journal)	Late 50s	M	No		None
(Kim Yŏng-dae)	K4	Former secretary general of KCTU (1998–2001)	Late 50s	M	No	Yes, ran as a candidate for Open Uri Party	None
(Kim T'ae-hyŏn)	K5	Current KCTU Policy Unit director	Late 50s	M	Yes	None	None

(*continued*)

A.1. (continued)

Name	ID	Role & Affiliation	Age	Gender	Going-Under-ground Activity	Party Involvement	Civic Involvement
(Pae Ki-nam)	K6	Current KCTU Seoul Regional Center vice-president	Mid-50s	M	Yes	Yes, ran as a candidate for DLP	None
(Kang Ch'ang-gu)	K7	Former president of RHCS and KHMU/former secretary-general of NCHIU	Late 50s	M	No	None	Chief secretary-general of NCHIU
(Sin Ŏn-jik)	K8	Former chief officer of KCTU Organization and Strike Unit/current chief aide to Congresswoman Sim Sang-jŏng	Mid-50s	M	Yes	Yes, Founding team of DLP (from KCTU)	None
(Kim Yu-sŏn)	K9	Former KCTU Policy Unit analyzer/current vice-director of KLSI	Late 50s	M	No	None	Founding member of KLSI
(Han Sŏk-ho)	K10	Current chief of KCTU Strike/Struggle Unit	Early 50s	M	Yes	Yes, Founding team of DLP	None
(Chu Chin-u)	K11	Former KCTU Policy Unit analyzer/current director of Policy Unit of City Bureau of Seoul	Early 50s	M	Yes	None	None
(O Kŏn-ho)	K12	Former KCTU Policy Unit analyzer/current director of Institute for Global Political Economy	Early 50s	M	No	None	Representative of "The Welfare State I Make"

Name	Code	Position	Age	Gender		Political affiliation	Other
(Hyŏn Chŏng-gil)	K13	Former vice-president of KCTU Pusan Regional Center/current advisor for Pusan City Educational Superintendent (elected position)	Early 50s	M	Yes	None	Former representative of Workers' Co-op
(Kim T'ae-gŭn)	K14	Current secretary of PSPD Ulsan Regional Branch	Late 40s	M	Yes	None	Former secretary of CCEJ Ulsan Regional Branch
(Ha Pu-yŏng)	K15	Former vice-president of Hyundai Automobile Union (1999)/former president of KCTU Ulsan Regional Center (2006)	Late 50s	M	No	None	None
(Yi Yŏng-do)	K16	Former vice-president of KCTU Ulsan Regional Center	Early 50s	M	No	Yes, ran as a candidate of PNP (Ulsan)	None
(Kim Chŏng-ho)	K17	Current director of Ch'angwŏn Institute for Labor Education	Mid-50s	M	Yes	None	None
(Im Yŏng-il)	K18	Former sociology professor at Kyŏngnam Univ./founder of Yŏngnam Labor Institute/current director of Institute for Korean Labor Movements (under KCTU Seoul Center)	Early 60s	M	No	Advisor for early DLP	None
(Pak Yu-ho)	K19	Former chief of Metal Union Organizational Unit/former director of UPP (Unified Progressive Party) Ch'angwŏn Regional Branch	Early 50s	M	Yes	One of leaders of UPP	None

(continued)

Name	ID	Role & Affiliation	Age	Gender	Going-Under-ground Activity	Party Involvement	Civic Involvement
(Yŏ Yŏng-guk)	K20	Founding member of former Kyŏngnam Workers' Association/Ma-Ch'ang Union Confederation/NCTU	Early 50s	M	No	Former DLP regional leader	Regional-level coalitions with religious orgs
(Ch'oe Yong-guk)	K21	President of Daewoo Automobile Sales Company/KCTU founding team/president of KCTU Pusan Regional Center	Early 60s	M	No	None	Representative of Pusan Workers Co-op
(Na Sang-yun)	K22	Has been a paid official of KRWU/current member of Policy Committee of KRWU	Mid-50s	M	Yes	None	Representative of House of People in Kangsŏ area
(Kim Ch'ang-bo)	K23	Former secretary of the Health Rights Network/current director of Welfare Policy Unit in City Bureau of Seoul	Mid-40s	M	No	None	Student (SNU) founder of the Health Rights Network
(Kim Chun-hyŏn)	K24	Current secretary of Health Rights Network	Late 40s	M	No	None	
(Kim Ki-sik)	K25	Former PSPD secretary-general/ current Congressman	Late 40s	M	Yes	None	Founder of PSPD/ founder of "The World I Dream of"
(Kim Yong-ik)	K26	Former NCHIU leader/current Congressman	Mid-60s	M	No	None	One of the founders of NCHIU

(continued)

K27	(Yi Ŭn-gu)	Former President of Daewoo Automobile Union	Late 50s	M	No	None	None
K28	(Yang Kyu-hyŏn)	Former president of NCTU/one of founding leaders of KCTU	Late 60s	M	No	None	None
K29	(Pak Nae-gun)	Current president of Human Rights Solidarity	Mid-50s	M	Yes	None	Founder of "Club for Human Rights Movements"
K30	(Chŏng Mun-ju)	Current FKTU chief of Policy Unit	Late 40s	M	No	None	None
K31	(Yi Chŏng-sik)	Current FKTU secretary-general	Late 50s	M	No	None	None
K32	(No Chin-gwi)	Current FKTU advisor	Early 60s	M	No	None	None
K33	(Kim Yŏn-myŏng)	Commissioner of Social Welfare Unit of PSPD/professor in Dept. of Social Welfare, Chungang Univ.	Early 50s	M	No	None	Involved in PSPD since mid-1990s
K34	(Chŏng Kyŏng-sŏp)	Current chairperson of Map'o Regional Branch of PNP(Progressive New Party)	Early 40s	M	No	PNP official	Representative of Map'o House of People
K35	(Ch'oe Yong)	Former KHMU paid official/current secretary for Congresswoman Chang Ha-na (DP)	Early 40s	M	No	Official of DLP Regional Office	None
K36	(Chŏng Chin-u)	Worked at National Laid-Off Workers' Association/current PNP vice-president	Early 40s	M	No	DLP Regional Office	None
K37	(Pak Jun-wu)	Current president of NPS Union	Mid-50s	M	None	None	Kim Kwan-jin (Pak Jun-wu)

Name	ID	Role & Affiliation	Age	Gender	Going-Under-ground Activity	Party Involvement	Civic Involvement
(Cho Kyŏng-ae)	K38	Former secretary of HCASR/ representative of HRN/ representative of Citizens' Solidarity against Privatization of Health Care	Early 50s	F	No	None	Founder of several consortium orgs for Health Rights
(Kim Kyŏng-ja)	K39	President of KHMU/vice-president of KCTU/ current co-president of Citizens' Solidarity against Privatization of Health Care	Late 40s	F	No	None	None
(Yi Ŭn-ju)	K40	Former vice-president of New Progressive Party (split from the DLP)	Early 40s	F	No	None	None
(No Ok-hŭi)	K41	Former Ulsan City Education Committee member/current chairperson of PNP Ulsan Branch	Late 50s	F	Yes	PNP	Ulsan Tonggu Residents' Association
(Yi Hyang-wŏn)	K42	Former KCTU vice-president/ director of Women's Committee	Late 40s	F	Yes	None	None
(Kim So-yŏn)	K43	Former chief officer of KCTU Metal Union Kiryung Branch/ 2012 independent presidential candidate (no party base)	Mid-40s	F	No	None	None
(Kim Sŏn-jŏng)	K44	Former KCTU union organizer/ current activist in city-based agriculture movement	Late 40s	F	No	Former DLP activist	City-based small agriculture movements

			Age	Gender			
(Sim Chae-ok)	K45	Former chief of KRWU Women's Unit/current planner for Non-standard Worker Center at KCTU Seoul Regional Center	Early 50s	F	No	None	None
(Ch'oe Hye-yŏng)	K46	Secretary of KCTU Kyŏnggi North Regional Office	Early 50s	F	Yes	None	Representative of Women's Committee at Ŭijŏngbu City
(Hwang Hye-wŏn)	K47	Current representative of "Place for Talk" (Base Community for House of People)/former director of Environmental Committee of the New Progressive Party	Early 50s	F	No	None	Founder of region-based community associations in Yongsan (Seoul) area
(Han Chŏng-hŭi)	K48	Former journalist/former secretary of Hot Line for Women in Kangsŏ area (Seoul)/current member of Founding Committee for House of People in Yangch'ŏn Area	Early 50s	F	No	Ran as a DLP candidate in 2006	Region-based Community Associations
(Im Chin-hŭi)	K49	Current secretary of Institute for Labor Education for Equality Society (the KCTU)	Late 30s	F	No	None	None
(Pak Sŏn-min)	K50	Worked at National Peasants Association (NPA) Chŏnbuk region/former assistant for DLP Congressmen/current chief aide for Congressman Pak Wŏn-suk (Justice Party)	Early 40s	F	No	None	Regional peasants' movements

(continued)

Name	ID	Role & Affiliation	Age	Gender	Going-Underground Activity	Party Involvement	Civic Involvement
(Kim Yŏng-gyŏng)	K51	Former president of Youth Community Union	Early 30s	F	No	None	SNS communities for non-standard youth Workers in services
(Kim Ha-nŭi)	K52	Current president of Solidarity for Hope Union	Late 30s	F	No	None	Region-based union–civic solidarity movements
(An Yŏng-sin)	K53	Current executive director of Citizens' Association, "Joyful Imagination"	Early 40s	F	No	None	Community-based education/co-op movements with unions
(Cho Kŭm-dŭk)	K54	Current president of a care cooperative/former chief officer of Youth Union	Mid-30s	F	No	None	Youth Workers' Union/youth co-op movements
(Na Kyŏng-ch'ae)	K55	Representative of Policy Think Tank, "Today"	Mid-40s	F	No	Workers' Party, Kwanak Region	House of People movement
(Kim Myŏng-sin)	K56	Current policy aide (social policy areas) for Congressman Ch'oe Tong-ik (DP)	Early 40s	F	No	None	None

Name	ID	Role & Affiliation	Age	Gender	Going-Under-ground Activity	Party-Involvement	Civic-Involvement
(You-lian Sun)	T1	Secretary-general, Taiwan Labor Front	42	M	Yes (activities as unregistered organization)	No	Union participation since the 1990s
(Ying-gui Su)	T2	Lawyer (former legislator and head of Department of Labor, Taipei City)	56	M	No	TSU (Taiwan Solidarity Union) legislator	Civic participation since the 1990s
(Xu-zhong Zhang)	T2	Chair, Chunghwa Telecom Workers' Union, Kaohsiung Branch	56	M	Yes ("unregistered")	No	Union leader since the late 1980s
(Ya-ping Liu)	T4	Chair, Kaohsiung Education Union	50s	M	No	No	Union leader since the 1990s
(Rui-fang Chen)	T5	Chair, Bank of Kaohsiung Workers' Union	50s	M	No	No	Union/movement participation since the 1990s
(Jian-yi Liu)	T6	Chair, Formosa Plastics Workers' Union	60s	M	Yes	No	Union/movement participation since the 1990s
(Zong-hong Lin)	T7	Researcher, Academia Sinica	50s	M	No	No	Movement participation since the 1990s
(Yao-zi Wang)	T8	Chair, Serve the People Association	60s	M	Yes	No	Union participation since the 1990s
(Feng-yi Zhang)	T9	Executive director, Taiwan Labor and Social Policy Research Association	50s	M	No	No	Civic participation since 1990s

(continued)

A.2. (*continued*)

Name	ID	Role & Affiliation	Age	Gender	Going-Under-ground Activity	Party-Involvement	Civic-Involvement
(Zhen-fei Mao)	T10	Honorary chair, Taoyuan County Confederation of Trade Unions (former TCTU position)	60s	M	Yes	No	Union participation since the 1980s
(Lian-xing Cai)	T11	Chair, Kaohsiung City Occupation Union	60s	M	No	Yes (DPP Labor Headquarters. Self-identified DPP)	Movement/union participation since the 1980s
(Jian-xing Jiang)	T12	Chair, Kaohsiung City Confederation of Trade Unions	60s	M	No	No	Movement/union participation since the late 1980s
(Mei-wen Luo)	T13	Honorary chair, Taiwan Labor Party (former Yuandong Petrochemical employee)	64	M	Yes	Taiwan Labor Party	Union leader since the 1970s
(Kun-quan Yan)	T14	Self-employed, Haomei Trucks (former Formosa Plastics/Nan Ya Plastics employee)	60	M	No	Taiwan Labor Party	Union/movement leader since the 1980s
(Qing-xian Huang)	T15	Consultant, Taiwan Petroleum Workers' Union (former TCTU chair)	65	M	No	No	Union leader since the 1980s
(Zheng-xian Bai)	T16	Consultant, Tatung Union (former TCTU, Taiwan Labor Front secretary-general)	63	M	No	No	Union participation since late 1980s

(Guo-xi Ceng)	T17	Chair, Kaohsiung City Federation of Petrochemical Industrial Unions	50s	M	No	Union participation since late 1980s
(Jin-quan Tang)	T18	Lawyer (former DPP Legislator, Kaohsiung City Councilor, Deputy Mayor)	68	M	Yes	DPP (Legislator)	Union participation since the early 1980s/ former lawyer
(Jue-an Zhuang)	T19	Chair, TCTU	51	M	No	Union/movement participation since 1990s
(He-zong Huang)	T20	Former managing director, Taichung Bus Workers' Union	60s	M	No	Union/movement participation since 1980s
(Hui-ling Wu)	T21	Director-general, Taiwan Provincial Machinery Workers' Union	50s	F	No	Union participation since 1990s

A.3. *Brazil (N = 43)*

Name	ID	Role & Affiliation	Age	Gender	Going-Underground Activity	Party-Involvement	Civic-Involvement
(João Avamileno)	B1	Current chancellor of the Department of Human Rights in local government of Santo André	Early-70s	M	Yes	Workers' Party	Metalworkers' civic leader since late 1970s
(Sergio Novais)	B2	Current coordinator of the Department of Business	57	M	No	Workers' Party	Chemical workers' civic leader since 1990s
(Alemão Duarte)	B3	Current city councilman in Santo André	51	M	No	Workers' Party	Metalworkers' civic leader since 1990s
(João Cayres)	B4	Current general secretary and international relations director at CNM – Confederação Nacional dos Metalúrgicos (National Confederation of Metallurgists)	46	M	Yes	Workers' Party	Metalworkers' civic leader since late 1980s
(Sergio Ricardo Antiqueira)	B5	Current president of the Sindicato dos Servidores Municipais de São Paulo – SINDSEP	45	M	No	Workers' Party	Education workers' civic leader since late 1990s
(Waldemar Rossi)	B6	Retired metalworker/ member of Pastoral Operária	82	M	Yes	Not a member of Workers' Party anymore	Member of Pastoral Operária/ Metalworkers' civic leader since 1960s/ was a member of Oposição Sindical de São Paulo and Juventude Operária Cristã (JOC)

Name	Code	Occupation	Age	Gender		Party	Notes
(Elias Stein)	B7	Retired metalworker	75	M	Yes	Not a member of Workers' Party anymore	Metalworkers' civic leader since the 1960s/was a member of Oposição Sindical de São Paulo and Juventude Operária Cristã (JOC)
(Remígio Todeschini)	B8	Current executive director of the Santo André Social Security Institute (Instituto de Previdência de Santo André)	61	M	Yes	Workers' Party	Was leader of Petrochemical workers, treasurer of CUT and member of Juventude Operária Cristã (JOC)
(Leandro Horie)	B9	DIEESE at CUT Nacional (scientific/technical board)	37	M	No	Not a member	Student movement during undergraduate studies
(Expedito Solaney)	B10	Current Secretário de Políticas Sociais e Direitos Humanos (secretary of social policy and human rights) of CUT-National	48	M	Yes	Workers' Party	Was member of the executive of the Sindicato dos Bancários
(José Gaspar)	B11	Current executive counselor of the Força Sindical	67	M	Yes	Democratic Labour Party	Former executive secretary of Força Sindical
(Paulo Mattos Skromov)	B12	Retired from leather industry	68	M	Yes	Workers' Party	Former president of Leatherworkers' Union and civic leader since 1960s/was one of the creators of the PT, chairing the plenary of its foundation, on February 10, 1980

(continued)

A.3. (continued)

Name	ID	Role & Affiliation	Age	Gender	Going-Underground Activity	Party-Involvement	Civic-Involvement
(João Carlos Gonçalvez – Juruna)	B13	Current general secretary of National Força Sindical	62	M	Yes	Democratic Workers' Party	Former part of Catholic Workers' Youth (JOC)/ former Sao Paulo Metalworkers' director during dictatorship in Brazil
(Geraldino dos Santos)	B14	Current union relations secretary of Força Sindical	63	M	Yes	Solidariedade Party	Former Sao Paulo Metalworkers' executive director during dictatorship in Brazil/ affiliated with clandestine Communist Party during dictatorship
(Diógenes Sandim)	B15	Current executive counselor of the Força Sindical	65	M	Yes	Solidariedade Party	Member of clandestine Communist Party during dictatorship
(Aparecido Donizeti da Silva)	B16	Current assistant director of the Department of Business and Finances of National CUT	54	M	No	Workers' Party	Chemical workers' civic leader since 1990s
(Vicente Cândido)	B17	Current Congressman elect for Sao Paulo	54	M	No	Workers' Party	Former Pastoral Youth member (Pastoral da Juventude)/one of the founders of Workers' Party (PT)

(Paulo Roberto Salvador)	B18	Current director of Rede Brasil Atual (one of the main left media vehicles in Brazil)	60	M	Yes	Workers' Party	Former member of Sindicato dos Bancários/participated in the student movement in 1970s
(Valter Sanches)	B19	Director of communication of Sindicato dos Metalúrgicos do ABC and Executive Director of CNM/CUT – Confederação Nacional dos Metalúrgicos da CUT	51	M	Yes	Workers' Party	Sindicato dos Metalúrgicos do ABC/participated in the student movement in early 1980s
(Artur Henrique da Silva Santos)	B20	Currently secretary of development, labor and entrepreneurship of Prefeitura of Sao Paulo (municipality)	54	M	No	Workers' Party	Former president of CUT (2006–12) and former president of Sindicato dos Eletriciários
(Valdenilson Alves de Lira)	B21	Union coordinator of Federação dos Sindicatos de Metalúrgicos da CUT/SP (FEM-CUT/SP)	66	M	Yes	Workers' Party	Former director of Sindicato dos Metalúrgicos do ABC/former director of CNM/CUT
(Adi dos Santos)	B22	Current president of CUT-SP	59	M	Yes	Workers' Party	Executive director of the ABC Union, 1999–2000/former president of DIEESE, 2001–02/general secretary of CUT-SP, 2006–09

(continued)

A.3. (continued)

Name	ID	Role & Affiliation	Age	Gender	Going-Underground Activity	Party-Involvement	Civic-Involvement
(Walter Barelli)	B23	Retired professor/worked at DIEESE for 23 years	76	M	Yes	Not a member of Brazilian Social Democracy Party anymore	President of DIEESE, Minister of Labour in the Franco government (October 1992 to April 1994)/secretary for Emprego e Relações do Trabalho de São Paulo (1995 to 2002)/Congressman from the PSDB-SP (2003–07)
(Célia Regina Costa)	B24	General secretary of National Confederation of Workers in Social Security CNTSS/CUT	57	F	Yes	Workers' Party	Former president of the Union of Public Health Workers of São Paulo (Sindsaúde-SP/CUT)
(Sônia Auxiliadora Vasconcelos Silva)	B25	Secretary of politics for women at CUT/SP (Secretaria da Mulher Trabalhadora) and general coordinator of the Union School of São Paulo (Escola Sindical São Paulo)	51	F	No	Workers' Party	Former member of Ecclesial Base Communities of the Catolic Church (Comunidades Eclesiais de Base)/president of the Union of Municipal Public Employees of Presidente Prudente, SP (SINTRAPP-CUT)

Name	ID	Position	Age	Gender		Party	Description
(Maria Ozaneide de Paulo)	B26	Secretary of politics for women at CUT/Ceará and director of the Federation of Workers of the Public Municipal Service of Ceará (FETAMCE)	50	F	No	Workers' Party	Former president of the Union of Municipal Public Employees of Aquiraz/CE (SINSEPUMA/CUT)
(Renato Carvalho Zulato)	B27	Director of Finance and Administration of the CUT/SP and administrative coordinator of the Union School of São Paulo (Escola Sindical São Paulo)	58	M	No	Workers' Party	Former secretary of communication of the National Confederation of Chemical Workers (Confederação Nacional do Ramo Químico/CUT)/former director of communication of Diretório Municipal do PT-SP/former director of finance and administration of Union of Chemical and Plastics workers in São Paulo
(Rafael Marques da Silva Junior)	B28	President of Sindicato dos Metalúrgicos do ABC	51	M	No	Workers' Party	Member of Workers' Party since his youth/former director and vice-president of Sindicato dos Metalúrgicos do ABC/former president of Agência de Desenvolvimento Econômico do Grande ABC (Economic Development Agency of ABC area)

(*continued*)

A.3. (*continued*)

Name	ID	Role & Affiliation	Age	Gender	Going-Underground Activity	Party-Involvement	Civic-Involvement
(Carlos Grana)	B29	Mayor of Santo André -SP	49	M	Yes	Workers' Party	Former member of Sao Paulo state Legislative Chamber/former General Secretary of Central Única dos Trabalhadores, Confederação Nacional dos Metalurgicos and Federação Estadual dos Metalurgicos
(Teonílio Barba)	B30	Member of Legislative Chamber of Sao Paulo State Government	52	M	No	Workers' Party	Discharged director of administraion of MetalWorkers Union of ABC/former director of Confederação Nacional dos Metalurgicos and president of Central Unica dos Trabalhadores Audit Committee

Name	Code	Position	Age	Gender		Party	Notes
(Rosane Bertotti)	B31	National secretary of Communications of the Workers Central Union (CUT)	49	F	No	Workers' Party	Was part of Pastoral da Juventude, Comunidades Eclesiais de Base (Basic ecclesial Community), and Movimento das Mulheres Campesinas (Women Peasant Movement) in the state of Santa Catarina/secretary of formation at CUT-SC (three terms)/since 2006, national secretary of communication at National CUT/National
(Chico Vigilante)	B32	Member of Legislative Chamber of Distrito Federal	60	M	No	Workers' Party	Creator of the Union of Security Guards of DF/founder and president of CUT-DF/founder and president of PT–DF/federal Congressman elect for Distrito Federal (1990–98 and 2010–14)
(Erika Kokay)	B33	Current federal Congresswoman elect for Distrito Federal	57	F	Yes	Workers' Party	Former president of Sindicato dos Bancários de Brasília (1992–98)/former president of CUT-DF (2000–02)/federal Congresswoman in 2010–14

(continued)

Name	ID	Role & Affiliation	Age	Gender	Going-Underground Activity	Party-Involvement	Civic-Involvement
(Rose Pavan)	B34	Advisor to the secretary of international relations at the CUT and director of the Cooperation Institute	67	F	Yes	Workers' Party	Has been director of the Department of Communication and Department of Social Policy at CUT-SP
(Lucineide Varjão)	B35	Currently president of the CNQ-CUT (National Chemical Workers' Confederation/ Confederação Nacional dos Químicos)	47	F	No	Workers' Party	Has been part of the Chemical Workers from ABC and São Paulo/in 2013, was the first woman elected president of the National Chemical Workers' Confederation (Confederação Nacional dos Químicos)
(Luci Paulino de Aguiar)	B36	Former secretary of social relations from Lula's and Dilma's tenure	65	F	Yes	Workers' Party	Former director of Metalworkers Union of ABC/first women on the board of directors of CUT Nacional as well as one of founders of National Confederation of Metalworkers
(Rosane da Silva)	B37	Current Women Worker director at National CUT	45	F	No	Workers' Party	Director at Shoemaker's Union of Rio Grande do Sul/former part of Coletivo Nacional da Juventude Trabalhadora at National CUT

(Juncia Batista)	B38	Current Worker's Health director at National CUT/ current Women Worker director at International Union of Public Service	57	F	No	Workers' Party	Current Women Worker director at International Union of Public Service/ current licensed director at Public Service Union of São Paulo (SINSEP-SP)/one of the founders of FETAM-SP, and CONFETAM
(Antônio Carlos)	B39	Current general secretary of Public Service Union of Sao Paulo (SINDSEP)	61	M	Yes, as a student	Workers' Party	Was part of the student movement and the underground communist party in Brazil during the military regime/ part of Health Popular Movement in Sao Paulo/ former Coordinator of South City neighborhood at his union
(Cida Trajano)	B40	President of the National Confederation of Apparel Workers (Confederação Nacional dos Trabalhadores no Vestuário – CNTV/CUT)	53	F	No	Workers' Party	Has been president of the ABC Apparel Union and Executive Secretariat for Women at CUT

(continued)

Name	ID	Role & Affiliation	Age	Gender	Going-Underground Activity	Party-Involvement	Civic-Involvement
(Licilene Binsfeld)	B41	Current secretary of international relations and cooperation (Secretária de Relações Internacionais e de Cooperação) fo CONTRACS	44	F	No	Workers' Party	Former president of the National Confederation of Workers in Commerce and Services (Confederação Nacional dos Trabalhadores no Comércio e Serviços – CONTRACS-CUT)
(José Drummond)	B42	Adviser to the CUTs International Relations Secretariat and coordinator of the project CUTMulti	68	M	Yes	Workers' Party	Former director of the Chemical Workers' Union/member of the pro-CUT commission/in August 1983, leading figure in the foundation of CUT. Performs several activities today: Bilateral Project coordinator with foreign central trade union/advice on union negotiations and planning/execution and monitoring of international projects
(Wagner Santana)	B43	Currently the secretary-general of the Sindicato dos Metalúrgicos do ABC	53	M	Yes	Workers' Party	Former director of DIEESE

A.4. *Argentina (N = 23)*

Name	ID	Role and Affiliation	Age	Gender	Going-Under-ground Activity	Party Involvement	Civic Involvement
(Lorenzo Pepe)	A1	Union leader, Railroad Workers' Union (Unión Ferroviaria-CGT)	Mid-80s (Born 1931)	M	Yes	Congressional representative, PJ Party (1983–2003); president, Peronist Party Council (1990–98)	Educational foundation with three schools (for disabled and low-income groups, as well as a vocational school)
(Oraldo Britos)	A2	Union leader, Railroad Workers' Union (Unión Ferroviaria-CGT); former Minister of Labor (2002)	Early 80s (Born 1933)	M	Yes	Senator (1973–76; 1983–2003), PJ Party; Congressional representative, PJ Party	Social assistance foundation "Eva Perón, San Luis Province"/ computer and trade school courses
(Omar Plaini)	A3	National general secretary, Newspaper Vendors' Union (CGT)	Mid-60s (Born 1950)	M	Yes	Congressional representative FPV-PJ (2009–11) and Congressional representative for CGT (dissident but Peronist) (2011–15)	Union financed 35 high schools for marginalized social sectors
(Francisco Gaitán)	A4	Union leader, Marine and Ship Workers' Union (CGT)	Early 80s (Born 1935)	M	Yes	Former leader in the leftist Peronist guerrilla group Montoneros, union sector	National director of the educational department of CLAT and INCASUR
(Rodolfo Díaz)	A5	Labor lawyer/former Minister of Labor (1991–92)	Early 70s (Born 1943)	M			Student movement (1960s and 1970s)

(continued)

A.4. (continued)

Name	ID	Role and Affiliation	Age	Gender	Going-Under-ground Activity	Party Involvement	Civic Involvement
(Guillermo Carrasco)	A6	Grassroots Peronist activist/ journalist (underground)/ government official, internal security	Early 60s (Born 1954)	M	Yes	Local leader (conurbano sur), PJ Party (1973–2015)	Student movement (1970s)/Peronist Youth
(Roberto Digón)	A7	Union leader, Tobacco Factory Workers' Union (CGT)	Late 70s (Born 1938)	M	Yes	Diputado Nacional 80s and 90s (PJ)/soccer clubs (Boca Junior)	None
(Carlos Holubica)	A8	National director of relations between the state and Catholic Archdiocese, Ministry of Foreign Affairs and Worship/journalist and former director of magazine *Justicia Social*	Mid 60s (Born 1950)	M	Yes	National government official (1990s and 2000s)	None
(Susana Rueda)	A9	Union leader, health workers' unions/former leader, CGT	Early 60s (Born 1953)	F	Yes	Party leader at province level, PJ-Santa Fe (1990s and 2000s)	None
(Arnaldo Goenara)	A10	Union adviser/former adviser to Perón/ director of two Peronist magazines	Mid 70s (Born 1940)	M	Yes	Representative at provincial level, PJ Party (1983–87)	None
(José Castillo)	A11	Union leader, Ship Workers' Union (CGT)	Late 70s (Born 1936)	M	Yes	Congressional representative, PJ Party (1980s–1990s)	None

(Carlos Gandsky)	A12	National representative, Metalworkers' Union (CGT)	Mid 70s (Born 1946)	M	Yes	Congressional representative, PJ Party (2000s)	None
(Roberto Baschetti)	A13	Writer	Mid 60s (Born 1950)	M	Yes	None	Grassroots groups
(Nora Patrich)	A14	Artist	Mid 60s (Born 1952)	F	Yes	Former member of leftist Peronist guerrilla group Montoneros (1972–83)	Radical student groups/human rights movement
(María Elena Naddeo)	A15	Union leader, Teachers' Union (CTA)	Mid 60s (Born 1958)	F	Yes	Representative at provincial level (Capital Federal), 1990s and 2000s	Union feminist groups
(Horacio Caminos)	A16	Union leader, Train Drivers and Operators' Union (La Fraternidad-CGT)	Mid 60s (Born 1958)	M	Yes	Member, Partido Intransigente (PI) (1980s)/ local Peronist leader, FPV-PJ Party (2000s)	Leftist union groups
(Jorge Lobais)	A17	Union leader, Textile Workers' Union (AOT-CGT)	Mid 60s (Born 1950)	M	Yes	Peronist party leader, 2000s	Leader of CGT
(Mario Oporto)	A18	Congressional Representative, FPV-PJ/president, National Commission of Communications (Comisión de Comunicaciones)/former Minister of Education	Mid 60s (Born 1952)	M	No	Peronist party leader, 1990s and 2000s	Party leader
(Inés Pérez Suárez)	A19	Former Secretary of Human Rights (1990s)	Mid 70s (Born 1948)	F	Yes	Concejal (1980s)/Congressional representative (1990s), PJ Party	Women's movement organizations/ human rights organizations

(continued)

A.4. (continued)

Name	ID	Role and Affiliation	Age	Gender	Going-Under-ground Activity	Party Involvement	Civic Involvement
(Abel Cabrera)	A20	Union leader, Textile Workers' Union (AOT-CGT)	Mid 70s (Born 1948)	M	Yes	None	Local union networks
(Alejandra Estoup)	A21	Union leader, Bank Employees' Union (La Bancaria-CGT)/president, Uni Mujeres América	Mid 50s (Born 1963)	F	Yes	None	Feminist union networks
(Armando Caro Figueroa)	A22	Former Minister of Labor (1993–97)	Mid 70s (Born 1944)	M	Yes	Peronist (1960s–70s)/ neo-liberal (1980s–2000s)	Intellectual supporting unions
(Victor De Gennaro)	A23	Founder, CTA/leader of public sector workers' union ATE (Asociación Trabajadores del Estado)/congressional representative (Diputado Nacional)	Late 60s (Born 1948)	M	Yes	Peronist leader, 1970s–1990s/ Peronist opposition leader, 1990s	National union leader/CTA ties to civil society

Appendix B

Measurements of Embeddedness and Cohesiveness in Associational Network Data (used in Chapter 9)

In order to measure the structure of associational communities in four developing countries, I utilize data on memberships of voluntary associations in three waves of World Values Surveys, 1995, 2005, and 2014. Membership questionnaires contained in these three waves provide important information by asking whether respondents are active or non-active members for a specific association.[1] The individual-level survey data on memberships with voluntary associations allow me to build an analytical map of each national associational community to explore "how individuals in a society are affiliated with different types of voluntary organizations," "how these individuals and organizations are connected to each other through co-memberships," and "how these affiliation networks are aggregated into a distinctive pattern of organizational power structure and configuration" (Lee 2007, p. 594).

Then, based on the two-mode information (m individuals * n associational types), I built an n*n co-affiliation matrix (Borgatti *et al.* 2002; Breiger 1974) using UCINET 6. The matrix is composed of diagonal elements representing the number of memberships for each association and non-diagonal elements representing the number of co-memberships between two associational types. With this co-membership matrix, I calculated the measures of cohesiveness and embeddedness as follows.

Cohesiveness of Formal Organizational Sphere
$$= \Sigma(CM_{i,j}) / M(min)_{u,pa,pr}$$
$$(i \neq j; i,j = \text{any formal civic associations})$$
$$= [(CM_{u,pa} + CM_{u,pr} + CM_{pa,pr})] / M(min)_{u,pa,pr}$$

Where $CM_{u,pa}$, $CM_{u,pr}$, and $CM_{pa,pr}$ denote co-membership between unions and parties, co-membership between unions and professional associations, and co-membership between parties and professional associations, respectively. $M(min)_{u,pa,\,pr}$ denotes a membership count of three key formal organizations, excluding any redundant memberships (e.g. even though a respondent is co-affiliated with all three associations, only one membership will be recorded for the respondent).

Embeddedness of Formal Organizational Sphere
$$= \Sigma(CM_{i,k}) \,/\, M(min)_{u,pa,\,pr}$$
(i ≠ k; i = any formal civic association,
k = any non-formal civic association)
$$= [\Sigma(CM_{u,k}) + \Sigma(CM_{pa,k}) + \Sigma(CM_{pr,k})] \,/\, M(min)_{u,pa,\,pr}$$

Where the numerator denotes the sum of all co-membership counts between formal civic associations and informal civic associations. More specifically, the numerator includes the sum of co-memberships between unions and all informal civic associations ($\Sigma(CM_{u,k})$), the sum of co-memberships between parties and all informal civic associations ($\Sigma(CM_{pa,k})$), and the sum of co-memberships between professional associations and all informal civic associations ($\Sigma(CM_{pr,k})$).

Similarly, cohesiveness of unions can be measured as the co-membership density of unions with other formal-sector associations, while being normalized by unions' own membership value. The formula for cohesiveness of unions is as follows:

$$\text{Cohesiveness}_u = \Sigma\left(CM_{u,\,pa\,or\,pro}\right) / U_i,$$
$$\text{Cohesiveness}_u = \Sigma\left(CM_{u,lp}\right) / U_i,$$
$$\text{Cohesiveness}_u = \Sigma\left(CM_{u,ip}\right) / U_i,$$

where $CM_{u,pa\,or\,pro}$ is the size of co-membership of unions with parties (pa) and professional associations (pro), and U_i is the membership of unions. In narrower definitions, $CM_{u,lp}$ is the size of co-membership of unions with labor parties, while $CM_{u,ip}$ is the size of co-membership of unions with incumbent parties. The first one captures the general lobbying channels of unions to all political parties regardless of partisanship. The measure also captures unions' coalitional ties with professional associations, signifying 'working class/middle class coalitions' (Esping-Andersen 1990; Baldwin 1990). The second one captures the social democratic cohesiveness between unions and labor-based parties (Stephens 1979; Korpi 1983; Esping-Andersen 1985), while the last one captures unions' negotiation power with/against the state/incumbent parties.

Finally, embeddedness of unions can be calculated as the co-membership density of unions with other non-formal-sector organizations such as peace, human rights, environmental, cultural, and religious associations. It is expected to capture unions' trust relationship with informal civic associations and their potential encapsulation of non-unionized sectors' interests.

$$\text{Embeddedness}_u = \Sigma \left(CM_{u,k} \right) / U_i$$

Where $CM_{u,k}$ denotes the size of co-membership between unions and all other informal civic associations and unions' embeddedness is the co-membership normalized by union density (U_i).

Appendix C

Network-Informed Strategic Actions of the State and Unions: The Structures of Retrenchment and Expansion Games

Appendix C.1 Retrenchment Games: Initial Set-Up

I consider a game in which the state moves first and the union responds. I start with a set of assumptions about the state and unions. I initially assume that the state, facing pressures from international competition (often in the form of economic crisis), has preferences about appropriate levels of union activity, and shapes its first actions in response to unions' (possible) actions. The state has three options regarding reform agendas: no reform, moderate reform, or radical reform. 'Radical reform' is representative of market-oriented labor-repressive reforms of labor rights and 'moderate reform' is representative of moderate adjustment of labor rights. I assume that the state has the option of 'no reform', which implies that unions preserve status quo rights, but under intensified pressures for market reforms from global market and financial institutions, the state will be pressured to introduce some level of market reform. Next, I assume that the union, as a unitary actor representing multiple unions and workers, has preferences about levels of state action on labor and welfare policies. If the state chooses either 'moderate reform' or 'radical reform,' then the union responds by either choosing either 'militancy' or 'restraint.'

Figure C.1 describes a game tree with two status quo income/asset levels – that of employers (y^E) and that of workers (y^W). Here I assume, in general, that the unions' payoff represents workers' welfare, while the state's payoff represents employers' welfare. I normalize the status quo payoffs so that $y^W = 0$ and $y^E = 0$, respectively. Therefore, when the state chooses 'no reform,' both the state and the unions receive payoff zero.

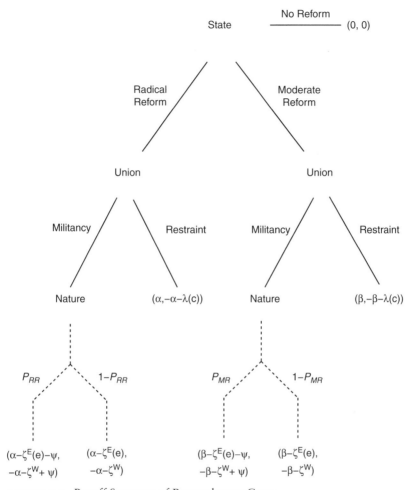

FIGURE C.1. Payoff Structure of Retrenchment Game

I assume that the state reforms will be realized through transfers of some income from workers to employers. With either radical or moderate transgression, workers (as a social class) will be deprived of initial assets and income by the lowered income or social wage. Let α and β denote the sizes of the transfers for the radical and moderate reforms, respectively, in which α is greater than β.

After each type of reform, if the unions choose 'restraint', then the reform does not incur any cost for the state. Therefore, the state's payoff following 'radical reform' and 'restraint' is α, and its payoff following 'moderate reform' and 'restraint' is β. As the unions' restraint incurs cost

$\lambda(c) > 0$ to the unions, the unions' payoffs following the 'restraint' path under radical reform and moderate reform are $-\alpha - \lambda(c)$ and $-\beta - \lambda(c)$, respectively. I assume that the unions' restraint cost depends on cohesiveness $c \in [0, +\infty)$. Taking into account Burgess' (2004) 'loyalty dilemma,' I assume that $\lambda(\cdot)$ is strictly decreasing in c. That is, the more cohesive the relationship between unions and the incumbent party, the less costly it will be for unions to accept the state-driven market reforms.

Next, I assume that unions' militancy results in costs to the state (and employers) through contentious politics. Such costs can be denoted as $\zeta^E(e) > 0$, which strictly increases with unions' embeddedness $e \in [0, +\infty)$. I also assume that unions' militancy involves costs, $\zeta^W > 0$, which is fixed in embeddedness and cohesiveness, to workers and union organizations by either depleting their existing resources or resulting in coordination problems (Olson 1965).

I also assume that it is randomly determined whether unions' resistance will be successful or not. In the case of its success, the state will make concessions to the union through lump-sum compensatory transfer. I denote this concession amount as $\psi > 0$. I introduce the probability of successful protest after either radical or moderate reform, $p^{RR}(e) \in (0, 1)$ and $p^{MR}(c) \in (0, 1)$, with which unions will win the war against the state and eventually draw a concession package, while with the probability $(1 - p)$, unions will not. Then, the state's payoff following 'radical reform' and 'militancy' is $\alpha - \zeta^E(e) - p^{RR}(e)\psi$, and unions' payoff under the same situation is $-\alpha - \zeta^W + p^{RR}(e)\psi$. The state's payoff under the moderate reform and militancy path is $\beta - \zeta^E(e) - p^{MR}(c)\psi$, while unions' payoff in the same situation is $-\beta - \zeta^W + p^{MR}(c)\psi$.

Finally, I assume that unions' high embeddedness will induce the state and employers to perceive or observe a high threat of strong militancy, which implies that $p^{RR}(e)$ is strictly increasing in e. However, unions' high cohesiveness will induce the state to decrease the probability p^{MR} in a way that punishes unions' opportunism in seeking militancy against MR, which implies that $p^{MR}(c)$ is strictly decreasing in c. In other words, with high embeddedness, unions have more resources with which to punish the state, especially under RR, while with high cohesiveness, the state has more leverage to punish unions under MR. We assume that all functions of e or c are continuous.

Analysis

The game can be solved through backward induction. I first consider unions' choice after the state chooses 'radical reform.' The unions' payoff from choosing 'militancy' is $-\alpha - \zeta^W + p^{RR}(e)\psi$, and their payoff from choosing 'restraint' is $-\alpha - \lambda(c)$. Under a radical reform path in the bottom decision nodes in Figure C.1, unions will wage militancy if and only if

$$p^{RR}(e)\psi + \lambda(c) > \zeta^W \qquad (C.1\text{-}1)$$

We are interested in comparative statics with respect to cohesiveness and embeddedness. Given that the left-hand side of C.1-1 is strictly increasing in e, while strictly decreasing in c, I assume that, for any level of e, the inequality condition binds as long as c is sufficiently low, but the inequality will be reversed if c is sufficiently high. Then, for each e, let $\hat{c}(e)$ be such that $p^{RR}(e)\psi + \lambda(\hat{c}(e)) = \zeta^W$.

The function $\hat{c}(\cdot)$ is continuous. Since p^{RR} is strictly increasing in e and λ is strictly decreasing in c, $\hat{c}(e)$ is strictly increasing in e. The unions choose 'militancy' if and only if $c < \hat{c}(e)$.

Next I consider the unions' choice under a 'moderate reform' path. The unions' payoff from choosing 'militancy' is $-\beta - \zeta^W + p^{MR}(c)\psi$, and their payoff from choosing 'restraint' is $-\beta - \lambda(c)$. Then, the unions choose 'militancy' if and only if:

$$p^{MR}(c)\psi + \lambda(c) > \zeta^W \qquad (C.1\text{-}2)$$

The left-hand side of the inequality condition is strictly decreasing in c. We assume that if cohesiveness is sufficiently low, the inequality does not hold. If cohesiveness is sufficiently high, the inequality does not hold either. Let $\bar{c}$ be such that $p^{MR}(\bar{c})\psi + \lambda(c) = \zeta^W$. Then, the unions choose

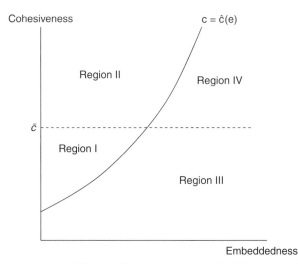

FIGURE C.2. Unions' Choice Space by Embeddedness and Cohesiveness

'militancy' if and only if c < c̄. Figure C.2 illustrates the unions' choices by embeddedness and cohesiveness, with the former being measures on the horizontal axis and the latter being measures on the vertical axis. The two conditions partition the parameter space into four subsets. In region I, the unions choose 'restraint' after radical reform and 'militancy' after moderate reform. In region II, the unions choose 'restraint' in both situations. In region III, the unions choose 'militancy' in both situations. In region IV, the unions choose 'militancy' after radical reform and 'restraint' after moderate reform. We now consider four cases in order.

Retrenchment Game 1: Low Cohesiveness and Low Embeddedness
Now I consider how changes in embeddedness and cohesiveness result in different strategies and retrenchment outcomes. I start with a game in which unions and the state are scarcely linked to each other and unions have weak linkages to broader civil society. I consider the case in which $c < \bar{c}$ and $c \geq \hat{c}(e)$. The unions choose 'restraint' after radical reform and 'militancy' after moderate reform. If the state chooses 'radical reform,' then its payoff is α, while its payoff is $\beta - \zeta^E(e) - p^{MR}(c)\psi$ for moderate reform. Clearly, the former is greater than the latter, and therefore the state will choose 'radical reform.'

Retrenchment Game 2: High Cohesiveness and Low Embeddedness
In the second senario, in which unions have strong linkages to the incumbent party but are weakly embedded in wider civil society, I consider the case in which $c \geq \bar{c}$ and $c \geq \hat{c}(e)$. In this case, without a commitment to wider civil society, union leaders endorse the necessity of the reforms, choosing 'restraint' whichever reform is implemented. Given that unions acquiesce under both paths, the state will compare payoffs under the RR-R path with those under MR-R. Since $\alpha > \beta$, the state will choose radical reform.

Retrenchment Game 3: Low Cohesiveness and High Embeddedness
In the next game, the configuration of the networks in which unions are situated is opposite to that of the previous game: unions do not have strong linkages with the incumbent party, but are deeply embedded in wider civil society. I consider the case in which $c < \bar{c}$ and $c < \hat{c}(e)$. The unions choose 'militancy' for both radical and moderate reforms. Then, the state compares payoff from the radical reform, $\alpha - \zeta^E(e) - p^{RR}(e)\psi$,

with that from the moderate reform, $\beta - \zeta^E(e) - p^{MR}(c)\psi$. Then, the state will choose moderate reform if and only if

$$[p^{RR}(e) - p^{MR}(c)]\psi \geq \alpha - \beta \tag{C.1-3}$$

The left-hand side is strictly increasing in e and c. For each e, let $\check{c}(e)$ be such that $[p^{RR}(e) - p^{MR}(\check{c}(e))]\psi = \alpha - \beta$. Then, $\check{c}(e)$ is strictly decreasing in e. The state chooses moderate reform if and only if $c \geq \check{c}(e)$. Since $c < \bar{c}$, moderate reform occurs only when embeddedness is fairly high.

Retrenchment Game 4: High Cohesiveness and High Embeddedness

I consider the final case in which $c \geq \bar{c}$ and $c < \hat{c}(e)$. The unions choose 'militancy' after radical reform and 'restraint' after moderate reform. Then, the state's payoff from radical reform is $\alpha - \zeta^E(e) - p^{RR}(e)\psi$ and its payoff from moderate reform is β. The state chooses moderate reform if and only if

$$p^{RR}(e)\psi + \zeta^E(e) \geq \alpha - \beta \tag{C.1-4}$$

Let $\bar{e}$ be such that $p^{RR}(\bar{e})\psi + \zeta^E(\bar{e}) = \alpha - \beta$. Then, the state chooses moderate reform if and only if $e \geq \bar{e}$. Figure C.3 summarizes the state's reform choices in the given parameter space.

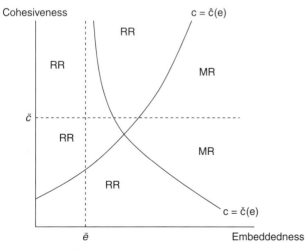

FIGURE C.3. The State's Choice Space by Embeddedness and Cohesiveness

Appendix C.2 Union-led Expansion Games: Initial Set-Up

In the expansion games, the initiator of the game is unions rather than the state (and employers). With the game tree in Figure C.4, I introduce a model with two income/asset levels, as in the retrenchment games – that of the state representing employers (y^E) and that of the union representing workers (y^W), respectively. I again normalize these payoffs at zero. Thus, if the unions choose 'no reform,' both players receive payoff zero. If the unions choose 'no reform,' then the game ends. If the unions choose either 'universal reform' or 'selective reform,' then, after observing the unions' choice, the state chooses either 'rebuff' or 'accept.'

As with retrenchment games, I start with a set of assumptions about the state and unions. Unions, facing pressures for social reforms, have preferences about the appropriate level of state action and make their first move with expectations about the (potential) state responses. Unions hold three options regarding their social reform agendas: no reform, universal reform, and selective reform. With selective reform, unions act to launch social (or labor market) policies that are beneficial only or primarily to their members (i.e., the organized middle and working classes in core industries and the public sector). With universal reform, unions are expected to pursue social policies serving a wider constituency, including non-unionized (non-standard) workers, the urban poor, peasants, and the self-employed. If the state accepts either type of the reforms, the reform initiated by the union will be implemented. With selective reform, β amount of income will be transferred from employers to organized workers. Therefore, the unions' payoff will increase by β, but non-organized outsiders will be excluded from the selective redistributive reform,[1] which makes the state's payoff at the same node $-\beta$. With universal reform, the employers' burden is larger since redistribution to a broader constituency must be made. I assume that the cost of universal reform for employers is γ, but the benefit for organized workers will increase only by α, in which $\alpha < \gamma$, while payoffs for non-organized workers and labor market outsiders will also see an increase by $\gamma - \alpha$. In addition, I assume that $\alpha < \beta < \gamma$. That is, I assume that 'universal reform' is sufficiently universal, with its encompassing benefits outweighing those of selective reform. However, simultaneously, its benefit for the organized workers, α, is smaller than that of selective reform, β.

Then, I assume that the state has preferences about the appropriate levels of union action. The state forms its actions in response to one of the two union actions: selective or universal reform. However, in contrast to the retrenchment game, the state implicitly considers the 'no reform' option of the unions, which is one of the realistic options for unions, depending upon the state's responses. The state's options are either to accept or to rebuff the unions' two reform agendas. If the state accepts, the game ends. If the state chooses 'rebuff,' then the outcome depends on how potential confrontation between the unions and the state plays out. Implicitly, the unions may punish the state after the state's rebuff, and I model this as a randomized event. If the state rebuffs the unions' policy suggestions, unions immediately punish the state with the probability p, or do not punish with the probability $(1-p)$; p may be regarded as 'the probability that the state's rebuff decision will draw unions' militancy.' I again differentiate the probability p, making it contingent upon the union's choice between UR and SR: $p^{UR}(e)$ and $p^{SR}(c)$ are probabilities that unions will engage in militancy after the state rebuffs UR and SR, respectively. I assume that $p^{UR}(\cdot)$ is continuous and strictly increasing in the unions' embeddedness, e, while $p^{SR}(\cdot)$ is strictly increasing in the unions' cohesiveness, c. On the one hand, unions' high embeddedness will increase p^{UR} because highly embedded unions and their allied civil society forces are more likely to encapsulate each other's interests as universal citizens'

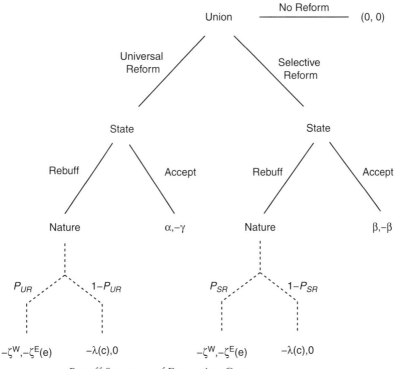

FIGURE C.4. Payoff Structure of Expansion Game

rights. This may lead them to collectively resist the state's rebuff decision on UR. On the other hand, unions' high cohesiveness will increase p^{SR}, because the state/employers and unions disarticulated from non-organized workers or labor market outsiders may pursue their own collusive interests, which may induce unions to respond to the state's rebuff decision on SR in more militant ways. Such a tendency will be more noticeable when unions' embeddedness is low. The paths and payoffs of the game based on these assumptions are summarized in Figure C.4.

The militancy with which unions seek to punish the state (and employers) also results in collective action costs for unions themselves (due to difficulty in internal coordination and mobilization). Such costs will be denoted as ζ^W, which is constant in embeddedness and cohesiveness. If unions relinquish the punishment of the state, they will have to face challenges from grassroots members for inaction (a loyalty dilemma), which incurs cost to the unions $\lambda(c)$. Thus, the unions' payoff following 'universal reform' and 'rebuff' is $-p^{UR}(e)\zeta^W - (1 - p^{UR}(e)) \lambda(c)$, while their payoff following 'selective reform' and 'rebuff' is $-p^{SR}(c)\zeta^W - (1 - p^{SR}(c)) \lambda(c)$. As in the retrenchment game, $\lambda(\cdot)$ is continuous and strictly decreasing in union's cohesiveness, c.

Through their militancy, unions will punish the state by not only damaging employers' production procedures through strikes, but also encroaching upon the state's economic performance, and their political performance in their electoral campaigns and public opinion strategies. The costs to the state will be systemized as $\zeta^E(e)$, which increases in embeddedness. Therefore, the state's payoff under the 'universal reform' and 'rebuff' path is $-p^{UR}(e)\zeta^E(e)$, while its payoff following 'selective reform' and 'rebuff' is $-p^{SR}(c)\zeta^E(c)$. I again assume that $\zeta^E(\cdot)$ is continuous and strictly increasing in unions' embeddedness, e.

Analysis
I first explore the state's choice after the unions choose 'universal reform.' The state compares payoff from rebuffing, $-p^{UR}(e)\zeta^E(e)$, with that from accepting, $-\gamma$. Assuming that the state will accept when indifferent, I conclude that the state rebuffs if and only if

$$p^{UR}(e)\zeta^E (e) < \gamma \qquad\qquad\qquad (C.2\text{-}1)$$

I now investigate comparative statics with respect to cohesiveness and embeddedness. Given that the left-hand side of C.2-1 is strictly increasing in e, we assume that the inequality condition holds when $e = 0$, and will be reversed when e is sufficiently high. Let $\hat{e}$ be such that $p^{UR}(\hat{e})\zeta^E(\hat{e}) = \gamma$.

Then, in equilibrium, the state chooses 'rebuff' after 'universal reform' if and only if $e < \hat{e}$.

Next, I consider the state's choice after the unions choose 'selective reform.' The state compares payoff from rebuffing, $-p^{SR}(c)\zeta^E(e)$, with that from accepting, $-\beta$. Then, the state rebuffs if and only if

$$p^{SR}(c)\zeta^E(e) < \beta \qquad\qquad\qquad\qquad\qquad\qquad\qquad\text{(C.2-2)}$$

The left-hand side is strictly increasing in c and e. We assume that, for each e, the inequality holds if c is sufficiently low, and the inequality will be reversed if c is sufficiently high. Then, for each e, let $\dot{c}(e)$ be such that $p^{SR}(\dot{c}(e))\zeta^E(e) = \beta$. In equilibrium, the state chooses 'rebuff' after 'selective reform' if and only if $c < \dot{c}(e)$. The function $\dot{c}(\cdot)$ is strictly decreasing in e.

In Figure C.5, embeddedness is measured on the horizontal axis, while cohesiveness is measured on the vertical axis. The two conditions above partition the parameter space into four subsets. In region I, the state rejects both universal and selective reform. In region II, the state rejects universal reform but accepts selective reform. In region III, the state accepts universal reform but rejects selective reform. Finally, in region IV, the state accepts both universal and selective reform.

Expansion Game 1: Low Cohesiveness and Low Embeddedness

In the first scenario, unions are weakly connected to both the state and broader civil society. I consider the first case (region I) in which $e < \hat{e}$ and $c \geq \dot{c}(e)$. The state chooses 'rebuff' following the unions' 'universal reform' and 'selective reform.' Then, the unions' payoff will be $-p^{UR}(e)\zeta^W - (1 - p^{UR}(e))\lambda(c)$ for universal reform, and $-p^{SR}(c)\zeta^W - (1 - p^{SR}(c))\lambda(c)$ for selective reform. As both payoffs are negative, 'no reform' is the optimal choice for the unions.

Expansion Game 2: High Cohesiveness and Low Embeddedness

In the second game, unions have durable channels to the state (cohesiveness) but are not well embedded in civil society. Then, I primarily consider the second case (region II) in which $e < \hat{e}$ and $c \geq \dot{c}(e)$. The state chooses 'rebuff' after the unions' 'universal reform' and chooses 'accept' after the unions' selective reform. Then, if the unions choose universal reform, their payoff is $-p^{UR}(e)\zeta^W - (1-p^{UR}(e))\lambda(c)$. If they choose selective reform, their payoff is β. As the latter ($>$o) is clearly better than the former ($<$o) and no reform (o), the unions will launch selective reform. However, if $c < \dot{c}(e)$ at a medium level of cohesiveness (as in the box area in Figure C.6), the state will rebuff both UR and SR, then unions will choose no reform.

Expansion Game 3: Low Cohesiveness and High Embeddedness
In the third game, unions have strong linkages to wider civil society but do not have channels to the incumbent party. I analyze the third case (region III) in which $e \geq \hat{e}$ and $c < \dot{c}(e)$. The state chooses 'accept' after the unions' universal reform, ending up with its payoff α. If the unions choose selective reform, then their payoff is $-p^{SR}(c)\zeta^{W} - (1 - p^{SR}(c))\lambda(c)$. Universal reform is clearly better than selective reform and 'no reform.' Therefore, the unions will launch universal reform.

Expansion Game 4: High Cohesiveness and High Embeddedness.
In the fourth game, unions have strong linkages to both the state and civil society. In the final case (region IV) in which $e \geq \hat{e}$ and $c \geq \dot{c}(e)$, the state chooses 'accept' after the unions' 'universal reform' and 'selective reform.' Then, the unions' payoff will be α for universal reform and β for selective reform. As $\beta > \alpha > 0$, the unions will launch selective reform. Figure C.5 summarizes the state's reform choice in the parameter space.

However, there is a caveat in interpreting the final case. In reality, C.2-2 inequality condition, $p^{SR}(c)\zeta^{E}(e) < \beta$, is not easily breakable, because $p^{SR}(c)$ and $\zeta^{E}(e)$ are not likely to increase simultaneously, but are likely to be inversely correlated. In other words, under the SR sub-game, labor–civic solidarity will be turned off by unions' SR proposal, as civil society refuses to join labor–civic solidarity, which is unlikely to increase $\zeta^{E}(e)$. Then, the inequality condition C.2-2 is likely to persist especially under high embeddedness as $p^{SR}(c)$ is suppressed by $\zeta^{E}(e)$. In this case, the state will choose UR, while rebuffing SR. Unions will eventually choose UR, at the top of the information set. Then, region IV is theoretically present, but empirically unlikely, because c and e constrain each other. Embedded cohesiveness, therefore, may imply 'cohesiveness constrained by embeddedness', as a high level of embeddedness prevents cohesive collusion from occurring (or evolving) between the state and unions toward selective reforms (at too high a level of cohesiveness).

In a sense, it is medium-level cohesiveness (as illustrated in a range of boxes in Figure C.5) in combination with high embeddedness that achieves the best outcome, UR, for labor–civic solidarity. When unions maintain both cohesive ties and some autonomy from the state, being undergirded by strong embeddedness, as illustrated by the Brazilian CUT–PT relationship (see Chapter 7), embedded cohesiveness is most likely to lead to universal social policy reforms. In Figure C.6, cases of embedded cohesiveness, therefore, may be located just below the $\dot{c}(e)$ line in which medium-level cohesiveness is combined with high embeddedness, which achieves the best outcome, UR, for the unions.

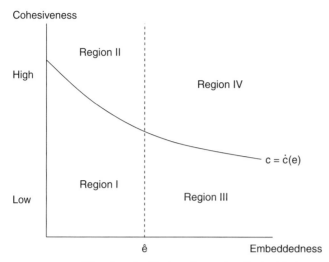

FIGURE C.5. The State's Choice Space by Embeddedness and Cohesiveness (Expansion Game)

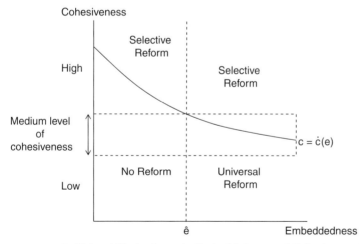

FIGURE C.6. Unions' Choice Space by Embeddedness and Cohesiveness (Expansion Game)

Appendix D

Supplementary Analyses: South Korean Associational Networks in the 2000s

In order to illustrate the structure of associational networks in the critical era of the 2000s in South Korea, I analyze a dataset on civic associational networks. The network data I utilize in this book for mobilization and policy embeddedness were originally constructed by Ŭn (2005a) in her dissertation (waves 1991, 1997, and 2001), and then updated later by a journalist, Kang (2006).[1] I used all four waves of associational data in constructing Figures 4.4 and 4.5 in Chapter 4. For the other network diagrams and analyses in Chapters 5 and 6, I primarily used Ŭn's 1997 and Kang's 2006 data, with my own cleaning and re-compilation of key attribute data. For the purpose of cross-national and over-time comparison of associational networks, however, I used associational co-membership data constructed from World Values Surveys (1995, 2005, and 2014 modules) in Chapter 9.

In particular, Kang's 2006 dataset was built upon two modes of information consisting of 1,744 civic, political, and labor associations' co-affiliation records with 361 major political and civic events (which are composed of 52 solidaristic demonstrations and organizing efforts, 85 symposiums/seminars/petitions for legislative efforts, and 224 press conferences and declarations), which occurred from Jan 1 to Dec 31, 2005.[2] The dataset is one of the most comprehensive efforts to compile associational activities by including not only major central organizational actors in civil and political societies but also larger numbers of smaller, non-political, issue-based associations and region-specific associations in major cities such as Pusan, Kwang-joo, Dae-koo, and Incheon. Therefore, the dataset enables me to analyze deep and detailed structures of South Korean associational community life during the critical era of democratic consolidation in the mid-2000s.

TABLE D.I. *Key Solidaristic Events on Social Welfare and Health Issues and Participating Civic and Labor Organizations in 2005*

No.	Time	Content of Solidaristic Organizing Efforts, Co-Demonstrations, and Petitions	Examples of Participating Organizations
6	Feb 23	Actions against law on non-standard employment and petition for rights of non-standard workers	The KCTU-Seoul, the DLP-Seoul, Solidarity for Progress, Student Councils-Seoul, National Student Solidarity Councils, Democratic Workers' Solidarity, Railroad Union, National Civic Servant Union, etc.
12	April 16	The 3rd Annual Convention for Disabled Women	Sympathy for Disabled Women, Korean Federation for Children with Cerebral Palsy, Federation for Disabled Women, Seoul Task Force for Human Rights of Disabled, etc.
14	April 20	National Convention on Action for Democratization and Social Provision of Welfare Facilities	Workers' Power, DLP, Socialist Party, Disabled Friends, Korean Public Service and Transport Worker's Union (KPTWU), Korean Gov. Employee's Unions (KGEU), Disabled Friends, Health Professionals for Action, Civic Coalition for Welfare, Sarangbang, Seoul Metal Union, Network for Autonomous Life, etc.
15	April 20	4.20 Action for Anti-Discrimination of the Disabled	Kyungnam Action for Anti-Discrimination of Disabled, **DLP, KCTU**, Minkahyup Human Rights, Korean People's Solidarity against Poverty, Socialist Party, Solidarity for Progress, Workers' Coalition for Industrial Accidents, KGEU, Korean Teachers' Union, etc.

(continued)

TABLE D.1. (*continued*)

No.	Time	Content of Solidaristic Organizing Efforts, Co-Demonstrations, and Petitions	Examples of Participating Organizations
25	June 30	Solidarity for anti-liberalization of childcare expenses and action for social provision of child care facilities	Cooperative Childrearing and Community Education, KCTU, Parents' Association for Childcare, Korean Childcare Workers' Union, PSPD, FKTU, Women's Associations United, etc.
28	July 17	Civic solidarity for action for rights of migrant workers	**KCTU**, FKTU, Women's Union, KCTU-Seoul, PSPD, Lawyers for Democracy, Coalition for Migrant Workers' Rights, Migrant Workers' Union, Solidarity for Progress, etc.
29	July 21	Launch of solidarity network of regional welfare organizations	Kyungki Citizens' Solidarity for Welfare, Citizens for Welfare Society, Share and Solidarity, Civic Coalition for Welfare, PSPD, Action for Welfare Solidarity, etc.
42	Oct 21	Launch of civic solidarity for legislation of compensation in medical malpractice	Health Rights Network, Coalition for Economic Justice, YMCA-Seoul, Medical Consumers, Korean Good Samaritan Network, etc.
47	Nov 24	Solidaristic Convention for Long-Term Care	HRN, Medical Consumers, KHMU, SIU, Institute for Poverty Research, Social Cooperative for Medical Welfare, etc.

Table D.1 presents exemplary mobilization-oriented events in civil society and organizations participating in those events. The data are initially constructed as two-mode data, an organization-by-event matrix (Breiger 1974), and then converted into one-mode network data in which organizations comprise nodes and each event serves as a tie linking participating organizations. The process implies that a matrix, X, in which the row represents organizations and the column represents events, is multiplied by its transpose matrix X' (P = XX'). A large value of XX'$_{ij}$ indicates that there exists a strong linkage between a pair of organizations (Borgatti and Everett 1997, p. 246). The bulk of network analyses using sub-group cohesion, centrality measures, and graphs are based on the second, one-mode matrix.

The nine events in Table D.1 were held to formulate executive committees for organizing demonstration/petition efforts or actual solidaristic demonstrations in the fields of social welfare and health. Many national centers of political, civic, and labor organizations such as the DLP, the KCTU, and the PSPD (bold), can be found in the table, but many issue-specific specialized unions and civic associations are also present. By investigating distinctive community environments and structures in which these general or issue-based labor and civic organizations are embedded, I assume that it is possible to reveal unique associational structures that play decisive roles in shaping social policy outcomes.

In the following sections, I initially display basic centrality measures built upon all three types of events, but in subsequent sections, I differentiate my analyses along two types of events by treating one (52 solidaristic demonstrations and organizing efforts) as 'mobilization-oriented events,' while considering the other (85 symposiums/seminars/petitions for legislative efforts) as 'policy-oriented events.' I contend that affiliation networks based on these two types of events greatly operationalize two concepts I developed in Chapter 3: the mobilization-oriented embeddedness and policy-oriented embeddedness of unions. After discussing general patterns and findings focusing upon the associational structure around labor unions and core civic associations (primarily relevant to Chapter 4), I discuss different structures between mobilization networks and policy networks in the 2000s. The findings provide convincing evidence on the organizational heterogeneity and inequality that have emerged in labor-linked civil and political society in the 2000s.

Contrasting Trends: Mobilization Capacity and
Policy Capacity

Table D.2 summarizes several centrality measures of the top 15 associations ranked by the two-mode centrality measures without any discrimination based on the kinds of events.[3] The three columns present
the top 15 associations (out of 1,744) in terms of their number of ties
with other associations (degree), their relative status as a function of
other influential actors (eigenvector), and their bridging roles in linking
other associations (betweenness) through their participation in contentious mobilization, policy-making, and formation of public opinion. For
instance, as for betweenness, the top three associations are the PSPD,
Cultural Coalition (CC), and Green Coalition (GC), while two representative labor organizations, the KCTU and the DLP, are ranked at
fourth and sixth. Five other popular civic associations represent several
key sub-fields of civic associational life, including human rights (Lawyers
for a Democratic Society, Minbyun), youth development (YMCA), economic justice (CCEJ), environmental movements (Korea Federation for
Environmental Movement, KFEM), and women's movements (Korean
Women's Association United, KWAU).

The KCTU's overall tie strength, status, and bridging roles for other
civic associations are prominent when they are compared to those of the
FKTU (twentieth, twenty-fifth, and seventeenth). The KCTU's regional
headquarters and industrial unions were separately counted as independent associations, with two of them being ranked within the top 30
and seven of them ranked within the top 200 in terms of betweenness
centrality, while none of the FKTU's regional and industrial unions were
present in those ranges. This finding lends credible support to the strong
social movement origin of the KCTU and its deep embeddedness in civic
associational networks. At the same time, however, the FKTU's embeddedness in the civic associational sector in 2005 is quite impressive, given
its corporatistic origin during the authoritarian developmental era. Its
fairly high rankings in the associational field in 2005, if inferior to those
of the KCTU, reflect its internal ideological and organizational re-orien-
tation toward a more reformist platform in the 2000s, as discussed in
Chapters 4 and 8.

Table D.3 displays rankings of civic and labor organizations based on
two different sub-events: mobilization-oriented events (demonstrations,
sit-ins, or organizational conventions for solidaristic collective action) and
policy-oriented events (symposiums and legislative petitions), excluding

TABLE D.2. *Ranking of Top 15 Associations for Three Centrality Measures (based on 361 Events and 1,744 Organizations)*

Rank	Degree Centrality	Eigenvector Centrality	Betweenness Centrality
1	*PSPD*	Federation of Peasants	*PSPD*
2	Cultural Coalition	*PSPD*	Cultural Coalition
3	Green Coalition	*KCTU*	Green Coalition
4	Lawyers for Democracy	Green Coalition	*KCTU*
5	Women's Association United	Coalition for Democratic Journalism	Lawyers for Democracy
6	Professors for Democracy	Cultural Coalition	*DLP*
7	*KCTU*	People's Solidarity	YMCA
8	Coalition for Democratic Journalism	Workers' Solidarity	Coalition for Economic Justice
9	*DLP*	Lawyers for Democracy	Women's Association United
10	Federation for Environmental Movements	Women's Association United	Federation for Environmental Movements
11	Federation of Peasants	Federation for Foreign Workers	Professors for Democracy
12	Federation for Foreign Workers	Federation of the Poor	Federation of Peasants
13	Women Link	Women for Anti-American Actions	Coalition for Democratic Journalism
14	People's Solidarity	Association for Migrant Workers' Rights	Spec (Speculation) Watch
15	Workers' Solidarity	Solidarity for Screen Quarter	Differently Abled Person's Right

joint press conferences and joint releases of counter-declarations. Co-affiliation networks based on these two types of events closely match the policy and mobilization capacities – policy-oriented embeddedness and mobilization-oriented embeddedness – which I discussed in Chapter 3. These two types of events are conceptually and substantially different

TABLE D.3. *Ranking of Top 15 Associations for Three Centrality Measures (based on 52 Mobilization-Oriented Events and 85 Policy-Oriented Events, 1,744 Organizations)*

Rank	Mobilization-Oriented Events		Policy-Oriented Events	
	Eigenvector Centrality	*Betweenness Centrality*	*Eigenvector Centrality*	*Betweenness Centrality*
1	Federation of Peasants	Cultural Coalition	People's Solidarity	Cultural Coalition
2	Workers' Solidarity	*PSPD*	Green Coalition	Green Coalition
3	Cultural Coalition	Green Coalition	Federation of Peasants	*PSPD*
4	Coalition for Democratic Journalism	*KCTU*	Workers' Solidarity	Lawyers for Democracy
5	*KCTU*	Women's Association United	*PSPD*	Women's Association United
6	Federation for Foreign Workers	Federation of Peasants	Cultural Coalition	Fed for Environmental Movements
7	Professors for Democracy	*FKTU*	Lawyers for Democracy	Coalition for Economic Justice
8	People's Solidarity	YMCA	*KCTU*	YMCA
9	Federation of the Poor	Lawyers for Democracy	Women's Association United	Federation of Peasants
10	Association for Migrant Workers' Rights	Minkahyup Human Rights	Citizens' Action	Citizens' Action
11	Korean Labor and Society Institute	*DLP*	Coalition for Democratic Journalism	Greenfuture
12	Federation of University Students' Councils	Coalition for Economic Justice	Fed for Environmental Movements	People's Solidarity
13	Women for Anti-American Actions	Catholic Committee for Human Rights	Fed of University Students' Councils	Professors for Democracy
14	Solidarity for Screen Quarter	Differently Abled Person's Right	Labor Pastoral Commission (Catholic)	Federation for Foreign Workers
15	Reunification Plaza	*KHMU*	Solidarity for Screen Quarter	Workers' Solidarity

not only from each other but also from the third 'weak-tie' or 'low-cost' events. First, mobilization-oriented events require much higher organizing costs (or the capacity to shoulder such costs) than the excluded weak-tie events. Second, in order to participate in policy-oriented events, any organization needs professional expertise in each field of policy or law, which is equivalent to policy capacity. Both events require participant organizations to accumulate, invest, and cultivate mobilization and policy resources in advance or in the future. The third type (press conferences and joint declarations), however, involves the least cost to an organization: all an organization has to do is to put its name on it when there is a press conference.

When the three types of events are discriminated and analyzed separately in Table D.3, the rankings of organizations significantly differ from those of Table D.2, in which results were dominated by weak-tie, low-cost events. The KCTU's status was about the same for mobilization-oriented events (fifth for eigenvector centrality and fourth for betweenness), but significantly dropped for centrality measures built upon policy-based events (eighth for eigenvector centrality and seventeenth for betweenness). The DLP's roles are weakly present for mobilization-oriented ties (twenty-sixth for eigenvector centrality and eleventh for betweenness centrality), but completely disappear from the (top 30) scene for policy-oriented linkages.

With the same data, Tables D.4 and D.5 present sub-group cohesion statistics in which 1,744 associations are classified along nine sub-groups. The tables report the density measures of networks within each group (diagonal elements) and between the nine sub-groups (non-diagonal elements). Each cell is the total sum of all actual ties divided by the number of all theoretically possible ties. In Table D.4, popular-sector associations exhibit the highest within-group density (0.186), while right-wing civic associations show the lowest (0.006). As for unions, they show the strongest mobilization-oriented linkages with the DLP (and popular-sector associations), while there is no linkage between unions and the incumbent Open Uri party (which does not have any ties with any other associations in the sample).[4] This simple sub-group analysis supports my claim that the KCTU strengthened its cohesiveness with the labor party.[5] However, in Table D.5, which reports within- and between-group density measures of the same nine groups for policy-oriented events, unions show the second lowest within-group density (0.005) and generally low levels of density outcomes with other types of associations.

TABLE D.4. *Sub-Group Cohesion Density (Mobilization-Oriented Events): South Korean Civic Networks, 2005*

	Civic Left	Civic Center	Civic Right	Unions	Labor Orgs	Popular Sector	DLP	Incumbent Open Uri Party	Professional Orgs
Civic Left	0.088	0.039	0.018	0.045	0.102	0.114	0.087	0	0.034
Civic Center	0.039	0.033	0.015	0.017	0.034	0.04	0.03	0	0.032
Civic Right	0.018	0.015	0.006	0.007	0.014	0.014	0.006	0	0.014
Unions	0.045	0.017	0.007	0.038	0.061	0.064	0.066	0	0.015
Labor Orgs	0.102	0.034	0.014	0.061	0.139	0.157	0.134	0	0.032
Popular Sector	0.114	0.04	0.014	0.064	0.157	0.186	0.16	0	0.043
DLP	0.087	0.03	0.006	0.066	0.134	0.16	0.055	0	0.031
Incumbent Open Uri Party	0	0	0	0	0	0	0	0	0
Professional Orgs	0.034	0.032	0.014	0.015	0.032	0.043	0.031	0	0.033

TABLE D.5. *Sub-Group Cohesion Density (Policy-Oriented Events): South Korean Civic Networks, 2005*

	Civic Left	Civic Center	Civic Right	Unions	Labor Orgs	Popular Sector	DLP	Incumbent Open Uri Party	Professional Orgs
Civic Left	0.047	0.023	0.01	0.016	0.048	0.048	0.026	0.001	0.024
Civic Center	0.023	0.024	0.009	0.009	0.02	0.025	0.017	0	0.028
Civic Right	0.01	0.009	0.002	0.004	0.008	0.01	0.004	0	0.01
Unions	0.016	0.009	0.004	0.005	0.014	0.017	0.014	0.002	0.01
Labor Orgs	0.048	0.02	0.008	0.014	0.058	0.057	0.039	0	0.021
Popular Sector	0.048	0.025	0.01	0.017	0.057	0.054	0.042	0	0.029
DLP	0.026	0.017	0.004	0.014	0.039	0.042	0.018	0	0.021
Incumbent Open Uri Party	0.001	0	0 0.	2	0	0 0	0	0	
Professional Orgs	0.024	0.028	0.01	0.01	0.021	0.029	0.021	0	0.034

Appendix E

Generalization: Findings from Cross-National Quantitative Analyses

This appendix presents quantitative analyses of associational networks and the development of welfare states in both developed and developing countries. While the previous chapters explored through qualitative analysis how embeddedness and cohesiveness have shaped social policies in South Korea and three other countries, this appendix extends its scope to the entire globe. To what extent does the EC approach account for variations in social spending across countries? Does it provide a broader explanatory framework that may be applicable to a wider range of societies beyond the four countries under investigation in this study?

For the dependent variable, I employ public health care expenditure as a percentage of GDP, one of the widely available cross-national social spending measures, extracted from the latest World Social Protection Report 2014–15 (ILO). For the main independent variable – embeddedness – I continue to use the same measure as in Chapter 9. In order to measure 'governance' or 'the rule of law,' I use the Latent Judicial Independence (LJI) scores (Linzer and Staton 2011). The measure is a standardized latent score built upon eight different measures of governance and the rule of law used in the previous studies via an Item Response Theory (IRT) model. It ranges from zero to one (the highest level of rule of law). I introduce several control variables which have been used in the previous studies as key variables representing major theories of the welfare state. I introduce GDP per capita (logged) and the population share aged 65 or over in the baseline model. Both variables are drawn from World Development Indicators (World Bank 2016). I expect that the level of economic development will have positive effects on both dependent variables, as economic development itself brings higher demands

344

TABLE E.1. *Unstandardized Coefficients from the Linear Regression (Using HC3[a]) of Social Spending on Embeddedness and Control Variables*

VARIABLES	Model (1)	Model (2)	Model (3)
Former Soviet Union	−0.637	−0.543	−0.249
	(−0.740)	(−0.633)	(−0.276)
Age 65 or over	0.189***	0.188**	0.147
	(2.721)	(2.162)	(1.517)
GDP per capita	0.521*	0.272	0.333
	(1.988)	(1.055)	(1.330)
Trade Openness	−0.00799	−0.00751	−0.00825
(% of GDP)	(−1.279)	(−1.367)	(−1.511)
Union Density	1.671	1.092	1.362
	(0.646)	(0.442)	(0.528)
Union Embeddedness	−0.0317	−0.139	−0.167
	(−0.0596)	(−0.267)	(−0.317)
High Governance		−1.602	
(dummy)		(−1.130)	
Embeddedness*Governance		2.593**	
		(2.501)	
Institutional Democracy			−2.085
(dummy)			(−1.623)
Embeddedness*Democracy			3.238***
			(4.152)
Constant	2.481**	2.570**	2.890**
	(2.023)	(2.030)	(2.253)
Observations	50	50	50
R-squared	0.641	0.668	0.690

Note[a]: HC3 is a variant of heteroskedasticity consistent covariance matrix (HCCM) (Long and Ervin 2000); t-statistics in parentheses; *** $p<0.01$, ** $p<0.05$, * $p<0.10$.

for social welfare due to urbanization and industrialization (which tend to generate a higher risk of income and job losses). The higher presence of an older population will also result in higher social spending, because of its strong interest group politics (Pampel and Williamson 1989). I also include economic openness, measured by the share of exports and imports as a percentage of GDP. I hypothesize that the variable will have a positive impact on social spending, because economic openness increases the vulnerability of lower classes to job and income loss due to economic fluctuations and market instability (Katzenstein 1985). I include union density as one of the control variables. I predict that the variable will have a positive effect on social spending measures, as stronger union power tends to channel working-class interests into political parties and pressure them to build more universal and generous social programs (Korpi 1983; Huber and Stephens 2001).[1]

Table E.1 presents results for the effects of unions' embeddedness on public health care spending. All models include the following baseline controls: logged GDP per capita, population over 65, trade openness, and union density. Each variable represents major theories of welfare state development, respectively: industrialization, changing demographic structure and interest group politics, economic openness, and power resource theory.[2] As Wilensky (1975) and Pampel and Williamson (1989) observed earlier, logged GDP per capita and population over 65 were two strongly significant variables in the baseline model (model 1).

In models 2 and 3, I introduce two interaction models to account for variations in public health care expenditure (as a percentage of GDP): the 'embeddedness-governance' model in model 2 produces impressive results: unions' embeddedness has a significant positive effect on public health spending at a high level of governance (the rule of law), while the positive effect of embeddedness disappears with a low level of governance. In a similar vein, the 'embeddedness-democracy' model in model 3 generates even more impressive results: unions' embeddedness has a strong positive effect on public health spending in societies in which democracy is well institutionalized.[3] The results are in strong accordance with my earlier qualitative findings and support my hypothesis that unions' embeddedness leads to larger welfare states in the field of basic security (health) under good governance or highly institutionalized democracy.

Notes

Chapter 1: Introduction

1 The unit of analysis and the coverage of the sample will vary across chapters throughout the book. For instance, in Chapters 4 to 6, the unit of analysis is primarily associations (labor unions and civic associations), but often gets down to individual-level leadership. In Chapters 7 and 8, the unit of analysis is at a confederation level, while it is at a countrylevel in Chapter 9. The coverage and scope of the sample is a single case study of South Korean labor and civic movements in Chapters 4 to 6, but it is a comparative case study of four countries (and eight union confederations) in Chapters 7, 8, and 9.

2 Zhao (2015) describes Mann's notion of "interstitial development" as "evolutionary impetuses" that do not originate from dominant species, but come from species residing interstitially at peripheral spaces which later emerge as dominant forces in new ecological environments. In my own terms, most innovative solidarity movements may evolve from actors interstitially embedded in both formal and informal civil society (see Chapter 3 for further discussion).

3 For instance, labor parties of New Zealand and Britain certainly made such turns in the 1980s and the 1990s, respectively (Castles *et al.* 1996; Huber and Stephens 2001). Especially, the labor party of New Zealand and its neo-liberal allies in the treasury introduced the most radical market-oriented reform in rich democracies in the 1980s. In two consecutive terms they liberalized the currency, privatized state-owned firms, lifted tariffs, eliminated subsidies to industries, and deregulated banks. Most importantly, they made significant cuts in pensions, health care, and unemployment benefits (Huber and Stephens 2001, pp. 292–307), thereby ending the era of the "wage-earner welfare state" (Castles 1985).

4 I use multi-organizational fields, associational fields, or associational networks interchangeably in this book. By associational field, I refer to an organizational field in which diverse forms of civic and labor organizations "interact with knowledge of one another under a set of common understandings about the purposes of the field, the relationships in the field … and the field's rules."(Fligstein and McAdam 2011, p. 3). The notion will be discussed in detail in Chapter 3 (in the section, "The Emergence and Consolidation of Associational Networks").

5 For the sources and contents of the network datasets, please refer to Appendix D.

6 All field work was funded by the National Science Foundation (Award No. 1260191, "Identity, Networks, and The Origins of Participatory Democracy"). Also see Appendix A for positions and roles of these leaders.

7 The other important 'preference-shaping' mechanism is media, which will not be discussed in this study.

8 Cognitive and moral legitimacy imply that citizens or voters accept these embedded leaders' actions and positions as 'taken for granted,' 'appropriate,' and 'right,' thereby being committed to them.

9 When this embeddedness is absent, unions with only cohesive ties to the state often resort to 'selective reforms' in collaboration with or through co-optation by the ruling block (which will be posited as the second proposition in Chapter 3).

Chapter 2: Revisiting Theories of the Welfare State in Developing Countries

1 Indeed, South Korea and Taiwan have rapidly become aged societies in the 2000s and after, with both countries reaching 10% of total population over 65 in the late 2000s (World Bank 2016) and passing 15% in the late 2010. Therefore, some may attribute the recent growth of the welfare state in these countries to rapidly growing elderly populations and their increased need for social safety nets.

2 One 'corrective' variant of this policy-legacy approach would be the constraint on the direction of future policy by a group of (economic) experts and voters who are more concerned about the financial cost of a social policy (fiscal conservatives). In a more mature welfare state, the consideration of this financial cost and actuarial projection of social insurance may decisively affect the direction of a social policy (See Barr 1992 for this perspective). For instance, the current debates in many rich democracies as well as South Korea and Taiwan on the sustainability of national pensions in light of declining fertility and (different) financial projections on the timing of fund depletion play central roles in setting limits on attempts toward expansionary reforms.

3 As I noted in the introduction, many developing societies have suffered deep and radical retrenchment of their social policies and labor market institutions. In contrast to rich democracies, therefore, scholarly focus on the politics of retrenchment in developing countries has been primarily centered on 'under what conditions are retrenchments more likely to occur?' For instance, Brooks (2008) effectively applied Pierson's blame avoidance framework to pension reforms in developing countries. In her comprehensive sample of 71 developed and developing nations, she found that funded defined contribution pension schemes (FDC), which involve higher sunk-cost and political burden compared to notional defined contribution systems (NDC), are more likely to be adopted in middle-income developing countries or post-communist countries via peer-pressure mechanism.

4 Haggard and Kaufmann (2009) indeed find in their quantitative analyses of developing countries that democratic regimes redistribute more in general compared to their authoritarian counterparts, while intermediate authoritarian regimes spend more on social protection than their hard authoritarian counterparts. More specifically, they find that democratization did so in East Asia but didn't contribute much in Eastern Europe, while it affected social spending negatively in Latin America. Huber and Stephens (2012) also found that "cumulative years of democracy" is one of the most consistent determinants of social security and welfare spending in Latin America, along with urbanization and aging population. They conclude, "Democracy makes the rise of actors committed to redistribution and the pursuit of actions aimed at redistribution possible"(p. 11). These findings generally lend support to the idea that exploring the distinctive trajectories of

civil society development under democracy over a relatively long time-span is critical for understanding social policy regimes. Many autonomous civic and labor organizations built their solidaristic linkages during authoritarian eras or in the democratization movements. Therefore, 'years of democracy' is a necessary time dimension for the early fermenting of 'equality projects' that then erupted during democratization movements. During these periods of democratic change, leaders and the supporters of labor and civic associations go through a trial-and-error process, gradually improving their practical knowledge regarding policy-shaping and lobbying channels as well as punishment and negotiation mechanisms with the state and capital – processes which will be delineated in the next chapter. However, the variable 'years of democracy' only captures the duration of an 'opportunity structure' for civil society forces that must already be formed, and so leaves unanswered the question of where the capacities of civil society for social policy development, expansion, and defense come from.

5 Persson and Tabellini (1999, 2003) propose that PR systems help center-leftist governments take power, because voters' choices based on candidates on party lists in a national district may favor the parties in support of universal redistributive programs. In contrast, voters' choices on individual candidates in regionally segmented districts with a first-past-the-post system may lead to geographically targeted programs. In the former, minority candidates are more likely to survive through coalitional politics, while in the latter, they may not easily survive, as party leaders are more reluctant to nominate minority candidates.

6 See Brady *et al.* (2005) for globalization's mixed, curvilinear effects on the welfare state.

7 South Korean pension programs have the same structure as those of Nordic countries, with three levels: (1) earnings-related social insurance (National Pension); (2) individualized accounts (Retirement Pension); and (3) flat-rate benefits as social assistance (Basic Pension). In contrast, Taiwanese pension programs are more market-oriented, individualized, and fragmented: their earnings-related social insurance has been converted into individualized accounts by individual choice from 2005; their basic pension is voluntary contribution, not universal basic social assistance; and therefore, the self-employed are largely not covered by the existing pension scheme. The South Korean health care program is virtually universal as the entire population is covered, while the Taiwanese counterpart covers only employees in firms with five or more employees, while leaving the rest of the population in the shadows of 'voluntary coverage.' These critical institutional differences will be discussed in more detail in Chapter 9.

8 Argentina had the highest level of aged population (9.6 percent) among four countries, when the radical retrenchment of pensions occurred, while Brazil had the smallest aged population (5 percent). In South Korea, the strongest opponent group of welfare state expansion has been older people (those in their 60s or over), who have been strongly aligned with the conservative party.

9 This state-centric reform (after transition to democracy) will be discussed as a subsumed case of the larger EC framework (in Chapter 9 and the Conclusion), in which unions have close 'subordinate' ties with the incumbent party (the state), while they are disarticulated from other civil society forces.

10 *Chaebol* is the term given to Korean big business conglomerates.

11 Despite these limitations, one should not underestimate the VoC school's focus on 'institutional complementarities' in which different sub-systems of firm governance, training, social protections, and financial institutions are systematically coordinated.

12 Indeed, the size of the welfare state in Latin American countries is much larger than in East Asian countries, which may be attributable to the underdevelopment of leftist parties in East Asia due to the limited role of PR. In the two East Asian countries, social spending barely reaches above 10 percent of GDP, while it has reached about 20 percent

of GDP in Argentina and Brazil (and many other Latin American countries such as Costa Rica and Uruguay).

13 Nevertheless, I do not completely reject the argument that neo-liberal reforms divide and individualize workers by increasing heterogeneity within the working classes, which leads to a significant weakening of labor movements over time. This issue will be further investigated in Chapter 8, which analyzes the decline of South Korean labor politics.

14 Kwon (2005) labels these intellectuals 'advocacy coalitions,' while Wong (2004) calls them 'policy groups.' But they neither further delve into the structures and contents of those coalitions or networks to explore why they were successful or unsuccessful regarding specific policy reforms, nor investigate how and when existing unions build 'policy-wise coalitions' with these intellectuals in civil society and what the (social policy) outcomes of such coalitions are.

15 Exceptions are Skocpol (1992) and Amenta (1998, 2006).

16 Revealing the mechanism of this process has been studied recently by scholars associated with the emotion school of social movements (Jasper 1998; Polletta and Jasper 2001). Such a tradition may define collective identity as (a group of) individuals' "cognitive, moral, and emotional connection(s) with a broader community" (Polletta and Jasper 2001). However, given that 'collective identity formation process' implies a historical construction process of cognitive, moral, and emotional perception systems among (a group of) individuals sharing "common interests, experiences, and solidarity"(Taylor 1989), it is hard to separate 'a cognitive awareness of common interests' from 'an emotional experience of linkages to a larger group.' This study uses the notion of solidarity as a collective identity as an equivalent to a cultural and economic cognitive system. In this sense, it implies a strong, solidaristic identity in a group that collectively informs each member of not only "who you are"(Laitin 1998) but also 'what they(we) share' based on shared meanings and interests.

17 In these two usages, political opportunities could mean either 'enabling forces driven by structure' at a mezzo-level or 'overwhelmingly dominant external pressures' at a macro-level. In the former, opportunity structure encourage a certain social or political group to take advantage of better opportunities to build allies, while in the latter, opportunity structure forces a specific movement force to move in a particular direction.

18 The same external conditions may also deter social movements by greatly increasing the organizing costs or by simply relegating movement agendas to trivial episodes: laws, policies, and institutions deeply entrenched upon deep social cleavages such as wealth, religion, and cultural traditions or strong public opinions may work as powerful veto points deterring movement forces. In rapidly changing societies, the social and economic terrain that has enabled movements could suddenly change or disappear altogether. These new political and economic conditions will not wait for movement forces to adjust.

19 At this point, I use the existing notion of "organizational community" (Suchman 1995) to describe a "field" (Bourdieu 1993) in which a movement organization is embedded. Later, I use my own terminology with a specific definition for this – 'associational network' or 'associational field' – which is equivalent to the conventional notion of 'civil society.'

20 In this sense, an opportunity structure is open to various movement outcomes depending upon actors' capacity for interpretation, strategy-making, and execution.

Chapter 3: Theoretical Discussion: The Structures of Associational Networks and the Politics of the Welfare State

1 The notion of 'associational networks' parallels several notions in social movements and organizational theory literature, such as "organizational fields" (DiMaggio and Powell 1983) or "fields" (Bourdieu 1993; Martin 2003). Elsewhere, I defined an 'associational field' as "a type of organizational field comprised of civil society organizations" (Akchurin and Lee 2013, p. 697, fn. 1) that "interact with knowledge of one another under a set of common understandings about the purposes of the field, the relationships in the field … and the field's rules"(Fligstein and McAdam 2011, p. 3). Associational networks/fields are not only a given structure by which actors are constrained regarding the degree and scope of available resources, but also a "tool-kit" (Swidler 1986) with which actors embedded in such networks could better organize their resources with respect to policy-crafting and constituency/advocacy mobilization. I claim that labor unions in each society-specific associational field will develop distinct "organizational repertoires" (Clemens 1993, 1997) consisting of "models of mobilization with different key actors, patterns of inter-organizational ties, and ways of making claims" (Akchurin and Lee 2013, p. 697). In order to understand such repertoires, this study focuses, first, on the emergence of key actors in the associational field, and second, on the way they consolidate their models of issue-making, resource mobilization, organizational linkages, and claim production. I use 'associational networks' and 'associational fields' interchangeably in the rest of the book.

2 See Lee (2016) for more detailed theoretical and empirical discussions on divergent forms of going-underground activities.

3 Refer to Appendix B for detailed explanations of the measurement of cohesiveness. See Chapter 9 also for further explanations regarding the measurement of interorganizational ties in a co-membership matrix.

4 The linkage between labor unions and professional associations represents cross-class organizational coalitions between the working and middle classes. There are many historical instances and theories demonstrating that strong working- and middle-class coalitions are more conducive to implementing and sustaining universal social policies. Historically, coalition-building was one of the main driving forces behind welfare state development. The celebrated social democratic welfare states were indeed built upon the cross-class political alliance of working-class movements and farmer organizations (Esping-Andersen 1990). As the new middle classes emerged in post-industrial economies, Nordic social democracy anchored its political base on a new coalition of the working classes and the emerging middle classes. Often, the middle-class segments of the population played a key role in creating social democracy and universal welfare states (Baldwin 1990; Luebbert 1991). The most stable and successful welfare programs were the ones that served the interests of the middle classes. In other words, creating political coalitions that embrace not only the demands of the needy and the poor but also the demands of the middle classes for insuring themselves from certain risks will be the most effective strategy for building universal welfare states. In such societies, with their strong linkages between unions and professional associations, the middle classes are likely to have greater sympathy for the idea of pursuing and defending universal social policies. Finally, even though it is unclear whether linkages between middle class-oriented professional associations and political parties necessarily defend or promote 'universal' social policies, professional organizations in advanced industrial democracies have historically played positive roles in claiming welfare state benefits for the middle classes and in defending

professional interests in the provision of welfare state services (Baldwin 1990; Huber and Stephens 2001). In addition, some professional associations, such as those of lawyers, professors, and doctors, have played significant roles in introducing social policies in some developing countries (for example, the PSPD in South Korea and the sanitarista movement in Brazil) by formulating advocacy coalitions for the legislation of specific social policies (Kwon 2003; Wong 2004; Falleti 2010).

5 One may be reminded of the distinction between state-led corporatism and societal corporatism conceptualized initially by Schmitter (1974) and then later by other scholars of 'neo-corporatism' (Calmfors and Driffill 1988; Crouch 1993; Traxler 1996). The corporatism literature highlighted the importance of close cooperative relationships between the state and interest organizations in the makings of wage, labor market, and social policies. In my framework, cohesiveness is akin to the notion of corporatism (which could be either state-led or interest group-led), but the embeddedness of the formal sphere (or unions) is a broader concept, absent in the corporatist literature, that underscores the linkages between interest organizations and informal civil society.

6 Refer to Appendix B for detailed measurement of embeddedness. Informal civic associations include churches, cultural clubs, environmental associations, sport clubs, and charity clubs.

7 There exists a considerable amount of literature in which this political leader–voter relationship is depicted as a 'patron–client' relationship (Kitschelt and Wilkinson 2007; Stokes 2007). Note, however, that the 'trust relationship' based on formal–informal associational linkages discussed in this study should be distinguished from the relationship of "a repeated game between voters and parties embedded in social networks"(Stokes 2007, p. 615). Such clientelistic relationships are more personal, non-associational, and "hierarchical/vertical networks" (Putnam 1993) between unconstrained party brokers and isolated local voters who lack other organizational resources. In a sense, clientelisic brokerage may abound in a society in which formal-sector leaders are not constrained by local civic associations. In this sense, Kitschelt and Wilkinson's "programmatic, indirect exchange relationships" are more likely to emerge in a society with embedded cohesiveness, while "clientelistic direct exchanges" are more prevalent when formal-sector leaders are disarticulated from informal civic associations.

8 Suchman defines legitimacy as "a generalized perception that the actions of an entity are desirable, proper, or appropriate within some socially constructed system of norms, values, beliefs, and definitions" (p. 574).

9 This notion of unions' embeddedness also has relevance to the Olsonian logic of labor unions (Olson 1965). Olson argued that smaller unions might be able to overcome "collective action problems" by institutionalizing two mechanisms: union members' social incentives (informal friendships and small-group norms) and a federated union system consisting of smaller unions in the same industry (Olson 1965, pp. 62–67). A third mechanism is 'closed shop', but this concept is not vital to this argument. Although Olson is unclear about the origin and mechanism of such social incentives and federated systems, it may be possible to invoke these mechanisms in developing the notion of union-linked social solidarity. When union activists/leaders are well-linked to local communities and other civic associations, they may be less likely to serve their own interests or free-riding society-wide policy-making efforts. In addition, unions may be 'federated with' not only similar unions in the same industry but also other civic associations and their leaders from the same policy arena. These other associations, leaders, and unions may have similar expectations, creating possibilities for long-term benefits through solidarity and exchange of resources, which may lead them to play a significant role in social policy development. In this way, the notion of 'embeddedness' may be regarded as a quasi-institutional mechanism deterring free-riding in multi-organizational fields.

10 In Habermas' terms, these embedded formal-sector leaders will not only "develop the communicative infrastructure of the lifeworld" but also institutionalize "the interplay of a public sphere based in civil society with the opinion- and will-formation" (Habermas 1996, pp. 370–1). Embedded formal-sector leaders are those who realize a sociological version of 'deliberative politics' by linking the lifeworld to the political action system. In Bourdieu's terms, these embedded leaders are the representatives of civil society working in each issue-/policy-specific associational field in which relevant stakeholders consisting of incumbents and challengers interact with a shared understanding of the goals and rules of the field. They are the ones who lead negotiation and deliberation, while creating new discourse for mobilization in the field. These 'embedded leaders' are akin to Morris's (1984) black ministers "rooted in indigenous organizations" or Robnett (1996)'s "bridge leaders" who hold linkages to a broader mass community base, guarding against the potential co-optation of formal leaders. Good examples are presented in Chapters 5, 6, 7, and 8, which describe the bridging roles of South Korean and Brazilian embedded civic and union leaders in health policy fields.

11 Collier and colleagues' project (e.g., Collier and Handlin 2009) also attempts to develop a theoretical framework that utilizes these two dimensions in similar ways (in their terminology, Up-hub and A-net, denoting union–party linkage and associational networks, respectively). However, there are fundamental differences between their approach and this study: (1) they do not theorize the linkage between Up-hub and A-net (embeddedness), as I do here; (2) they do not consider associational embeddedness as a (political) trust relationship; and (3) they do not investigate the causal impacts of associational structures (interactions of the two dimensions) on social and labor market policy outcomes.

12 It should be noted that these two sub-dimensions/components of embeddedness and cohesiveness were acquired through my field interviews and observations of about 150 labor leaders. In particular, most South Korean activists and some Brazilian activists explicitly and frequently used these two notions in their meetings, conferences, and informal gatherings. Thus, while my initial theoretical framework – embedded cohesiveness – was primarily built upon existing theoretical literature, my in-depth, ongoing communications with activists allowed me to deepen my theory. Therefore, the main components and arguments of the EC approach rest "on a dialectic between the deductive and the inductive, between the concept and the concrete, between its objectives and its subjects" (a remark by John Comaroff, in Ragin *et al.* 2004, p. 37).

13 One may argue that the size of unions, measured by union density (the share of union membership over the total labor force), should be the primary factor for explaining variations in welfare state reforms. I do not deny this conventional wisdom (originating from the power resource approach) with respect to the roles of centralized, large, encompassing unions in building universal welfare states in Nordic social democratic countries (Korpi 1983; Stephens 1979). However, I find that the size of unions does not account for much variation in welfare states when union density ranges from low to medium. Small to medium-sized union organizations have widely different levels of internal and external social institutions that compensate for their sizes, which explains why it is necessary to draw attention to unions' linkages as well as their size. Small union organizations, when they are well linked to wider civic communities, may generate remarkable achievements in social policy reforms. Conversely, some unions may contribute to very limited reforms or even retrenchments in social policies, when they are isolated from wider civil society. Empirically, at least for the four countries being investigated here, union density is not necessarily a critical factor in accounting for the variations in unions' influences on social policy reforms. From a cross-national perspective, countries with stronger and more influential labor movements in social policy

reforms (Brazil and South Korea) had much lower union densities (20.9 percent in 2007 and 10 percent in 2006, respectively; ILO 2011) than their regional counterparts (37.6 percent in 2006 in Argentina and 35.9 percent in 2006 in Taiwan). Over time, within each of these countries, union densities were relatively stable (only gradually declining) for the two decades under investigation in this study, while there were considerable variations in welfare state expansion and neo-liberal market reforms within each country. For instance, union density remained stable throughout the 2000s and after (from 13.8 percent in 1995 to 10.3 percent in 2013) in South Korea (Republic of Korea, Ministry of Employment and Labor 2015), and it also remained stable at 29.4 percent in 2013 in Taiwan (Republic of China, Council of Labor Affairs 2015).

14 Cohesiveness relates to Burgess's (2004) "loyalty dilemma," in which union leaders are torn between their political ally (the incumbent party) and grassroots workers regarding the state's retrenchment attempt. Under high cohesiveness, grassroots union members (who are also incorporated under the ideological and organizational umbrella of the incumbent party) will forgive union leaders for their restraint or no-punishment decisions in case of the state's radical retrenchment or rebuff of unions' request for social policy expansion. However, under low cohesiveness, grassroots union members (without any loyalty to the incumbent party) will punish union leaders for their opportunism. In a sense, union leaders can be exempt from a loyalty dilemma (and its costs) through unions' pre-existing ties to the party's leadership. Pre-existing ties between union leaders and party leaders will also relieve union leaders of the costs of their lobbying efforts.

15 Cress and Snow (2000) classify "movement resources" as moral, material, informational, and human. Just as "moral support" (endorsement by external organization) is similar to my general notion of embeddedness, so too are "informational resources" (strategic and technical support) very akin to the 'policy capacity' theorized in this study. Edwards and McCarthy (2004) formulate a general theory of "SMO resource" and "resource access," explicating four general modes: self-production, aggregation, appropriation, and patronage. Intra-organizational mobilization and policy capacity (represented in my framework in Figure 3.3) is largely in accordance with 'self-production,' while interorganizational capacities roughly correspond to 'aggregation' and 'appropriation.' Therefore, the sub-dimensions of embeddedness and cohesiveness – policy and mobilization capacities, which I developed through conversations with labor activists and studying their everyday activities — are in line with the resource mobilization tradition of social movement scholarship. The other closest deployment of these concepts can be found in Heller's work (1999) on Kerala, India, in which he briefly uses "the mobilizational and strategic capacity of a programmatic and pragmatic left-wing party"(p. 17). For further works in this tradition, defining resources and using them in empirical analysis, see Jenkins 1983; Jenkins and Eckert 1986; Jenkins and Perrow 1977; Oberschall 1995; Oliver and Marwell 1992.

16 Typically, middle- and upper-class associations have more abundant resources compared to poor and working-class associations (Edwards and McCarthy 2004). They are more likely to rely on professionalized knowledge networks and to utilize "institutional tactics" (Staggenborg 1991). Thus, when unions build policy-wise embeddedness with middle-class associations, they are more likely to gain access to such networks and to the political processes in the relevant issue fields.

17 One last point regarding mobilization or policy-wise embeddedness is that very large union confederations may internalize these needs for solidaristic linkages. For instance, unions in some Nordic countries, such as Sweden and Finland, two of the highest union density nations in the world (counting 82 percent and 76 percent of the total dependent labor force as union members, respectively, circa 2010), may not have an urgent necessity to build coalitions with civic associations representing other social forces. In such cases, middle-class white-collar workers, unskilled, non-regular workers, and even the

unemployed, are mostly organized by unions. Because of their comprehensive coverage of labor market outsiders as well as the middle classes and the working classes, maintaining their internal coherence will be more essential than reaching out to other social groups. As the size of a centralized union confederation becomes larger, its cohesiveness with the state, and with leftist, centrist, and right-wing parties, will become more complex: a large union confederation may have diverse political ideologies and alliance mechanisms under its umbrella, which may encourage its leaders to pursue more diverse lobbying and negotiation channels along different dimensions of cohesive ties.

18 In Appendix C, I formulate four different structures of extensive games in which unions and the incumbent party make strategic decisions regarding market reforms of social policies (C.1). Then, I build another four sets of extensive games to illustrate how unions and the state interact under expansionary social policy reforms (C.2).

19 In the EC approach, Burgess' loyalty dilemma (2004) will be resolved as follows: the relative capacity of the political party and workers to punish labor leaders is contingent upon the degree of labor leaders' embeddedness and cohesiveness. Under strong cohesiveness, the political party will have capacity to reward or punish labor leaders (which may lead union leaders to be loyal to the party), while under strong embeddedness (without cohesiveness), union leaders will put more weight on grassroots union members who are historically linked to other social movement actors in civil society. Under embedded cohesiveness, union leaders may find a balanced position between the party and grassroots workers.

20 However, if the state has sufficient information on the potential costs of contentious politics waged by society-wide labor–civic solidarity, the state may not introduce radical reforms at all, instead seeking negotiations with the embedded unions for moderate reforms. See more detailed discussion on this issue in Appendix C.1 (retrenchment game 3).

21 Also, at a fairly high level of cohesiveness, there is a chance that the state and unions will exploit cohesiveness over embeddedness, thereby launching selective reform (see game 4 in Appendix C.2 for further discussion). For universal reform (UR), therefore, the best configuration of associational network will be high embeddedness and medium cohesiveness, in which unions build strong labor–civic networks, but maintain a certain level of autonomy from the state.

22 One may find that the state (or the incumbent party) is depicted as a passive responder in the expansion game and, in contrast, as an implicit collaborator with capital in the retrenchment game. But the state is treated in diverse ways in the models presented in Appendix C. I assume that in the retrenchment game, the state, regardless of its partisanship, may be pressured to be a representative of the interests of capital – especially during periods of economic crisis or of the global spread of market-oriented reforms. However, this initial assumption does not necessarily mean that the overall framework follows a Marxist version of the state–capital relationship. Even during economic crises, the model allows for greater divergence and offers more flexibility in conceptualizing that relationship, as strong embeddedness may draw the state's ex ante moderation of its reform level or ex post concession. In the expansion games, the state is not necessarily the representative of capital, either, as it may coalesce with unions either for universal or for selective reforms, depending upon levels of cohesiveness and embeddedness. It is also completely possible to devise games in which the state (or its autonomous bureaucrats) is an initiator of universal policies (in which the state redistributes the gains or outputs of growth to different social forces (capital, unions, and non-organized civil society actors), as state-centered theories of the welfare state argue (Heclo 1974; Weir *et al.* 1988; Skocpol 1992). In other words, depending upon the levels of embeddedness and cohesiveness, the state may behave as a universal coordinator/redistributor/defender for the entire citizenry or as a strategic collaborator for certain segments of capital and labor,

or as a pure representative of capital. In both expansion and retrenchment games, capital is not explicitly present in the model, but the state will implicitly conduct distributional decisions between capital and labor, of which core parameters will be determined by the embeddedness and cohesiveness. In short, it is ultimately unions' structural position in an associational community that determines whether the state coalesces with unions or capital in both union-initiated and state-initiated expansion games. As this study does not delve into the empirical cases of state-initiated expansionary social policy reforms, I do not explain in detail how state-initiated games could be set up in Appendix C. See Chapters 9 and the Conclusion for further discussion on the implication of the state-centric theory under the EC approach.

23 I define UR as expansionary social policy reform that benefits all of civil society, embracing both organized and non-organized labor market outsiders, while SR is expansionary social policy reform that targets the privileged organized union members. See Appendix C.2 for the more specific definition and usage of UR vs. SR.

Chapter 4: The Origin of Top-Down Solidarity in South Korea

1 This section (about the next 15 pages) is for those who do not have knowledge about South Korean democratization and labor movements in the 1970s and 1980s. Those who do may skip the section and move to "Growth in Embededdness 1: Union Side Stories".

2 He also left a message saying, "I wish I had a college-student friend" (who could teach him labor laws and workers' rights). The message impressed many college students, and led them to devote their lives to labor movements from the early 1970s.

3 However, most missionary workers withdrew from workplaces in the early 1980s, criticizing the leftist, revolutionary turn of union movements (Suh, 2012). The missionaries could not coexist with new waves of radicalized leftist student activists who were not only armed with Leninist revolutionary ideals but also antagonistic to religion-based missionary works. As a result, young Protestant activists had no choice but to yield their hegemony in the movement to a new generation of radicals. The underground strategy of more serious student activists later became an important option, as the entire oppositional forces were radicalized with the Kwangju uprising in 1980.

4 The quote is from an interview with one of the former KCTU strategiests. The majority of labor activists who had such going-underground careers recount the same story. One labor leader who came from Seoul National University, the most prestigious university in South Korea, said, "it was a kind of declaration that an activist would give up a prestigious career opportunity and devote oneself to 'a (labor) movement,' so that one intentionally stops oneself from returning back to a normal life." (Kim Yu-sŏn).

5 Most (students-turned-)labor activists whom I interviewed addressed how they collectively made decisions to go underground, and the fact that they were easily able to find several others in the same factory. Although interviewees were not selected at random based on a complete list of activists, I attempted to take some stratifying variables into account by balancing the distribution of the cases by gender, age, and ideological factions. Refer to Appendix A for the distribution of interviewees' characteristics by demographic and political variables.

6 Although this last group of activists, those who quit their careers as activists, are not systematically followed or investigated by researchers, many of them later became professionals such as lawyers, professors, doctors, judges, prosecutors, journalists, and bureaucrats. It is not difficult to imagine that these remote 'sympathizers'(McCarthy

and Zald 1977) have played significant roles in helping workers defend their rights from their positions by 'endorsing' demands, 'conveying' information, and 'teaching' histories and justice.

7 However, the composition of actual members was not necessarily in accordance with that of its (non-member) electoral base. It is not a proletariat's party, but rather a social reformist, programmatic party that attracts votes from a wide range of reform-oriented social forces that cut across different social classes (Sin 2004).

8 Theorists of social corporatism proposed that the South Korean labor–capital relationship is too costly due to the two parties' antagonistic confrontations, and therefore that they should move to a democratic class compromise between labor and capital, even if indirectly mediated by the state (Crouch 1993; Katzenstein 1985). Ch'oe (1996), however, argued that European corporatism driven by a centralized union confederation and a (centralized) capitalists' association is unrealistic in South Korea, because large conglomerates and their state allies have been able to hold a hegemonic position, thereby preventing capital–labor compromise pushed from below. He therefore proposed that a comprehensive solidaristic movement composed of multiple classes and diverse social forces should be fostered to confront such a strong state–capital alliance. Ch'oe and other proponents of social or progressive corporatism (e.g. Kim 1992) argued that, in order to form such a wide range of solidarities, labor movements needed to moderate and become more inclusive of other social forces' interests. Im (1997) highlighted the centrality of democratic class politics, however, by emphasizing the central role in waging both militant struggles and negotiations of labor activists drawn either from student-movement origins or working-class origins.

9 This collective dissolution of top-down solidarity at the local factory level after such a short duration has important short-term and long-term consequences for the structure of the labor-linked associational network in South Korea. First, such a sudden collective dissolution of underground activities led to a burgeoning of civic and political institutions and a pouring of converted intellectuals into the existing political parties. Therefore, organizational density among civic and political society greatly increased in the 1990s. Second, local grassroots workers' communities and radical intellectuals did not have much time to solidify their bonds and trust. They built friendships as well as leadership-supporting base relationships, but their collective departures (to quit or to build higher-order organizations at the center) left local grassroots workers' societies without intellectual leadership. This dualism later results in thick and dense embeddedness at the movement center (in metropolitan Seoul), but very shallow and weak embeddedness among local societies.

10 The PD faction typically supports giving intellectuals a leading role in mobilizing the working classes, and once sought working-class-centered revolutionary change of Korean society. The NL faction pursues more moderate and comprehensive reforms based on larger social and political bases, and considers the reintegration and reunification of the two Koreas their single most important political goal. The NL segment typically asserts that US influence in the Korean peninsula deters the reunification project, which leads them to seek a unified front (embracing wide ranges of class segments beyond the working classes) against the United States and its domestic allies. This argument has been known to be closely linked to North Korea's official ideology, 'Juche sasang' (The ideology of self-reliance). In the 1980s, the NL faction emphasized the importance of popular movements, while the PD faction devoted its energy to reinforcing political movements. The differences in organizational strategies originate in the difference in their revolutionary theories: the NL faction sought a 'popular class struggle,' in which peasants, urban intellectuals, workers, and even reformist petty-bourgeois comprised a wide-ranging solidarity. In contrast, the PD faction sought a Leninist top-down working-class-centered revolution led by 'vanguard intellectuals,' taking the

view that the working classes would be 'galvanized' and 'instigated' by such leaders' revolutionary struggles.

11 In the labor movement, the popular leaders of the NL faction have been called 'Kungminp'a' (which implies the party of 'nation' or 'people'), the origin of which is known to be those who worked for Kwŏn Yŏng-gil's campaign organization in the 1997 presidential election, where the election motto was 'With People.' This faction is presumed to find 45 to 55 percent of its supporters among grassroots and industry-level union leaders. Labor leaders of the PD faction were divided into two major factions: 'Chungangp'a' (implying the party of 'center') and 'Hyŏngjangp'a' (implying the party of 'rank-and-file floor leaders'). The former label designates those who once worked with Tan Pyŏng-ho in the early KCTU era at the center office. The latter label is for those who contend that the labor movement should persistently wage uncompromising militant struggles against both employers and the state. Union officials account for about 25 to 30 percent of supporters among each segment. The KCTU center has been mainly managed by the coalitions between the party of 'nation' and the party of 'center', with the exception of the early years, when the PD factions dominated the chief secretary positions. In contrast to the DLP, which has been split into several parts since 2008, the KCTU leadership has preserved its core leadership structure around the coalition of the two majority factions, although the NL faction has mostly taken over the chief executive positions in the central office.

12 Some of the pre-existing structures still persist and operate. Regional branches of the KCTU function as another layer of union structure, whose main agendas and roles are not effectively covered by industrial unions. Even each industrial union has its own regional branch organizations.

13 It turned out that these efforts to bargain at industry level have largely failed for the last two decades, as not only did most employers not respond to the unions' requests, but individual firm-level unions in large manufacturing also refused to even join the industry-level collective bargaining.

14 The DP has almost always changed its label whenever it has absorbed external allies or coalition partners (National Conference, Unification Democratic Party, New Millennium Democratic Party, Open Uri Party, New Political Alliance (for) Democracy, etc.) However, as there is little change in its electoral base, platform, and personnel, I consistently use the term DP in this book regardless of frequent changes in labeling over time.

15 The cost of unilaterally relying on the DLP for policy-channeling was not negligible, especially since the 2000s. This issue will be discussed in further detail in the next two chapters.

16 In the late 1980s and the entire 1990s, it was not unusual to witness workers and students holding demonstrations together on the main streets in downtown Seoul.

17 Most labor activists whom I interviewed addressed the existence of the strong alliance between labor movements and other social movement associations in the late 1980s and early 1990s. Most of them, however, simultaneously discounted the implications of such alliances as specifically attributable to the democratization movements of the era.

18 Nearly all labor activists I interviewed proudly addressed that 1996–7 Anti-Labor Law Struggle as the most memorable moment of all the events and achievements in which they had participated.

19 I asked every interviewee when the KCTU had had the strongest policy and mobilization capacities since the 1990s. Nearly all respondents answered that both capacities reached their highest points in the late 1990s and the early 2000s (without clear distinction between the two capacities).

20 In Chapter 6, I will discuss how such stunningly growing embeddedness and cohesiveness tragically faltered during the supposedly labor-friendly regime in the 2000s.

21 I tentatively use this term, 'policy specialists' or 'policy circle,' as they were not systematically institutionalized as 'policy networks' in the 1990s. These policy specialists later institutionalized themselves through labor-based think tanks in the 2000s.

22 The data were built by recording divergent affiliation patterns of hundreds of labor and civic associations with dozens of critical events as 'ties' or 'networks' between them. For a more detailed description of the data sources and specific analytical techniques I used to create the figures, see Appendix D. Please see the introductory paragraphs for the source of the network data and refer to Table D.1 for exemplary mobilization-oriented events in civil society and participating organizations in those events. For more detailed ranking information on centrality measures, see Tables D.2 and D.3 (for the year 2005). In the relevant discussion of these tables in Appendix D, I justify how and why these network data successfully capture the notion of mobilization embeddedness and policy embeddedness developed in Chapter 3.

23 I also checked other centrality scores such as degree centrality or eigenvector centrality, but the results were largely similar (producing very high correlations among centrality measures: corr > 0.7). For simplicity, I report betweenness centrality because it measures an association's 'bridging roles' among other associations.

24 Some may find that the creation and electoral success of the DLP diversified the needs for policy deliberation and lobbying, which may have led to the declining KCTU role in channeling policy demands from civil society. The DLP was indeed ranked 10th for degree centrality, which partially supports this scenario. But, it is ranked fairly low at 34th for betweenness centrality (see Appendix D). Also note that the general decline of the KCTU does not represent entire episodes of success and failure in social policies in South Korea. In some policy fields, industrial unions and empowered civic associations successfully coordinated their resources and strategies, which not only launched expansionary social policy reforms but also succeeded in defending existing social policy schemes against retrenchment attempts, of which processes will be discussed in the next two chapters.

25 The latter group of activists was a little bit (five to ten years) younger than the former group of the going-underground generation. This cohort consists of those who entered colleges after the transition to procedural democracy in 1987.

26 When it was established in 1994, it had only five branches (Center for Monitoring Congress, Center for Human Rights, Center for Monitoring Courts, Center for Public Lawsuits, and Center for Supporting Whistle-Blowers). In 2004, however, its organizational form was greatly expanded to embrace nearly all areas of state and congressional activities, thereby being able to match all levels and fields of the formal institutional legal and policy procedures of government and congress. It had nine sub-fields of activist organizations: economy, court, congress, tax, peace and disarmament, environment, small-rights, social welfare, and international solidarity. It also had its own internal bureaucracy composed of nine units: policy, planning, administration, social and human rights, economic reform, anti-corruption, civic rights, civic participation, and civic monitoring. Importantly, it also advanced its own democratic mobilization of resources and opinions through members' small associations and a representative system: 12 members' associations with their own committees, which sent their representatives to the central administrative apparatuses. Finally, the PSPD had its own research institutes and educational centers. For the ten years of its activities, it not only differentiated and specialized its functions and roles (Kim and Chŏng 2004) but also developed its own coordination devices within its organizational form to maximize its internal democratic governance, innovative policy production, and effective policy-monitoring of government and congress. I find that the formation of the PSPD was nearly a process of party-building, only without elected politicians within it.

27 Like many other politicized civic associations in South Korea, it is hard to judge whether the PSPD belongs to the formal civic sectors or the informal civic sectors in Figure 3.1. On one hand, it doesn't necessarily belong to 'professional associations' in the sense that it is not a lobbying or certifying association that serves its insiders' (members') interests. On the other hand, it doesn't necessarily belong to 'informal civic sectors' in the sense that its core activities are not necessarily relevant to citizens' lifeworld matters (religion, culture, or health-related issues). It is engaged in the functions of formal civic sectors, as its organizational functions are more focused upon policy-crafting, governance-monitoring, and coalitional activities with unions, parties, and other professional associations. It is also engaged, however, in mobilizing informal civic sectors' lifeworld concerns in politically meaningful ways. Therefore, it should be treated as a professional brokerage association that links formal and informal civic sectors.

28 Hong's (2007) assessment is that the D. J. Kim's labor market and social policy reform under the financial crisis was a critical moment in which civic movements and Minjung movements (labor, peasants', and students' movements) turned from a relationship of "collaboration" to one of "tension and competition" (pp. 102–6).

29 An important point regarding the origin of the NCHIU solidarity network is that it also evolved from health professionals' going-underground activities on more moderate religious bases. Physicians and their apprentices in the CMAP and the CAUP were engaged in voluntary medical services to the peasants and the urban poor uncovered by health insurance in the 1970s and the 1980s. Although the radical intellectuals went underground in the same period with revolutionary agendas for radical social transformation, these health professionals went partially underground with more moderate, but more specific and concrete goals – enhancing the health conditions of the socially and economically marginalized through volunteering. With the democratization in the late 1980s, these associations formed the prototype of the NCHIU-NAHC.

30 The corporatist health care management system originates from German- and Japanese-style occupation-based fund mobilization and management. Each health care society (corporation) is financially independent, and their contribution and benefit structures differ.

31 Note that the NCTU (the antecedent body of the KCTU) was ranked at the top in 1991 in terms of mobilization embeddedness (in Figure 4.3).

32 Yong-Ik Kim, who played a crucial role in bridging labor unions and the solidarity network as the executive commissioner of the NCHIU, addresses the importance of labor unions as follows: "At the time, health care funds of large conglomerates were managed by the employers. With this (absurd) reality, I persuaded union leaders and workers to accept the logic of the integration movement. The funds should belong to workers, but they were in the pocket of the firm. If the divided health care providers are integrated, then, it is possible to extend the coverage up to the level of 'complete universal health care.' By highlighting that the issue of integration is indeed a matter of 'class,' I thought it would be possible to persuade workers to play a leading role in the integration movement"(NSIU and HPACA 2010, p. 93; also confirmed in an interview with Yong-Ik Kim).

33 The Physicians' Association for Action for Human Rights (PAAHR), the Korean Pharmacists for Democratic Society (the KPDS), and The Korean Dentists for Healthy Society (the KDHS) participated in the NAHC from the start.

34 Kyung-Ae Cho testifies that the role of the two unions was as follows: "labor leaders' roles were decisive in the NCHIU movement, as they had all the necessary data showing huge inequality between rich and poor corporations, including the reserved resources in large conglomerates such as Samsung. Based on the data, we were able to develop logics to persuade politicians and citizens."

35 Yong-Ik Kim, one of the renowned leaders of the NAHC and the NCHIU and the current congressman of the DP (Democratic Party), also points out that policy specialists of the NCHIU discovered (through their internval investigation of the HCSE) that the Health Care Service for Employees (the HCSE) had been accumulating a considerable amount of reserve funds inside the corporation, hiding its fiscal stability and superiority over the Regional Health Care Services (the RHCS).

Chapter 5: Embeddedness, Cohesiveness, and the Politics of Social Policy Expansion in South Korea: Universal vs. Selective Reforms

1 This long background history section is for those who do not have knowledge of South Korean politics and economy in the 1990s. Therefore, those who do may pass this section and proceed to the next section, "Labor Unions and Universal Welfare States."

2 For careful descriptions of such processes in the construction of labor parties, see Cho 2009; Im 2009. For the parting and reorganizing processes of factions in building union confederations, see articles in Cho and Yi 2008. For the roles of cultural and ideological differences of factions in the founding process of the DLP, see Chŏng 2011.

3 There are numerous studies on the founding process of the KCTU, which will not be repeated in this study. See Cho and Yi 2008; Im 1997. For the pre-history of the KCTU in the 1970s and 1980s, see Koo 2001.

4 Other than the direct, formal cohesive ties with the DLP, the KCTU also developed informal ties with the incumbent reformist liberal party, the DP, in the late 1990s. Many union leaders, especially those who belonged to the NL faction (the faction of 'nation'), tended to be supportive of the Kim Dae-jung regime and therefore attempted to build informal lobbying channels with individual politicians and the assistants of a few labor-friendly legislators. The diversity of the cohesiveness to different parties, however, played contradictory roles: on one hand, it helped the KCTU to lobby and negotiate important policy agendas with multiple parties from the left to the center, but on the other hand, it is one of the main reasons that the KCTU has become divided along factional lines.

5 The president-elect, Kim Dae-jung, was ultimately a liberal democrat who deeply trusted the virtue of a liberal market economy, while nonetheless being aware of the necessity to regulate it with generous social safety nets and fair and sound governance systems. Historically, the party had cultivated its electoral bases among the middle-class white collars, small entrepreneurs, the urban poor, younger generations, and south-western regions of the country. Therefore, the regime was hardly a labor-based party and so, from labor's point of view, cohesiveness with the state was partial and limited only to an alliance with the DP for specific agendas (such as social policy expansion).

6 The DP was able to win the close-call election primarily thanks to the division of the ruling party, from which two candidates, Yi Hoe-ch'ang and Yi In-je, competed in the presidential race. Also, the sudden and astonishing collapse of the South Korean economy just a month before the presidential election decisively encroached upon the legitimacy of the ruling conservative party. Therefore, the DP's platform and electoral strategy was simply to attack the ruling party over its responsibility for the unprecedented economic crisis.

7 The Kim Dae-jung regime had a coalition partner, the Free Democratic Alliance (the FDA), a right-wing party led by Kim Jong-Pil, a collaborator in former dictator Park Chung-hee's coup and a long-term subordinate during the Park dictatorship. Kim Jong-Pil formerly led a conservative coalition in the late 1980s, which led to the incumbency of another opposition leader, Kim Young-sam, in 1992. However, he became increasingly excluded from the regime, which led to his departure from the coalition and alliance with Kim Dae-jung.

8 The convention was filled with and surrounded by workers and students who were opposed to the agreement. The votes were made by representatives standing up, which meant that the ballot was obviously not secret but open to the whole audience.

9 Many policy experts I interviewed lamented that this disapproval at the ad hoc convention prevented labor from establishing more constraining devices for the lay-off law and the dispatch (of workers) law. As a result, labor movements did not obtain anything from the tripartite committee (in the sense that labor market reforms, the core interest of workers, were made in the way employers desired, and while labor unions helped to pass all the other welfare reforms, they did not perceive these as directly relevant to workers' core interests).

10 Gould and Fernandez (1989) proposed five brokerage roles: the 'coordinator' role refers to the case where all nodes belong to same group (A→A→A where the second node is the broker); 'gatekeeper' refers to the case where only the source belongs to a different group (B→A→A); 'representative' refers to the case where recipient belongs to a different group (A→ A→ B); 'consultant' refers to the case in which the broker belongs to a different group, while both the source and the recipient belong to the same group (A→ B→A); finally, 'liaison' refers to the case in which all three nodes belong to different groups (B→A→C). I used Ŭn (2005a)'s original scheme of groupings in which 210 organizations are sorted into eight groups to calculate the number of total brokerage roles: vanguard labor organizations, labor unions, labor-support institutes, peasants and poor people's organizations, progressive civic associations, non-ideological civic associations, right-wing civic associations, and popular-sector associations.

11 This impressive bridging role of the KDMU completely disappeared in the 2000s once it turned its position from universal reform seeker to selective reform seeker.

12 The Ministry of Health and Welfare, the most conservative veto group in the government against the integration movement, at the time viewed the union both as a trouble-maker and as a centerpiece of the integration movement, and so they harshly suppressed it using financial assessments and personnel management (lay-offs).

13 The RHCS union initially did not participate in the solidarity network when it was first formed in 1988.

14 The KCTU's deep engagement in the NCHIU in 1995 and its adoption of health care reform as a part of wage bargaining was also confirmed by several top-ranked officials and strategists (e.g. K2 Yi and K5 Kim). In the third central executive committee (January 27, 1995), the KCTU leaders agreed to pursue health care as the first social reform initiative as a part of wage bargaining, and 69 hospital unions, 27 construction unions, 10 automobile unions, 10 metal unions, and several other public firm unions requested health care reform in their firm-level wage bargaining, which drew considerable attention from media, politicians, and the state.

15 In an important way, with the launch of the KCTU, the core leadership group needed 'issues' that would justify the establishment of the national center of the several industrial confederations and regional organizations. The launch of the integrated national health care movement exactly fitted that need of the union center. KCTU leaders actively embraced the health care issue and promoted it as the primary policy agenda for labor to pursue in its negotiation with employers and the state. Several policy folks and experts who were dispatched from the KHMU to the KCTU played a decisive role in persuading union leaders of Chaebol companies and smaller manufacturing firms to take up the issue in their negotiations.

16 The solidarity network had allies in both the reformist incumbent and the conservative opposition parties. Kang, in my interview with him, picks up two congressmen, Yi Sŏng-jae (DP) and Hwang Sŏng-gyun (GNP), as primary channels who not only listened to NCHIU and unions' request for integration, but also actively persuaded their colleagues to support reform. He points out that Hwang, a former chief of Health Insurance for

Civil Servants (with 5 million members), played a decisive role in spreading the necessity for integration reform within the GNP. Not only reformist congressmen but also those from rural districts actively supported the bill. "Even within the Congressional Committee on Health & Welfare, the majority [out of 16] was on our side; all 7 DP and three GNP legislators supported the integration bill, while 3 were supportive or neutral and there were 3 or 4 who were linked to FKTU and adamantly opposed to it ... but it is not possible to pass such a bill only with our efforts. It would be more correct to say that the congress and we [civil society and unions] had a common thought on it ... [but behind such an atmosphere] there already existed a public mood that was strongly in favor of the integration of health care services. We mobilized such a mood from grassroots, and no politician was able to resist it in order to get elected in the next term." Kang also addresses the fact that that the Kim Dae-jung regime accepted and agreed to implement such a policy if there was a reasonable level of consensus between politicians and civil society actors (despite internal resistance from conservative bureaucrats). This implies that under the Kim Dae-jung regime, political opportunities were greatly widened and civil society actors had ample room to be engaged in policy formation, especially through congressional institutions (more than under any other regimes after democratization).

17 It is important again to point out that "discovery of a common interest"(Baldwin 1990, p. 292) between working and middle classes does not arise automatically. It is more important to ask under what conditions and by whom such a discovery is made than simply to assert that 'the risk solidarity' matters. The most important 'conscious solidaristic efforts' were made in the South Korean health solidarity movement by the leadership of the NCHIU, between progressive health professionals and new union leaders of the KCTU. They persuaded leaders and members of privileged large conglomerate unions (who already had good quality health care systems within their industries and occupations and therefore did not necessarily have to switch to a universal integrated single-pillar system) to share a common interest with farmers and the self-employed, the disadvantaged in the existing system.

18 This point (the role of labor) has been seriously underestimated in the literature on the development of the welfare state in South Korea. Both Kim T'ae-hyŏn and Kang Ch'ang-gu, who played key roles in the solidarity movement and negotiation with the government and the opposition party testified to this, and I was able to corroborate their arguments through other figures in civil society: "It was the KCTU, especially the RHCU and the KHMU, that led the solidarity movement for health care reform ... It was the KCTU's struggle and agreement through the tripartite committee in 1998 that decisively enabled the integration of health care providers. We, unionists in the area of medicine and health, led the discussion, and it was the KCTU that first integrated social policy reform movements in the context of popular union movements, even though the FKTU also raised the issue before. Even the KEF established a separate social welfare-related unit within its organization, while it had only employee–employer relationship or wage-related parts." (Kim T'ae-hyŏn, a current chief of the KCTU Policy Unit)

19 The HCSE union was an influential member of the FKTU. Its bureaucrats and union leaders were closely linked to conservative politicians, professors, bankers, and leaders of the former military regimes through numerous positions and financial resources within the differentiated corporatist management systems (Yi 2009). Therefore, it is not surprising that the FKTU, which had grown under the authoritarian corporatism, represented the HCSE union and its allies' interests.

20 The National Pension was first introduced in 1988 for workers in firms with more than ten employees. The entitlement was extended to peasants in 1995, and then to the self-employed and urban residents in 1999. It eventually became extended in 2006 to all citizens working in a business employing at least one person.

21 By 'cultural barrier', he meant that Korean existing pension recipients (of the time) did not want to reveal that they had an additional source of money 'in their pockets.' In a situation where receiving a pension is regarded as a 'privilege,' it may be difficult, in the traditional Korean culture, for a small number of recipients to speak up and defend their rights.

22 In contrast to health care reform, where the KCTU had already acquired a considerable level of policy capacity thanks to the activists in the RHCS union and KHMU, as well as dense networks with civil society leaders and intellectuals in the 1990s, pension reform was a new issue for labor unions: the KCTU leaders had not developed appropriate strategies and positions. As late as 2004, the KCTU hadn't developed a specialized task force on pension reform within the national center (an internal strategy report written in 2004 urged the leadership to develop a task force and mobilize opinions from grassroots unions; one of the key strategists, who specialized in pensions in the early 2000s testified in an interview with me that he was not initially an expert in the field). At the grassroots level, many member unions of the KCTU were opposed to the National Pension, perceiving it as a tax that could not be returned to workers. Grassroots workers and their leaders, after having witnessed mass lay-offs of their co-workers during the financial crisis, did not consider the National Pension a realistic safety net after retirement, as it required at least 20 years of contributions for a person to be eligible for the benefits. Instead, they pursued a short-term strategy – seeking maximization of their basic wages and overtime payments in firm-level bargaining.

23 This later led the NPS union to fight against the 2007 retrenchment of pensions without any support from other unions and civil society organizations (discussed in Chapter 6).

24 Scholars in the field are still debating whether the 1998 reform could be deemed a cornerstone of universal 'social rights' or not (Kim 2009). Economists in the regime primarily supported the World Bank model (World Bank 1994), which focused on the fiscal soundness and balance of the pension fund (as it faced demographic crisis), as well as its conduciveness to economic development. On the other side, policy-makers in the Ministry of Social Welfare and allied reformist researchers (in academia) supported the 'ILO model' emphasizing 'minimum replacement' (for living) and 'universal entitlement.'

25 In a joint press conference on July 24, 1998, the three organizations strongly criticized the government's plan for its indifference to their earlier requests for a more thorough income investigation of the self-employed, legal and institutional independence of the pension funds from other government fiscal policies, and a democratic management and monitoring system for the funds. The two unions showed somewhat strong resistance to universal coverage for those self-employed whose income was not accurately documented under the government tax monitoring system, fearing that the under-reporting of incomes by the self-employed would lead to 'reverse redistribution' from (honest) wage earners to the (dishonest) self-employed. The government's indifference to this issue later ignited popular discontent, confusion, and condemnation of the entire pension plan. In the context of this crisis, the PSPD durably supported the main framework of the reform and helped the reform bill to survive the popular dissatisfaction (Kim 2004). The central union eventually supported universal coverage, but grassroots discontent with the National Pension (driven by rumors of the potential depletion of the fund in the near future) was present in the early 2000s. The pension reform of the late 1990s, after all, left the status of the self-employed and of region-based residents unclear, allowing them to avoid contributing to the fund when they reported that they did not have any income. As a consequence, more than half of the self-employed and region-based residents remained virtually unaffiliated (due to making no contribution) and became vulnerable to poverty in their old ages. In this sense, both KCTU and FKTU implicitly sought an SR strategy rather than a UR strategy with respect to the coverage and entitlement scope of the National Pension.

26 As one policy expert laments, "we gave social policies to all [citizens], but failed to get something for ourselves." Indeed, members of unions sacrificed themselves for universal social policies benefiting the general public, but more radical members and leaders of the KCTU still criticize its national leadership for their actions during the tripartite committee: "How can a national center of labor unions accept the lay-off law? They should've fought against it."

27 The non-existence of any empirical examples in South Korea for the bottom-left cell of Figure 5.4 does not necessarily disqualify the theoretical prediction made in expansion game 3 (Appendix C.2). The cohesive ties of the NCHIU were developed at the very last stage of the reform as ad-hoc lobbying channels, and their strength and efficiency did not reach the same levels as those of traditional corporatistic party–union linkages, as illustrated in Table 5.1. In this sense, the labor–civic solidarity of the NCHIU could be located somewhere between the bottom-left and the bottom-right cells in Figure 5.4 (medium-level of cohesiveness).

28 Universal pension coverage had been postponed until the recent controversial reform was introduced by the conservative party in 2014, in which basic allowances were provided to older people, but disproportionally given to those covered by the National Pension. This regressive pension reform will be discussed in Chapter 6.

Chapter 6: The Politics of Retrenchment under Market Reforms

1 Many labor activists whom I interviewed expressed this point. Especially, those who worked in the policy-crafting and negotiation lines, so-called 'policy folks,' lamented the prevalence of such an atmosphere in the late 1990s and early 2000s.

2 The FKTU dramatically transformed itself from a corporatist subsidiary partner of authoritarian regimes for several decades to a center-left policy-centered union under two reformist regimes. As a result, it increased its cohesiveness with the incumbent parties in the late 1990s and the early 2000s. Therefore, the FKTU's collaboration with the Rho Mu-hyun regime regarding labor market reforms is an exemplary case of cohesiveness without embeddedness under the retrenchment games.

3 On labor's side, union leaders did not make conscious efforts to further cultivate their linkages to civil society, especially during the Rho regime and subsequent two conservative regimes. For the first couple of years of the conservative Lee regime, they were directly or indirectly involved in the brawls in the DLP, and the split, merger and subsequent re-split of DLP remnants. While their capacity to organize national- or industrial-level general strikes kept declining, their capacity to coordinate and craft policy agendas among divergent social and political forces was also dwindling due to the departure of key policy experts and the incorporation of civil society allies into the DP.

4 In appearance, these sudden moves of policy folks from the KCTU to the National Assembly and other institutions look coincidental, but there existed factional power struggles within the KCTU and internal disputes regarding how to restructure policy units within the KCTU. Especially, several prominent policy specialists who were well versed in policy-making, data management, and report production left the KCTU around 2004–05. Kim moved to the KLSI (Korea Labor and Society Institute), while Mr. O moved to the National Assembly to serve as an assistant (for congresswoman Sim Sang-jŏng Shim) and Chu eventually joined the mayoral election campaign camp for Pak Wŏn-sun, the founder of the PSPD. These policy folks desired to build an independent policy institute within the KCTU which would not be swayed by factional regime changes, but failed to do so. Unfortunately, with their abrupt departures, their expert

know-how in labor issues and their lifetime networks densely covering unions, parties, and other civic associations were all gone. Many KCTU activists lamented the loss, and testified that the KCTU did not recover for the next decade from this sudden dissolution of the policy unit.

5 They were Pak T'ae-ju, the chief labor advisor to President Roh; Yi Chŏng-u, the chief policy advisor of the Blue House; Chŏng T'ae-in, the secretary of the economic advisory committee for the president; and Kim Yŏng-dae, a team leader of the society-labor unit of the presidential transition committee.

6 A KCTU leader of that time lamented of that moment, "to be honest, unions went too far by repeated, prolonged strikes during the first couple of months. The president started considering unions as 'a group of whining people having a tantrum.' I personally have a thought that the NTU strike was unnecessary. It was a system to keep a couple of very basic personal records, not even a serious violation of human rights. Why should the unions disrupt the first year [of the supposedly labor-friendly regime] with such a small matter and aggravate the relationship with the regime? … After the impeachment, as a consequence, the president and his party became an island, detached from civil society and unions. *They increasingly relied on the bureaucrats* [emphasis added]. They didn't talk to us after the second year." When I asked whether the president and union leaders had any single channel through which to coordinate and fill such differences and cleavages, he answered briefly, "No, we didn't." I conclude that unions had little 'institutionalized cohesiveness' from the very beginning of the regime, if there were some pro-labor intellectuals within the regime whose base was indeed unstable and unorganized. Indeed, the KCTU did not have any institutionalized ties or units for consulting on policy with the Rho regime. A former KCTU top leader who served as one of the early 'labor-issue' advisors to the president Rho (who also quit in less than a year) recalled that, after the second truck drivers' strike, "I tried to explain why unions behaved that way and what they expected from the president, but he and his close circle refused to talk about it, saying that they didn't want to listen to my accounts."

7 In a press conference, Rho addressed his intention to help the ruling party in the coming election and mentioned, "I would like to do everything I can do to help the Open Uri Party (the ruling party)." The opposition parties protested the president's remark as a potential violation of election law and requested the president to issue an apology. Rho refused and three opposition parties passed the impeachment bill in March, 2004. It was overturned in the Constitutional Court in May, while the Open Uri Party recorded a decisive win in the general election with 152 seats (out of 299) in April.

8 Why did the 'reformist' government, which was supposed to be labor-friendly, take such an abrupt neo-liberal turn? Was it driven by an unavoidable external economic pressure or the president's own political will? What was the role of state bureaucrats and larger conservative forces in creating a crack in the (short-lived) embedded cohesiveness? These are questions that may naturally arise with the EC approach, as the approach puts its emphasis on labor–civic solidarity rather than state actors. First, it is important to point out that conservative forces, employers (large conglomerates), and market-oriented bureaucrats, were increasingly solidifying their own coordination institutions at multiple informal levels. Many activists whom I interviewed expressed that they were able to perceive increasingly coordinated lobbying efforts toward the presidential office by employers (especially Samsung), through conservative bureaucrats in the Ministry of Finance and Economy. A former adviser to President Rho, one of the leaders of the NCHIU movement, commented that he often observed the president being briefed by his conservative economists regarding the social policy issues he wanted to promote. Obviously, this glimpse of observational information does not help much. In order to understand the deep latent and systematic processes of the emergence and operation of employers' lobbying mechanisms, one would need a separate project to investigate

them through employers' internal documents and close interviews. Second, many activists pointed out that President Rho (and his close internal circle), even though he was engaged in labor and human rights issues as a lawyer and a congressman, was not ready for the commander-in-chief job. They claim that the president had neither a good understanding of social policy issues nor a deep philosophy toward the socially disadvantaged and those in need of social policies. The EC approach, however, does not consider individual-level capacity or the personal will of leadership as a truly exogenous factor in social policy-making, but regards them as endogenous factors that tend to be shaped by contending civic and political forces. As I addressed in this section, the KCTU's unilateral alliance with the DLP (therefore declining cohesiveness with the state), its own internal fragmentation due to factional strife (therefore declining embeddedness), and the co-optation of surrounding progressive civic associations into the Rho regime (also causing declining embeddedness) all contributed to the Rho regime's departure from embedded cohesiveness. This further allowed it to be penetrated by the efforts of employers lobbying for privatization drives. Note that it was also the KCTU member unions' militant strikes during the first six months of the regime that separated it from the Rho regime. Unions' declining cohesiveness with the state led to penetration of the Rho regime's decision-making processes by employers' lobbying power and processes, not vice versa.

9 In spite of these retrenchments in health care and pensions, the Rho regime also implemented three key expansionary reforms in other social welfare areas: (1) it introduced the basic pension (basic old-age allowances) for the elderly poor, even if with means testing; (2) it also introduced long-term care insurance for the elderly; and (3) it expanded family allowances for child care. "Within the regime, despite a lot of constraints, we worked hard to transfer budget from economy to social welfare"(Kim Yong-ik). In this sense, the Rho regime deserves to receive recognition for introducing important institutional reforms for marginalized populations (especially the elderly) as well as criticism for opening up room for market reforms in major social insurance fields.

10 Yi Sŏng-jae (a congressman who played a key role in passing the integration bill under the Kim Dae-jung regime) was the chief of the NHIS, while Yi Sang-i was the chief of the National Institute for Health and Insurance. Kim Yong-ik was one of the chief advisors for President Rho.

11 There was a policy specialist within the KCTU policy unit who was specializing in the new pension, but he started this only in 2001 under Byung-Ho Dan's leadership (2001–04) and quit his role in 2004. "I sought to expand the policy unit to an independent policy institute with its head not influenced by internal regime changes, but they did not listen to me. When I quit the job, I was unable to transfer to the next person my networks and know-how I had built for the three years in the KCTU. The level of knowledge could not be deepened, because I had to run everywhere, from other civic associations to the congress, by myself. There was no supporting cast. Like my case, when other important policy folks moved out of the KCTU for different reasons, their expertise was completely gone with their departure. There was little effort to institutionalize such networks and experiences."

12 The NPS union leaders had little significant experience of solidarity with the KCTU leaders due to the NPS's membership in the FKTU for more than a decade in the 1990s. Additionally, while it remained a subsidiary organization of the FKTU, the NPS union did not have the chance to develop its organizational networks with other civic associations and experts in pension fields (low embeddedness).

13 The union president stated that they were left alone when they waged their first strike and demonstration in 2007 against the retrenchment of the National Pension. They then realized the need to build solidarity with other unions and civil society organizations to exert any influence on political society.

14 There are studies that compare a specific insurance company (Samsung Life Insurance Co.'s report) with the government's privatization drives and conclude that the government has been adopting Samsung's plans with little change (Sin 2010).

15 According to Kim Yong-ik, the reasons why large hospitals desperately sought to become profit-oriented date back to the institutional setting of the health care system when it was first introduced: health care first began in firms with more than 500 employees in 1964, and then was extended to civil servants and soldiers in 1970 and peasants in 1988. As a result, under the old system, health care providers (hospitals and physicians) had to suffer a heavy loss for the insured (due to low reimbursements for treatment under insurance), while gaining profits from the uninsured as well as from high charges for treatments covered by insurance. As the National Health Insurance covers all citizens (since the universal integration), health care providers were no longer able to impose excessive charges on the uninsured, and so they had to rely on high medical fees for treatments not under insurance coverage, which caused serious conflict between consumers and providers, while the low medical fee covered by state insurance contributed to incessant negotiations and conflict between the state (NHCS) and providers. As labor and civil society forces (SHR) gradually pushed the state to raise the coverage of health insurance, providers were pressured to generate profits either by generating new treatments not covered by insurance or by generating new businesses not regulated by the current health care laws (summarized by the author based on an interview with him). Thus, it was not only private insurance companies but also large health care providers who desired to launch privatized health care systems independent of the national health care system.

16 The mandate requires health care service providers (all hospitals and individual physicians) to accept patients under the national health insurance, which implies that their services would be priced by the National Health Insurance Service (NHIS). The KMA (the Korean Medical Association) filed suits at the CCK (Constitutional Court of Korea) twice against this mandate, in 2002 and 2012, with the rationale that the mandate encroached upon not only the 'free business activities' of medical institutions but also the 'free choices' of customers. The CCK declared that the current mandate was constitutionally sound and should be maintained to defend citizens' (universal) health rights. The abrogation of this mandate would be an opening for launching an American-style private health care system.

17 In 2009, after its success in defeating the Lee regime's privatization attempt, SHR was in jeopardy of being split, by serious disagreement regarding the financing of health care, between two segments, one called "Go with One Health Care" and the other "People's Solidarity for Free Health Care." The former sought to raise premiums to increase the coverage and benefits of national health insurance, while the latter was opposed to such a solution, arguing that such a raise without constraints on health care providers would only contribute to increasing revenues for providers. The two camps bitterly fought within the solidarity network, then requested the KCTU to intervene and mediate in order to maintain solidarity. KHMU officials persuaded the two camps not to break up the solidarity organization, suggesting that they could remain in the solidarity to the degree to which they found a policy consensus. More accurately speaking, the HRN has been converted into one permanent organization, the Solidarity Network of Health and Medical Associations (SNHMA), and another temporary movement organization, People's Movement against Privatization of Health Care (PMPHC). Unions play central coordinating roles in both solidarity networks (summarized based on an interview with a KMHU leader). For simplicity, I call all these movements and associational activities "Solidarity for Health Rights (SHR)."

18 A bigger incident in 2008 was the introduction of supplementary indemnity insurance by private insurance companies, which, regardless of its awkward name, was meant to

serve as a primary private health insurance to quietly replace the roles of public health insurance. Thanks to the Candlelight Demonstration, nobody paid attention to the advent of this product in May 2008.

19 As the conservative party won both general and presidential elections in 2012, however, the privatization torch was passed along to the Park regime, and the second round of clashes between the government and labor–civic solidarity began. Under the Park regime, further aspects of privatization of health care were added to the government list (in addition to the existing profit-oriented hospitals in Cheju Island). In particular, the idea of developing and introducing remote-controlled medical devices, which was conceived under the Lee regime, emerged as one of the primary policy agendas, as Samsung Electronics Company announced it as one of its future 'profit-generating blue ocean' ideas. The Park regime declared that it would advance the new medical industry projects relentlessly against any obstacles. Kim Mu-sŏng, one of the representative proponents of the privatization of the medical industry, became the leader of the SP (Saenuri Party, the former GNP) in 2014 and won the decisive supplementary election to fill 15 seats in congress in July. Nevertheless, SHR activists and its supporting base, in collaboration with the opposition parties (the Democratic Party and the Justice Party), successfully defeated the Park regime's legislation attempts during the government's first two critical years.

20 Refer to Appendix C.2 for detailed definitions of unions' universal vs. selective reform strategies. KHMA has been one of the rare unions in South Korea in which industry-level wage bargaining has been underway in the 2000s.

21 The list of the member organizations included the KCTU, the PSPD, the FKTU, the KWAU (Korean Women's Associations United), the KPTSU (Korean Public Transportation and Service Union), the NPSU (National Pensions Service Union), the KPU (Korean Public Union), the KFIU (Korean Financial Industry Union), the KFSW (Korean Finance and Service Workers' Union), the NPA (National Peasants' Association), the Old Age Union, and the Youth Union, among others.

22 Even considering the short lifetime of Korea's pension system, it is surprising that Korea's elderly haven't developed their own interest organization to defend their pension rights. The lack of a single recipients' interest group, like the AARP (American Associations of Retired Persons) in the US, made it difficult for unions to build a durable solidarity consisting of current and future recipients across generations. This absence enabled the conservative government and private insurance companies to manipulate the pension structure at ease without serious resistance or political costs.

Chapter 7: Market-Oriented Reforms of the Welfare State and Union Responses in Brazil and Argentina

1 In some countries, the state merely implemented labor-repressive labor market policies or coercive measures to suppress demands for better working conditions and wage increases (e.g. in Taiwan and South Korea in the 1980s). In the rest of this and following chapters, I treat these repressive labor policies as equivalent to state-driven market reform to confiscate labor's assets.

2 In order to further explore how different forms of labor–civic solidarity emerged during the authoritarian eras, see Lee (2016).

3 The CUT-MST alliance is still in the making: "The popular movements of fighting for housing have an historical partnership with the CUT, [under] the National Fight for Housing Movement ... MST was born soon after the CUT and is directly related to our fight. Our fight for agrarian reform is classic at the CUT" (Expedito Solaney). In this sense, the CUT-MST alliance is comparable to the red-green alliance (Esping-Andersen 1990), which contributed to the long-term incumbency of the Social Democratic Party

in Sweden. An important difference is that the MST in Brazil is based on landless work-ers, while the green component in the Swedish alliance was mainly composed of inde-pendent small farmers.

4 In competition with the CUT, Força Sindical solidified its position among more mod-erate unions in the manufacturing and construction sectors (e.g. the Metalworkers of São Paulo, Civil Construction, Federation of Chemical Workers, the Federation of Nutrition, and the Union of Workers). It later strengthened its social movement base as well, primarily working with the women's, black, human rights, and environmental movements.

5 In a similar strategic move, the leadership of the central unions also concentrated on elected positions. A former union militant, Rogério Magri, the CGT president in 1989, was nominated to head the Ministry of Labor in 1991 under the Collor government. Similarly, Luiz Antônio de Medeiros, a founder of the Força Sindical in 1991, became a federal lower house representative for the state of São Paulo in 1999. Former unionists entering the government signaled a trend of increased collaboration between unions and the state.

6 Many CUT leaders listed the passage of the minimum wage law as a more significant achievement made by unions than Bolsa Familia.

7 However, during the interview period (2013–15), the Dilma regime increasingly deteri-orated due to its declining public support, poor governance, rampant corruption scan-dals, and increasingly remote relationships with the CUT and social movements. Many union leaders were critical of the regime, addressing concerns about the CUT-PT relation-ship: "there's guilt in the evolution of Dilma's government. There's a backing away and lack of dialogue with activist movements and the youth. That's a mortal sin." "The Party needs to reconnect to people … They need to know what the angriest demands are and which problems are still the same." "The PT made a mistake in these 12 years of govern-ment. If you don't have a strategy, you're at risk of just administration, and workers will only get leftovers and that's what happened" (Anonymous former CUT leaders).

8 However, about this time, when more leftist unionists realized that Lula was going to remain on the track of (moderate) market reforms, many activists and union leaders/members left the CUT to establish a new independent union confederation, the National Coordination of Struggles (Conlutas, or CSP-Conlutas).

9 The list of allying organizations is as follows: ACFTU, CSP-Conlutas, the National Union of Teachers of Higher Education Institutions (ANDES-SN), CNTA (National Confederation of Food Workers), COBAP (Brazilian Confederation of Retirees and Pensioners) CONDSEF (National Federation of Federal Public Servants), MST, FERAESP (Federation of Rural Workers of the State of São Paulo), ADMAP (Democratic Association of Retirees and Pensioners), RING (National Assembly of Students – Free), and other popular movement organizations (ANDES-SN 2013).

10 Argentine union leaders whom I interviewed were mostly raised in Peronist families and became involved in Peronist informal circles from their youth (e.g. 'Peronist Youth Worker').

11 Some may say this is not 'striking' because Menem was one of the *renovadores* who wanted to weaken the PJ's ties with unions. What matters here, however, is that there was a huge discrepancy between Menem's electoral platform favoring labor and the neo-liberal economic policies of Cavallo, Menem's economic brain.

12 Most Peronist union leaders (whom I interviewed) under the CGT tradition either said "no" or did not have clear answers to the questions asking whether they were involved in joint activities or coalitional politics with other non-union organizations and their causes. They rarely had relationships with other civic association such as human rights

groups, environmental groups, and other advocacy groups, which is in sharp contrast to the Brazilian union leaders who were proud of and well versed in their long history of collaboration with other social movement organizations. If students or professionals joined union activities, however, they showed some interest and respect, but such ties were neither systematic nor institutionalized at collective organizational levels. Only a few union leaders highlighted unions' close collaboration with human rights associations (primarily over human rights abuses during the military dictatorship). In general, it is hard to find meaningful civic associations, because most associational activities are organized around either unions or parties. One intellectual laments, "as soon as there emerge new cultural or intellectual movements, they tend to become linked to the state through [Peronist] party organizations."

13 Among 23 union leaders and strategists whom I interviewed, 14 worked for the PJ either at the central or the local municipal levels and 6 of them eventually became congressional representatives.

14 Some scholars (e.g. Huber and Stephens 2012) describe Menem's pension reform as 'concessions' to the unions, as the regime stepped back from its initial full privatization, making considerable modifications in the face of strong opposition from unions (Madrid 2003). However, launching a mixed system that introduced Chilean-style individual accounts, while simultaneously allowing employees to choose between the public system and individual accounts, should be considered a significant retrenchment of the public pension system.

15 Indeed, Argentinian CTA leaders often addressed their formal and informal ties to Lula and CUT leaders during the interviews. They invited each other to their rallies as speakers. "Miguel Rossetto invited me for the 1994 federal march ... Grasso had already begun with the real plan [the Plano Real: a stabilization measure conducted under the Franco and Cardoso regimes] and was hooking people. Lula wanted to fight. As we were coming from four years of Cavallo [his currency stabilization measure in Argentina] and we knew the consequences of it ... we went to Brazil and did a campaign against it with the CUT" (One of the CTA leaders). In a sense, the diffusion of market reforms in Latin America fueled new social movement unions to build their own cross-border solidarity to share knowledge, experiences, and common ideological ground.

16 Nevertheless, the CTA is still a much smaller union confederation compared to the CGT. Given weaker civil society in Argentina, it would be an exaggeration to say that Argentine unions boosted their embeddedness thanks to the emergence of the CTA. After its first creation in 1991, the CTA was divided into two smaller confederations: CTA de los Trabajadores and CTA Auténtica.

17 Under the Kirchners' regimes, the CTA developed as strong cohesiveness with the government as the CGT had. It supported the (re)nationalization of pensions (2008–14), parts of the airline industry (Aerolíneas Argentinas, 2008), energy companies, and railway systems (2003–14). It also waged coalitional campaigns with civil society organizations in defense of public hospitals, while playing a significant role in creating universal child allowance (Asignación Universal por Hijo) under the Kirchners' regimes. The CTA also engaged in broad campaigns to defend public schools and human rights (UTE-CTERA-CTA).

18 However, this successful expansion of the welfare state in Argentina has been achieved at the expense of sound budget and the flight of international investors. Therefore, the lingering balance-of-payment crises in Argentina since the early 2000s suggest that too-strong embedded cohesiveness may have negative impacts on economic performance in the globalized economy. This negative impact of too-strong embedded cohesiveness may be a separate topic to be discussed in more detail, given that many Latin American countries under leftist regimes, including Brazil, suffered from similar currency crises in the 2010s.

Chapter 8: Market-Oriented Reforms of the Welfare State and Union Responses in South Korea and Taiwan

1 As I addressed earlier, few intellectuals went underground in Taiwan compared to in South Korea in the late 1970s and early 1980s. While South Korean intellectuals became disguised workers to organize and mobilize workers, Taiwanese intellectuals remained 'outside the factories,' self-limiting their role as a 'midwifery' rather than an 'incubator,' a role employed by South Koreans.

2 This can be seen from the press releases of both the CFL and the TCTU (the TCTU in particular).

3 Several dissident grassroots unions and some county-level confederations (such as the Taipei Confederation of Trade Unions and Taoyuan Confederation of Trade Unions), most of which were dissatisfied with the TCTU's moderate position toward the DPP or critical of its non-militant stance, formed the National Federation of Independent Trade Unions (NAFITU). They sought to develop an independent, national-level union confederation not under the control of any political party. NAFITU and member unions fought for the Labor Standard Act amendments, flexible working hours amendments, the Act for Settlement of Labor–Management Disputes amendments, paid leave, unemployment insurance/benefits, and pensions amendments. One of the former NAFITU union leaders laments, however, that "there is hardly any political party that truly takes the labor stance [in Taiwan]," and that "the biggest setback is that it [NAFITU] is not performing as expected … because people at the top involve their own self-interests."

4 Since 2009, when the KMT returned to power, the TCTU has showed its militancy again, if shortly, in support of improving unemployment benefits and reducing youth poverty.

5 The TCTU's recent (in the 2010s) lack of funding and the lack of personnel in its central office limited its role as a national center of labor movements and labor policies: "It doesn't have enough funding, hence lack of human resources. After my departure, they only have three full-time staff members. How can a national-level labor union have only three full-time staff to promote efficient [policy] activities? We have a formal structure within the TCTU, such as a policy department … If you don't have enough funding, you won't be able to do research work; hence you won't be able to finalize a good macro labor policy. Then, your organization will lack sufficient negotiation power. This becomes a vicious cycle" (former secretary-general of the TCTU).

6 The origin, development, and decline of the KCTU have been discussed at length in Chapters 4 to 6. In this section, therefore, I pay more attention to a comparative analysis of the FKTU and the KCTU's responses to the state's market reforms.

7 "We had about 420,000 members in our metal union only. However, from the early 1990s, we began to lose about 100,000 members [of the metal union] to KCTU every year [until it lost more than half of its members]"(Chŏng Mun-ju, chief of FKTU policy headquarters).

8 "Since the late 1990s, FKTU ended its traditional emphasis on 'negotiation-centered strategy' and employed other principles and strategies such as militant struggles and solidarity with other unions and civic associations" (former secretary-general of FKTU). During this time, FKTU adopted 'social reformist unionism,' which is almost identical to the unionism of KCTU. "Currently, there is little difference between FKTU and KCTU, as KCTU has recently lost its mobilization capacity [in the early 2010s]" (member of FKTU senior advisory committee).

9 However, when the decade-long incumbency of the reformist regimes (1998–2007) ended, the FKTU quickly turned its back on the DP and aligned again with the conservative candidate, Myung-Bak Lee. The FKTU, therefore, has attempted to stand by the ruling party, regardless of the incumbent's ideological stance, in order to maintain its cohesiveness. Since 2011, however, it has concluded that it cannot tolerate the ruling

conservative party's anti-labor stance, and so it closely coalesced with the DP in the next two elections (general and presidential elections in 2011 and 2012, respectively).

10 Note that, despite the convergence in their stance against the government, their organizational capacity in terms of embeddedness did not change: the KCTU emerged with its strong mobilization capacity and durable labor–civic networks originating from democratization movements, while the FKTU had few civil society allies.

11 This national center-level politics does not necessarily coincide with industrial union-level or policy domain-level politics. As described in Chapters 4 to 6, the KHMU's embedded cohesiveness or embeddedness with weak to moderate cohesiveness through the KFMA kept operating and maintained its influence throughout the 2000s.

12 The pursuit by South Korean leftist intellectuals of a mass-bureaucratic labor party began to crumble just as it reached its most promising moment. The DLP split into two parties just four years after it had its most remarkable electoral success in 2004 and immediately before a general election (in 2008). After the split, both parties witnessed striking shrinkages of both their party bases and popular electoral support. The division of the DLP into two factions also divided its social bases and created deep skepticism about the party leadership. The dissolution of the DLP in 2008, therefore, marked the failure of KCTU and DLP leaders' conscious experiment to build a social democratic, programmatic party model similar to the Brazilian PT-CUT model. The implosion of the DLP due to factional politics left reformist citizens and workers deeply frustrated and disenchanted with leftist politics. The internecine warfare among activists severely damaged mobilization and policy networks and lead to the loss of internal capacity. It occurred at a time when workers and the socially marginalized most needed a well-organized labor movement – in other words, when the neo-liberal structural transformation of the workplace, labor markets, and social policies severely affected Korean society, and when workers desperately needed a party that could represent and defend their interests. The dissolution of the DLP, most importantly, compelled grassroots unions to find their own, local solutions, as opposed to engaging in broader solidaristic and cooperative endeavors to defend their rights and channel their collective interests. Grassroots workers and union leaders were unable to find political agents in the local and national politics to promote universal, nationwide solutions for the crises in employment and the social safety net. Therefore, unions further focused on advancing their narrow, short-term economic interests at their individual firms.

13 If an average worker hired in a large firm (with more than 500 workers) as a standard worker affiliated with a union received '100', an average worker hired in a small to mid-sized firm as a non-standard worker without union affiliation received merely 38.6 in South Korea in 2014 (it was 44 in 2004). Even among workers hired in large firms, non-standard workers' average wage over that of standard workers decreased from 73.8 in 2004 to 66.1 in 2014. Among workers hired in small to mid-sized firms, the ratio diminished from 78.1 in 2004 to 68.4 in 2014 (Kim 2015).

14 A KCTU strategist asserted, "We have no choice but to wage movements to increase benefits [for non-standard workers]. They are unorganized. Among 150,000 [metal] workers [under the KCTU], the number of organized non-standard labor is merely 2–3,000. We need to provide those unorganized with models to organize themselves and develop policies for them."

15 Indeed, large manufacturing unions did not have to sacrifice any material gains in their turn to SR strategy, as the KCTU and metal unions have not established any institutionalized punishment mechanisms for defection, such as a reduction of strike funds or exclusion from collective bargaining. Unions at large firms have their own resources for mobilization and are content with firm-level bargaining. Individual union leaders, who are mostly of worker background, are only thinly and 'ideologically' connected to the students-turned-labor activists who dominate the KCTU national center and

industrial union offices. As grassroots union leaders are more sensitive to workers' votes in upcoming elections, it is natural for them to serve their workers' narrow material interests rather than those of their long-term ideological collaborators (who once went underground to organize and educate rank-and-file workers and their leaders) at upper-level union organizations. An (anonymous) industrial union leader's retrospective account illustrates well the changing relationship between going-underground activists and the leaders of grassroots workers over time in Korean labor movements: "I lived with one of the famous Hyundai Automobile union's presidents as a roommate and studied together for years in the late 1980s. I virtually taught him everything on labor movements [as a mentor of revolutionary movements] until I left Ulsan. He followed me calling me '[elder] brother' … Recently I met him, but he won't listen to what I am saying. He outgrew."

16 This is the core argument of Yoonkyung Lee's book, *Militants or Partisans* (2011).

17 Nearly 72 percent of voters over 60 supported the conservative candidate Park, while about 67 percent of voters under 40 supported the opposition party candidate Moon, in the 2012 presidential election. Such generational voting patterns have been reinforced in recent elections in South Korea (source: three major broadcasting companies' exit polls).

18 Assessments of overall union strategies, including their own efforts for expansionary reforms, will be made in country-level comparative analyses in the next chapter.

19 As the unit of analysis is at the confederation level, this study cannot fully address heterogeneity among individual unions, especially that of industrial unions and grassroots unions. The different levels of centralization and coordination within unions across societies are important determinants of unions' capacity for mobilization and bargaining against the state (and employers). Considering this aspect of internal cohesion of a union confederation and its leadership structure, we control for the 'coherence' of a union confederation in our causal model (in factor 3 in Tables 8.2 and 8.3), which captures the degree to which a union confederation can manage different segments of member unions' heterogeneous interests and ideological trends. When this variable has a low value for a confederation, individual unions under such a confederation may have divergent, uncoordinated strategies and directions in their relationships to the state, civil society, and employers, which may weaken the leadership and bargaining power of the confederation. In a similar vein, Murillo (2001) theorized and operationalized this dimension with 'union competition for members.' The other variable she developed to operationalize internal labor politics is 'leadership competition' among union leaders who are linked to different political parties. This variable seems similar to the cohesiveness dimension of this study, but is different as it systemizes whether unions are dominated by one party or divided into several segments (while cohesiveness taps into unions' ties to the incumbent party or leftist party).

20 One explanation for this deviance (from the models of this study) is that, thanks to Taiwan's small firm sizes, and their flexibilities and early exposure to (and the division of labor with) mainland China, the Taiwanese state has been less under pressure for neo-liberal market reforms, compared to its South Korean and Latin American counterparts, especially in the 2000s. Therefore, the Taiwanese case indicates that the proposed framework needs a certain level of economic crisis as a necessary condition for radical market reform. Without it, the state does not have an incentive to introduce radical market-oriented reform. Another simple explanation is that the state's moderate reform is a response to growing labor-civic solidarity (TCTU elements' embeddedness without cohesiveness).

21 The Taiwanese case in the 2000s is not a perfect case for MR-R, but is a very close case. The TCTU's linkage to civil society was considerably weakened in the 2000s, but its close relationship with the DPP contributed to MR. But the Taiwanese case could be

interpreted as being a result of weak market reform pressure (due to relatively milder economic pressure).

22 It is therefore uncertain whether we should assign the primary partnership of the incumbent PJ to the CGT or to the CTA in Table 8.2. If the CGT is the primary negotiator with the PJ, then the outcome, 'moderate reform-restraint', is inconsistent with the expectation (cohesiveness without embeddedness). If the CTA is the primary responder to the incumbent PJ, 'moderate reform-restraint' is consistent with the initial hypothesis (embedded cohesiveness).

Chapter 9: Associational Networks and the Welfare State in Argentina, Brazil, South Korea, and Taiwan

1 This chapter is an extended version of the empirical analysis part of my earlier work published in *World Politics* (2012, pp. 522–54), based on further archival and field interview data as well as updated network data. While the earlier version analyzes the associational networks and the politics of the welfare state in the 1990s and up to the mid-2000s, the current version extends its time scope up to the early 2010s. In contrast to Brazil and Taiwan, Argentina experienced a radical reversal of welfare politics from retrenchment to expansion, while South Korea experienced a moderate reversal from expansion to retrenchment or stagnation, due not only to regime changes, but also to the changing structures of associational networks.

2 This chapter extends the definition and measurement of cohesiveness. Unlike the previous chapters on South Korea and Chapters 7 and 8, in which two definitions of unions' cohesiveness – unions' ties with incumbent political parties and unions' ties with labor parties – are consistently used, this chapter focuses on (1) both unions and parties' cohesiveness and embeddedness; and (2) their cohesive ties with not only parties but also professional associations within formal sectors. The purpose of extending and diversifying cohesiveness in this way is to understand the larger and higher national-level politics beyond specific union confederations and partisan affiliations of unions. See Appendix B for detailed discussion on the measurement of cohesiveness and embeddedness.

3 While the South Korean case study in the previous chapters delved into the deep underlying dimensions of cohesiveness and embeddedness – policy and mobilization capacities – this chapter is content to measure the cohesiveness and embeddedness of unions (and parties) in associational fields using 'co-membership' data available in World Values Surveys. The South Korean case shows that the qualitative assessments of policy and mobilization capacities of cohesiveness and embeddedness are highly correlated with social network measures based on co-affiliation data.

4 The ensuing four Tables based on World Values Survey provide a cursory comparison of the structures of associational networks in four countries. For more detailed illustration and analyses of labor–civic networks built upon detailed organizational events, see Chapters 4 to 6, in which I investigate how evolving union-linked associational networks led to the provision of universal social protection in South Korea.

5 See columns A and C in Table 9.2 and column A in Table 9.3. The bold italics in columns B and C in Table 9.3 indicate where the incumbent party belonged to (either leftist or non-leftist parties). For Argentina, it was mostly under the PJ, while in Brazil, the PSDB (Cardoso) was in power in the 1990s, and the PT (Lula) and its center-left coalition took over the government in the 2000s and after. Unions' ties with either leftist incumbent parties in the 2000s or non-leftist incumbent parties in the 1990s were largely similar (0.10 in 1995 and 0.09 in 2005) in Brazil, which is in great contrast to the significant decrease in union-incumbent leftist party linkage in Argentina. Overall,

both unions' cohesiveness with the incumbent party (and leftist parties) and unions' embeddedness declined in Argentina, but were intact in Brazil in the 1990s and 2000s.

6   The Workers' Party has a very peculiar organizational structure and culture: (1) it was established by two workers' movements (Central Unica dos Trabalhadores, CUT and Movimento dos Trabalhadores Rurais Sem Terra, MST) and activists from the Catholic Church. CUT is a newly established strong trade union confederation and MST is a nationwide landless workers' association. Both organizations share the same members and leaders with the PT, but the PT is not officially funded by these organizations. Rather, the progressive wing of the Catholic Church, being influenced by the critical pedagogy and the liberation theology of Paulo Freire (who joined the PT in 1980), has played a critical role in financially supporting the party and in culturally shaping the party's unorthodox and progressive ethic codes (for example, it approves gay and abortion rights) (Branford and Kucinski 2003; Keck 1992).

7   It started in 1994, but several ensuing adjustments were made and further legislation passed in 1999, 2004, and 2008.

8   See Auyero 1999 for the form and functions of Peronist broker–client networks in urban slums.

9   This reciprocal, feedback effect of neo-liberal reform on cohesiveness suggests that disarticulated cohesiveness may not necessarily persist in the long term, and therefore, transformative politics by the PJ were destined to oscillate between populist co-optation (of the working class) and neo-liberal reform (aiming to attract support from the middle class), depending upon economic and electoral cycles. Indeed, after the center-left components of the PJ had been newly mobilized by the Kirchners, the party reinforced the public component in the pensions system in 2007 (Brooks 2008) and conducted several universal social policy reforms to win back the disenchanted former party base.

10 The linkages of the PJ and its ally Peronist unions (CGT) to informal civil society have been primarily based on numerous soccer clubs, which have played critical roles in delivery of social welfare, political mobilization of votes and candidates, and social integration in Argentina. In spite of their 'depth' of embeddedness within Peronist cliques, however, the PJ and CGT's 'scope' of embeddedness in other civic associations is unimpressive, compared to that of Brazilian parties/unions. Especially during processes by which CGT split into several segments (engendering CTA and MST), more 'solidarity-oriented' elements broke away from the original CGT, seeking more determined resistance against Menem's neo-liberal reforms.

11 See note A, Table 9.3 regarding caveats over the interpretation of findings for Argentina (and also those for Taiwan).

12 These results are consistent with Etchemendy and Collier's (2007) contrast of densely connected social movement unionism in Brazil and Peronist top-down, disconnected unionism in Argentina.

13 Among major Latin American countries, only Chile and Uruguay experienced similar setbacks during that time.

14 Gini index increased from 44 in 1991 to 52 in 2002 (WIID, World Income Inequality Database), while the poverty rate skyrocketed from 21.5 percent to 54.3 percent (of individuals in the greater Buenos Aires area) during the same period (SEDLAC, Socio-Economic Database for Latin America and the Caribbean). Both have made great 'u-turns' in the 2000s under the Kirchners. See Huber and Stephens 2012 for more systematic cross-national time-series analyses.

15 However, it is unclear yet whether leftist upsurge in Argentina since the 2000s can be classified as embedded cohesiveness, based on Table 9.3, as the labor–civic solidarity is neither deeply rooted in informal civil society nor composed of a wide range of different social groups, compared to its Brazilian counterpart. On one hand, Kirchnerism

seems to be a revival of Peronism in the form of leftist populism without a thick, voluntaristic civil society base, a configuration which has been endemic for decades in weakly institutionalized Argentine politics. On the other hand, the Kirchners' regimes and their impacts on social policies demonstrate that changes in cohesiveness may be driven by changes in leadership structure (which is not necessarily implied in the EC framework). Therefore, one may argue that it was the Kirchners' leftist, top-down mobilization capacity that drove expansionary social policy reforms in Argentina, rather than the bottom-up social mobilization process implied by the changes in embeddedness and cohesiveness. Overall, (abrupt) social policy expansion in Argentina during the Kirchners' regimes leaves room for alternative explanations such as the (autonomous) roles of partisan bureaucrats and politicians.

16 As the South Korean universal pension program has not yet fully developed, its public pension spending has stayed at a fairly low level (2.2 percent of GDP in 2011, the third lowest among the OECD countries; OECD 2016). In the latest publication by ILO (2014–5), the two countries spent roughly identical amounts on social protection (9.30 percent of GDP for South Korea and 9.58 percent for Taiwan)

17 However, the coverage of National Health Insurance was limited to employees in firms with five or more employees in the private sector, with employees in firms with fewer than five being left as 'voluntary coverage' and public sector workers, teachers, and farmers belonging to separate special systems (USA Social Security Adminstration 2014/15). Therefore, like its pension system, Taiwan's 'National' Health Insurance is hardly a universal system in terms of its coverage, but a fragmented system for different social groups and occupations.

18 One may wonder about the effect of the prior level of civic associational membership stock (Putnam 2000) on welfare states. However, the level of and change in associational membership, as shown in Table 9.1, do not significantly contribute to explaining variations in the welfare states of the four countries. They simply capture the rich stock of social capital in Brazil, and indicate little difference among Argentina, South Korea, and Taiwan. South Korea holds slightly higher stock (especially stock II) than the other two, but there is little change over time in each of the three countries. In contrast to this stability in membership stock, embeddedness captured by intersectoral co-memberships vary noticeably over time in all three countries, where there are dramatic changes in their welfare states. The South Korean case, showing different directions of membership stock and co-membership linkages during the course of institutionalization of associational spheres, highlights the importance of the 'relational' approach over a conventional 'stock'-based approach.

19 The difference is less pronounced compared with the Argentina–Brazil contrast, but the parties and unions are clearly more densely connected to each other and with other non-formal civic associations in South Korea than in Taiwan during this period.

20 See Chapters 4 and 5 for the PSPD's role in reforming National Pension in late 1990s.

21 As for the National Pension (introduced in 2007), the newly added scheme for the former noninsured does not require any contributions from employers; the insured person's flat rate contribution (60 percent) is combined with the government's flat rate funding (40 percent).

22 The details of the process of expansion of pensions in the late 1990s in South Korea are provided in Chapter 5. Although Chapter 5 highlighted the difference in the roles and capacities of advocacy coalitions in the enactment processes of national pensions and national health care systems within South Korea, in this chapter I focus on (wider) cross-national variations in the institutional features of social policy programs in the two countries.

23 In contrast to pensions, in which the PSPD played a central role, the integration of health care societies would have been impossible without the core KCTU unions (the

KHMU and the KFMA) playing leading roles, and without agreements from large conglomerate unions, as described in details in Chapters 4 to 6.

24 During the period of 'expansion' of social policy regimes, public social protection expenditure precipitously increased from 2.25 percent (as a percentage of GDP) in 1990 to 9.4 percent in 2009 in South Korea (leveling off during the conservative Lee regime until 2012), it did not change much in Taiwan (8.0 percent in 1990, 10.13 percent in 2005, and 9.68 percent in 2010). However, Chi and Kwon (2012), after analyzing market income inequality and disposable income inequality data in the two countries, report that Taiwan did a better job in decreasing market income inequality. They estimated that "nearly two-thirds of the increase in wage inequality has been reduced by government taxation and transfer policies" in Taiwan (p. 905).

25 While it is too early to judge, the Taiwanese case in the 2010s, in which a leftist candidate, Tsai Ing-wen, took over the presidential office in 2016, could potentially be another case of embedded cohesiveness.

26 Note that the cohesiveness measure in Figure 9.8 and Table 9.4 is based on the broad definition – unions' ties with all political parties and professional associations – not the narrow definition used earlier – unions' ties with the incumbent party. Therefore, its values are not necessarily in accordance with (qualitative) cohesiveness values in Chapters 7 and 8.

27 Under limited democracy or transition to democracy, in which formal and informal organizations are not yet fully developed, a (former authoritarian) incumbent rightwing party may have the autonomy to initiate policy reforms even without allies in the formal sector, as the KMT'S 1995 health care reform illustrates. This path is often utilized by state-centric theory as an illustration of the critical role of state bureaucrats in initiating expansionary social policy reforms.

28 The KCTU's participation in the NCHIU in 1998 could be a case of embedded cohesiveness, while the general strike jointly led by the KCTU and the FKTU in South Korea in 1996–7 is a typical case of embeddedness without cohesiveness. Also, the integration of health care societies in the late 1990s and early 2000s in South Korea could be a case of embedded cohesiveness. In Chapter 8, however, I treated the KCTU in the 1990s as a case of 'embeddedness without cohesiveness.'

29 These over-time changes of cohesiveness and embeddedness are built upon columns A and D in Table 9.3, when data are present for all four countries (1995–2005).

30 This stronger role of embeddedness (than cohesiveness) in social policy reforms is well in accordance with the game theoretical models in Appendix C and results from the tentative regression analyses in Appendix E.

31 Under East Asian developmental state tradition, expansion game 2 can be easily transformed into a 'state-initiated game' in which the state initiates selective reform and unions respond to it with acquiescence.

32 As I discussed in Chapter 8, these recent reversals of labor politics in the two countries are fairly in line with the ones described in Lee's (2011) recent work, which highlights the relative success of Taiwanese labor movements' institutional politics over the record of their South Korean counterparts.

33 Some may wonder if the EC approach can be generalizable to a wider range of countries, e.g. rich democracies. In a separate cross-national study in Appendix E with a larger set of both developed and developing countries (N = 50), I found that higher embeddedness leads to bigger welfare states in countries with good governance or highly institutionalized democracy. Although the governance issue itself is an intriguing and an important topic to explore, I decided not to delve into it in this book, and therefore limited the scope to the four recently democratized, more advanced developing societies.

Chapter 10: Conclusion

1 The congruence between Esping-Andersen's and Baldwin's perspectives on class alliance become more obvious in Esping-Andersen's 1999 book, where he fully embraces Baldwin's 'risk class category,' discounting laborists' 'class position category.' In contrast, Korpi and Palme (2003) and Huber and Stephens (2001) stick to the more traditional sociological notion of 'class positions' and a 'class-based power resource model' and their significance in accounting for welfare state outcomes.

2 Huber and Stephens (2001) point out that, in Sweden, the agrarians "were not the policy initiators, but once a policy was initiated they sought to ensure that its structure was favorable to their primary constituency, family farmers" (p. 118). In South Korea, however, the agrarian class and allied intellectuals were the initiators of the universal scheme, while the working class (unions) joined the movement later with the KCTU's conscious efforts to embrace social reforms. The unions then played a decisive role in letting the universal plan pass the legislative bar (Chapter 5). In both cases, if the reform movements had been led only by farmers, nothing would have happened.

3 While Thelen's coalitional politics is limited to active/passive labor market policies and training, my notion of embeddedness implies broader coalitions with civil society groups in the fields of social welfare, environmental, and human rights policies, as well as labor market policies.

4 The sociology of neo-institutionalism may call this move 'institutional isomorphism' (DiMaggio and Powell 1983; Meyer *et al.* 1997; Boli and Thomas 1997) in the sense that a local actor attempts to converge to a 'global norm.' But under the EC approach, it is still a specific instance of four ideal spaces determined by cohesiveness and embeddedness. For instance, under embedded cohesiveness, both union leaders and partisan state elites (of Brazil) do not have any incentive to imitate 'rationalized world culture.' Even for disarticulated cohesiveness, an ultimate driving force of importing neo-liberal market reform or expansionary welfare reform is a strategic move of partisan politicians to attract newly emerging median voters who may align with new market-oriented principles (in Menem's Argentina) or to allure relatively impoverished median voters who may desire more redistribution from the fruits of long-term economic growth (in democratized Taiwan and South Korea). For this reason, I did not rely on the notion of a 'world society' or similar variant in this book, which compounds actors' different incentives and structural conditions under the notions of 'isomorphism' and 'imitation.'

Appendix B

1 I only utilize 'active members' to construct a co-membership matrix among eight associational types (church, cultural clubs, labor unions, political parties, professional associations, environmental associations, sport clubs, and charity groups) for each country module. I believe that when I use active members, excluding non-active members, I can capture the structure of 'leadership networks' of civic associational community more accurately. I also investigate 'active members' with 'social movement experiences' using other questionnaires on having joined demonstrations/strikes/occupation/petitions, and the results were largely identical with the ones presented in the current chapter.

Appendix C

1 Another implicit assumption is that non-organized workers such as precarious irregular workers or labor market outsiders, by definition, do not have a centralized bargaining

unit, thereby being deprived of the chance to take part in the negotiation between the state and unions. Therefore, implicitly, there is one more actor in the model who has a payoff function, but the game is only conducted between two actors.

Appendix D

1 I made additional efforts to add more data to classify attributes, and then reanalyze the updated version. I am also updating the latest 2014–15 data, which I did not include in this book project. I thank both Dr. Ŭn and Kang for not only granting me access to their datasets, but also helping me update the data by providing necessary information. Kang originally constructed the 2005 dataset with the advice of Dr. Ŭn, who collected the same structure of associational co-affiliation networks in the 1980s and the 1990s in her dissertation (I do not use 1985–86 data because of the too-small number of associations). I also appreciate two graduate students, Myŏng-Sŏn Mun and Bo-Yŏng Pak, for having spent significant time on re-compiling (updating and arranging) Kang's data.
2 The year is the third year of the reformist M. H. Rho regime, and one year after the DLP's historic success in the general election.
3 All measures were calculated by UCINET 6 (ver. 6.592); see Borgatti *et al.* (2002).
4 One may interpret these multiple zeros for the cells of the incumbent (Open Uri) party as clear evidence that unions' and progressive civic associations' cohesive ties with the incumbent reformist party evaporated in the 2000s. However, it is cumbersome to treat all of these multiple zeros as signs of 'no linkages' between the incumbent party and the 1,744 associations. These events were ultimately 'petitions' to the state, and therefore the incumbent party may not have formally taken part in them, as participating in any of these events itself could have signaled endorsement of that petition. For this reason, vertical, cohesive linkages between the state and unions/civic associations must have been operating through more informal channels. In Chapter 6, I contended that cohesive ties between the reformist incumbent party and unions/progressive civic associations significantly declined based on my qualitative data, but would not utilize these multiple zeros to support such argument.
5 The results do not change significantly even if the FKTU is excluded from the data.

Appendix E

1 Other than these variables in the baseline model, I also tested the effects of electoral system (Iversen and Soskice 2009) and cumulative left party incumbency (Huber and Stephens 2001) on welfare state size, along with regional indicators (Africa, South Asia, and Middle East). These variables were statistically non-significant in any meaningful way, and were therefore dropped from the models with consideration of the small sample size.
2 The other most prominent measure of power resource theory, (cumulative) left party incumbency, which has been one of the most consistent predictors of welfare state size for rich democracies (Huber, Ragin, and Stephens 1993; Huber and Stephens 2001), was tested but non-significant.
3 Note that the high vs. low dichotomous measure worked as a conditional switcher of the relationship only when the threshold was set at a fairly high level for both governance and democracy indicators (high governance countries if legal justice index is equal to or bigger than 0.7, while high democracy countries if polity II index reaches the full score, 10). Note also that the formerly significant GDP per capita and population over 65 became non-significant in model 3.

Bibliography

Abbott, Andrew. 2016. *Processual Sociology*. Chicago: University of Chicago Press.

Acemoglu, Daron, and James A. Robinson. 2005. *Economic Origins of Dictatorship and Democracy*. New York: Cambridge University Press.

Acemoglu, Daron, Simon Johnson, and James A. Robinson. 2012. "The Colonial Origins of Comparative Development: An Empirical Investigation: Reply." *The American Economic Review* 102, no. 6: 3077–110.

Acemoglu, Daron, James A. Robinson, and Dan Woren. 2012. *Why Nations Fail: The Origins of Power, Prosperity and Poverty*. New York: Crown Business.

Ahlquist, John S., and Margaret Levi. 2013. *In the Interest of Others: Organizations and Social Activism*. Princeton, NJ: Princeton University Press.

Akchurin, Maria, and Cheol-Sung Lee. 2013. "Pathways to Empowerment Repertoires of Women's Activism and Gender Earnings Equality." *American Sociological Review* 78: 679–701.

Alavi, Hamza. 1972. "The State in Post-Colonial Societies: Pakistan and Bangladesh." *New Left Review* 74, no. 1: 59–81.

Aldrich, Howard E., and Martin Ruef. 2006. *Organizations Evolving*, 2nd ed. Thousand Oaks, CA: Sage.

Alexander, Jeffrey C. 2006. *The Civic Sphere*. New York: Oxford University Press.

Almeida, Paul. 2008. "The Sequencing of Success: Organizing Templates and Neoliberal Policy Outcomes." *Mobilization: An International Quarterly* 13, no. 2: 165–87.

Alvarez, R. Michael, Geoffrey Garrett, and Peter Lange. 1991. "Government Partisanship, Labor Organization, and Macroeconomic Performance." *The American Political Science Review* 85, no. 2): 539–56.

Amenta, Edwin. 1998. *Bold Relief: Institutional Politics and the Origins of Modern American Social Policy*. Princeton, NJ: Princeton University Press.

2006. *When Movements Matter: The Townsend Plan and the Rise of Social Security*. Princeton, NJ: Princeton University Press.

Amenta, Edwin, and Michael P. Young. 1999. "Making an Impact: Conceptual and Methodological Implications of the Collective Goods Criterion." Pp. 22–41 in *How Social Movements Matter*. Edited by Marco Giugni, Doug McAdam, and Charles Tilly. Minneapolis: University of Minnesota Press.

Amenta, Edwin, Neal Caren, and Sheera Joy Olasky. 2005. "Age for Leisure? Political Mediation and the Impact of the Pension Movement on U.S. Old-Age Policy." *American Sociological Review* 70, no. 3: 516–38.

Amenta, Edwin, Neal Caren, Elizabeth Chiarello, and Yang Su.. 2011. "The Political Consequences of Social Movements."*Annual Review of Sociology* 36: 287–307.

Ames, Barry. 2001. *The Deadlock of Democracy in Brazil: Interests, Identities and Institutions*. Ann Arbor: University of Michigan Press.

ANDES-SN (Sindicato Nacional dos Docentes das Instituições de Ensino Superior). 2013. "Mais de 20 Mil Trabalhadores Ocupam a Esplanada em Marcha Vitoriosa." [More than 20 thousand workers occupy the Esplanade in March Victorious]. São Paulo, April 24, 2013. Available at www.andes.org.br/andes/print-ultimas-noticias.andes?id=5987 (accessed October 24, 2014).

Andrews, Kenneth T. 2001. "Social Movements and Policy Implementation: The Mississippi Civil Rights Movement and the War on Poverty, 1965 to 1971." *American Sociological Review* 66, no. 1: 71–95.

2004. *Freedom is a Constant Struggle: The Mississippi Civil Rights Movement and its Legacy*. Chicago: University of Chicago Press.

Arellano, Karina, and Lucia De Gennaro. 2002. *Identidades, Palabras, e Imaginarios. Entrevistas y Análisis*. [Identities, Words, and Imaginary. Interviews and Analysis] Buenos Aires: Instituto de Estudios y Formación de la CTA.

"As manifestações no Brasil" [Demonstrations in Brazil]. 1997. *Jornal Folha da Tarde*, São Paulo, July 26.

Auyero, Javier. 1999. ""From the Client's Point(s) of View': How Poor People Perceive and Evaluate Political Clientelism." *Theory and Society* 28, no. 2 (April): 297–334.

2000. *Poor People's Politics: Peronist Survival Networks and the Legacy of Evita*. Durham, NC: Duke University Press.

Avelino, George, David S. Brown, and Wendy Hunter. 2005. "The Effects of Capital Mobility, Trade Openness, and Democracy on Social Spending in Latin America, 1980–1999." *American Journal of Political Science* 49, no. 3: 625–41.

Avritzer, Leonardo. 2009. *Participatory Institutions in Democratic Brazil*. Baltimore, MD: Johns Hopkins University Press.

Axelrod, Robert. 1984. *The Evolution of Cooperation*. New York: Basic Books.

Babb, Sarah. 2001. *Managing Mexico: Economists from Nationalism to Neoliberalism*. Princeton, NJ, and Oxford: Princeton University Press.

Baiocchi, Gianpaolo. 2005. *Militants and Citizens: The Politics of Participatory Democracy in Porto Alegre*. Stanford, CA: Stanford University Press.

Baiocchi, Gianpaolo, Patrick Heller, and Marcelo Silva. 2011. *Bootstrapping Democracy: Transforming Local Governance and Civil Society in Brazil*. Stanford, CA: Stanford University Press.

Baldwin, Peter. 1990. *The Politics of Social Solidarity: Class Bases of the European Welfare State 1875–1975*. Cambridge: Cambridge University Press.

Barr, Nicholas. 1992. "Economic Theory and the Welfare State: A Survey and Interpretation." *Journal of Economic literature* 30, no. 2: 741–803.

Becker, Gary S. 1976. *The Economic Approach to Human Behavior*. Chicago: University of Chicago Press,.

1985. "Public Policies, Pressure Groups, and Dead Weight Costs."*Journal of Public Economics* 28, no. 3: 329–47.

Berman, Sheri. 1997. "Civil Society and the Collapse of the Weimar Republic." *World Politics* 49: 401–29.

Boito Jr., Armando. 1991. *O Sindicalismo de Estado no Brasil: Uma Análise Crítica da Estrutura Sindical* [The State of Trade Unionism in Brazil : A Critical Analysis of the Trade Union Structure]. São Paulo: Unicamp, Hucitec.

Boito, Armando, and Paula Regina Pereira Marcelino. 2011. "Decline in Unionism? An Analysis of the New Wave of Strikes in Brazil." *Latin American Perspectives* 38, no. 5: 62–73.

Boli, John, and George M. Thomas. 1997. "World Culture in the World Polity: A Century of International Non-Governmental Organizations." *American Sociological Review* 62, no. 2: 171–90.

Borgatti, Stephen, and Martin G. Everett. 1997. "Network Analysis of 2-Mode Data." *Social Networks* 19: 243–69.

Borgatti, Stephen, Martin G. Everett, and Linton C. Freeman. 2002. UCINET 6 (Manual) for Windows: Software for Social Network Analysis. Harvard, MA: Analytic Technologies.

Bourdieu, Pierre. 1993. *The Field of Cultural Production: Essays on Art and Literature.* Edited by Randal Johnson. New York: Columbia University Press.

Brady, David, Jason Beckfield, and Martin Seeleib-Kaiser. 2005. "Economic Globalization and the Welfare State in Affluent Democracies, 1975–2001." *American Sociological Review* 70, no. 6: 921–48.

Branford, Sue, and Bernardo Kucinski. 2003. *Politics Transformed: Lula and the Workers' Party in Brazil.* New York: The New Press.

Breiger, Ronald. 1974. "The Duality of Persons and Groups." *Social Forces* 53: 191–90.

Brooks, Sarah M. 2008. *Social Protection and the Market in Latin America: The Transformation of Social Security Institutions.* New York: Cambridge University Press.

Burgess, Katrina. 2004. *Parties and Unions in the New Global Economy.* Pittsburgh, PA: University of Pittsburgh Press.

Burgess, Katrina, and Steven Levitsky. 2003. "Explaining Populist Party Adaptation in Latin America: Environmental and Organizational Determinants of Party Change in Argentina, Mexico, Peru, and Venezuela." *Comparative Political Studies* 36, no. 8: 881–911.

Burstein, Paul. 1991. "Legal Mobilization as a Social Movement Tactic: The Struggle for Equal Employment Opportunity." *The American Journal of Sociology* 96: 1201–25.

Burt, Ronald S. 1992. *Structural Holes.* Cambridge, MA: Harvard University Press.

Calmfors, Lars, and John Driffill. 1988. "Bargaining Structure, Corporatism and Macroeconomic Performance." *Economic policy* 3: 13–61.

Calvo, Ernesto, and M. Victoria Murillo. 2013. "When Parties Meet Voters Assessing Political Linkages Through Partisan Networks and Distributive Expectations in Argentina and Chile." *Comparative Political Studies* 45: 851–82.

Cameron, David R. 1978. "The Expansion of the Public Economy: A Comparative Analysis." *American Political Science Review* 72, no. 4: 1243–61.

Carey, John M., and Matthew Soberg Shugart. 1994. "Incentives to Cultivate a Personal Vote: A Rank Ordering of Electoral Formulas." *Electoral Studies* 14, no. 4: 417–39.

Carpenter, Daniel. 2012. "Is Health Politics Different?" *Annual Review of Political Science* 15: 287–311.

Castles, Francis Geoffrey. 1985. *The Working Class and Welfare: Reflections on the Political Development of the Welfare State in Australia and New Zealand, 1890–1980.* Wellington: Allen and Unwin.

Castles, Francis, Rolf Gerritsen, and Jack Vowles. 1996. "Introduction: Setting the Scene for Economic and Political Change." Pp. 1–21 in *The Great Experiment: Labour Parties and Public Policy Transformation in Australia and New Zealand.* Edited by Frances Castles, Rolf Gerritsen, and Jack Vowles. St. Leonards: Allen & Unwin Pty Ltd.

Central Única dos Trabalhadores (CUT). 2003a. *A Revista: Central Única dos Trabalhadores.* São Paulo: Takano.

2003b. "CUT Comanda Protesto contra Reforma da Previdência."[Command Protest against Pension Reform] Portal Terra, June 10, 2003. Available at http://noticias.terra.com.br/brasil/noticias/0,,OI112342-EI1194,00CUT+comanda+protesto+contra+reforma+da+Previdencia.html (accessed September 9, 2014).

2009. *Cronologia das Lutas (1981–2009)* [Chronology of the Struggles, 1981–2009]. São Paulo: CUT.

2013. "Dia Nacional de mobilização contra o fator previdenciário." [National Day of Mobilization against Pension Reform]. São Paulo, CEDOC, December 11, 2013. Available at http://cedoc.cut.org.br/cronologia-das-lutas (accessed October 20, 2014).

Cerutti, Paula, Anna Fruttero, Margaret Grosh, Silvana Kostenbaum, Maria Laura Oliveri, Claudia Rodriguez-Alas, and Victoria Strokova. 2014. "Social Assistance and Labor Market Programs in Latin America Methodology and Key Findings from the Social Protection Database." *Social Protection and Labor Discussion Paper Series* No. 1401. Available at www.worldbank.org/servlet/WDSContentServer/WDSP/IB/2014/06/27/000470435_20140627092449/Rendered/PDF/887690WP0P1321085243B00PUBLIC001401.pdf (accessed June 18, 2016).

CFL. 2005–2013. Press releases and event listings. Available at www.cfl.org.tw/page1.aspx-?no=100100204112638212 (accessed February 1, 2013). In Chinese.

Chalmers, Douglas A., Scott B. Martin, and Kerianne Piester. 1998. "Associative Networks: New Structures of Representation for the Popular Sectors?" Pp. 543–82 in *The New Politics of Inequality in Latin America: Rethinking Participation and Representation*. Edited by D. A. Chalmers *et al.* New York: Oxford University Press.

Chang, Chi-yŏn, *et al.* 2011. *Nodong sijang kujo wa sahoe pojang ch'egye ŭi chŏnghapsŏng* [The Consistency between the Structure of Labor Market and Social Welfare System]. Seoul: Han'guk Nodong Yŏn'guwŏn.

Chang, Chi-yŏn, Ch'oe Yŏng-jun, Kim Ki-sŏn, and Kang Sŏng-t'ae. 2012. *OECD chuyoguk ŭi koyong poho wa sahoejŏk poho* [Employment Protection and Social Protection in Rich OECD Countries]. Seoul: Han'guk Nodong Yŏn'guwŏn.

Chen, Chien-Hsun. 2005. "Taiwan's Burgeoning Budget Deficit: A Crisis in the Making?" *Asian Survey* 45, no. 3 (May–June): 383–96.

Chi, Eunju, and Hyeok Yong Kwon. 2012. "Unequal New Democracies in East Asia: Rising Inequality and Government Responses in South Korea and Taiwan." *Asian Survey* 52, no. 5: 900–23.

Cho, Hyo-rae. 2010. *Nodong chohap minjujuŭi* [Union Democracy]. Seoul: Humanit'asŭ.

Cho, Hyŏn-yŏn. 2009. *Han'guk chinbo chŏngdang undongsa* [A History of Korean Progressive Parties]. Seoul: Humanit'asŭ.

Cho, Ton-mun, and Yi Su-bong, eds. 2008. *Minju nojo undong 20-yŏn* [Twenty Years of Democratic Labor Movements]. Seoul: Humanit'asŭ.

Ch'oe, Chang-jip. 1996. *Han'guk minjujuŭi ŭi chogŏn kwa chŏnmang* [The Condition and Prospect of Korean Democracy]. Seoul: Nanam Ch'ulp'an.

Choi, Young-Jun. 2008. "Pension Policy and Politics in East Aisa." *Policy & Politics* 36: 127–44.

Chŏng, I-hwan. 2013. *Han'guk koyong ch'ejeron* [A Theory of the Korean Employment Regime]. Seoul: Humanit'asŭ.

Chŏng, Yŏng-t'ae. 2011. "Raibŏl chŏngch'i undong tanche ŭi yŏnhap e ŭihan chŏngdang kŏnsŏl" [Formation of a Political Party through the Merger of Political Movement Organizations: The Case of the Democratic Labor Party of Korea]. *Han'guk Chŏngch'i Yŏn'gu* 22, no. 2: 79–106.

Chu, Yin-wah. 1996. "Democracy and Organized Labor in Taiwan: The 1986 Transition." *Asia Survey* 36, no. 5: 495–510.

Clark, Terry Nichols, and Seymour Martin Lipset. 2001. *The Breakdown of Class Politics: A Debate on Post-Industrial Stratification*. Baltimore, MD: Johns Hopkins University Press.

Clawson, Dan. 2003. *The Next Upsurge: Labor and the New Social Movements*. Ithaca, NY: Cornell University Press.

Clawson, D., and M. A. Clawson. 1999. "What Has Happened to the US Labor Movement? Union Decline and Renewal." *Annual Review of Sociology* 25: 95–119.

Clemens, Elisabeth S. 1993. "Organizational Repertoires and Institutional Change: Women's Groups and the Transformation of US Politics, 1890–1920." *American Journal of Sociology* 98: 755–98.

   1997. *The People's Lobby: Organizational Innovation and the Rise of Interest Group Politics in the United States, 1890–1925.* Chicago: University of Chicago Press.

Coleman, James S. 1988. "Social Capital in the Creation of Human Capital." *American Journal of Sociology* 94: 95–120.

   1990. *Foundations of Social Theory.* Cambridge, MA: Belknap Press of Harvard University Press.

Collier, David. 1995. "Trajectory of a Concept: 'Corporatism' in the Study of Latin American Politics." Pp. 135–62 in *Latin America in Comparative Perspective.* Edited by P. H. Smith. Boulder, CO: Westview.

Collier, Ruth Berins. 1999. *Paths Toward Democracy: The Working Class and Elites in Western Europe and South America.* New York: Cambridge University Press.

Collier, Ruth B., and David Collier. 1991. *Shaping the Political Arena: Critical Junctures, the Labor Movement, and Regime Dynamics in Latin America.* Princeton, NJ: Princeton University Press.

Collier, Ruth Berins, and Samuel Handlin. 2009. "General Patterns and Emerging Differences." Pp. 293–328 in *Reorganizing Popular Politics: Participation and the New Interest Regime in Latin America.* Edited by Ruth B. Collier and Samuel Handlin. University Park: Pennsylvania State University Press.

Cornwell, Benjamin, and Jill Ann Harrison. 2004. "Union Members and Voluntary Associations: Membership Overlap as a Case of Organizational Embeddedness." *American Sociological Review* 69: 862–81.

Cress, Daniel M., and David A. Snow. 2000. "The Outcomes of Homeless Mobilization: The Influence of Organization, Disruption, Political Mediation, and Framing." *American Journal of Sociology* 105: 1063–104.

Crouch, Colin. 1993. *Industrial Relations and European State Traditions.* Oxford: Oxford University Press.

Curtis, Russell L., and Louis A. Zurcher. 1973. "Stable Resources of Protest Movements: The Multi-Organizational Field." *Social forces* 52, no. 1: 53–61.

Cutright, Phillips. 1965. "Political Structure, Economic Development, and National Social Security Programs." *American Journal of Sociology* 70: 537–50.

Dark, Taylor E. 1999. *The Unions and the Democrats.* Ithaca, NY: Cornell University Press.

De La O, Ana. 2011. *The Politics of Conditional Cash Transfers.* New Haven, CT: Yale University Press.

Del Campo, Hugo. 2005. *Sindicalismo y Peronismo: Los Comienzos de un Vínculo Perdurable* [Trade unionism and Peronism: The Beginning of a Lasting Tie]. Buenos Aires: Siglo XXI Editores.

Diamond, Larry, and Gi-Wook Shin. 2014. "Introduction." Pp.1–26 in *New Challenges for Maturing Democracies in Korea and Taiwan.* Stanford, Stanford University Press.

Diani, Mario. 2003. "Introduction." Pp. 1–20 in *Social Movements and Networks: Relational Approaches to Collective Action.* Edited by M. Diani and D. McAdam. New York: Oxford University Press.

DiMaggio, Paul. 1990. "Cultural Aspects of Economic Action and Organization." Pp.113–36 in *Beyond the Marketplace.* Edited by R. Friedland and A. F. Robertson. New York: Aldine de Gruyter.

   1997. "Culture and Cognition." *Annual Review of Sociology* 23, no. 1: 263–87.

DiMaggio, Paul and Walter W. Powell. 1983. "The Iron Cage Revisited: Institutional Isomorphism and Collective Rationality in Organizational Fields." *American Sociological Review* 48: 147–60.

Dixon, Marc, Vincent J. Roscigno, and Randy Hodson. 2004. "Unions, Solidarity, and Striking." *Social Forces* 83: 3–33.

Economist, The. 2010. "Brazil's Bolsa Familia: How to Get Children out of Jobs and into School." July 29. Available at www.economist.com/node/16690887 (accessed June 22, 2016).

Edwards, Bob, and John D. McCarthy. 2004. "Resources and Social Movement Mobilization." Pp. 116–52 in *The Blackwell Companion to Social Movements*. Edited by D. A. Snow, S. A. Soule, and H. Kriesi. Malden, MA: Blackwell.

Eimer, Stuart. 1999. "From 'Business Unionism' to 'Social Movement Unionism': The Case of the AFL-CIO Milwaukee County Labor Council." *Labor Studies Journal* 24: 63–81.

Eisinger, Peter K. 1973. "The Conditions of Protest Behavior in American Cities." *American Political Science Review* 67, no. 1: 11–28.

Elster, Jon. 1998. "A Plea for Mechanisms." Pp. 45–73 in *Social Mechanisms: An Analytical Approach to Social Theory*. Edited by P. Hedström and R. Swedberg. New York: Cambridge University Press.

Emirbayer, Mustafa. 1997. "Manifesto for a Relational Sociology." *American Journal of Sociology* 103: 281–317.

Esping-Andersen, Gøsta. 1985. *Politics against Markets*. Princeton, NJ: Princeton University Press.

　1990. *The Three Worlds of Welfare Capitalism*. Princeton, NJ: Princeton University Press.

　1999. *Social Foundations of Postindustrial Economies*. New York: Oxford University Press.

Estevez-Abe, Margarita, Torben Iversen, and David Soskice. 2001. "Social Protection and the Formation of Skills: A Reinterpretation of the Welfare State." Pp. 145–33 in *Varieties of Capitalism: The Institutional Foundations of Comparative Advantage*. Edited by Peter Hall and David Soskice. New York: Oxford University Press.

Etchemendy, Sebastián, and Ruth Berins Collier. 2007. "Down but Not Out: Union Resurgence and Segmented Neocorporatism in Argentina (2003–2007)." *Politics and Society* 35, no. 3 (September): 363–401.

Etchemendy, Sebastián, and Candelaria Garay. 2011. "Argentina's Left Populism in Comparative Perspective." Pp. 283–305 in *The Resurgence of the Latin American Left*. Edited by S. Levitsky and K. Roberts. Baltimore, MD: Johns Hopkins University Press.

Evans, Peter B. 1995. *Embedded Autonomy: States and Industrial Transformation*. Princeton, NJ: Princeton University Press.

Evans, Peter, Evelyne Huber, and John D. Stephens. Forthcoming. "The Political Foundations of State Effectiveness." In *State Building in the Developing World*. Edited by Miguel Centeno, Atul Kohli, and Deborah Yashar. Unpublished manuscript.

Falleti, Tulia. 2010. "Infiltrating the State: The Evolution of Healthcare Reforms in Brazil." Pp. 38–62 in *Explaining Institutional Change: Ambiguity, Agency, and Power*. Edited by J. Mahoney and K. Thelen. Cambridge: Cambridge University Press.

Fantasia, Rick and Judith Stepan-Norris. 2004. "The Labor Movement in Motion." Pp. 555–75 in *The Blackwell Companion to Social Movements*. Edited by D. A. Snow, S. A. Soule, and H. Kriesti. Malden, MA: Blackwell Publishing.

Fantasia, Rick, and Kim Voss. 2004. *Hard Work: Remaking the American Labor Movement*. Berkeley and Los Angeles: University of California Press.

Fearon, J. D. 1995. "Rationalist Explanations for War." *International Organization* 49: 379–79.

Fell, Dafydd. 2005. *Party Politics in Taiwan: Party Change and the Democratic Evolution of Taiwan, 1991–2004*. New York: Routledge.

Fligstein, Neil. 1997. "Social Skill and Institutional Theory." *American Behavioral Scientist* 40, no. 4: 397–405.

Fligstein, Neil, and Doug McAdam. 2011. "Toward a General Theory of Strategic Action Fields." *Sociological Theory* 29: 1–26.

Franklin, Mark N., Thomas T. Mackie, and Henry Valen. 1992. *Electoral Change*. Colchester, UK: ECPR Press.

Fraser, Nancy. 1990. "Struggle over Needs: Outline of a Socialist-Feminist Critical Theory of Late-Capitalist Political Culture." Pp. 199–225 in *Women, the State, and Welfare*. Edited by L. Gordon. Madison: University of Wisconsin Press.

French, John D. 1992. *The Brazilian Workers' ABC: Class Conflict and Alliances in Modern São Paulo*. Chapel Hill: University of North Carolina Press.

Ganz, Marshall. 2000. "Resources and Resourcefulness: Strategic Capacity in the Unionization of California Agriculture: 1959–1966. *American Journal of Sociology* 10. No. 4: 1003–62.

Garrett, Geoffrey. 1998. *Partisan Politics in the Global Economy*. New York: Cambridge University Press.

Gerhards, Jurgen, and Dieter Rucht. 1992. "Mesomobilization." *American Journal of Sociology* 98: 555–95.

Giugni, Marco G. 2004. "Personal and Biographical Consequences." Pp. 489–507 in *The Blackwell Companion to Social Movements*. Edited by D. A. Snow, S. A. Soule, and H. Kriesi. Malden, MA: Blackwell.

Godio, Julio. 1987. *El Movimiento obrero Argentino (1955–1990)* [The Argentine Labor Movement]. Buenos Aires: Fundación Fiedrich Ebert.

Goldstone, Jack A. 1991. *Revolution and Rebellion in the Early Modern World*. Berkeley and Los Angeles: University of California Press.

Gordillo, Marta, Víctor Lavagno, and Antonio Francisco Cafiero. 1987. *Los Hombres de Perón: el peronismo renovador* [The Men of Peron: The Peronism Renovator]. Buenos Aires: Puntosur.

Gould, Roger V. 1989. "Power and Structure in Community Elites." *Social Forces* 68, no. 2: 531–52.

1991. "Multiple Networks and Mobilization in the Paris Commune, 1871." *American Sociological Review* 56: 716–29.

1995. *Insurgent Identities: Class, Community, and Protest in Paris from 1848 to the Commune*. Chicago: University of Chicago Press.

Gould, Roger V., and Roberto M. Fernandez. 1989. "Structures of Mediation: A Formal Approach to Brokerage in Transaction Networks." *Sociological Methodology* 19: 89–126.

Gramsci, Antonio. 1971. *Selections from the Prison Notebooks*. New York: International Publishers.

Granovetter, Mark. 1985. "Economic Action and Social Structure: The Problem of Embeddedness." *American Journal of Sociology* 91, no. 3: 481–510.

2002. "A Theoretical Agenda for Economic Sociology." Pp. 35–60 in *The New Economic Sociology: Developments in an Emerging Field*. Edited by Mauro F. Guillén, Randall Collins, Paula England, and Marshall Meyer. New York: Russell Sage Foundation.

Grossman, Gene M., and Elhanan Helpman. 2002. *Special Interest Politics*. Cambridge, MA: MIT Press.

Guidry, John A. 2003. "Not Just Another Labor Party The Workers' Party and Democracy in Brazil." *Labor Studies Journal* 28: 83–108.

Gutiérrez, Ricardo. 1998. "Desindicalización y cambio organizativo del peronismo Argentino, 1982–1995." XXI Latin American Studies Association Conference, September 1998, Chicago.

Habermas, Jürgen. 1984. *The Theory of Communicative Action I: Reason and the Rationalization of Society*. Boston, MA: Beacon Press.

1987. *The Theory of Communicative Action II: Lifeworld and System: A Critique of Functionalist Reason*. Boston, MA: Beacon Press.

1991[1962]. *The Structural Transformation of the Public Sphere: An Inquiry into a Category of Bourgeois Society*. Cambridge, MA: The MIT Press.

1996. *Between Facts and Norms: Contributions to a Discourse Theory of Law and Democracy*. Translated by William Rehg. Cambridge: Polity Press.

Hacker, Jacob. 2002. *Divided Welfare State: The Battle over Public and Private Social Benefits in the United States*. New York: Cambridge University Press.

Haggard, Stephen. 2004. "Institutions and Growth in East Asia." *Studies in Comparative International Development* 38, no. 4: 53–81.

Haggard, Stephen, and Robert Kaufmann. 2008. *Development, Democracy, and Welfare States: Latin America, East Asia, and Eastern Europe*. Princeton, NJ: Princeton University Press.

Hall, Anthony. 2008. "Brazil's Bolsa Familia: A Double-Edged Sword?" *Development and Change* 39, no. 5 (September): 799–822.

Hall, Peter A., and Daniel W. Gingerich. 2009. "Varieties of Capitalism and Institutional Complementarities in the Political Economy: An Empirical Analysis." *British Journal of Political Science* 39, no. 3: 449–82.

Hall, Peter A., and David Soskice, eds. 2001. *Varieties of Capitalism: The Institutional Foundations of Comparative Advantage*. New York: Oxford University Press.

Hall, Peter A. and Rosemary C. R. Taylor. 1996. "Political Science and Three New Institutionalisms." *Political Studies* 44: 936–57.

Han, Tzu-Shian, and Su-fen Chiu. 2000. "Industrial Democracy and Institutional Environments: A Comparison of Germany and Taiwan." *Economic and Industrial Democracy* 21: 147–182.

Hardin, Russell. 2002. *Trust and Trustworthiness*. Russell Sage Foundation.

Hayter, Susan and Valentina Stoevska. 2011. "Social dialogue Indicators: International Statistical Inquiry 2008–9, Technical Brief." International Labour Office, Geneva.

Heclo, Hugh. 1974. *Modern Social Politics in Britain and Sweden*. New Haven, CT: Yale University Press.

Hedström, Peter, and Richard Swedberg. 1998. *Social Mechanisms: An Analytical Approach to Social Theory*. New York: Cambridge University Press.

Heller, Patrick. 1999. *The Labor of Development: Workers and the Transformation of Capitalism in Kerala, India*. Ithaca, NY, and London: Cornell University Press.

Hicks, Alexander M. 1999. *Social Democracy and Welfare Capitalism: A Century of Income Security Politics*. Ithaca, NY: Cornell University Press.

Hicks, Alexander, and Lane Kenworthy. 1998. "Cooperation and Political Economic Performance in Affluent Democratic Capitalism." *American Journal of Sociology* 103: 1631–72.

Higgins, Sean. 2012. "The Impact of Bolsa Família on Poverty: Does Brazil's Conditional Cash Transfer Program Have a Rural Bias?" *The Journal of Politics and Society* 23: 88–125.

Hirsch, Eric L. 1987. *The Theory of Communicative Action II: Lifeworld and System: A Critique of Functionalist Reason*. Boston: Beacon Press.

1990. *Urban Revolt: Ethnic Politics in the Nineteenth-Century Chicago Labor Movement*. Berkeley: University of California Press.

Ho, Ming-sho. 2003. "Democratization and Autonomous Unionism in Taiwan: The Case of Petrochemical Workers." *Issues and Studies* 39, no. 3: 105–36.

2006. "Challenging State Corporatism: The Politics of Taiwan's Labor Federation Movement." *China Journal* 56: 107–27.

2008. "A Working-Class Movement without Class Identity: Taiwan's Independent Labor Union Movement and the Limit of Brotherhood." *Taiwan: A Radical Quarterly in Social Studies* 72. In Chinese.

Hong Il-p'yo. 2007. *Kiro e sŏn simin ippŏp: Han'guk simin ippŏp undong ŭi yŏksa, kujo, tonghak* [Civic Legislation at the Crossroads]. Seoul: Humanit'asŭ.

Houtzager, Peter P. 2001. "Collective Action and Political Authority: Rural Workers, Church, and State in Brazil." *Theory and Society* 30: 1–45.

Howell, Chris, Anthony Daley, and Michel Vale. 1992 "Introduction: The Transformation of Political Exchange." *International Journal of Political Economy* 22, no. 4: 3–16.

HRN (Health Rights Network). 2010. *Healthy World (Kŏnkang Sesang) 2010: Activity Report.* Seoul: HRN.

Hsiao, Michael Hsin-huang. 1992. "The Labor Movement in Taiwan: A Retrospective and Prospective Look." Pp. 151–68 in *Taiwan: Beyond the Economic Miracle.* Edited by D. F. Simon and M. Y. M. Kau. New York: M. E. Sharpe.

Huang, Changling. 2002. "The Politics of Reregulation: Globalization, Democratization, and the Taiwanese Labor Movement." *The Developing Economies* 40, no. 3: 305–26.

Huber, Evelyne, and John D. Stephens. 2001. *Development and Crisis of the Welfare State: Parties and Policies in Global Markets.* Chicago: University of Chicago Press.

2012. *Democracy and the Left.* Chicago: University of Chicago Press.

Huber, Evelyne, Charles Ragin, and John D. Stephens. 1993. "Social Democracy, Christian Democracy, Constitutional Structure, and the Welfare State." *American Journal of Sociology* 99: 711–49.

Huber, Evelyne, François Nielsen, Jenny Pribble, and John D. Stephens. 2006. "Politics and Inequality in Latin America and the Caribbean." *American Sociological Review* 71: 943–63.

Hunter, Wendy. 2010. *The Transformation of the Workers' Party in Brazil, 1989–2009.* New York: Cambridge University Press.

ILO (International Labor Organization). 2010–11 and 2014–15. *World Social Security Report: Providing Coverage in Times of Crisis and Beyond.* Geneva: ILO. Available at www.ilo.org (accessed June 22, 2016).

Im Hyŏn-jin. 2009. *Han'guk ŭi sahoe undong kwa chinbo chŏngdang: "Han'gyŏrye Minjudang," "Minjungdang," "Kaehyŏk Minjudang," Minju Nodongdang'" ŭl chungsim ŭro* [Korean Social Movements and Progressive Parties]. Seoul: Sŏul Taehakkyo Ch'ulp'anbu.

Im, Hyŏn-jin and Kim Pyŏng-guk. 1991. "Nodong ŭi chwajŏl, paebandoen minjuhwa [Labor Frustrated, Democratization Betrayed: Korean Reality of State-Capital-Labor Relationship]." *Kyegan Sasang* (Winter).

Im, Yŏng-il. 1997. *Han'guk ŭi nodong undong kwa kyegŭp chŏngch'i, 1987–1995: Pyŏnhwa rŭl wihan t'ujaeng, hyŏpsang ŭl wihan t'ujaeng* [Korean Labor Movements and Class Politics, 1987–1995]. Kyŏngnam Masan-si: Kyŏngnam Taehakkyo Ch'ulp'anbu.

2005. "Nodong undong kwa nodong chŏngch'" [Labor Movement and Labor Politics]. *Kyŏngje wa Sahoe* 64, no. 4: 64–83.

Isaac, Larry, and Lars Christiansen. 2002. "How the Civil Rights Movement Revitalized Labor Militancy." *American Sociological Review* 67: 722–46.

Iversen, Torben. 1999. *Contested Economic Institutions: The Politics of Macroeconomics and Wage Bargaining in Advanced Democracies.* New York: Cambridge University Press.

Iversen, Torben, and David Soskice. 2001. "An Asset Theory of Social Policy Preferences." *American Political Science Review* 95: 875–94.

2009. "Distribution and Redistribution: The Shadow of the Nineteenth Century." *World Politics* 61, no. 3: 438–86.

James, Daniel. 1988. *Resistance and Integration: Peronism and the Argentine Working class, 1946–1976.* Cambridge: Cambridge University Press.

Jasper, James M. 1998. "The Emotions of Protest: Affective and Reactive Emotions in and around Social Movements." *Sociological Forum* 13, no. 3: 397–424.

Jenkins, J. Craig. 1983. "Resource Mobilization Theory and the Study of Social Movements." *Annual Review of Sociology* 9: 527–53.

Jenkins, J. Craig, and Craig M. Eckert. 1986. "Channeling Black Insurgency: Elite Patronage and Professional Social Movement Organizations in the Development of the Black Movement." *American Sociological Review* 51: 812–29.

Jenkins, J. Craig, and Charles Perrow. 1977. "Insurgency of the Powerless: Farm Worker Movements (1946–1972)." *American Sociological Review* 42: 249–68.

Jessop, Robert Douglas. 2002. *The Future of the Capitalist State*. Cambridge: Polity Press.

Kang, Kookjin. 2006. "Analyses on Civil Society Network." Featured as a special theme article in *The Korean NGO Times (Citizens' Newspaper)*, January 2 and January 16 (no. 630 and no. 632).

Katzenstein, Peter J. 1985. *Small States in World Markets: Industrial Policy in Europe*. Ithaca, NY: Cornell University Press.

Keck, Margaret. 1992. *The Workers' Party and Democratization in Brazil*. New Haven, CT: Yale University Press.

　1995. *The Workers' Party and Democratization in Brazil*. New Haven, CT: Yale University Press.

Kenis, Patrick, and Volker Schneider. 1991. "Policy Networks and Policy Analysis: Scrutinizing a New Analytical Toolbox." Pp. 25–62 in *Policy Networks: Empirical Evidence and Theoretical Considerations*. Edited by Bernd Marin and Renate Mayntz. Boulder, CO, and Frankfurt: Campus and Westview Press.

Kim, Dong-chun. 1995. *Han'guk sahoe nodongja yŏn'gu* [A Study on Korean Workers]. Seoul: *Yŏksa Pip'yŏngsa*.

　2001. "Nodong undong, sahoe undongsŏng hoebok haeya" [Labor Should Recover Its Social Movement Unionism]. *Nodong Sahoe* 51, no. 2: 16–23.

Kim, Ho-gi and Chŏng Tong-ch'ŏl. 2004. "Ch'amyŏ Yŏndae ŭi ŭisa kyŏlchŏng kujo wa chojik unyŏng pangsik [The PSPD's Decision-Making Structure and Organizational Management]." Pp. 131–52 in *Ch'amyŏ wa yŏndae ro yŏn minjujuŭi ŭi sae chip'yŏng: Ch'amyŏ Yŏndae ch'angsŏl 10-chunyŏn kinyŏm nonmunjip* [The New Vision of Democracy via Pariticipation and Solidarity]. Edited by Hong Sŏng-t'ae. Seoul: Arŭk'e.

Kim, Hyŏng-gi. 1992. "Chinbojŏk noja kwan'gye wa chinbojŏk nodong chohapjuŭi rŭl hyanghayŏ" [Toward Progressive Labor-Capital Relationship and Progressive Labor Unionism]. *Kyŏngje wa Sahoe* 15 (Fall): 14–32.

Kim, Junki. 2001. "The Emergence of a Third Party Government in Korea: Contents and Consequences." *International Review of Public Administration* 6, no. 1: 95–108.

Kim, Pok-sun. 2015. "Saŏpch'e kyumobyŏl imgŭm mit kŭllo chokŏn pigyo" [A Comparison of Wage and Working Condition by Firm Size]. *Wŏlgan Nodong Ribyu* (February): 43–59.

Kim, Wŏn-sŏp. 2009. "Han'guk esŏ sahoe chŏngch'aek kaehyŏk kwa chŏngch'aek hwaksan" [Social Policy Reform and Policy Diffusion in South Korea]. Pp. 681–722 in *Han'guk pokchi kukka sŏngkyŏk nonjaeng II* [Debates on the Characteristics of the Korean Welfare State II]. Edited by Chŏng Mu-gwŏn. Seoul: In'gan kwa Pokchi.

Kim, Yŏn-myŏng. 2004. "Ch'amyŏ yŏndae 10-yŏn ŭi sŏngkwa wa ŭiŭi" [The Achievements and Agendas of the PSPD Social Welfare Committee for 10 Years]. Available at www.peoplepower21.org/Welfare/655774 (accessed June 9, 2016). In Korean.

King, Brayden, and Nicholas Pearce. 2010. "The Contentiousness of Markets: Politics, Social Movements, and Institutional Change in Markets." *Annual Review of Sociology* 36: 249–67.

King, Brayden, Marie Cornwall, and Eric Dahlin. 2005. "Winning Women's Suffrage One Step at a Time: Social Movements and the Logic of the Legislative Process." *Social Forces* 83, no. 3: 1211–34.

Kitschelt, Herbert. 1994. *The Transformation of European Social Democracy*. New York: Cambridge University Press.

Kitschelt, Herbert, and Steven I. Wilkinson. 2007. "Citizen–Politician Linkages: An Introduction." Pp. 1–49 in *Patrons, Clients, and Policies: Patterns of Democratic Accountability and Political Competition*. Edited by Herbert Kitschelt and Steven I. Wilkinson. New York: Cambridge University Press.

KLI (Korea Labor Institute). 2010. *2010 KLI nodong t'onggye* [2010 KLI Labor Statistics]. Seoul: Han'guk Nodong Yŏn'guwŏn. Available at www.kli.re.kr (accessed June 22, 2016).

Knoke, David. 1990. *Political Networks: The Structural Perspective*. New York: Cambridge University Press.

Knoke, David, Franz Urban Pappi, Jeffrey Broadbent, and Yutaka Tsujinaka. 1996. *Comparing Policy Networks: Labor Politics in the U.S., Germany, and Japan*. New York: Cambridge University Press.

Kollman, Ken. 1998. *Outside Lobbying: Public Opinion and Interest Group Strategies*. Princeton, NJ: Princeton University Press.

Kollock, Peter. 1994. "The Emergence of Exchange Structures: An Experimental Study of Uncertainty, Commitment, and Trust." *American Journal of Sociology* 100, no. 2: 313–45.

Koo, Hagen. 2001. *Korean Workers: The Culture and Politics of Class Formation*. Ithaca, NY: Cornell University Press.

Korpi, Walter. 1983. *The Democratic Class Struggle*. London: Routledge and Kegan Paul.

   2006. "Power Resources and Employer-Centered Approaches in Explanations of Welfare States and Varieties of Capitalism: Protagonists, Consenters, and Antagonists." *World Politics* 58, no. 2: 167–206.

Korpi, Walter, and Joakim Palme. 2003. "New Politics and Class Politics in the Context of Austerity and Globalization: Welfare State Regress in 18 Countries, 1975–95." *American Political Science Review* 97, no. 3: 425–46.

Korpi, Walter and Michael Shalev. 1980. "Strikes, Power and Politics in the Western Nations, 1900–1976." Pp. 301–34 in *Political Power and Social Theory*, vol. I. Edited by M. Zeitlin. Greenwich, CT: JAI Press Inc.

Kuo, Cheng-hsien. 2005. "Deconstruction of the Labor Process of the Long-Distance Bus Drivers." Masters Thesis. Institute for Labor Research, National Chengchi University: Taiwan. Available at http://nccuir.lib.nccu.edu.tw/handle/140.119/34453 (accessed April 1, 2013).

Kwon, Huck-Ju. 2003. "Advocacy Coalitions and the Politics of Welfare in Korea after the Economic Crisis." *Policy and Politics* 31, no. 1: 69–83.

   2005. "An Overview of the Study: The Developmental Welfare State and Policy Reforms in East Asia." Pp. 1–26 in *Transforming the Developmental Welfare State in East Asia*. Edited by H.-J. Kwon. New York: Palgrave MacMillan.

   2007. "Advocacy coalitions and health politics in Korea." *Social Policy & Administration* 41: 148–61.

Kwon, Huck-Ju, and Fen-ling Chen. 2007. "Governing Universal Health Insurance in Korea and Taiwan." *International Journal of Social Welfare* 17, no. 4 (September): 355–64.

Kwon, Hyeok Yong, and Jonas Pontusson. 2010. "Globalization, Labour Power and Partisan Politics Revisited." *Socio-Economic Review* 8, no. 2: 251–81.

Laitin, David D. 1998. *Identity in Formation: Russian-Speaking Populations in the Near Abroad*. Ithaca, NY: Cornell University Press.

Laumann, Edward O., David Knoke, and Yong-Hak Kim. 1985. "An Organizational Approach to State Policy Formation: A Comparative Study of Energy and Health Domains." *American Sociological Review* 50: 1–19.

Laumann, Edward O., Peter V. Marsden, and Joseph Galaskiewicz. 1977. "Community–Elite Influence Structures: Extension of a Network Approach." *American Journal of Sociology* 83: 594–631.

Lee, Cheol-Sung. 2005. "Income Inequality, Democracy, and Public Sector Size." *American Sociological Review* 70, no. 1: 158–81.

   2007. "Labor Unions and Good Governance: A Cross-National, Comparative Study." *American Sociological Review* 72, no. 4: 585–609.

2012. "Associational Networks and Welfare States in Argentina, Brazil, South Korea, and Taiwan." *World Politics* 64: 507–54.

2016. "Going Underground: The Origins of Divergent Forms of Labor Parties in Recently Democratized Countries." Forthcoming in *Sociological Theory*.

Lee, Cheol-Sung, Young-Beom Kim, and Jae-Mahn Shim. 2011. "The Limit of Equality Projects: Public Sector Expansion, Sectoral Conflicts, and Income Inequality in Post-Industrial Democracies." *American Sociological Review* 76: 100–24.

Lee, Namhee. 2007. *The Making of Minjung: Democracy and the Politics of Representation in South Korea*. Ithaca, NY: Cornell University Press.

Lee, Yoonkyung. 2006. "Varieties of Labor Politics in Northeast Asian Democracies: Political Institutions and Union: Activism in Korea and Taiwan." *Asian Survey* 46, no. 5: 721–40.

2011. *Militants or Partisans: Labor Unions and Democratic Politics in Korea and Taiwan*. Stanford, CA: Stanford University Press.

Levitsky, Steven. 2003a. "From Labor Politics to Machine Politics: The Transformation of Party–Union Linkages in Argentine Peronism, 1983–1999." *Latin American Research Review* 38, no. 3: 3–36.

2003b. *Transforming Labor-Based Parties in Latin America: Argentine Peronism in Comparative Perspective*. New York: Cambridge University Press.

Levitsky, Steven, and Maria Victoria Murillo. 2008. Argentina: From Kirchner to Kirchner. *Journal of Democracy* 19, no. 2: 16–30.

Levitsky, Steven, and Kenneth M. Roberts. 2011. *Latin America's Left Turn*. Baltimore, MD: Johns Hopkins University Press.

Lieberson, Stanley. 1991. "Small Ns and Big Conclusions: An Examination of the Reasoning in Comparative Studies Based on a Small Number of Cases." *Social Forces* 70: 307–20.

Linz, Juan J. 1978. *The Breakdown of Democratic Regimes: Crisis, Breakdown, and Re-equilibration*. Baltimore, MD: Johns Hopkins University Press.

Linzer, Drew A., and Jeffrey K. Staton. 2011. "A Measurement Model for Synthesizing Multiple Comparative Indicators: The Case of Judicial Independence." Presentation to the 2011 Annual Meeting of the American Political Science Association, September.

Lipset, Seymour Martin. 1960. *Political Man: The Social Bases of Politics*. Garden City, NY: Doubleday.

Lipset, Seymour M. and Stein Rokkan. 1967. "Cleavage Structures, Party Systems, and voter Alignments. An Introduction." Pp. 1–64 in *Party Systems and Voter Alignments: Cross-National Perspectives*. Edited by S. M. Lipset and S. Rokkan. New York: The Free Press.

Lipton, Michael. 1977. *Why Poor People Stay Poor: Urban Bias in World Development*. Cambridge, MA: Harvard University Press.

Lomeli, Enrique Valencia. 2008. "Conditional Cash Transfers as Social Policy in Latin America: An Assessment of Their Contributions and Limitations." *Annual Review of Sociology* 34: 475–99.

Long, J. Scott, and Laurie H. Ervin. 2000. "Using Heteroscedasticity Consistent Standard Errors in the Linear Regression Model." *The American Statistician* 54: 217–24.

Lopez, Steven Henry. 2004. *Reorganizing the Rust Belt: An Inside Study of the American Labor Movement*. Berkeley and Los Angeles: University of California Press.

Luebbert, Gregory M. 1991. *Liberalism, Fascism, or Social Democracy: Social Classes and the Political Origins of Regimes in Interwar Europe*. New York: Oxford University Press.

Madrid, Raúl L. 2003. *Retiring the State: The Politics of Pension Privatization in Latin America and Beyond*. Stanford, CA: Stanford University Press.

Mahoney, James. 2003. "Knowledge Accumulation in Comparative Historical Research: The Case of Democracy and Authoritarianism." Pp. 131–74 in *Comparative Historical Analysis in the Social Sciences*. Edited by J. Mahoney and D. Rueschemeyer. Cambridge: Cambridge University Press.

Mahoney, James, and Dietrich Rueschemeyer. 2003. *Comparative Historical Analysis in the Social Science*. New York: Cambridge University Press.

Mahoney, James and Kathleen Thelen. 2010. *Explaining Institutional Change: Ambiguity, Agency, and Power*. New York: Oxford University Press.

Mainwaring, Scott. 1984. "The Catholic Church, Popular Education, and Political Change in Brazil." *Journal of Inter-American Studies and World Affairs* 26: 97–124.

   1999. *Rethinking Party Systems in the Third Wave of Democratization: The Case of Brazil*. Palo Alto, CA: Stanford University Press.

Malloy, James M. 1979. *Politics of Social Security in Brazil*. Pittsburgh, PA: University of Pittsburgh Press.

Mann, Michael. 1986. *The Sources of Social Power, vol. 1, A History of Power from the Beginning to AD 1760*. New York: Cambridge University Press.

Mannheim, Karl. 1993 [1932]. "The Sociology of Intellectuals." Transl. D. Pels. *Theory, Culture and Society* 10: 369–80.

Marcelino, Paula Regina Pereira. 2008. "Terceirização e ação sindical: a singularidade da reestruturação do capital no Brasil." [Outsourcing and Union Action: The Uniqueness of the Restructuring of Capital in Brazil]. PhD dissertation, University of Campinas.

Mares, Isabela. 2003. *The Politics of Social Risk: Business and Welfare State Development*. Cambridge: Cambridge University Press.

Mares, Isabela, and Matthew E. Carnes. 2009. "Social Policy in Developing Countries." *Annual Review of Political Science* 12: 93–113.

Marks, Gary. 1989. *Unions in Politics: Britain, Germany, and the United States in the Nineteenth and Early Twentieth Centuries*. Princeton, NJ: Princeton University Press.

Marques, Rosa Maria, and Áquila Mendes. 2004. "O governo Lula e a contra-reforma previdenciária." [Lula Government and Counter-Pension Reform]. *São Paulo em Perspectiva* 18, no. 3, July.

Martin, Isaac. 2010. "Redistributing toward the Rich: Strategy Policy Crafting in the Campaign to Repeal the Sixteenth Amendment, 1938–1958. *American Journal of Sociology* 116: 1–52.

Martin, John Levi. 2003. "What Is Field Theory?" *American Journal of Sociology* 109, no. 1: 1–49.

McAdam, Doug. 1982. *Political Process and the Development of Black Insurgency, 1930–1970*. Chicago: University of Chicago Press.

   1996. "Conceptual Origins, Current Problems, Future Directions." Pp. 23–40 in *Comparative Perspectives on Social Movements: Political Opportunities, Mobilizing Structures, and Cultural Framings*. Edited by D. McAdam, J. McCarthy, and M. Zald. New York: Cambridge University Press.

McAdam, Doug and W. Richard Scott. "Organizations and Movements." Pp. 4–40 in *Social Movements and Organization Theory*. Edited by G. F. Davis, D. McAdam, W. R. Scott, and M. N. Zald. Cambridge: Cambridge University Press.

McAdam, Doug, John D. McCarthy, and Mayer N. Zald, eds. 1996. *Comparative Perspectives on Social Movements: Political Opportunities, Mobilizing Structures, and Cultural Framings*. New York: Cambridge University Press.

McAdam, Doug., Sidney Tarrow, and Charles Tilly. 2001. *Dynamics of Contention*. Cambridge and New York: Cambridge University Press.

McCammon, Holly, Karen Campbell, Ellen Granberg, and Christine Mowery. 2001. "How Movements Win: Gendered Opportunity Structures and U.S. Women's Suffrage Movements, 1866 to 1919." *American Sociological Review* 66, no. 1: 49–70.

McCammon, Holly, Soma Chaudhuri, Lyndi Hewitt, Courtney Sanders Muse, Harmony Newman, Carrie Lee Smith, and Teresa Terrell. 2008. "Becoming Full Citizens: The U.S. Women's Jury Rights Campaigns, the Pace of Reform, and Strategic Adaptation." *American Journal of Sociology* 113, no. 4: 1104–47.

McCann, Michael W. 1994. *Rights at Work: Pay Equity Reform and the Politics of Legal Mobilization*. Chicago: University of Chicago Press.

McCarthy, John D., and Edward T. Walker. 2004. "Alternative Organizational Repertoires of Poor People's Social Movement Organizations." *Nonprofit and Voluntary Sector Quarterly* 33: 97S–119S.

McCarthy, John D., and Mayer N. Zald. 1977. "Resource Mobilization and Social Movements: A Partial Theory." *American Journal of Sociology* 82, no. 6: 1212–41.

McGuire, James W. 1997. *Peronism Without Peron: Unions, Parties, and Democracy in Argentina*. Stanford, CA: Stanford University Press.

2010. *Wealth, Health, and Democracy in East Asia and Latin America*. New York: Cambridge University Press.

Meltzer, Allan H., and Scott F. Richard. 1981. "A Rational Theory of the Size of Government." *The Journal of Political Economy* 89: 914–27.

Melucci, Alberto. 1980. "The New Social Movements: A Theoretical Approach." *Social science information* 19, no. 2: 199–226.

1989. *Nomads of the Present*. London: Hutchinson Radius.

Memoria dos Metalurgicos do ABC. "Protesto Brasil, Cain a Real – S.B.C.: Contexto." [Protest Brazil, Cain Real – S.B.C.: Context]. Available at www.abcdeluta.org.br/materia.asp?id_CON=1039 (accessed June 22, 2016).

Meyer, David S. 2004. "Protest and Political Opportunities." *Annual Review of Sociology* 30: 125–45.

Meyer, David S., and Nancy Whittier. 1994. "Social Movement Spillover." *Social Problems* 41: 277–98.

Meyer, John W., John Boli, George M. Thomas, and Francisco O. Ramirez. 1997. "World Society and the Nation-State." *American Journal of Sociology* 103, no. 1: 144–81.

Michels, Robert. 1962. *Political Parties: A Sociological Study of the Oligarchical Tendencies of Modern Democracy*. New York: The Free Press.

Minkoff, Debra C., and John D. McCarthy. 2005. "Reinvigorating the Study of Organizational Processes in Social Movements." *Mobilization: An International Quarterly* 10, no. 2: 289–308.

Mische, Ann. 2007. *Partisan Publics: Communication and Contention across Brazilian youth Activist Networks*. Princeton, NJ: Princeton University Press.

2008. *Partisan Publics: Communication and Contention across Brazilian Youth Activist Networks*. Princeton, NJ: Princeton University Press.

MOEL (Ministry of Employment and Labor). 2012. *2011 Chŏn'guk Nodong chohap Chojik Hyŏnhwang* [2011 Trends of Union Densities]. Report No. 11-1492000-000049-10. Available at http://www.moel.go.kr/ (accessed June 22, 2016).

Molin, Naira Dal. 2011. "As Reformas Trabalhalista e Sindical no Brasil nos Governos Cardoso e Lula: Conflitos e Consensos." [Trade Union Reform in Brazil in governments Cardoso and Lula: Conflict and Consensus]. PhD dissertation, Universidade Federal do Rio Grande do Sul, Brazil.

Montgomery, James D. 1998. "Toward a Role-Theoretic Conception of Embeddedness." *American Journal of Sociology* 104, no. 1: 92–125.

Morris, Aldon D. 1984. *Origins of the Civil Rights Movements*. New York: The Free Press.

Mosley, Layna, and Saika Uno. 2007. "Racing to the Bottom or Climbing to the Top? Economic Globalization and Collective Labor Rights." *Comparative Political Studies* 40, no. 8: 923–48.

Murillo, María Victoria. 2000. "From Populism to Neoliberalism: Labor Unions and Market Reforms in Latin America." *World Politics* 52: 135–68.

2001. *Labor Unions, Partisan Coalitions, and Market Reforms in Latin America*. New York: Cambridge University Press.

Murillo, María Victoria, and Andrew Schrank. 2005. "With a Little Help from my Friends – Partisan Politics, Transnational Alliances, and Labor Rights in Latin America." *Comparative Political Studies* 3, no. 8: 971–99.

NCHIU. 1994–5. Conference Reports nos 1 to 8 (internal documents).

1999. NCHIU Task Report I and II (commercially unavailable).

Nee, Victor, and Paul Ingram. 1998. "Embeddedness and Beyond: Institutions, Exchange, and Social Structure." Pp. 19–45 in *The New Institutionalism in Sociology*. Edited by Victor Nee. Stanford, CA: Stanford University Press.

No, Chung-gi. 2008. *Han'guk ŭi nodong ch'eje wa sahoejŏk habŭi* [Korea's Labor Regime and Social Consensus]. Seoul: Humanit'asŭ.

NSIU and HPACA (National Social Insurance Union and Health Policy Association for Critiques and Alternatives). 2010. *A History of the Foundation of National Health Insurance*. Kungmin Kŏngang Bohŏm Chaeng-chwi-sa. Seoul: NSIU and HPACA.

Oberschall, Anthony. 1995. *Social Movements: Ideologies, Interests, and Identities*. New Brunswick, NJ: Transaction Publishers.

OECD. 2016. *OECD Social Expenditure Database*. Available at https://data.oecd.org/socialexp/pension-spending.htm (accessed June 22, 2016).

Offe, Claus. 1985. "New Social Movements: Challenging the Boundaries of Institutional Politics." *Social Research* 52, no. 4: 817–68.

Oliver, Pamela E., and Gerald Marwell. 1992. "Mobilizing Technologies for Collective Action." Pp. 251–72 in *Frontiers in Social Movement Theory*. Edited by A. D. Morris and C. M. Mueller. New Haven: Yale University Press.

Olson, Mancur. 1965. *The Logic of Collective Action: Public Goods and the Theory of Groups*. Cambridge, MA: Harvard University Press.

"Oposição faz ato contra FHC na rampa do Planalto" [Opposition Acts against FHC at Planalto Ramp]. 1998. *Jornal Folha de São Paulo*, January 22.

Ostrom, Elinor. 1990. *Governing the Commons: The Evolutions of Institutions for Collective Action*. New York: Cambridge University Press.

Pak, T'ae-ju. 2014. *Hyundai Chadongch'a enŭn Han'guk nosa kwan'gye ka itta* [One Can Find Korean Industrial Relations in Hyundai Automobile Company]. Seoul: Maeil Nodong Nyusŭ.

Palomino, Héctor. 2005. "Los sindicatos y los movimientos sociales emergentes del colapso neoliberal en Argentina." [Unions and Social Movements Emerging from Neo-Liberal Collapse in Argentina]. Pp. 19–52 in *Sindicatos y nuevos movimientos sociales en América Latina*. Edited by CLACSO (Consejo Latinoamericano de Ciencias Sociales).

Pampel, Fred, and John Williamson. 1989. *Age, Class, Politics and the Welfare State*. New York: Cambridge University Press.

"Passeata de metalúrgico para Via Anchieta." [Metalworker's Protest March Via Anchieta]. 1998. *Jornal Diário do Grande ABC*, São Bernardo, February 11.

Passos, Najla. 2012. "Entidades de servidores públicos querem anulação da Reforma da Previdência." Revista Carta Maior, São Paulo, October 11, 2012.

Paula *et al.* 2014. *Social Assistance and Labor Market Programs in Latin America: Methodology and Key Findings from the Social Protection Database*. World Bank Discussion Paper No. 1401. World Bank.

Paxton, Pamela. 2002. "Social Capital and Democracy: An Interdependent Relationship." *American Sociological Review* 67: 254–77.

Persson, Torsten, and Guido Tabellini. 1999. "The Size and Scope of Government: Comparative Politics with Rational Politicians." *European Economic Review* 43, no. 4: 699–735.

2003. *The Economic Effects of Constitutions*. Cambridge, MA: MIT Press.

Pierson, Paul. 1994. *Dismantling the Welfare State? Reagan, Thatcher and the Politics of Retrenchment*. New York: Cambridge University Press.

1996. "The New Politics of the Welfare State." *World Politics* 48, no. 2: 143–79.

2004. *Politics in Time: History, Institutions, and Social Analysis*. Princeton, NJ: Princeton University Press.

Podolny, Joel M. 2001. "Networks as the Pipes and Prisms of the Market." *American Journal of Sociology* 107: 33–60.

Polanyi, Karl. 2001 [1944]. *The Great Transformation: The Political and Economic Origins of our Time*. Boston: Beacon Press.

Polletta, Francesca. 1999. "'Free Spaces' in Collective Action." *Theory and Society* 28: 1–29.

Polletta, Francesca, and James M. Jasper. 2001. "Collective Identity and Social Movements." *Annual Review of Sociology* 27: 283–305.

Pontusson, Jonas, and Peter Swenson. 1996. "Labor Markets, Production Strategies, and Wage Bargaining Institutions: The Swedish Employer Offensive in Comparative Perspective." *Comparative Political Studies* 29, no. 2: 223–50.

Portes, Alejandro, and Julia Sensenbrenner. 1993. "Embeddedness and Immigration: Notes on the Social Determinants of Economic Action." *American Journal of Sociology* 98, no. 6: 1320–50.

Przeworski, Adam. 1985. *Capitalism and Social Democracy*. New York: Cambridge University Press.

1991. *Democracy and the Market: Political and Economic Reforms in Eastern Europe and Latin America*. New York: Cambridge University Press.

Putnam, Robert. 1993. *Making Democracy Work: Civic Traditions in Modern Italy*. Princeton, NJ: Princeton University Press.

2000. *Bowling Alone: The Collapse and Revival of American Community*. New York: Simon and Schuster.

Ragin, Charles, Joane Nagel, and Patricia White. 2003. Workshop on Scientific Foundations of Qualitative Research. Washington, DC: National Science Foundation. Available at www.nsf.gov/pubs/2004/nsf04219/nsf04219.pdf (accessed June 22, 2016).

Ramesh, M. 2004. *Social Policy in East and Southeast Asia: Education, Health, Housing, and Income Maintenance*. New York: RoutledgeCurzon.

Rauber, Isabel, ed. 1997. *Profetas del Cambio: CTA, una Experiencia de Construcción de Poder Popular en Argentina* [An Experience of Construction of Popular Power in Argentina]. Havana, Cuba: Centro de Recuperación y Difusión de la Memoria Histórica del Movimiento Popular Latinoamericano.

Rawlings, Laura B. 2005. "A New Approach to Social Assistance: Latin America's Experience with Conditional Cash Transfer Programmes." *International Social Security Review* 58, no. 2–3: 133–61.

Republic of China, Council of Labor Affairs. 2015. "Table 20: Important Labor Force Status. Statistics from Statistical Bureau. Available at http://eng.stat.gov.tw/public/data/dgbas03/bs2/yearbook_eng/y020.pdf (accessed Oct 22, 2015).

Republic of Korea, Ministry of Employment and Labor. 2015. "Statistics on Employment and Labor". Available at http://laborstat.moel.go.kr/ (accessed Oct 22, 2015). In Korean.

Riley, Dylan. 2005. "Civic Associations and Authoritarian Regimes in Interwar Europe: Italy and Spain in Comparative Perspective." *American Sociological Review* 70: 288–310.

Roberts, Kenneth M. 2002. "Social Inequalities Without Class Cleavages: Party Systems and Labor Movements in Latin America's Neoliberal Era," *Studies in Comparative International Development* 36: 3–33.

2006. "Populism, Political Conflict, and Grass-Roots Organization in Latin America." *Comparative Politics* 38, no. 2 (January): 127–48.

Robnett, Belinda. 1996. "African-American Women in the Civil Rights Movement, 1954–1965: Gender, Leadership, and Micromobilization." *American Journal of Sociology* 101: 1661–93.

Rocca Rivarola, María Dolores. 2009. "Protagonista opositor, peronista desplazado: la CGT durante el gobierno de Raúl Alfonsín." *Revista Mexicana de Ciencias Políticas y Sociales* 207: 137–54.

Rochon, Thomas R. 1998. *Culture Moves: Ideas, Activism, and Changing Values.* Princeton, NJ: Princeton University Press.

Roscigno, Vincent J., and William F. Danaher. 2001. "Media and Mobilization: The Case of Radio and Southern Textile Worker Insurgency, 1929–1934." *American Sociological Review* 66: 21–48.

Rose, Fred. 2000. *Coalitions across the Class Divide: Lessons from the Labor, Peace, and Environmental Movements.* Ithaca, NY: Cornell University Press.

Rosenthal, Naomi, Meryl Fingrutd, Michele Ethier, Roberta Karant, and David McDonald. 1985. "Social Movements and Network Analysis: A Case Study of Nineteenth-Century Women's Reform in New York State." *American Journal of Sociology* 90: 1022–54.

Rudra, Nita. 2007. "Welfare States in Developing Countries: Unique or Universal?" *Journal of Politics* 69, no. 2: 378–96.

2008. *Globalization and the Race to the Bottom in Developing Countries: Who Really Gets Hurt?* New York: Cambridge University Press.

Rueda, David. 2005. "Insider–Outsider Politics in Industrialized Democracies: The Challenge to Social Democratic Parties." *American Political Science Review* 99: 61–74.

2007. *Social Democracy Inside Out: Partisanship and Labor Market Policy in Advanced Industrialized Democracies.* Oxford: Oxford University Press.

Rueschemeyer, Dietrich, Evelyne Huber Stephens, and John D. Stephens. 1992. *Capitalist Development and Democracy.* Chicago: University of Chicago Press.

Sabatier, Paul A. 1986. "Top-Down and Bottom-Up Approach to Implementation Research: A Critical Analysis and Suggested Synthesis." *Journal of Public Policy* 6, no. 1: 21–48.

Sandbrook, Richard, Marc Edelman, Patrick Heller, and Judith Teichman. 2007. *Social Democracy in Global Periphery: Origins, Challenges, Prospects.* New York: Cambridge University Press.

Scharpf, Fritz W. 1994. "Games Real Actors Could Play: Positive and Negative Coordination in Embedded Negotiations." *Journal of Theoretical Politics* 6: 27–53.

1997. *Games Real Actors Play: Actor-Centered Institutionalism in Policy Research.* Boulder, CO: Westview Press.

Schmitter, Philippe C. 1974. "Still the Century of Corporatism?" *The Review of Politics* 36, no. 1: 85–131.

Schneider, Ben Ross, and David Soskice. 2009. "Inequality in Developed Countries and Latin America: Coordinated, Liberal and Hierarchical Systems." *Economy and society* 38: 17–52.

Scipes, Kim. 1992. "Understanding the New Labor Movements in the 'Third World': The Emergence of Social Movement Unionism." *Critical Sociology* 19, no. 2: 81–101.

Scott, W. Richard. 2008. *Institutions and Organizations: Ideas and Interests,* 3rd ed. Thousand Oaks, CA: Sage.

Seidman, Gay. 1994. *Manufacturing Militance: Workers' Movements in Brazil and South Africa, 1970–1985.* Berkeley and Los Angeles: University of California Press.

Sen, Amartya. 1999. *Development as Freedom.* New York: Oxford University Press.

Shugart, Matthew Soberg, and John M. Carey. 1992. *Presidents and Assemblies: Constitutional Design and Electoral Dynamics.* New York: Cambridge University Press.

Silver, Beverly J. 2003. *Forces of Labor: Workers' Movements and Globalization since 1870.* New York: Cambridge University Press.

Sin, Kwang-yŏng. 2004. "Han'guk chinbo chŏngdang ŭi chonjae chokŏn" [The Existential Condition of Progressive Parties in Korea]. *Yŏksa Pip'yŏng* 68, no. 3: 41–64.

Sin, Yŏng-jŏn. 2010. "Ŭiryo minyŏnghwa chŏngch'aek kwa i e taehan sahoejŏk taeŭng ŭi yŏksajŏk maengnak kwa chŏn'gae" [Privatization Policy of Health Fields and Historical Context and Development of Social Responses]. *Sanghwang kwa Pokchi* 29: 45–90.

SINDUSP (Sindicato dos Trabalhadores da USP). 2012. "Vem aí Novamente a Reforma da Previdência." [Here Comes the Pension Reform Again]. São Paulo, July 24.

Skocpol, Theda. 1979. *States and Social Revolutions: A Comparative Analysis of France, Russia and China*. New York: Cambridge University Press,.

  1992. *Protecting Mothers and Soldiers*. Cambridge, MA: Harvard University Press.

  1999. "How Americans Became Civic." Pp. 27–80 in *Civic Engagement in American Democracy*. Edited by T. Skocpol and M. P. Fiorina. Washington, DC: Brookings Institution Press/Russell Sage Foundation.

Skocpol, Theda, Peter Evans, and Dietrich Rueschemeyer, eds. 1985. *Bringing the State Back In*. New York: Cambridge University Press.

Skocpol, Theda, Marshall Ganz, and Ziad Munson. 2000. "A Nation of Organizers: The Institutional Origins of Civic Voluntarism in the United States." *American Political Science Review* 94: 527–46.

Snow, David. 2004. "Framing Processes, Ideology, and Discursive Fields." Pp. 380–412 in *The Blackwell Companion to Social Movements*. Edited by D. A. Snow, S. A. Soule, and H. Kriesi. Malden, MA: Blackwell.

Snow, David, and Robert D. Benford. 1988. "Ideology, Frame Resonance, and Participant Mobilization." *International Social Movement Research*: 197–217.

Snow, David, E. Burke Rochford, Jr., Steven K. Worden, and Robert D. Benford. 1986. "Frame Alignment Processes, Micromobilization, and Movement Participation." *American Sociological Review* 51: 464–81.

Soule, Sarah, and Brayden King. 2006. "The Stages of the Policy Process and the Equal Rights Amendment, 1972–1982." *American Journal of Sociology* 11, no. 6: 1871–909.

Southworth, Caleb, and Judith Stepan-Norris. 2003. "The Geography of Class in an Industrial American City: Connections Between Workplace and Neighborhood Politics." *Social Problems* 50: 319–47.

Staggenborg, Suzanne. 1991. *The Pro-Choice Movement: Organization and Activism in the Abortion Conflict*. New York: Oxford University Press.

Stearns, Linda Brewster, and Paul D. Almeida. 2004. "The Formation of State Actor–Social Movement Coalitions and Favorable Policy Outcomes." *Social Problems* 51, no. 4: 478–504.

Steinmo, Sven. 2002. "Globalization and Taxation Challenges to the Swedish Welfare State." *Comparative Political Studies* 35, no. 7: 839–62.

Stephens, John D. 1979. *The Transition from Capitalism to Socialism*. London: Macmillan.

Stokes, Susan C. 2007. "Political Clientelism." Pp. 604–27 in *The Oxford Handbook of Comparative Politics*. Edited by Carles Boix and Susan C. Stokes. New York: Oxford University Press.

Strange, Susan. 1997. *Casino Capitalism*. Manchester: Manchester University Press.

Suchman, Mark C. 1995. "Managing Legitimacy: Strategic and Institutional Approaches." *Academy of Management Review* 20: 571–610.

Suh, Myung-Sahm. 2012. "The Political Turn as an Act of Transgression: The Case of Left-Turned-Right Christian Activists." Paper presented to the conference "Transgression as a Secular Value: Korean in Transition?" Nam Center for Korean Studies, University of Michigan, October 25–27.

Swank, Duane, and Sven Steinmo. 2002. "The New Political Economy of Taxation in Advanced Capitalist Democracies." *American Journal of Political Science* 46, no. 3: 642–55.

Swenson, Peter. 1991a. "Bringing Capital Back In, or Social Democracy Reconsidered: Employer Power, Cross-Class Alliances, and Centralization of Industrial Relations in Denmark and Sweden." *World Politics* 43, no. 4: 513–44.

1991b. "Labor and the Limits of the Welfare State: The Politics of Intraclass Conflict and Cross-Class Alliances in Sweden and West Germany." *Comparative Politics* 23: 379–99.

Swidler, Ann. 1986. "Culture in Action: Symbols and Strategies." *American Sociological Review* 51: 273–86.

Taylor, Verta. 1989. "Social Movement Continuity: The Women's Movement in Abeyance." *American Sociological Review* 54: 761–75.

TCTU. 2000–2005. "Timeline of TCTU's Assistance of or Support for Labor Conflicts." Available at www.tctu.org.tw/front/bin/ptdetail.phtml?Part=achieve009&Category= 173835 (accessed February 1, 2013). In Chinese.

2005–2013. Press releases. Available at www.tctu.org.tw/front/bin/ptlist.phtml?Category= 1737199 (accessed February 1, 2013). In Chinese.

Terra. 2003. "Lula é vaiado e ovacionado em congresso da CUT." [Lula is Booed and Cheered in CUT Congress]. Portal Terra, June 4, 2003. Available at http://noticias. terra.com.br/brasil/noticias/0,,OI110888-EI1194,00 Lula+e+vaiado+e+ovacionado+ em+congresso+da+CUT.html (accessed October 1, 2014).

Thelen, Kathleen. 2004. *How Institutions Evolve: The Political Economy of Skills in Germany, Britain, the United States, and Japan.* New York: Cambridge University Press.

2014. *Varieties of Liberalization and the New Politics of Social Solidarity.* New York: Cambridge University Press.

Tilly, Charles. 1978. *From Mobilization to Revolution.* New York: McGraw-Hill.

1993. "Contentious Repertoires in Great Britain, 1758–1834." *Social Science History* 17: 253–80.

2005. *Trust and Rule.* New York: Cambridge University Press.

Torre, Juan Carlos. 1990. *La vieja guardia sindical y Perón. Sobre los orígenes del peronismo.* Buenos Aires: Siglo XXI.

"Trinta mil protestam contra o desemprego." [Thirty Thousand Protested against Unemployment]. 1995. *Jornal da Tarde,* São Paulo, August 25.

Traxler, Franz. 1996. "Collective Bargaining and Industrial Change: A Case of Disorganization? A Comparative Analysis of Eighteen OECD Countries." *European Sociological Review* 12 (3): 271–87.

Ŭn, Su-mi. 2001. "Han'guk nodong undong kwa simin undong ŭi kyŏngjaeng kŭrigo hegemoni." [Competition and Hegemony between Labor and Civic Movements in South Korea]. Master's thesis, Seoul National University.

2005a. "Han'guk nodong undong ŭi chŏngch'i seryŏkhwa yuhyŏng yŏn'gu." [Political Empowerment Modes of the Korean Labor Movement: An Analysis of the Relational Structure between the Labor Movement and the Civic Movement]. PhD dissertation, Seoul National University.

2005b. "Yŏn'gyŏlmang chŏpkŭn ŭl t'onghaesŏ pon sahoe undongjŏk nodong undong ŭi kanŭngsŏng." [Possibility of Social Movement Unionism in Korean Labor Movement]. *Nodong Chŏngch'aek Yŏn'gu* 5: 43–73.

UNCTAD (United Nations Conference on Trade and Development). 2008. "Domestic and External Debt in Developing Countries." Discussion Paper no. 188, March. Data available at http://ideas.repec.org/p/unc/dispap/188.html (accessed June 22, 2016).

USA Social Security Adminstration. 2014/15. "Social Security Programs throughout the World: Asia and the Pacific, 2014. The Americas, 2015." Available at www.ssa.gov/ policy/docs/progdesc/ssptw/ (accessed June 2, 2016).

Uzzi, Brian. 1997. "Social Structure and Competition in Interfirm Networks: The Paradox of Embeddedness." *Administrative Science Quarterly* 42: 35–67.

Vedres, Balazs, and David Stark. "Structural Folds: Generative Disruption in Overlapping Groups." *American Journal of Sociology* 115: 1150–90.

Voss, K., and R. Sherman. 2000. "Breaking the Iron Law of Oligarchy: Union Revitalization in the American Labor Movement." *American Journal of Sociology* 106, no. 2: 303–49.

Waisman, Carlos H. 1999. "Argentina: Capitalism and Democracy." Pp. 71–130 in *Democracy in Developing Countries: Latin America*. Edited by L. Diamond, J. Hartlyn, J. J. Linz, and S. M. Lipset. Boulder, CO: Lynne Rienner Publishers.

Walzer, Michael. 1984. *Spheres of Justice: A Defense of Pluralism and Equality*. New York: Basic Books.

Waterman, Peter. 1993. "Social-Movement Unionism: A New Union Model for a New World Order?" *Review (Fernand Braudel Center)* 16, no. 3: 245–78.

Weingast, Barry R. 1997. "The Political Foundations of Democracy and the Rule of Law." *American Political Science Review* 91, no. 2: 245–63.

Weir, Margaret, Ann Shola Orloff, and Theda Skocpol. 1988. "Introduction: Understanding American Social Politics." Pp. 3–36 In *The Politics of Social Policy in the United States*. Edited by Margaret Weir, Ann Shola Orloff, and Theda Skocpol. Princeton, NJ: Princeton University Press.

Western, Bruce. 1995. "A Comparative Study of Working-Class Disorganization: Union Decline in Eighteen Advanced Capitalist Countries." *American Sociological Review* 60, no. 2: 179–201.

1997. *Between Class and Market*. Princeton, NJ: Princeton University Press.

Weyland, Kurt. 1996. *Democracy without Equity: The Failure of Reform in Brazil*. Pittsburgh, PA: University of Pittsburgh Press.

Wibbels, Erik. 2006. "Dependency Revisited: International Markets, Business Cycles, and Social Spending in the Developing World." *International Organization* 60, no. 2: 433–68.

Wibbels, Erik, and John S. Ahlquist. 2011. "Development, Trade, and Social Insurance." *International Studies Quarterly* 55, no. 1: 125–49.

Wilensky, Harold. 1975. *The Welfare State and Equality*. Berkeley: University of California Press.

Wong, Joseph. 2004. *Healthy Democracies: Welfare Politics in Taiwan and South Korea*. Ithaca, NY: Cornell University Press.

Wood, Geoffrey. 2002. "Organizing Unionism and the Possibilities for Perpetuating a Social Movement Role: Representivity, Politics, and the Congress of South African Trade Unions." *Labour Studies Journal* 26: 29–49.

World Bank. 1994. *Averting the Old-Age Crisis: Policies to Protect the Old and Promote Growth*. New York: Oxford University Press.

2016. *World Development Indicators*. Washington, DC. Available at http://data.worldbank.org (accessed June 22, 2016).

Wright, E. O. 2000. "Working-Class Power, Capitalist-Class Interests, and Class Compromise." *American Journal of Sociology* 105: 957–1002.

Yang, Jae-Jin. 2004. "Democratic Governance and Bureaucratic Politics: A Case of Pension Reform in Korea." *Policy & Politics* 32, no. 2: 193–206.

2010. "Korean Social Concertation at the Crossroads: Consolidation or Deterioration?." *Asian Survey* 50, no. 3: 449–73.

Yi, Kwang-ch'an. 2009. *Kungmin kŏn'gang pojang chaengch'wisa: Minju pokchihwa ch'amsam ŭl hyanghan kongin ŭi yŏjŏng* [A History of the Winning of National Health Care]. Kyŏnggi-do P'aju-si: Yangsŏwŏn.

Yu, Hyŏng-kŭn. 2012. "Han'guk nodong kyegŭp ŭi hyŏngsŏng kwa pyŏnhyŏng" [The Formation and Transformation of the Korean Working Class: A Case of Workers of Large Conglomerates in Ul-San area, 1987–2010]. PhD dissertation, Seoul National University.

Zald, Mayer N., and John D. McCarthy. 1979. *The Dynamics of Social Movements*. Cambridge, MA: Winthrop.

1987. *Social Movements in an Organizational Society: Collected Essays*. New Brunswick, NJ: Transaction Books.

Zhao, Dingxin. 2015. *The Confucian-Legalist State: A New Theory of Chinese History*. New York: Oxford University Press.

Index

Associational Networks based on Comembership Data for South Korea, 2005, 251f.9.5.
Associational Networks based on Comembership Data for Taiwan, 2005, 248f.9.4.
authoritarian regimes, 22, 23, 35, 39, 41, 115, 116, 150–51, 265, 267
authoritarian repression, 184, 206, 291
authoritarian rule, 5, 28
Auyero, Javier, 193
Avelino, George, 38

Babb, Sarah, 38, 283
Baldwin, Peter, 18, 131, 277–78, 282, 287, 289
ballots, 12–13
Banco do Brasil, 191
Bank-Chaebol relationships directed by the government in South Korea, 40
Bankers' Union, 191
Barrington Moore tradition, 288
Basic Economic, Demographic, and Social Spending Data for Four Countries in the 1990s and 2000s, 225t.8.1.
basic pensions 157–58, 161, 167–68, 169, 174, 202, 262; *see also* pensions
Bastos, Márcio Thomas, 188
Becker, Gary S., 21, 75
Berman, Sheri, 15
Boito, Armando, 186, 189
Bolsa Familia, 8t.1.1., 242–43, 263
bonds, 160, 164t.6.2.
Borgatti, Stephen, 54, 235
Brazil, 6–8, 30–31, 43, 182–83, 186–87, 224–26, 228t.8.2., 232–38, 257–59, 266–67; and unions in INAMPS, 281; case studies in the 1990s, 200; economy of, 263; labor activists in, 24; labor movements in, 43, 183; leftist parties in, 249; petroleum mines, 190; state-union relationships, 188; union confederations, 189; unions, 12, 182–83, 184, 187, 195, 238, 241, 276
Brazilian Labor Party, 42, 239t.9.2.
Brazilian Social Democracy Party, 183
Breiger, Ronald, 54, 235
Britos, Oraldo, 192
brokerage role of labor unions in civic associational networks, 121

Brokerage Roles of Key Labor Unions and Civic Associations across Sub-Groups, 124f.5.3.
Brooks, Sarah M, 194, 244
Burgess, Katrina, 61

Calmfors, Lars, 20, 55
Cameron, David R., 37, 39
campaigns, 114, 162, 166, 169, 199; anti-privatization, 165; electoral, 62, 91, 162, 206, 232; national, 162; policy-based solidarity, 28; political, 14, 85; presidential, 114; public, 272; public awareness, 174
Candlelight Demonstration, 162–65
capacity, 20–21, 47–48, 56, 62–63, 64–66, 72, 165, 278–79, 285–86; civil society's, 24; coalitional, 286; collective bargaining, 39; expanded state, 178; institutional, 47, 208; long-term planning, 35; mobilization and policy, 61, 63, 65f.3.3., 66, 139, 162, 168–69, 175, 176, 284; of unions, 63, 169; social movement, 24; working-class, 278
Cardoso regime, 187–88, 191, 200, 231, 238, 258, 266
Cardoso, Fernando Henrique, 7, 183, 187, 188, 190, 242, 259, 263
Carneiro, Gilmar, 185, 191
case studies, 24, 25–26, 28, 111, 139, 142, 200–02, 235–36, 270–71, 276; archival, 144; comparative, 31, 111, 181, 234, 274, 275; historical, 14, 25, 50, 54, 75, 111, 235; in-depth, 271; multi-level, 31; network-informed, 50, 54, 235
Catholic Association for the Urban Poor, 105
Catholic Church, 6, 188
Catholic Peasant Association, 105
Catholic priests, 197
Causal Argument, 271f.10.1.
Causal Combinations: Determinants of the State-Union Interactions in the 1990s (Time of Economic Crisis) at Confederation Level, 228t.8.2.
Causal Combinations: Determinants of State-Union Interactions in the 2000s (Time of Growth) at Confederation Level, 229t.8.3.
Causal Sequences, 22f.1.1.
Cayres, João, 12, 190